PRIVATE OPTIONS:
TOOLS and CONCEPTS for LAND CONSERVATION

MONTANA
LAND
RELIANCE

LAND
TRUST
EXCHANGE

Island Press   Covelo, California

Volume editors: Barbara Rusmore, Montana Land Reliance
      Alexandra Swaney, Montana Land Reliance
      Allan D. Spader, Land Trust Exchange

Production coordinator: Judith Chaffin
Text designer: Li Greiner
Cover designer: Li Greiner
Type: Journal Roman with Berling and Baskerville Old Face for display
Compositor: Lexis Press, San Francisco, Calif.
Printer and binder: Banta Company, Menasha, Wis.

Library of Congress Cataloging in Publication Data
Main entry under title:

Private options.

    Papers from two conferences organized by the Montana Land Reliance and the Land Trust Exchange.
    Bibliography: p.
    Includes index.
    1. Land use—United States—Planning—Congresses. 2. Soil conservation—United States—Congresses. 3. Nature conservation—United States—Congresses. 4. Conservation of natural resources—United States—Congresses. I. Montana Land Reliance (Trust) II. Land Trust Exchange (U.S.)
HD191.P74 1982   333.73'16'0973   82-13070
ISBN 0-933280-15-7

Printed in the United States of America.

CONTENTS

CONTENTS

CONTENTS

CONTENTS

PREFACE

In picking up this book, you are putting yourself in touch with a growing number of people across the country who share a desire and commitment to innovative, locally responsive land preservation. They have a wide range of goals, but they share a common desire: to maintain the land base of their community in a productive open space use.

The people introduced in this book are not waiting for someone else to protect the land. They are determined to make their hopes an economically viable reality and are using private enterprise techniques to accomplish their goals. In these days of diminishing governmental support and the tight dollar, these people are creatively and effectively protecting land in their communities through private means. If this approach intrigues you, this book will give you insight into these people's thoughts, their concerns for their community, and the techniques they use in their work. Perhaps you may wish to adapt some of this information for your own situation; it is presented here with that hope.

> The task ahead is for local citizens to learn how to rebuild a community with a plan that includes reverence for and care of the land that is their "place." I see the community land trust as an act of reconciliation between mankind and land. It is a peaceful solution to rebuilding an industrially destroyed community. (Marie Cirillo, *Rural American Women*)

Who are these local citizens? They are farmers and ranchers trying to hold on to their land; they are town and city residents wanting to protect land for habitat and recreation. They have a wide variety of land preservation objectives. Some are real estate brokers, lawyers and accountants, but many have no technical background for the work they now do. Through the technique of forming nonprofit tax-exempt organizations, they set about the complex task of land preservation. These grass-roots organizations are little known outside their own communities. Scattered across the country, springing up in uncommon places as citizens felt the need and inspiration, these organizations have been emerging rapidly in the last five years. The Land Trust Exchange made a survey of these groups in 1981, and their diversity is described by Terry Bremer, who compiled the survey:

> The land's ability to sustain diversity in nature is being mirrored in the diversity of those 404 local groups dedicated to its conservation. Local land conservation organizations preserve land for food and shelter; land for wildlife, plants, and people; land for water quality, soil conservation, and water quantity; land to satisfy visual sensibilities and physical needs; land to learn from, to play on, and land to dream on—prairies, dunes, deserts, and coastlines; marshes, rivers and flood plains—land for folks rich and poor, urban, suburban, and rural; and, land for land's sake.
>
> The diversity of local land conservation organizations is their greatest strength because that diversity arises from the special local conditions of the land which surrounds each group. While safeguarding natural resources for the future, they can moni-

tor land resources and can creatively and flexibly organize local action when a threat to the environment is perceived.

How did this book come about? The Montana Land Reliance, one of the two sponsoring organizations, is a local land trust formed in 1976 and granted tax-exempt status in 1978 to undertake land conservation activities and education and research on land use problems. As much of the critical lands in Montana are in agricultural use, this has been the focus of the Reliance's work. Barbara Rusmore established the Reliance and currently serves on the board of directors. Alexandra Swaney has worked for the Reliance for several years. The other sponsor, the Land Trust Exchange, was established in 1981 to provide a communications link for local land trusts around the country. The Exchange was formed through the efforts of Allan Spader, who currently serves as executive director.

During the fall of 1981, each of these organizations sponsored a major national conference for local land trusts. This book is a compilation of the proceedings from these two very different state-of-the-art conferences. The Land Trust Exchange sponsored the National Consultation on Local Land Conservation, which was held in Boston to define the common context of the diverse local land conservation organizations: Who are we? Where are we going? And can we help each other out? It was a very invigorating session for the forty people attending.

The recent National Consultation was a real milestone for those of us involved in private land conservation efforts. It was the first time, I believe, that those of us in the West had the opportunity to sit down with our eastern colleagues to examine our common needs, goals, and directions and to share ideas. A real strengthening of the private land conservation movement began to emerge during those two days. (Jean Hocker, Jackson Hole Land Trust)

The combined papers written for the Consultation provide an excellent insight into the theories, strategies and organizational concerns faced by these groups.

A month later the Reliance sponsored a conference in San Francisco: Private Options for Land Preservation, a Conference for Practitioners. This conference focused on the techniques used in private land preservation. Practical workshops were held to allow participants to discuss the nuts and bolts of how to do it. As most of the techniques are still developing, the aim of the workshops was to provide for an interchange among peers. The proceedings of that conference present a state-of-the-art roundup of a wide variety of techniques.

Local land trusts are just beginning to realize that they are in the land preservation *business*. Will they really be able to develop the business acumen, the political savvy to become a truly effective force for land preservation, or will their work result in isolated, individual properties being preserved? That largely depends on how effectively the tools of the trade are developed. It is not an easy task to put together an economic tool or technique that creates financial benefit while preserving land; at times it appears to be a dichotomy of concepts. Yet the conference revealed an incredible array of tools and techniques for private land saving.

Land preservation is an exciting and promising field. One of the questions we asked at these conferences is, How can we, as members of the local land trust profession, strengthen our capability to use these tools and techniques? How can we develop them most effectively? Each organization has its own unique goals, its own environment that it is working in and trying to preserve. Each situation provides a different problem to solve and calls for a slightly different application of an existing technique or the development of a new technique. In this diversity lies our greatest strength and potential. The best way to further the private land preservation movement is for each group to get out there and do it, to try to apply the existing tools or see what new tool it can generate to add to the growing list of examples that others may build on. No one will find the perfect answer to all our problems, so the more tools we have to choose from, the more likely we are to create an effective solution to each land conservation problem.

Wrestling with economic realities is a tough business. Breaking new ground is always hard work, especially if you are trying to do it alone. Land trusts have tended to be isolated, separated by great distance from each other and with few means of communication, often not even knowing who else is concerned about the same things. That time is on its way out. We are now able to begin working together. The work that Allan Spader has done to create the Land Trust Exchange will prove to be most fruitful for those of us wanting to work cooperatively.

We now have the opportunity to work together, and our work will be much easier. We may not need to repeat mistakes that someone else has made, and we can build on one another's expertise. We can identify people who have dealt with similar problems and learn from their successes and perhaps more importantly, their failures.

The Montana Land Reliance and the Land Trust Exchange offer this book in the service of the private land conservation movement. Presented here is a smorgasbord of opportunities, a sample of what we can do when we set our minds to it. Better work than this can be done by working creatively together. The job is enormous, but these conferences reflect the great energy and capabilities of the people in this field.

Barbara Rusmore
Helena, MT, 1982

ACKNOWLEDGMENTS

MONTANA LAND RELIANCE

A conference like this is not the work of one or two people—it is the reflection of the qualities of those who are pioneering in the field of private enterprise land preservation. We all benefit from the coming together of such talent, and all participants deserve a heartfelt thank-you.

For the two of us who organized the conference [Barbara Rusmore and Alexandra Swaney], many individuals' contributions stand out. Without them, the conference could not have occurred. We would like to mention everyone here but will content ourselves with thanking by name only a few.

Special thanks are due to Terry Sedgwick of Island Foundation and Jennie Gerard of the Trust for Public Land. Both of them thought through this whole concept with us from beginning to end. Their vision, comments, and criticisms were absolutely vital in creating this event. We are also grateful for the financial support of the Island Foundation and the Columbia Foundation.

The assistance and advice of Allan Spader, who organized the National Consultation for Land Conservation Organizations in Boston in October, 1981, was also invaluable. Doug Horne and Douglas Wheeler from the American Farmland Trust arranged for the participation of Cecil Andrus and many of the resource people who added much to the conference. The staff at the Montana Land Reliance: Bill Dunham, Bill Long, Lisa Anderson, and Bill Yager worked with us constantly, to ensure a quality conference and proceedings.

The resource staff at the conference put forth a fantastic effort, each contributing many hours of preparation time and excellent presentations at the conference. Cecil Andrus started the conference on the right track with his opening address. Kingsbury Browne of Hill & Barlow in Boston and William Hutton with Hastings College of Law in San Francisco both gave us outstanding legal presentations. The workshops, brainstorming sessions, and private conversations were made possible by the continued good efforts of all of the resource people: Joseph Brooks, Emergency Land Fund; Paul Brunner, Eco Realty; Davis Cherington, Massachusetts Farm and Conservation Lands Trust; Jim Connor, Connor AgriResearch; Ben Emory, Maine Coast Heritage Trust; Jennie Gerard, Bill Gay, and Tom Mills, Trust for Public Land; Doug Horne, American Farmland Trust; Chuck Matthei, Institute for Community Economics; Steve Moody, United States Trust; Jon Roush, The Nature Conservancy and Montana Land Reliance; Don Rubenstein, California Coastal Conservancy; Allan Spader, Land Trust Exchange; Michael Swack, New Hampshire College; Ed Thompson, Jr., American Farmland Trust; Glenn Tiedt, National Park Service; and Douglas Wheeler, American Farmland Trust.

The actual staging of the conference was handled beautifully by Nancy Pine, Chuck Loomis, and Tom Drake of the Yosemite Institute in the face of incredibly inclement weather. The sound team, handling the taping of all sessions, managed to capture everything by constant monitoring and quick reflexes every time the electricity went out. A special thanks goes to Mary Jane Williams, Billie Miller, and their helpers; Terry Bremer of Lincoln Institute, and Mary Lester of Trust for Public Land for service beyond the call of duty.

Compiling, transcribing, writing, editing, typing, proofing, retyping, correcting, and at long last printing a document like this seems an interminable task. Fortunately for us, we had great help all the way. During the conference a crew of volunteer recorders was recruited to outline the salient points of the sessions. The walls of the conference halls were festooned with newsprint sheets colorfully scribbled with felt-tip pens. A generous thanks to you recorders: Jean Hocker, Jackson Hole Land Trust; Joan Vilms, Sonoma & Napa Land Trusts; Jennie Gerard, Trust for Public Land; Bill Long, Montana Land Reliance; Bob Augsburger, Peninsula Open Space Trust; Ellen Straus, Marin Agricultural Land Trust; and Don Rubenstein, the California Coastal Conservancy. Our typist, Jean Stephenson, did much more than type the voluminous transcriptions and numerous drafts. As a friend, she and her husband Alex often put forth the extra effort that makes a tough job enjoyable.

From start to finish, this conference has been a team effort. Thanks to everyone for making it a success.

LAND TRUST EXCHANGE

Fundamental support for the Consultation was provided by the Lincoln Institute of Land Policy as part of its ongoing education program providing for the exchange of ideas and information and the linking of theory and practice in a variety of land- and tax-related issues. Additional support came from the William and Flora Hewlett Foundation, the Fund for the Preservation of Wildlife and Natural Areas, the Island Foundation, the David and Lucile Packard Foundation, and an anonymous donor. Their generous contributions are gratefully appreciated and acknowledged.

This publication is the result of the enthusiasm, ideas, and hard labors of many individuals involved in land conservation. Their experience and enduring concern encourages and focuses new energy on land saving in the United States today. Special acknowledgment is made of the contributions of Kingsbury Browne, who provided inspiration, Jeff Cook, who steered us through the funding waters, and Don Rubenstein, who generated most of the ideas that made the conference work. Leonard Wilson of The Council of State Governments served as the conference reporter and drafted the paper "National Consultation on Local Land Conservation: A Review" and the chapter introductions.

INTRODUCTION:
LAND PRESERVATION by the
PRIVATE SECTOR

CECIL ANDRUS

Good afternoon, ladies and gentlemen, and welcome here this afternoon. When I received the brochure on the meeting here, it made me think back to similar conferences of days gone by, and I concluded that there is indeed something different here. Just look at the topics that are listed in that brochure. They are very practical. No longer are they simply buzz words or phrases that were philosophically sound and looked good as a headline: "toward a new land ethic"; "man and nature and approach to the future"; things of that nature. Instead, we see "marketing land preservation," "partial development options," and "pending tax initiatives for farmland." Something has changed. Something has really changed if you look at you people seated out there before me today. You are on the leading edge, you *are* the new wave. Many of you have been working on land preservation through private initiative for some time. I hope that you feel that your efforts, the techniques that you have originated, have been successful—at least most of them. But for those people who feel that some of them were not successful, let me remind you that if we sit still and we don't move and we don't try, we're not going to get anywhere.

In your opening remarks, comments were made here that you are a grass-roots organi-

This paper is a transcription of the keynote speech delivered by Cecil Andrus, governor of Idaho, to open the 1981 conference sponsored by Montana Land Reliance. In the editors' view, however, it provides a fitting introduction to the entire book, not just to the section that it originally introduced.

zation. Yes, you are, yet you are also beyond any grass-roots level in that you have been here long enough to be recognized as legitimate, and that makes a great deal of difference. You are really the third wave, the leading edge in conservation today.

Since I call you the third wave, let's quickly review the first two waves. The first wave of American conservationists grew out of the efforts clear back in the nineteenth century: Audubon, John Wesley Powell, Olmstead, Muir; and then into the political implementation: President Teddy Roosevelt, Gifford Pinchot, the beginning of the Forest Service, some of my predecessors in the Department of the Interior. All of these people took those ideas that were expressed and implemented them through the political spectrum. And then, there was a second wave. The second wave was probably the one that most of us were involved in, and I think you have to look back to Earth Day of 1970 if you want to pick a date when that second wave started. We were a little more astute and knowledgeable of the environment in which we live, and all those efforts in the second wave were then honed politically by people very similar in nature to those that were involved in the first wave—different names, different faces, different places, but the same philosophical approach. From that second wave, we got the NEPA Act, the Clean Air, the Clean Water Act.

We had the Coastal Zone Management Act, we had other monumental pieces of legislation that were able to protect some lands within America. I would say that the second wave was pretty good to most of us. And countless acres of the critical habitat were protected, but now I would submit to you that those days are basically behind us. Our national economy has faltered, and the public dollar is harder to find, particularly for our purposes. I am not making a political statement; it's a practical statement of the facts that face us. We are going to have to recognize that.

You are the third wave, we are the third wave, and you are a scrappy lot. You're resourceful. You have accepted the fact that you are in the business of conservation and for you, the land trust practitioners, this means that you are going to have to clearly establish the goals that you set. You're going to have to work to the light at the end of that tunnel because we are not going to have the support that I mentioned in other areas—it's just a political fact of life, and I say that we are going to have to accept it. It would be a *grave* mistake to view the position of the current administration in Washington as anything other than a challenge. You're not going to change it—I am not going to argue with them politically whether they're right or wrong. It's going to be a challenge, and that's exactly the way we should look at it, a challenge to your capabilities to act with efficiency and innovation. We are going to have to use and learn to use effectively all of the tools of the trades that you have. We are going to have to pursue means of support through private subscription and donations from private corporations, and we are going to have to go after those with a great deal of vigor and really a sense of purpose. In many instances, this means educating the boards of corporations, foundations, and the general public about the many activities that a land trust can pursue. I'll have to admit that I am a little bit delighted that the issue of marketing land preservation is being addressed at this gathering. I'd encourage you to think broadly about this. And let me explain to you why: The public-private partnership can achieve some of our most important savings goals, but we are going to have to work at it.

As you know, I've been speaking around the country about the farm conversion issue, and I believe this is one of the great issues of our time. I've been critical of the lack of a coherent federal policy to protect the productive farmland or even to scrutinize government's role in helping to destroy or change an agricultural usage to asphalt and concrete. I would like to direct your attention to a bill that is in conference committee right now. The Farmland Protection Policy Act would establish criteria to scrutinize the adverse effects of federal programs on the preservation of farmland to assure that such programs are compatible with state and, get this, *private* programs and policies to protect the farmland. That's the first time we have recognized in federal legislation that they must be compatible with private programs and policies to protect the farmland. Also in that act, the Department of Agriculture may make available information on the protection and restoration of farmland through state, local, and *private* organizations. There's that word again. That's you—that's you people—you, the practitioners. You're the people that will have a voice in it in the future if that bill is passed. The House version of the bill goes even further by encouraging the Secretary of Agriculture to provide technical assistance to any state or locality or qualifying nonprofit organizations. *Qualified nonprofit organizations.* Who is that again? That's us. So we've got some tools that we are going to be able to use if that legislation is passed. Now this language was included in the farm bills by virtue of the initiative that was taken on the hill before the Congress by the American Farmland Trust, and it represents the type of activity that must be made repeatedly to help develop a favorable climate for land trust programs through legislative initiative at all levels of government. So the challenge was to develop a legislative strategy for careful marketing of your services. It worked, and we have to continue to work to carve out a little niche for the land trust programs wherever we possibly can. Now I have said repeatedly that we cannot wait for the federal government to act or to slow down this conversion. Regardless of the success of that legislation I talked about, we're going to have to continue to mobilize all of our efforts. The times are such that the average person today will be a whole lot more receptive to what we have to say in selling our programs than they have been in the past.

Now let's take a minute to touch upon the National Agricultural Land Study. That study was put out about a year ago, in December of 1980, and it received a great deal of publicity in the press. I am going to assume that you are reasonably familiar with it, so I am just going to mention a few of the highlights that they found. First, we have a base-line file. Between 1967 and 1975, that eight-year period of time, 23 million acres of United States agricultural land were converted to nonagricultural uses. Subdivisions, highways, airports, roadways, supermarkets, parking lots, inundation by networks of dams, you name it. Since then it has been running at about 3 million acres per year of ag land being converted to another use. But that doesn't say anything about the leapfrog effect as they jump out from an urbanized area, pick up a parcel of land, and disrupt the agricultural climate, whether it be the waterworks or whatever, and it becomes racing for the horses of the urban cowboys and what have you. So it's larger than the 3 million acres, but certainly it is the full 3 million acres. Now anybody who works in Washington, D.C., quickly becomes almost immune to numbers like *millions* (except Mr. Stockman)!

What does the general in the Pentagon say? "A billion here and a billion there and a billion over here." Pretty soon that adds up to a whole bunch; but how much is 3 million acres? Three million acres is 12 sections a day, 12 square miles a day that is taken out. Let's take 3 million acres per year across the last decade: 30 million acres. That's the size equal to Vermont, New Hampshire, Massachusetts, Rhode Island, Connecticut, New Jersey, and Delaware all combined. That's how much land 30 million acres is. That's how much that we have taken out of productivity. Now does all of this say that the loss of agricultural land right now is a national crisis? No, I really don't think so. I can't say that to you. It's not a crisis yet. I've got a hunch that the American people are a little bit "over-crisised" right now. And if we try to sell it on a crisis basis and enlist their help, perhaps we would not succeed in procuring their battered and jaded sympathies. What we have, rather, is a tough but bad set of tendencies.

The issues are here: Are we going to recognize them now or are we going to wait until we are forced to recognize them by some outside variables that we don't have control of such as OPEC and the energy crunch? Crop land now in production totals 413 million acres nationwide. We've got another 127 million acres, and if you add that to the 413, it makes a total of 540. This would appear to be a sufficient cushion to guarantee future farm production and still permit commercial development. Not all of that 127 million acres is prime. It's not class 1; it does not have the productivity level; it doesn't have water on it for the most part (and to put water on it, you've got an economic and political situation so tough that I doubt that you could). So we don't have that cushion. Also we have variables that are not under our control. People migration is one. People in the North and Northeast are moving into the sunshine in the Southwest. That is going to require the use of land for another purpose. Another variable is the increase in world population. We figure in thirty-five years the world population is going to go from 4½ billion to 8, with a commensurate increase in food demands. Erosion is another variable. In Iowa they say a farmer loses 2 bushels of topsoil to erosion to get 1 bushel of corn. Climate is still another. All of these reduce that cushion we talked about. In my opinion, those statistics show that we will have a crisis if we don't do something about it.

Now in all fairness I have to tell you about the other side. There is at least one observer who disputes the speculations that I have just been giving you. Dr. Julian Simon is from the University of Illinois and has written articles in *U.S. News and World Report, Science Magazine,* and other periodicals. He points out that all of our urban conversions, all of the things—the cities, the highways and everything else—amount to only 2.7 percent of the land mass of America. Well, we've got 2 billion, 200 million acres on shore in America. And he also writes that we are adding 1.3 million acres a year from the draining of swamps and the irrigation of deserts, etc. An economist (as Dr. Simon is) might gain a little bit of confidence and comfort from those figures, but I doubt that very many farmers would, because the statistics about the total land area in America are irrelevant to agricultural production. It's farmland mass that counts. Unlike land for shopping centers, parking lots, and four-lane highways, ag land is not interchangeable with other lands. One million acres of the Grand Canyon, majestic as it is, isn't worth 100 acres of farmland in Iowa if you want to raise corn. They are not interchangeable. One of the anomalies of our system of economics is the assumption that enough demand can create a supply of anything, and I submit to you if there is enough demand out there, yes, it will create a supply of thumbtacks or panty hose; but it doesn't work for finite, irreplaceable resources such as our land. And that's exactly what it is. Once you pour asphalt or concrete on it, it's gone for any other purpose. That's a one-time crop and a one-time use. And you drain that wetland, and it's gone, its protein productivity with it.

Anyone who's looked as I have at the cost-benefit ratio of the irrigation of additional desert land with public works knows that is not exactly the way to go anymore with creating farmland. If money is no object, we all recognize that you can do some pretty extraordinary things—we could grow chickens, for example, on the top of the World Trade Center in New York City if we chose to. Drumsticks and thighs would cost you $50 apiece, but we could do it if money were not an object. But money *is* an object in the society in which we live. And what should we do? First, I think that we should probably stress that the conservation of prime land for agricultural purposes, for natural areas or wetlands or habitat, doesn't force us to adopt an antigrowth policy. We simply *cannot* be interpreted as such. The point is not to halt commercial development, but to direct commercial development to marginal land, the so-so land—the scab patches, the foothills, or what have you—that land that's not suitable for crops or is not deemed to be the supportive element of endangered species or that doesn't have to be drained. I submit to you that there is plenty of room on the other 1 billion, 700 million acres of land for all the hot-dog stands and dry cleaning establishments and parking lots that we need. We are not against the nail pounders that are out there building the homes. We are just saying, "Don't do it in these sensitive areas or in these highly productive farm areas. Do it over here." The profit in the development is still going to be there, so it's an educational process in many instances. No matter which organization or combination of techniques we use, the critical matter for all of us right now is to do something.

We must have this conference, you must use the tools that you have, you must hone the techniques and the knowledge. Listen to what Mr. Browne is going to tell you about the tax advantages of other ways of doing business, listen, be innovative, and in your work groups, decide whether you want to sustain the family farm. You know we should not have an adversarial position with ag land, but there are many instances in which we do and I don't know why. It's probably a failure to communicate. Failure to explain to the Farm Bureau that if they really want their children and their grandchildren to cast their shadow upon that farm ground the way they have for years, they are going to have to do something to protect it. We are not talking about taking away in value; we are talking about other ways to sustain their value. Give it to them now if you will take the developmental costs off the top; give them that money now or let them donate those developmental costs to sustain the family farm in perpetuity for growth by a donation if they choose—It's recognized by IRS—and they get compensated by that. So what we have to do is to communicate—you and I; we've got to be *communicators* with these people to show them that we all want the same thing, and that there is a way to get it. We can't wait for the federal government, ladies and gentlemen, can't even wait for the state government. But there isn't any reason why we can't do a great deal of it ourselves, and we can explain to state governments as we do to the federal governments that they have to get out of this program of subsidizing ill-conceived development and put that money into the budgets. Let us begin now, little by little, to gain and regain control over what we want to do; to make a decision as to what we want to do and then find out exactly how we are going to do it.

The third wave is building as we speak to one another here today; and in the history of the land trust movement, I believe that no time has been more crucial to our goals than the present time. The steps taken now by you gathered here today—you innovators, you practitioners of the art—are likely to shape the face of land conservation for many, many years to come, and I sure hope that you do. If you don't do it, I don't see anybody else out there in that horizon that's willing to do it. You've got change in your hands, and I hope that you will respond as you have in the past with a high level of excellence. Good luck to you!

5

PRIVATE OPTIONS for LAND PRESERVATION

MONTANA LAND RELIANCE

Gathering at the Yosemite Institute, Golden Gate National Recreation Area, on November 13, 1981, we were looking forward to three days of intensive interchange of ideas and information on land preservation techniques. Fortunately, we were all quite determined. The gale force winds and sheets of rain that greeted us as we converged from all parts of the country that day might have deterred a less hardy or dedicated group, but not these people concerned with land preservation. Later in the day, when the lights went out, both resource people and participants carried on with scarcely a change in schedule, while some of us made forays into Sausalito for flashlights and batteries. Those of us responsible for organizing the conference thanked our lucky stars for the resourcefulness of all concerned. The response of the participants was actually quite revealing and perhaps not surprising: It takes great resilience and perseverance to succeed in private enterprise land preservation.

How then did the Montana Land Reliance come to sponsor such a national conference on land preservation techniques? As with many events of some historic importance, this one had its origin in a fishing trip. Terry Sedgwick of Island Foundation came to Montana in October of 1980 to do some fishing. He spent some time at the Land Reliance talking with us about the problems we face in our situation: our frustrations, our felt isolation, and our needs for information. After listening to us, he suggested that a conference on practical techniques for organizations such as the Land Reliance would be very useful. We would gather together as many of the best and most experienced minds in the field as we could for a conference to present state-of-the-art information on methods for land preservation being utilized or developed by private nonprofit organizations around the country. The communication would be a source of real inspiration, breaking us out of our isolation; and the information would help us to develop our organizations in their on-the-ground programs. Conference material could then be made available in written form for wider distribution.

But, we all agreed, we didn't want just another conference. We want to talk to other organizations, to find out what *their* problems are, to make *sure* the meeting addressed the needs of the people it would be meant to serve: the practitioners of land preservation. So the Island Foundation funded a research survey to gather information about needs.

Alexandra Swaney then spoke to about thirty people from all over the country, all involved in some aspect of land preservation or related fields. They were very generous with their time and information, putting her in touch with other related people and organizations. She developed a questionnaire and sent it to fifteen organizations, following the survey with a telephone call to make sure the information was gathered. The questionnaire confirmed a desire on the part of our counterpart organizations for more knowledge about techniques. Based on their responses, tentative agenda items were selected, and resource people to present the material and guide the discussion contacted.

It was decided to hold the Conference in California. Though it would have been great to have held it in Montana, transportation costs would have been prohibitive for many individuals and organizations, and we wanted to have a fairly large group of people—to draw on their experience in solving land preservation problems as well as to use their current frustrations as raw material for the resource people.

It was also decided to present state-of-the-art material rather than material on a beginning level, as we felt this conference had the potential for generating some new thinking, and most of the organizations we talked to were eager for high-level information.

Based on the survey, a decision was also made to exclude organizational topics. Although many people expressed an interest in these topics, we felt it would have been too much to cover in two and a half days. As it is, there is a great deal of material here, representing the thinking of many enthusiastic people who are working very hard.

We believe that the Conference's success can be attributed largely to two factors: the high degree of participation from land trusts before and during the Conference *and* the incredible job done by resource people in preparing and presenting their material. We want to thank all of you for your time, your excellent work, and your encouragement. Without you, these pages would not exist. We offer these proceedings to all of you involved in making the preservation of this earth a positive and functioning part of your communities. We hope they will be of some use to you.

The SKILLS

CALL to ACTION
William H. Dunham

I would like to welcome you all here today. A month ago in Cambridge, about forty people, twenty of whom are here today, took part in the first National Consultation for Local Land Trusts. This was sponsored by the Lincoln Institute of Land Policy. It was a two-day meeting coordinated by Allan Spader, who is here today.

It was a very exciting event. That conference and this one both grew out of the same widespread feeling that the local land preservation movement needs more national coordination.

Two things are true: We have indeed become a grass-roots movement. I think that Allan, along with Kingsbury Browne, has identified over 500 different land preservation groups in thirty-five states across the country. The other thing that's very true is that we are at the point at which we need a national network. What we are hoping for today is that the momentum that was created at Boston last month will be transmitted right through this conference and some of the findings that came together there will be carried on and furthered.

In Boston the aim was really broader in scope. It was to examine the major issues, the problems, the concerns that the individual local land trusts face in the coming decade and try to reach some kind of consensus about the directions in which we individually and as a whole should be moving and what we need to become more effective. It was an attempt to share both our needs and our resources and to begin to build new cooperative structures. It won't be easy, but the need and the desire are there. And this weekend we have a chance to start putting this network together.

I am new to this land trust movement—and in many ways it reminds me of the farmers and ranchers across the nation. What I see in Montana is that the farmers and ranchers are receiving too little money for their crops; they know they need to unite in order to build their goals and reach them. But they have a lot of trouble doing so effectively because they are by nature so very independent. The same thing is true in the local land trust community. There is

9

enormous diversity, yet we do have some common goals. But without a united front I don't think that we are going to be able to realize them effectively. We are going to find ourselves increasingly stymied by Washington, on the state and local government level, and by the general public, because we have not effectively sold any of these other groups on the real importance of our work and the benefits of our efforts. We know our work is valuable, obviously. One of the people from Boston who has been in this work for many years said he felt that at the present time in this country the local land trust movement is probably the single most important thing happening in national resource preservation. We went to Boston hoping to break out of a strong sense of isolation that many people were feeling across the nation. We certainly feel isolated in Montana, and I have talked to a lot of other people who also feel that way.

We had the realization also that this movement faces both very real, immediate problems and also enormous opportunities in the decade ahead. The consensus that came out of Boston was that how well we survive and how effective we are in the next decade depends very much on how well we form a team and are able to work together toward a common goal. What came out of Boston was the decision, in my viewpoint, to form a national team because we decided that we have to play in the national arena.

As a widespread grass-roots community we are becoming more effective; we are attracting more attention, at the national, state, and local government levels. We are going to meet more obstacles, and we will continue to face them, but we can't win big unless we form a smart, tough, aggressive, professional team. What kind of team are we? Obviously, at this point, we are a young, rather amateurish, expansion team and are just starting to play in the big leagues. At this point I don't think we are being taken very seriously. We are going to have to prove ourselves, and we are going to have to win a few big victories to gain respect. I view today as the beginning of our first team practice. During the next two days we are going to focus on the state-of-the-art land preservation techniques that work. We are going to learn more about them, how they are evolving, and how to use them more effectively. We are also going to join together and brainstorm in an effort to come up with some new techniques to help solve some of the recognized problems. In effect, we are going to try and create some new plays. We are in a damn tough league, and it is imperative that we keep coming up with new, effective moves if we are going to keep on winning. What we are fighting for is obviously more important than winning any football game. We are fighting to preserve one of the three vital components of life: land, air, water. We know that all three of those things right now are under an increasingly steady onslaught. I can't believe the amount of change I have seen in Montana in the last nine years—when I moved there a few years ago I never thought that it could occur that quickly.

A great deal of effort has gone into this gathering; it's your conference, and we are looking for your help and direction. It's up to you to help keep this conference on track. As I said, it's a tight schedule. We need you to express your needs, and we need all of you to participate strongly. That's the only thing that is going to ensure that the published result of these two conferences will really be of substance.

It's also important, finally, to realize that all of you are breaking new ground. The Morrises, Kingsbury Browne, and a few other people were pretty much alone a few years ago when they started journeying out into this area of local land preservation. Gradually other people have joined in, and it is obvious today that many people in this room are five- to ten-year veterans. A great many of us are newcomers. We are here because we care deeply about the kind of detrimental changes that we see going on. We quickly find out when we get into this effort that wishing to preserve the land and actually being able to do it are two entirely different things. The keys that we have seen at the Montana Land Reliance are dedication, knowledge, persistence, and determination. The Reliance is only five years old, and we have a very tiny staff—most of this year it has been 1½ people. There have been recent times when we thought we would fold from lack of sustenance, but we are still here. But we have saved 16,000 acres of land this year, and now we are getting involved in helping to build this national team. I think that the secret we've learned is that we try hard to learn from our mistakes, and we never stop playing flat-out hardball. We play 110 percent day after day, month after month, and we never quit no matter how many times we get hit. We are constantly practicing our plays, trying to improve them, trying to execute every play we make to the very best of our ability. By utilizing the law of averages, by being out there in the field and hitting hard all the time, we end up scoring some points.

As we face the problems that we will confront in the next decade, it is important to realize that as small groups perhaps the biggest enemy is fear. Remember, courage is not the absence of fear, it is the conquest of fear. The best way to overcome fear when you are new in these preservation efforts is to get out there and try to do that which is new to you and seems rather frightening to attempt.

MARKETING LAND PRESERVATION

Benjamin R. Emory
and William H. Dunham

ABSTRACT

Ben Emory began the session by asking those present to state what they would like to get out of a workshop on marketing. Some of the questions raised were: How do you sell conservation buyers on the benefits of land conservation to both buyers and sellers? How do you get the private sector to recognize their own self-interest and needs in the preservation of open space? How do you get the support of your community behind your land trust?

The workshop did not answer all of these questions specifically. However, by examining land conservation as a marketing problem and then as a personal selling challenge, it did provide some tools and guidelines to individual organizations for answering these questions more fully in their own areas of operation. The reader is also referred to the workshop on conservation real estate for further discussion of "selling" land conservation.

MARKETING LAND PRESERVATION

LAND CONSERVATION AS A MARKETING PROBLEM—BEN EMORY

Many of us have been aware that we are dealing with a marketing problem, but have been slow to come to grips with the fact. The questions raised in the beginning of the workshop clearly reflect the need to connect with a wide variety of different audiences: landowners, communities, and land developers. But, for instance, how many of us have realized that our own board of directors is our most important audience. The extent to which our boards understand what we are doing and our potential can go a long way toward our organizations' success or failure.

An Example of Successful Marketing—The Nature Conservancy

The Nature Conservancy has been a great example of successful marketing. They have designed a host of techniques—which we might consider as their *products*—that fit many different markets. They have found ways to make these techniques work, to *distribute* the techniques; and their *communications* have been highly effective.

Marketing as an activity can be looked at in three categories. The product mix, the distribution mix, and the communication mix. Following is a discussion of those categories as illustrated by the experience of the Maine Coast Heritage Trust (MCHT).

The product mix. The MCHT was set up to promote conservation easements; that is its primary "product." But it also deals in gifts of land, sales of land, bargain sales, and helping landowners gain current use assessment (because it helps protect open space). The trust has also done some looking for conservation-minded buyers who might buy key properties on the market, and acts as a clearinghouse for planning and management advice. Look at what you do and determine what are your products, what are you trying to sell?

The distribution mix. How do we provide these services to the markets? One way is directly from ourselves. Staff and board members make available their knowledge and assistance. Another key way is to get the professional advisers of landowners—the bank trust officers, real estate appraisers, the lawyers—to be instrumental in working in whatever the conservation action is.

Another way MCHT brings its services to the customer is by referrals by government agencies and other nonprofit organizations. For example, very often The Nature Conservancy refers people to MCHT.

The communication mix. Following is a brief description of the kinds of communications used by the MCHT:

1. *Personal selling.* This is probably the most important form for the MCHT and for most other organizations. MCHT waited a long time before using a newsletter because they were doing so much personal selling and because their target audience was specific enough to make personal selling the primary vehicle for communication in the beginning.

2. *A newsletter.* Eventually, as the targeted audience broadened over time, the newsletter became a useful tool. It is published twice a year.

3. *Workshops and conferences.*

4. *Magazine articles.* Write some for magazines and arrange to have some written about you.

5. *Speaking opportunities.* Get out and talk to whatever groups you can.

6. *Public service spots on TV.* MCHT has used this primarily in promoting workshops and conferences. They can give good mileage and they are free.

7. *Pamphlets on land management issues.* MCHT is not usually directly involved in these kinds of issues, but felt that broadening the kind of information they were distributing increased the opportunity for personal interaction with landowners. For example, they published a pamphlet on forestry on islands. If they could meet an island owner through talking to them about forestry even though forestry wasn't MCHT's main concern, it might help the organization persuade the landowner to grant a conservation easement. The pamphlets are distributed by announcement through the newsletter, which goes to about 3,800 people.

PERSONAL SELLING AND LAND CONSERVATION—BILL DUNHAM

The land conservation movement is weak in the art and science of selling, according to Bill Dunham, of Montana Land Reliance. Dunham, who made an abrupt switch of life style—from academic to salesman—when he moved to Montana, was in direct sales for eight years prior to joining the Reliance staff. Bill discussed the ingredients necessary in becoming a successful salesperson.

Marketing in the sense that it concerns us is largely a euphemism for selling: selling our services or products to the landowner; selling the tools, goals, and benefits of our organization to the public and to the government on local, state, and federal levels; and fund raising. We all use persuasion daily without thinking much about it, but to really be effective there are certain laws and techniques one must obey, principles that are as true as 2 + 2 = 4. Excellence in marketing land preservation, like any other skill, requires diligent study and practice.

1. *Enthusiasm.* Enthusiasm is the biggest single factor in selling. You can't sell unless you believe intensely in the importance and benefits of whatever you are offering. To sell, you have to take your "prospect" from freezing to the boiling point. He will feel exactly what you feel and communicate; thus if you are medium warm when you reach the close, your prospect will be medium warm, and you will lose. To become enthusiastic, start today to force yourself to *act* enthusiastic. Resolve to double your enthusiasm for the next thirty days: You'll be surprised at the immediate improvement in all areas of your life.

2. *PMA.* Enthusiasm clearly goes hand in hand with *PMA*, positive mental attitude. You have to continually force the negatives out of your head and focus on the positive aspects of the situation. This is how teams who are two touchdowns behind with only two minutes left in the game come back to win, and it's the only way. Football and bull riding are extremely physical sports, yet no less than O. J. Simpson has said several times that successful playing is *90 percent* determination and mental concentration. A world champion bull rider says, "When you get up on one of them rank bulls, if you don't already have him ridden in your mind, you ain't got a chance." So true. If you don't have your prospect sold in your mind before you ever meet him, you're

dead in the saddle and you don't even know it. PMA, determination, and mental concentration are essential, but you can't acquire these things unless you have a fierce emotional commitment to your work and the services you are offering.

3. *Set specific goals.* No ship captain would ever venture out of harbor without a precise destination in mind and a way to measure his course. Set carefully thought-out five-year and one-year goals; then break them down month by month. It must be realistic but challenging, a goal you really believe you can reach. Once you set it, never let go of it; eat, breathe, and sleep it. Remember, lack of wholeheartedness is the biggest reason people fail.

4. *See the people.* The business of selling all boils down to this one thing. Put the law of averages to work for you. Tell your story with enthusiasm every day. Never stop doing it. You can't hit 'em if you don't swing at 'em, and every time you come to bat make sure you swing hard. You can't close until you make your presentation; you can't give a presentation until you make an appointment; and you can't make an appointment until you make a phone call. Selling is an easy job if you work hard at it, but it's an extremely hard job if you work easy at it. Furthermore, you can't be successful until you lose your fear of talking to important strangers. I recommend a good public speaking course, such as Toastmasters. Once you lose your fear of talking to audiences, you'll never be scared of talking to any single person, no matter how wealthy or powerful.

5. *Leads.* You must work at getting leads constantly. Any good pool player always plays position for the next shot. New supporters are your best source of new leads; pull six from each one, *without fail.* Cultivate these new centers of influence, and they will make your job much easier in the long run. Take care of them, turn them into friends, and they'll take care of you.

6. *Create a volunteer sales force.* Create a volunteer sales force of accountants, CPAs, and attorneys, the professionals landowners turn to for advice. Appeal to enlightened self-interest by showing how they can benefit their clients, themselves, and their state simultaneously. Combine individual contact with conservation law seminars to educate them on the legal-financial aspects of conservation giving. In each city select a few successful professionals with a good land ethic; then have them refer you to others.

7. *Perfect your presentation.* Your initial goal is to sell the interview, not your service or product. First sell the interview, *then* the product.

Your first job is to sell yourself, to create confidence. Look like a professional; unless you look the part, people won't trust you.

Your own attitude is everything. You must have confidence in yourself, and you get this via belief in what you are doing and knowledge of your field. Know your business thoroughly and keep up-to-date. You must be an authority. Honesty is the best policy: Use understatement and avoid exaggeration for it will soon catch up with you.

Become an astute human psychologist; learn the laws of human behavior and persuasion. Be keenly aware of the values, interests, and desires of your prospect. Will your manners, appearance, and speech please and create confidence with this particular person?

Get your mind off yourself and what you want and onto the prospect and how you can help him. Study and think about their situation in advance and develop some ideas you think might be of particular benefit to them.

Be brief and never interrupt. You can't know too much, but you can talk too much. Be sincerely interested in others and be a good listener.

Remember and use names: To do so, get a clear impression of his name and face, associate it with an action picture, and use repetition at short intervals.

Bring your witnesses personally or by phone or letter. They are a great way to create confidence, but you have to have done a fine job for them in the first place and have continued to cultivate the relationship.

Your second job in selling is to make the prospect perceive that he will be better off by doing what you suggest than by not doing it. Incorporate the universal motives of desire for gain and fear of loss in your sales talk, the desire to increase their happiness and well-being for themselves and their family.

Your job is to bring the prospect from freezing to boiling, recognize when he is at the boiling point, and then close him (persuade him to take action). The way to accomplish this is to sell while you tell, and to do this you must perfect your presentation and close through continual self-analysis, correction of mistakes, and, above all, practice.

Study your product/service and your sales story until you know it cold. You must have a planned outline because this gives you confidence, but it must flow smoothly and spontaneously. A well-planned presentation has more force.

Include three reasons why he should do as you suggest, three reasons why he should do it now. Season it well with questions such as, "Isn't it? Wouldn't you agree?" that give you commitments.

Then tailor your basic presentation to this specific prospect and situation. Show him a way to get it. Sell benefits, not features. When you find out what he wants, keep talking about it and never let him get away from it. Discover the most vulnerable point and stick to it.

Use "you" and "yours" often, for this will ensure that you are practicing the key principle of seeing things from his point of view, that you are talking in terms of *his* needs and desires. The only way to make anyone do what you want them to do is to make them want to do it, so don't talk about what *you* want.

Cultivate the art of asking questions: Inquire rather than debate.

After each presentation honestly evaluate what you did well and what you could have done better. Correct your mistakes. Strive constantly for improvement.

Enthusiasm, dedication, knowledge, and determination are the keys. And remember, your prospect will feel what you feel; you must reach his heart as well as his head. How well did you really *communicate* your intense belief in both the problem and then the benefits (the solution)?

8. *Perfect your close.* You hesitate to close if you don't know when or how to attempt it. Write out your close and memorize it so you know exactly where you are going step by step. This way you won't hesitate, stumble, and lose your momentum and thus the transaction.

A successful sale involves arousing attention, interest, desire, and then comes the close. Suppressed excitement and an assumed close are very important, and this is easy if you have brought them to the boiling point.

When you have received three commitments, it's time to close.

At the end of your presentation, summarize, then ask, "How do you like it?" If he answers, "I like it," or says to his wife, "What do you think?" you've got a *buying* sign. Act on it. "Well great, Bob, let's go ahead with it."

If he has objections, ask, "Why?" and, "In addition to that, Bob, isn't there something else that is causing you to hesitate?" These are great ways to find out the true objection. Remember, we usually have two reasons for doing or not doing anything: the reason that sounds good and the real one.

Your job in the close is to be an assistant buyer, to help them make the wisest decision, not to cram something down their throat. Never argue, never get angry, and never tell him he is wrong if you can possibly avoid it. Take control, but don't dominate.

Try to close several times before giving up. Use testimonial letters, a story of how it benefited someone else, a stress of the major benefit.

Read, study, and practice everything you can about closing techniques.

9. *Negotiating.* Negotiating is a form of closing. Deal only with the boss, never with his underlings, and be frank about money. These two things will save you a lot of wasted time, misunderstanding, and bad feeling. Any businessman knows there is no free lunch. If you have done him a big favor, ask for one in return.

10. *Don't be afraid to fail.* Fear of failure is the biggest stumbling block you face. Courage is not the absence of fear; it is the conquest of fear. No ski-jumping champion mastered his sport overnight. The first time he stood atop a big ski jump, his knees quaked, but he didn't quit after his first fall nor his hundredth. And neither did he ever slacken his effort.

Repeatedly do the very thing you fear, and your fear will subside. Expect failures and setbacks, take them in stride, and keep on swinging hard. Put the law of averages to work for you: Keep seeing the people steadily, give it 100 percent every time, and keep improving. When you aren't seeing enough people, you aren't giving the law of averages a chance to go to work for you. Lincoln suffered eight major failures in his life before he finally became president. Edison failed 10,000 times before finally inventing the light bulb. Both were determined that each attempt brought them that much closer to success. *They failed forward* by learning from their mistakes. So never allow your fear of failure to weaken your effort. Keep going and don't be afraid to lose today, because if you keep trying hard you'll succeed tomorrow.

EVALUATING AGRICULTURAL LAND for PRESERVATION

James M. Connor and Douglas R. Horne

ABSTRACT

Property location, land productivity, and farm management must be addressed before a land conservancy decides to acquire a property. Often significant liabilities are encountered through the acquisition of farmland or farmland preservation interests that are not always apparent at the outset to the conservancy or often even to the landowner.

This section presents an assessment methodology based on the approach used by American Farmland Trust and its consultants when considering farms for acquisition. While it is focused on acquisition, much of this evaluation process would be necessary in any land preservation transaction. Prime agricultural land preservation is the primary goal. The steps for evaluating a specific parcel are outlined. Some broader agricultural land conservation issues are raised followed by a list of information sources for local action. The section closes with four case studies of transactions.

STEPS IN THE PROCESS

This procedure is oriented to determining whether or not it makes sense to maintain a property in agricultural use and, if so, what kind of agricultural and compatible uses are appropriate. These steps are laid out in a general start-to-finish manner as a guideline, but in practice information often will turn up along the way that will change or add to an earlier step.

A land conservancy must be vigilant to avoid getting involved with an inappropriate property. Sometimes, even if a property is offered as a gift, it may be better to leave it alone. This following process will hopefully help organizations make the right choices.

Resource evaluation. First off we have to determine what the property can produce and the place to start is with the land resources, primarily the soils. A visit with the Soil Conservation Service (SCS) can quickly point out the capability of a place to produce. The SCS has detailed maps of the soils in most parts of the country and can give you maps and detailed information about most farms. This will give basic data on the productive capability of the place and its natural limitations, for example, water needs, alkaline soils, and location of fields and

17

woodlots. If they have done a detailed conservation plan of the property, they will have even better data, including management suggestions.

Productivity evaluation. Having determined the pluses and minuses of the resource in step 1, we now have to determine the best crop possibilities. This involves meshing the resource capability with management and marketing considerations. The management history of a place is our starting point. What has been produced? What were the objectives of the operator? How were the products marketed? What were the successes or failures? What kind of condition is the land in (e.g., overgrazed, weed problems, erosion control)? What is the condition of the improvements (e.g., fences, irrigation system, outbuildings)? At this point we are looking for a general evaluation of these factors to identify problems and the most likely crops.

The other major sources of information for this stage are the county farm adviser and the Agricultural Stabilization and Conservation Service (ASCS) as they work with operators on management concerns on a county basis. They can be particularly helpful in identifying the marketing potentials of certain crops.

Surrounding land use. Agricultural and other land uses can tell you much about the viability of continuing a place as a farm or ranch. What are the surrounding operators producing? Are they successful? Why or why not? Is the area experiencing development pressures? What is the current level of support services in nearby communities for machinery sales, repairs and parts, banking, markets, and so forth? What is the future community outlook? Are any surrounding uses in conflict with agricultural use (e.g., dogs)?

Lending institutions. If you are proposing a deal that will restrict the future land uses (e.g., through a conservation easement) or will entail an unusual leasing or management arrangement, it is important to talk to the most likely funders of the operation. Generally this will be the Federal Land Bank (FLB). Make sure they understand what you do as a land conservancy; they will generally be sympathetic, but it is a new concept and you need to make your case. The FLB can give you valuable information on:

1. The value of the land at its highest and best use. Because they are the biggest lender on agricultural properties, they can give you the best estimate short of an appraisal.

2. What they would loan on it if it were deed restricted.

3. People in the area who would want to buy and farm a deed-restricted property and that the FLB would be willing to loan to.

Determination of economic viability. By this point you should have a pretty good outline of the economics of the property. By working with different experts you will have figures for the production and income capability of the place, the land, improvement and machinery costs, the start-up production costs, and the fixed and variable operating costs. This will give you an economic profile of the place and an income-to-capitalization ratio. Use your local resources to help figure out the economics. Many federal and state agricultural services are free, and once they understand what you are doing will probably be very helpful. At this point you should be able to tell whether or not the property is appropriate for your goals and if someone can make a living on it.

Looking for the operator. When the research results are favorable and you decide to go ahead with the land acquisition and preservation project, the next step is finding an operator for the farm or ranch. Agricultural extension or ASCS may know of someone who would be good. The FLB is another good source. One could ask for proposals from neighboring farmers. If an objective is to get a young person started in agriculture, the land grant colleges might be a good place to start asking for an appropriate applicant. Evaluating and selecting potential operators is another task beyond the scope of the outline on evaluating land for conservation. This discussion is included because if one is going to preserve a piece of agricultural land, one must know that there will be someone willing to work it.

ISSUES NOT ADDRESSED

As stated at the beginning, this evaluation process is designed for an organization whose goal is prime agricultural land preservation. At least two other major issues were raised at the workshop. One, which received some peripheral discussion, was the issue of access to land, particularly by the beginning operator. The other issue, which was only briefly mentioned and could easily have taken a full workshop itself, is the compatibility of agricultural uses with more traditional conservation purposes, for example, the preservation of wildlife habitats.

A land conservancy dealing with agricultural land preservation must come to terms with both of these issues in formulating their goals and programs. An organization must develop goals and programs that are achievable; as Jim Connor said, "You can't chase too many rabbits at once or you'll never catch one." However, we are in the business of land preservation, and the issues of who will get the opportunity to use that land and what will be their management practices will continue to confront us. We had best be prepared to deal with the larger philosophical and practical questions these issues raise.

INFORMATION SOURCES FOR LOCAL ACTION

County farm adviser

Agricultural experiment stations

Soil Conservation Service

University departments and researchers

Agricultural Stabilization and Conservation Service

Federal Land Bank

Production Credit Association

Extension service (university)

All of these groups have local representatives by county or region who work extensively with agricultural operators. They know the area, its problems and strengths, and are concerned about its agricultural vitality. Their information is public, and generally they are interested in sharing it. A land trust is probably an unfamiliar entity for them, but once they understand it they will probably be some of your best allies.

EVALUATING AGRICULTURAL LAND for PRESERVATION

CASE STUDIES

Dairy

Size: 450 acres
Location: Michigan
Operation: Small dairy, designed 30–40 years ago; used as hobby operation; abandoned dairy 10 years ago, now just vacation place; three homes; mint condition.

The owners wanted to see it remain in agricultural use and were interested in donating it to the American Farmland Trust. The AFT had to determine if the property fit their objective of prime land preservation, if someone could make a living on it, and what it would cost to make the transaction.

They began by visiting the place, making a survey of the condition of the land and improvements and talking with the caretaker. They then went to the Soil Conservation Service and identified the property on aerial soil maps and researched the soil's productivity. It did not rate very highly. While the unit had been used as a dairy, it had not been modernized and could not be operated without a major capital outlay. In the meantime, many surrounding operations had turned to horse raising and training. The owners of this property did not like the horse operations and did not want to see horses on their place. Given this situation, the most logical future use of the place was hay production to be sold to the surrounding units. In conversation with the Federal Land Bank, AFT determined that the land was worth about $2,000–$2,200 per acre for its "highest and best" use and worth about $1,000–$1,200 restricted for agricultural use. The Land Bank was willing to lend to an operator at that price on a restricted property and knew of several people that they thought would be qualified. A major problem was posed by the three residences on the property. Only one made sense from the operator's perspective; the other two would have to be sold off separately. The proceeds from these sales would go into a fund to be used to preserve prime farmland. When the landowner and potential donor realized that their "farm" really couldn't support a very viable agricultural unit, they decided instead to give it to their favorite charity.

Partial Development—Example 1

Size: 130 acres
Location: New Jersey
Operation: A developer had award-winning plans for this place to combine clustered housing with a recycling system and organic vegetable operation. It was an abandoned, weed-infested, old pasture.

The developer was having trouble with the local rural community and had not been able to get a permit. He approached the Farmland Trust for assistance. AFT was interested in the concept and agreed to do some investigation on the place. The two main questions they needed resolved were the marketability of the housing and the validity of an organic vegetable farm. They undertook a housing-market analysis and an evaluation of the property's agricultural potential.

After checking the condition of the place and soil maps, it was clear that it would take a lot to set up a truck farm, especially an organic operation. There also were no readily available markets and though the plans called for roadside selling, they did not account for the complexity of such an operation. There was no capital available to back the establishment of the farmer, and he was expected to return money to the community of homeowners on the property. Starting out with a custom hay operation appeared to be the only feasible option from the agricultural viewpoint. The overall major problem, which proved unresolvable, was the desire of the developer to accomplish many different goals simultaneously.

Partial Development—Example 2

Size: 3,100 acres, two major parcels
Location: Illinois, Fox River area
Operation: A corporation had purchased several farms, put them together for a new town development. Good and prime soils for corn.

The market turned against these developers and AFT felt they could purchase the property at a bargain sale price and break it up into approximately 500-acre pieces, sell most to farmers deed restricted, and a small parcel to a developer.

By evaluating the soils and economics of agriculture in the area, AFT determined that parcels of approximately 500 acres were economically viable and that if they could purchase the property at $3,000–$3,100 an acre, they could sell it at $3,500 an acre, which would be an affordable price. The Federal Land Bank was willing to lend 80 percent of the land value on a deed-restricted property. They would sell the land to the highest bidder who wanted farmland.

Confined Hog Operation for Southern Agricultural Corporation

Size: 650 acres
Location: Georgia
Operation: Confined hog operation and corn ground to be operated by the Southern Agricultural Corporation.

The SAC has been involved with helping limited resource operators set up profitable hog operations. In order to become financially self-sufficient, they needed a property where they could locate more feeder units, grow some of their own corn, and eventually have several related facilities. They had located this 650-acre parcel and needed bridge financing to help them acquire it until a grant came through. AFT was asked to consider this bridge financing.

AFT had to evaluate the economic viability of their plans. Evaluation of the resources of the property indicated that it would fit their needs. Research into SAC's past management led AFT to the conclusion that SAC was undercapitalized but otherwise very competent. The grant seemed very secure; it was just a problem of timing. Therefore, AFT agreed to go ahead with the bridge financing.

MANAGEMENT IMPLICATIONS of LAND STEWARDSHIP: Focus on Conservation Easement Management

Benjamin R. Emory and Jon Roush

ABSTRACT

Identifying stewardship goals and management considerations are prerequisite to undertaking land protection activity. This workshop focused on the design of a stewardship program and dealt in depth with the management implications of conservation easements. While the workshop itself began with easement management and then moved into the conceptual and planning aspects of land stewardship, in written form the reverse presentation is more coherent. An excellent example of the complexities of stewardship, the discussion of easement management underscores the need for advance planning. Conservation easements, rather than another form of land protection, were selected because they are relatively new and are getting quite a bit of attention. Also for local trusts, donations of conservation easements are likely to be a major tool in implementing their preservation program.

This workshop brought together the expertise of Ben Emory of the Maine Coast Heritage Trust and Jon Roush, long-time staff of The Nature Conservancy and now on their executive board and the board of the Montana Land Reliance. Maine has probably had more experience with easements than anywhere else; over the last ten years, 188 easements have been conveyed/granted largely through the efforts of MCHT. The Conservancy has pioneered land stewardship through private trusts and utilizes a whole array of tools, including easements. A newcomer, the Reliance, has taken easements on agricultural properties for the last four years.

STEWARDSHIP—JON ROUSH

Land management and stewardship begin in planning. An organization must develop stewardship goals, a picture of their ultimate objective. *What is it* you are trying to protect? That's the first question to answer and the more specifically you can answer it, the easier your job will become. Then you can answer, "*How* can you protect this land, species, resource, and so forth?" and select the correct tools. Developing a comprehensive stewardship program is critical for effectively using your time and money. It may make the difference between a land trust that works and one that fails.

An outline of the questions that must be answered in designing a stewardship program follows:

1. *Objectives.* Why protect it? What is it that makes an area or property worth protecting? Is it a particular species, an ecosystem, a geologic feature, a productive human land use such as forestry, fisheries, or agriculture, or something else? Be specific.

2. *Boundaries.* What geographical area must be protected? What components of the area are critical, and do they have different boundaries? For instance, a water resource may require a very different protection area than an endangered plant species.

3. *Caretaking.* Who is going to take care of it? What are the options? Who else besides the land trust might be concerned about this resource? What are their capabilities and limitations? What are the tools that might be used by any and all of these concerned people to protect it?

4. *Strategies.* At this point, a land trust can really develop a working plan for protection. A selection of allies and strategies can be made and specific tools evaluated and implemented. Be thinking in terms of layers of protection. The more ways a resource is preserved the more secure it is. Zoning, easements, water rights acquisitions, rights of first refusal, for example, could all be used simultaneously to protect a designated area.

5. *Financing.* Think through the costs of different strategies, particularly the implications for the land trust's budget. A stewardship plan will have several financial components: How much will it cost to protect the resource? How much will ongoing stewardship cost and where will the funds come from? For example, acquisition is a very expensive means of protection. Not only does it cost a great deal to purchase a property, but it also places the entire management costs on the trust. There are times when acquisition provides the most appropriate protection, and there are ways of dealing creatively with the management responsibility and costs, but an organization must carefully plan for such an eventuality.

In summary, think about your long-range goals and how you will achieve them before settling on a specific technique. It makes me very nervous to hear so much emphasis on conservation easements. During the last few months I have heard several new land trusts describe their purpose as "to take conservation easements." That is a pretty poor purpose; it does not address any kind of stewardship goals, and it puts the cart before the horse.

Conservation easements are only one of the tools available for use by land trusts. If you want to maintain existing land uses, if the current landowner is doing an all-right management job now, then an easement *may* be the correct tool. But you might also consider voluntary agreements, securing rights of first refusal, a lease, or host of other possibilities depending on the situation. If there are heavy pressures for change in an area, perhaps an easement is not the correct tool; it will certainly be harder to achieve.

CONSERVATION EASEMENT MANAGEMENT—BEN EMORY

In the preceding section we addressed planning for stewardship. In this portion of the workshop, this approach is taken the next step and made specific to one stewardship technique:

conservation easements. Once you decide that an easement is the right tool for the job, what are the management concerns?

Easement Criteria

State your goals and evaluate your resources and capabilities to design a realistic set of criteria. These criteria will be your guide in selecting properties for acceptance of an easement. Some of the factors that could be covered in your criteria are:

1. Location of the property; traveling distance for monitoring; proximity to other preserved properties.

2. How well do the natural characteristics of the property fit your preservation goals?

3. Finances; cost of easement and monitoring; fund raising.

4. What are the benefits to the public?

5. What would be the likely public response to the easement?

6. Alternatives to accepting a conservation easement.

Criteria will also need to be developed for specific terms and restrictions in easements and for the base line study. While general restrictions are established by law and regulation, easement terms are developed individually for each property. A resource conditions study, or base line document, may be desirable as background data for each easement. Each organization will have to develop its own standards for base line studies and easements based on its stewardship objectives.

Problems in Design and Negotiation

This workshop did not address the specifics of what might be included in conservation easements, for example, the particular terms and restrictions over timber harvest practices or agricultural uses, with placement and design of housing. There are many examples of model easements available to people from various different organizations. What is addressed here are some of the problems that come up in developing an easement, both to make sure it is enforceable and to eliminate ambiguity.

Enforceability. It's important that an easement be enforceable. The kinds of restrictions that you take have to be something that you are capable of monitoring; for instance: An easement was granted in Maine prohibiting campfires and picnic fires above the high tide line. There was no way that the organization that accepted that easement could possibly monitor that area to ensure that there were no campfires. Another easement limited livestock except for pigs. It could be a problem to monitor that kind of an easement. There are no hard and fast rules about restrictions in easements; it's merely a matter of what you can and cannot police. It's dependent, therefore, on both your financial and personnel capabilities.

Ambiguities. In writing the terms of an easement, it is important to be as clear as possible. Ambiguities can surface after a period of time and be a source of serious problems.

Anticipate them as much as possible and clarify your terms where you can. If later on more information arises or a situation changes and more clarity in the terms is needed, it can be written up and attached to the easement at that time. During the workshop, three different areas of ambiguity were brought up:

1. *Surveys.* Where possible, try to avoid needing a survey of the easement or of a particular area within the easement that is restricted. It is *very* expensive and if there is another way to describe the property, use it. The need for a survey may vary from state to state, however, and should be checked into.

2. *Preservation clauses.* Within an easement, you may want to put in a preservation clause that will set standards beyond which the natural resource base cannot be degraded. For instance, in dealing with soil erosion and quality, it is possible to agree on a soil class level below which the soil quality cannot be degraded. A third party can be chosen to be an arbitrator should there be any questions.

3. *Reverter clauses.* As a young organization, you may have difficulties in negotiating with donors of conservation easements because a conservation easement is a long-term, perpetual agreement. You may find it useful to arrange with a more established organization to be your back-up donee for easement donations. This can provide you as well as the donor of the conservation easement with a measure of security.

Monitoring
Some easement terms may be relatively self-enforcing, such as restrictions over future lot splitting. However, most easement terms will require some level of monitoring. This section looks at five of the major monitoring concerns:

1. *Timing.* Most easement properties should be visited at least once a year. In some circumstances, it may be possible to monitor an easement from the air, but by and large an on-site ground visit is the best. During this visit the different base line categories should be checked and any problems that arise during the year can be further investigated. Depending on the easement terms, you may need to monitor or police the property more frequently than once a year.

2. *Documentation.* A clear, written documentation of your visit will be very important for the long-term monitoring of a property. The documentation can be visual as well. Photographs on a yearly basis can provide an excellent review of changes over time on a property. Your documentation of your monitoring should follow your base line study. The Nature Conservancy has put out a book called *Conservation Resource Evaluation Procedures.* It is a detailed analysis, perhaps more so than most need, but it is a good model to work from in developing your documentation procedures.

3. *Keep in touch with the landowner.* You have a detailed contract with the landowners about the usage of their property. It's important to keep in touch with them so that they do not forget the specifics of the agreement; and in fact if the property changes hands, the new owner may not know what the easement agreement really means. Though it is attached to the deed and should likely have turned up during the title search, the new owner may not really understand it, and the previous owner

probably will not have taken the time to discuss the easement in detail. If you can develop a mechanism to know when the property changes hands, you can arrange a visit with the new owners and explain to them the workings of the conservation easement. Some organizations send out a letter once a year to all landowners who have easements. Through this, they soon find out if a landowner has sold a property.

When visiting a property, try to inform the landowner of your plans and if possible, arrange to have the landowner go with you. This provides a personal touch and a continuing involvement that will pay off over the years.

4. *Pooling monitoring resources.* If you are in an area where several organizations hold easements, such as the National Park Service, The Nature Conservancy, your local fish and game department or parks department, you may be able to arrange for pooling of monitoring visits, particularly if you monitor your easements by plane. If you get involved in such a situation, make sure that you have a consistent written record format so that monitoring meets your standards. It may be possible for a land trust to arrange a contract with another organization for monitoring of easements where the land trust would undertake the actual site visit; or perhaps the reverse arrangement would be preferable.

5. *Failure to monitor.* The failure to monitor an easement may be interpreted by a court as grounds for legal abandonment of the easement. While this has never been tested, some lawyers feel that there is sufficient grounds for concern. This consideration makes it even more important to have easement terms that are enforceable and to have clear documentation of your visits to a property. The Maine chapter of The Nature Conservancy has just prepared a report on appropriate procedures for monitoring specific easement properties. It may provide a good model for other organizations as well and can be located through your local Nature Conservancy representative.

Violations of Easement Terms

The violation of an easement term is a breach of contract and is enforceable in court. Court proceedings, however, are very expensive. In some easements, the enforcement terms are written into the document where possible so that the restitution, should there be a violation, is clearly understood from the outset. If this is not sufficient and a court case must be pursued, the organization will have to pay the costs at least until the settlement of the terms. It is possible that the organization could sue not only for breach of contract but also for payment of court fees. However, if the case is not settled favorably for the organization, they will need to pay the court costs from their own resources. In many cases, an endowment is negotiated with the donor of the conservation easement. Because the donors generally are receiving a substantial tax saving through the contribution of the easement, they are often willing to also make a cash contribution from a portion of those tax savings. In some cases, this is negotiated for the same year as the easement donation; in other cases, it may be spread out over a period of years or even included in the donor's will.

It is also possible to raise money from other sources for a legal action. The Maine Coast Heritage Trust, for instance, has not set up an endowment fund or an easement management war chest, because they do not know when they might need it nor do they know which of the many organizations in the state currently holding easements will need it. None of these organizations has developed an endowment fund for this purpose. When the need arises, they plan to collectively raise the necessary funds.

Modifying Easement Terms

If your organization holds any easements, you will need at some time to make changes in those terms. However, don't set a precedent of making changes. An easement is a contract between the grantor and the grantee, and changes should be made only if absolutely necessary and a clear public benefit will be derived from the change. If the change is solely for the landowner's benefit, it could pose a problem both for the landowner and for many organizations taking conservation easements. Make sure that there is clear language in an easement about making changes. Arbitration procedures can be set up in an easement, and the arrangement for making changes should be spelled out.

Tax consequences. Changes in the terms of the easement may result in tax consequences to the landowner and perhaps to the tax-exempt status of the organization. If ambient conditions change and the circumstances surrounding the property are different, the terms of the easement may need to be changed as well. Possibly, and this has occurred in several cases, a landowner will wish to tighten up the easement terms. This could create a further tax deduction for the landowner. However, if the terms loosen and the easement is no longer as restrictive as it once was, this could jeopardize the tax status of the exempt organization holding the easement. No changes in the terms of an easement should be taken lightly.

OTHER ISSUES NOT COVERED

Two major issues that were not addressed thoroughly in this workshop and could easily have had an entire workshop devoted just to them, are *base line studies* and *specific easement terms.* It would be pertinent to discuss the design of a base line study and how it might best give information for designing easement terms and how to use it as the first step in your monitoring program.

INFORMATION SOURCES FOR LOCAL ACTION

Several documents have been mentioned throughout the course of this workshop. Those will be useful for organizations to review as they develop their land stewardship programs. Most established land trusts have dealt with this issue and for a new organization or for one evaluating their stewardship program, it would probably be worthwhile to contact similar organizations for their stewardship guidelines. One of the most obvious sources of information is The Nature Conservancy because they have wrestled with these problems for a longer period of time and probably in greater depth than most other organizations.

NEGOTIATING SKILLS
Jon Roush

ABSTRACT

Jon, an experienced negotiator for The Nature Conservancy, opened the workshop with a statement outlining the basic steps in the negotiation process, including points to check yourself on as you go through that process. Discussion centered around the experiences of several land trusts in getting to the negotiating stage. Suggestions were offered that would be helpful in bringing landowners to the bargaining table. Unless the experiences discussed here can be attributed to the fledgling status of these organizations, it would appear that, as in so many other activities, merely agreeing to negotiate is the most difficult step.

STEPS IN THE NEGOTIATION PROCESS

1. *Clarify your objectives.* In negotiation, there are usually two levels of objectives: those things that you would *like* to get and those you *must* get or it's not worth your while to continue negotiating. You come into negotiations having thought through your objectives so that they are clear, you know what they are, you know which objectives or which demands you are willing to give away and which ones you can't afford to give away.

Check out those objectives with everybody who has some influence over the negotiations process. One of the reasons PATCO employees were left high and dry by the Reagan administration was that their leadership thought they had an agreement but they hadn't checked with the membership and they rejected it. Whoever is doing the negotiating has to be as sure as possible that he or she knows everyone's bottom line.

2. *Analyze the other party.* Feel what it is like to be the other person, what it is that person wants. This is the place where role playing really helps. Try to really sit down and imagine what it is the other person wants. It's worth doing that. Find out what you can about what that person needs. What kind of stresses might he be under? Why is that person negotiating? What put him in the position that he feels it necessary to come and sit down at the table? How much time does he have? Who does he have

to answer to? What kind of control is he really likely to exercise? How much authority does he have? Is he likely to get up in the middle of the negotiation and say he'd like to agree to your demands but, unfortunately, he doesn't have the power to do so? Who are all the players and what are the roles going to be?

3. *Analyze yourself.* Ask yourself not only what your objectives are but what your hidden needs are. We all have them. What are your weaknesses? What are the things that people are likely to play on, that make you a less rational human being? If you are part of a group, what are the strengths and weaknesses of everybody in the group? What role is each person in the group going to play? When are they going to play it?

Once you have completed this basic procedure, you can begin to strategize. Here you will want to ask yourself a lot of questions, particularly about timing. How fast do you want the negotiations to proceed? Will it be useful to insist on some deadlines? Or create artificial deadlines? Or look for natural deadlines that you can use to force a conclusion? Or are you going to want a fairly leisurely, open-ended kind of process so people have time to go back and check with each other, their lawyers, and other advisers? You want to have as much control over the timing as you can.

Ask yourself when you are going to meet? Is the time of day or the time of month important? Sometimes it is, sometimes it isn't, but do remember to think about it.

Where are you going to meet? Your place or theirs? Or a neutral place? If you are going to meet at your place, the advantage is that you probably have a lot of information there that you can get at. The disadvantage is that you can't use *not* having that information as an excuse to stop negotiating, to slow things down if you need to.

The Strategy of Limited Authority

This is an important aspect of any negotiation. You usually don't want to walk into a negotiation with the complete power to make decisions. Nine times out of ten you want the other party to have the complete power to make decisions. You want to be able to nail them down, but you want to have an escape hatch if you need it: "Gee, I've got to go back and check with my board of directors—my lawyer—or my constituency." This is one of the advantages of negotiating in a neutral place.

Role Playing

You have already thought some about what your opposite number is likely to say. But now is a good time to sit down and really think through some various scenarios with somebody else about how the negotiation might go as a way of watching for pitfalls. Once you have gone through that kind of strategizing, then you are ready to negotiate.

Sitting Down at the Table—Look for Solutions

Most importantly, once you sit down at the table, keep your objectives in mind. The most important thing to do is to find solutions, not to get stuck on issues. Always be looking for solutions that move you toward the goal. If you find yourselves at loggerheads about something, say, "Let's set that aside and go on to something else."

Stay flexible. If you come in with one way you think things are going to go and you see that there is something else going on and things are going to go another way, go along with them. Just remember why you are there. It sounds elementary but the thing that upsets negotiations more than anything else is the people's inability to keep moving toward their objectives. Their egos get in the way. Or they fixate compulsively on some disagreement or other, enough to blow the whole thing up.

Keep calm. The attitude you want to maintain is a sort of disciplined passion. You are obviously there because you care about something enough to be there, especially in the kind of work we're doing. But you can't let your desire to have something good happen get in the way of your being in control. If you do find yourself getting emotionally involved or anxious that things aren't going well, step aside and ask somebody else to come in and negotiate. Stepping aside is not a bad idea; it is also a way of keeping the other party a little bit off balance. It is a sign of a mature negotiator that he or she recognizes when emotional involvement has become too great.

A two-person team allows you to defer to your teammate when this happens as well as presenting another mind to work with. It is also sometimes useful to have a third, neutral party present to help you verify what is going on.

It is very important to keep records. Keep notes of everything: what people said, what was agreed to.

Beginning negotiators often have a tendency to play it too close to the chest, or do something goofy, or bluff. All those things are almost always no good. If you bluff and you get caught, it is going to be (properly) interpreted as a sign of insecurity. If you do want to bluff, do it early on in the game, so if they do catch it, maybe they'll think you're a little bit wacky and it won't be quite so damaging as if you did it later in the game.

Be very thoughtful about what information you are going to reveal and when you are going to reveal it. It is quite true that very often there is information that you do not want the other party to know. That is quite appropriate. The tendency often is for people to be too coy, rather than recognizing that what you are both trying to do is find a workable solution. Usually the more information you have about each other, the better you are going to be able to work on a solution. You do have to judge what the tone is. If someone is intensely opposed to you, is an intense adversary, then obviously you have to play it differently.

SOME OBSERVATIONS ON THE USE OF ATTORNEYS AND OTHER ADVISERS IN NEGOTIATING

1. In general, keep legal and financial advisers *out* of negotiations. Too many deals get hung up on technicalities. It is useful to keep a distance from legal counsel.

2. Attorneys tend to be conservative and sometimes stifle creativity, particularly if they're not familiar with land trust activities.

3. However, you can use an attorney as a surrogate when you get a technical problem. Saying, "I have to check with my attorney," sometimes can give you the distance you need in the negotiation process.

4. Attorneys *can* be effective once you have settled the basic negotiation: the amounts of money involved and what will be happening.

5. Sometimes having a lawyer present can be a useful intimidation tactic.

CASE STUDIES

Golden Gate National Recreation Area. The property adjacent to where this conference was held, the Golden Gate National Recreation Area, was acquired by The Nature Conservancy after three years of negotiating with Gulf Oil, who wanted to put a residential development on the land. The Nature Conservancy had to use every trick in the book to accomplish this acquisition. The basic tactic, however, was to convince Gulf that they had to negotiate by keeping them off balance, really coercing them. The Conservancy tried to make it obvious to Gulf that they would never be able to put the proposed development on the land, or that if they did, it would be much more expensive than anticipated. They did this through helping to keep the Marin County legal pots simmering, letting Gulf know that development ordinances were in the works.

There are other examples of The Nature Conservancy and other good organizations using the good cop-bad cop routine. A fairly aggressive environmental organization will start pounding on the door of a corporate landowner (in this case) and making a lot of trouble for them. The negotiating organization, in this case, The Nature Conservancy, comes in with its briefcase and three-piece suit, and says, "Boy, you guys have a problem." They continue to say they don't have a problem, and you tell them they do until they know you know they do.

Problem. How do you get people to negotiate who have you at a disadvantage or who have no incentive to negotiate?

Suggestions. Bullying is not the answer. In some communities it could ruin your reputation. Try to do as much groundwork with the advisers of the landowners as you can. "Sell" their attorneys and accountants on land conservation deals.

Problem. How do you reach a landowner who just won't talk to you? Would knowing his financial status help put a package together?

A man owns a piece of property along a stream that a county parks department wants to buy as a connecting piece in a parks system bikeway. They have been trying to negotiate with him, but he will not sit down at the table with them. Although he is in violation of the law in channeling the stream and filling it and otherwise making a mess, no government agency will tell him he is in violation because there are too many overlapping areas of responsibility among them. He sold a large piece of land this year and perhaps could use a tax shelter. But he wants to develop an industrial site on one side of the creek, and it looks like he has his own time line in mind and won't discuss it at all until it suits him. The land conservation organization wants a small piece of property between the stream and the freeway. Although it could bring condemnation proceedings, the parks department does not want the public to associate any ill will with the project. There is a possibility that part of the freeway could be used as the connector instead of his property.

Suggestions.

1. It wouldn't hurt to give him an ultimatum. Tell him that the bikeway will go on the freeway unless he agrees to negotiate within a certain time frame.

2.   Also, pull out the legal stops. Encourage someone not associated with the parks department to bring an attorney general action against the landowner for his illegal tampering with the stream.

3.   In other cases where a person has no incentive to negotiate, one solution is sheer salesmanship. Develop a rapport with a person; don't give up on them. Get to know them through a hobby, for instance, and show them that you care about them as one human being for another. This isn't "bootlicking," just good human relations.

Problem.   A buyer and seller know one another. The property for sale is 800 acres in total, and 200 acres of it is agricultural land. The buyer wants to preserve the agricultural land and some historic features the land has. The two are very good friends with each other and with individuals in the land trust but are resistant somehow to the land trust concept. What the trust wants is to put a conservation easement on the property. The seller's advisers are not well informed about land conservation options, and this is part of the problem.

Suggestions.

1.   Find a way to educate their lawyers and other advisers. Get your land trust to offer educational workshops featuring highly experienced professionals in the field; or talk to them personally.

2.   Find a way to utilize both buyer's and seller's attachment to the property to ensure that it will stay as is.

Problem.   A farmer died without a will. The two heirs are elderly and not very energetic in terms of playing a critical role in how the estate is settled. They are concerned that it stay in one piece, but are also concerned for the financial situation of their children and want to dispose of the property as soon as possible. The land conservation organization representative has been trying to gain the trust of one heir who has the most to say in the affair. The administrator of the estate is probably making the decisions, but the heir has the option to make the decisions, even though he won't believe that he can really have an impact. The land trust would like to see the property sold with restrictions to another party or purchase it and do limited development on it in order to finance the transaction.

Suggestions.

1.   Your job is to make the heir feel more powerful, to make him heel the administrator.

2.   Present a credible package to the administrator, set up a deal that is appealing to them both, once you have got the heir's approval to work with them.

The TOOLS

INCOME TAX INCENTIVES for LAND CONSERVATION

William Hutton

You are aware that, for every triumph, for every transcendent moment of inspiration, there are hours and days and months of drudgery, of handholding with landowners, looking at family pictures, maybe having a drink or two. The corollary to that realization is that for every forty-five minutes of Cecil Andrus you get at least two hours of federal income tax.

I should say right off that there is no magic in tax learning, or tax principles, or tax rules. It is often the layman's assumption that a tax lawyer carries a bag of tricks, from which he can pull some magical solution. I sometimes think people save up their impossible cases until I am around, hoping for a magic trick. But there are a lot of things you can do with tax rules. I think of the Internal Revenue Code, or aspects of it that relate to this kind of work, as just a bag of tools, like mechanic's tools. If you are familiar enough with them you can do some interesting and good things . . . or at least you'll know what the possibilities are. That's my objective here—to create a sense of the possible—at least for those of you who have not had a great deal of experience in land preservation and conservation. Some of you may not yet have done a transaction, and for you, I would be entirely content if we can just alert you to possibilities for the use of tax incentives. (Some of the incentives are not quite what they used to be, due to the 1981 Economic Recovery Tax Act [ERTA].)

Let me spend a minute or two just talking about some basic structural principles before we get on to use some examples of transactions.

Our income tax is structurally very simple. It applies to whatever taxable entity or person we are dealing with: corporation, individual, trust, partnership. It starts with the computation of total income, "gross income," which is an all-inclusive term. Gambling winnings, lottery proceeds, you name it, anything that looks like income and actually has the effect of enriching you is income. Then from gross income certain deductions are taken, in the case of an individual, to reach a sort of midpoint that is extremely consequential for our purposes. It's called *adjusted gross income* (AGI). Adjusted gross income is a way station between all of the income of the person and the final income, which is called *taxable income,* on which tax liability is computed. The reason adjusted gross income is important is because it is a bench mark for the allowable charitable contribution. In an individual's case, the allowable deduction is dependent upon the amount of adjusted gross income.

33

The charitable contribution itself is taken as an itemized deduction from adjusted gross income. In 1981 it was a "below-the-line deduction," the "line" being adjusted gross income. Congress has, in its wisdom, seen fit to tinker with that concept and, beginning in 1982 and increasingly so for a period of five years, has moved the charitable contribution deduction above the line. However, it makes no difference for our purposes. We shall still use AGI as a bench mark. (As a matter of incentive to charitable giving, this change seems to be virtually irrelevant and as a matter of policy it's nonsensical, but it is an example of the fact that in the 1981 legislative process, nobody said no to anybody.) We are principally concerned with a person who is able to make a sizable charitable contribution and therefore would get the tax benefit of it whether it is itemized or not.

It is worth focusing virtually all of tax planning upon the notion of tax benefit. Tax benefit is simply the marginal rate applied to whatever deduction you are talking about—charitable contribution, tax shelter, depreciation, or what have you. Our graduated rate system really means that you start at a zero bracket. For example, in 1981, the married taxpayer is in a zero bracket for the first $3,400 of taxable income and then it graduates. Once taxable income hits $215,400, every dollar after that is taxed at 70 percent. To estimate the utility of a charitable contribution for any taxpayer, take the amount of the contribution and multiply it by the applicable marginal rate. For example, a $90,000 gift reduces taxable income from say $300,000 to $210,000. If the donation had not been made, that $90,000 would have been taxed at roughly 70 percent (a $63,000 tax) and the after-tax value would have been $27,000. The contribution is worth $63,000 of tax savings ($90,000 × 70 percent = $63,000).

Partnerships

Partnership donations offer the same possibilities for tax benefit as do individual gifts. In fact, where all the partners participate equally in the profits and losses of the partnership and there are no special allocations provisions made, each will take a share of the charitable contribution. But the partners don't have to allocate the charitable contribution in equal amounts. They can make special provisions that don't have to be preexisting special provisions. Through either a donation or a bargain sale, one or more partners can take a disproportionate part of that gift, and provided the arrangement has what is called *substantially economic effect*, the allocation will govern. *Substantial economic effect* means that investment in partnership capital will properly reflect the division of the charitable contribution. In the partnership setting you can tailor the contribution to the relative tax situations of the partners.

OPTIONS

Let's talk for a minute about something that often is the first step in an acquisition transaction. Until about a year and a half ago, we assumed that an option, in and of itself, didn't create any difficulties or raise any interesting questions. An option creates a binding legal obligation to sell property at a designated price in the event the optionee exercises. In our typical case, option periods don't run very long. I personally feel that long-term options are risky because in order to have the charitable contribution at all, you have to be able to show that there is donative intent that proceeds out of generosity. Once the option has been granted to purchase property at a price significantly below fair market value, it's a little difficult to see that at the subsequent exercise of that option and the closing of the transaction, that generosity continues to pervade the transaction. We have always blithely assumed that the charitable contribution takes place when the transaction closes, that is, when the environmental or conservation organization determines to exercise the option and receives the property for the bargain price.

About a year and a half ago the Internal Revenue Service issued a gift tax ruling, *Revenue Ruling 80-186*.[1] It is not a charitable contribution ruling but a gift tax ruling. It involved a family situation whereby a father granted a child an option to purchase property at a price $25,000 below fair market value. The ruling holds that a gift, subject to gift tax, takes place at the time of the grant of the option.

It wasn't long before people began to wonder whether or not that ruling could be transposed into the charitable context. If so, it creates some wonderful opportunities and also some horrendous scenarios. The opportunities involve alleged bargain options, whereby the donor or optioner takes a current write-off for the assumed bargain element. Then in some future year, when the option is not exercised, that "donor" conveniently forgets that a tax benefit flowed from the deduction. What I have just described has rather extraordinary potential for abuse. Over a year ago, the Internal Revenue Service was made aware of this and of the desire on the part of certain responsible organizations to have the closing of the transaction constitute the effective date of the charitable contribution. The Service has undertaken a rulings project that should clarify this issue, but we do not have any clarification yet.

DETERMINATION OF CHARITABLE DEDUCTION

Assuming that we don't use an option, let's consider the beginning point for the determination of a charitable contribution: the "amount." The amount of an outright gift of property is what a willing buyer will pay to a willing seller where there isn't any duress or other exigency. To determine the amount of charitable contribution, we are assuming a perfect market and infinite time to reach an accommodation. Of course that never happens. Since it's highly likely that appraised value is going to exceed actual sales value, bargain sales can create substantial outright gifts.

Let's assume that we deal here with land for which we have an "adjusted basis" of $10,000 (that adjusted basis is probably derived from, or maybe is exactly, the owner's original cost). The property has a $50,000 fair market value; that is, it is an appreciated property.[2] That property is the subject of the gift.

---

1. *Revenue Ruling 80-186*, 1980-2 C.B. 280, describes an option, granted January 2, 1978, by parent A to child B for $10, to purchase certain real property for $475,000. At the time of the grant, the property was worth $500,000; two years later, just before the option was to have expired, B exercised, paying A $475,000 for the property. The ruling holds that the transfer by A to B of an option that creates enforceable rights under local law is a taxable gift; the same result obtains, presumably, whether or not the optionee exercises the option. (The ruling does not determine the option's value, but it seems clear that the gift might be considerably more than $25,000; that is, the appreciation potential and the privilege of *not* exercising are relevant valuation factors.)

2. For substantial gifts of property not susceptible of ready valuation independent appraisal is essential. Many donors seek estimates of value from the donee organization; the IRS accords such evidence precisely the weight it deserves—none. Even where a representative of the donee offers an estimate of value, the taxpayer should be cautioned that such estimate will be of little use on audit. (The charity's subsequent sale of the donated property may furnish persuasive evidence of value, however.) On valuation generally, see Reg. 1.170A-1(c); also the Service's appraisal guidelines set forth in *Revenue Procedures 66-49*, 1976-2 C.B. 1257; and *79-24*, 1979-1 C.B. 565.

Criteria for Charitable Contributions

There are several questions we have to ask before we can make the conclusive assumption that a $50,000 charitable contribution has been achieved. First of all, is this long-term capital gain property? That question has three elements. (1) You need a capital asset, (2) you need a sale or exchange, and (3) you need a holding period in excess of a year. It wasn't that way before; most of this law on charitable contributions derives from congressional action in the 1969 Tax Reform Act.

The most difficult question you have is in determining whether the land is a capital asset. If the land was acquired and held either for personal use or for investment for a substantial period of time, there is ordinarily no problem. The precise statutory question is whether or not the would-be donor has held the property for sale principally to customers in the ordinary course of a trade or business. It is not possible to answer that question with any certainty, especially if the person has been heavily engaged in real estate activity. But there are some things that help and that may virtually guarantee that you will get the full market value deduction, even in the case of a dealer.[3]

A dealer can hold real estate for investment. Ordinarily investment intent should be evidenced by the separateness of investment activities from other real estate activities. For example, if he or she has typically dealt with business real estate in corporate or partnership entities with respect to developments, subdivisions, and sales, it is best that the gift property be held by the taxpayer individually, or maybe jointly with spouse. It is also preferable that no sales activities have been attempted and no improvements have been made. But in the final analysis, it is simply not possible to determine with great assurance that you come down on the investment versus the dealer side of the line.

Public Charity Status

Assuming we get over that hurdle, there are a couple of other possible statutory reductions you ought to be aware of. I assume that virtually all of you are representative of what we call public charities or, at worst, private operating foundations. *Public charity* is a generic term covering a lot of different categories and organizations having in common the ability to offer their contributors maximum contribution benefits.

Many of you are from fledgling organizations and are worried about—or will have to worry about in the years to come—maintaining your public support status. When you get an exemption as a new publicly supported organization, you get an exemption without investigation, on the representation that you expect to develop a significant breadth of public support. You can ask for that on a conditional basis for two or five years. Most organizations that I consult with ask for a five-year period because it simply gives you a longer time to develop the kind of support that you need. At the end of that two- or five-year period, the Service may or may not issue a final ruling that you are a publicly supported organization, depending on whether you have met statutory and regulations' standards. If you qualify, then you continue to offer your contributors maximum charitable contribution deductions. If you don't qualify, the amount of the gift will be reduced by 40 percent of the appreciation in the value of donated capital gain property. If you turn out to be a private foundation, then our $50,000 gift will have to be reduced by $16,000. The effect of that is that you are not going to be competitive with other organizations that have maintained their public status.

---

3. See George V. Buono, 74 T.C. 187 (1980).

The Internal Revenue Service does not appear to have taken a particularly aggressive audit stance as to public support. A lot of organizations feel that if they achieve over 10 percent of public support (which is measured in a fairly complicated way) that qualifies them to be judged favorably on facts and circumstances. I don't feel very comfortable with that. If you get up to one-third public support, then you are *guaranteed* to qualify, and to maintain your public charity tax status. It seems to me that this is the level of public support you should aspire to. It isn't all that difficult. Public support is possible to achieve if you can find as few as seventeen persons who are willing to support your organization in a more or less equal (and meaningful) way.

Let me illustrate why that is. Under the Code section that is most generally applicable to land trusts seeking public charity status, Section 170(b)(1)(A)(vi), those normally receiving a substantial part of their support from the general public and from governmental units qualify for public charity status. *Normally* is defined rather elaborately in the regulations: I mentioned that in order to be considered publicly supported you have to reach at least 10 percent of what I will call good support, but to be guaranteed you have to reach 33-1/3 percent.

Let's take an organization that has been in existence for the conditional ruling period of two years or five years. Suppose during that time its total support has been $45,000, which might be expected for a modestly funded land trust. That means to be guaranteed public charity status it is going to need $15,000 of good support. Now the hitch in the definition of *good support* is that no one individual or entity is permitted to be considered to have contributed more than 2 percent of total support. If you have a gift of $10,000 somewhere in this $45,000 support total, it can help only to the extent of $900. In other words, the $15,000 must come from a sufficient number of sources. Fifteen thousand dollars, or 33-1/3 percent, would need to be donated by individuals. By seventeen $900 contributions, your public support would be guaranteed. This might be accomplished by each of seventeen people contributing at least $180 annually over your entire five-year ruling period.

QUESTION: Do you mean that seventeen people have to give approximately equal amounts?

Hutton: No. But out of a $45,000 budget each one has to give at least $900; some of them could give $5,000 or $20,000. If you have twenty-five people who have given approximately $600 each you will be in just as favorable a position. All this is intended to do is to demonstrate that the public isn't as *public* as it may appear to be.

As regards public support computations, how do you handle the gifts of land or gifts of conservation restrictions, as opposed to operating grants? For gifts of land, the regulations provide an exception for unusual gifts. An unusual grant is essentially one that is unexpected in occurrence and is large relative to your total support. It would usually negatively affect your support calculation. The regulations are not as helpful as *Revenue Procedure 81-7*, published earlier this year in the Internal Revenue Bulletin. It sets out a list of factors, and if you can satisfy all of those factors as to a gift of land or an interest in land, including an easement, you'll be entitled to exclude that from the support calculation. That revenue procedure will cover nearly all large land gifts from persons who are not prior contributors or substantial contributors. It is a very, very useful procedure.

Regarding easements, the gift of an easement that produces a substantial deduction to the donor does not ordinarily produce any real support. If an easement reduces the value of the property by $100,000, there is no correlative $100,000 support. In fact, the easement produces a negative support item, as it carries the obligation to monitor the gift. So prior to *Revenue Procedure* 81-7, it seemed perfectly legitimate to me to carry the easement at *zero*. Now it is likely going to be treated as an unusual grant with the same result; that is, it need not be taken into account in your support calculation or you must use the revenue procedure.

QUESTION: Even if you have sought after it?

Hutton: That's right. Actively seeking a land or easement donation does not destroy the unusual nature of it under the revenue procedure.

TAX BENEFIT LIMITATIONS OF CHARITABLE CONTRIBUTIONS

Fifty Percent Limitation

The general or overall limitation on charitable contributions is 50 percent of adjusted gross income [Sec. 170(b)(1)(A)]. Whether a contribution will yield maximum tax benefits is dependent upon that adjusted gross income figure, that bench mark that determines the amount of contributions you qualify to deduct in any given year. Let's assume that adjusted gross income is $60,000 and we have a gift of $50,000. Then the overall limitation is $30,000, 50 percent of adjusted gross income.

Thirty Percent Limitation

On gifts of appreciated capital gain property—property that will yield long-term capital gain if sold—the limit is 30 percent [Sec. 170(b)(1)(C)]. The 50 percent limit is reached only where a substantial part of total contributions is made in cash or nonappreciated property. In our case, to reach a total deduction of $30,000, $12,000 would have to be contributions of cash or nonappreciated property. A land donation will be limited to 30 percent of adjusted gross income in this year, $18,000 with a carry-over of the excess. The carry-over lasts for five years or until it runs out, whichever comes first. So in the case of a $50,000 land donation, the donor would get a benefit in year one, 1981, of $18,000 times the marginal rate, and we carry over $32,000. If our adjusted gross income is the same next year, we use up another $18,000 and, finally, the last $14,000 in 1983.

Statutory election to reduce contributions of capital gain property. The Code permits an election whereby the amount of a contribution of capital gain property may be reduced by 40 percent of the potential long-term capital gain and the balance then permitted to be considered a gift of nonappreciated (50 percent) property [Sec. 170(b)(1)(C)(iii)].

Example: Assume a taxpayer with an AGI of $50,000 makes a gift of land appraised at $200,000 (adjusted basis $40,000). The 30 percent limit would produce a deduction of $15,000 per year for six years (assuming no change in income). But the election, although reducing the "amount" of the contribution to $136,000 (by 40 percent of $160,000), enables the donor to use $25,000 as a deduction each year for five years and the remaining $11,000 in the final carry-over year.

Although this example perhaps illustrates the most obvious use of the election—for a gift considerably larger than can be used otherwise—there are at least two other situations in which it should be considered: (1) where the gain potential is small relative to the size of the gift, so that, at the cost of a slight reduction in amount, the taxpayer accelerates tax benefits; and/or (2) where a decline in the taxpayer's marginal rate is expected for subsequent (carry-over) years.

QUESTION: Does the carry-over deduction change with the new law?

Hutton: It will not change. Charitable contributions will be subjected to the same percentage limitations. Congress didn't change that.

QUESTION: How will you know what percentage you can take?

Hutton: You compute AGI in the absence of charitable contribution as you did before.

Twenty Percent Limitation

There is yet another potential percentage limitation. It shows again the disadvantage of being other than a publicly supported charity, and that's a 20 percent limit. All gifts to private foundations are subject to a limit of 20 percent of adjusted gross income and, furthermore, there's no carry-over. Private foundation gifts that are gifts *inter vivos,* not by way of bequest, are subject to a 20 percent limit, in our case of a $50,000 donation, $12,000 with no carry-over. Furthermore, to use any of these private foundation gifts you first have to take into account against the 50 percent overall limitation all of the gifts made to public charities.

1981 TAX ACT

Now let's talk about how the new law affects charitable contributions after 1981. Congress, in the 1981 act, didn't directly change charitable incentives. But the maximum tax rate is 50 percent in 1982 and rate reductions go on in 1983 and 1984. The taxpayer who has an adjusted gross income of $200,000 and contributes property worth $50,000 has a charitable contribution amount of $50,000. This single taxpayer, in 1981, was a maximum, or 70 percent-bracket, taxpayer. Let's assume as well that his taxable income (before the gift) was $175,000. The $50,000 charitable contribution in 1981 would have reduced what would otherwise have been a taxable income of $175,000 to a taxable income of $125,000. The contribution produced a tax benefit of $35,000.

There's another way to look at it. The people in the Treasury would say it produced a tax expenditure of $35,000, and that's absolutely correct. A tax expenditure is an indirect government subsidy, and that's what a charitable contribution is. In this case, our taxpayer was out of pocket much less than the government's tax expenditure. And, in fact, if you consider the alternatives available to this taxpayer, a gift was about as good as a sale, maybe a little better.

For 1982, however, when the rates go down to 50 percent, the government's tax expenditure would similarly decline to $25,000 for exactly the same donation. We still have the same reduction in taxable income and we still have a $50,000 allowable contribution (note that this contribution doesn't exceed the 50 percent level) but the government subsidy is only going to be $25,000. This has *very serious ramifications,* for the kinds of transactions that we do, not just for outright gifts of land but for what has become really the garden variety of conservation transaction, the bargain sale.

Bargain Sales and Outright Gifts of Property

Bargain selling has become so attractive, so beneficial, that it has often raised the question in my mind as to whether the taxpayer is entitled to a charitable contribution at all. It has been possible, and in the future it will *not* be possible, to acquire computer programs that will allow you to tell a prospective donor or bargain seller exactly what bargain price will produce the same return that you could get through an outright sale. Those programs simply required you to plug in income levels or projected income levels, assume fair market value of the property, the basis of the property, and from that data, all of which is mechanical, you would get the appropriate bargain sales price.

That doesn't assume any charitability. That's very handy if you're dealing with the occasional donor who doesn't exhibit any inclinations toward charitability. We all know people in whom the random thought of charitability produces an immediate rush of white corpuscles to fight off the invasion. For those people you can actually do a bargain sale that looks very attractive.

Let me demonstrate a bargain sale for zero dollars with my 70 percent bracket taxpayer to show you the polar extremes. Let's assume you have a property with a very low adjusted basis of only $5,000 and a fair market value of $100,000. Virtually all of this property is appreciation and when an outright contribution is made the donor isn't taxed on that appreciation. The capital gain goes untaxed and the amount of the deduction, assuming we can avoid any of the reductions, is $100,000.

Then let's take it down lower and assume a single person with an adjusted gross income of $300,000, and that any sale of this land would involve a 10 percent combination of real estate commissions and other expenses of sale. A sale of this property in 1981 would produce an amount realized of $90,000. That's the fair market value minus the expenses of the sale. The adjusted basis is $5,000, so we have an $85,000 long-term capital gain. For transactions that take place after June 9, 1981, Congress has set a 20 percent maximum tax for capital gain; there is a 20 percent tax of $17,000. The after-tax value of the sale is $90,000 minus $17,000 or $73,000.

Now consider an outright gift of that property. What's the benefit? Our donor has few if any expenses, so with a $100,000 contribution amount, he has a 70 percent federal benefit, or a tax savings of $70,000. If he is in a state such as California, he is going to save another 5 or 5½ percent of state tax and perhaps a little bit of local tax in some places. You could hypothetically increase the tax benefits to $74,000.

We can show that a bargain sale at zero dollars or an outright gift, then, will produce a better return to this potential donor, who may not have a charitable bone in his body, than would a sale at fair market value, assuming a realistic real estate commission. He may even do better than that if the appraised value of the property is higher than the amount that could actually be realized on disposition.

What happens in 1982 on this same transaction is a bit discouraging, because the consequences of sale will be the same. We will still have the capital gain tax of 20 percent for this individual—a function of the capital gain deduction and the maximum rate of 50 percent. The reason that the capital gain rate will top off at 20 percent is that every capital gain (in our case the capital gain of $85,000) is subject to a deduction of 60 percent. Sixty percent is untaxed, in effect, and in this case that's a deduction of $51,000. The 40 percent remainder, $34,000, is taxed at 50 percent, leaving the seller, in the worst of cases, with a 20 percent capital gains tax. So for 1982 and thereafter, that's as much capital gains tax as can be suffered on the sale of appreciated long-term capital gain property. For all practical purposes, the people we are dealing with are apt to be at, or fairly close to, the 50 percent bracket after 1981; and the result is that their capital gains will be taxed at close to 20 percent. (Short-term capital gains don't qualify for any deduction; they are taxed just like earned income at as much as 50 percent.)

Right now we are just comparing contributions, an outright sale as opposed to a bargain sale. We saw that for this high-bracket taxpayer in 1981, we can achieve parity (an equal benefit) or maybe even a little better with an outright gift. We can induce an outright gift because the tax benefits are as good as the after-tax return on a sale. But for 1982, even assuming that we still have a 5 percent state and local tax burden, we are only going to get about $55,000 out of our charitable contribution of $100,000. We still effect the same reduction of taxable income, but we don't get the same tax benefit because those dollars of taxable income offset would otherwise have been taxed only at 50 percent plus the state and local tax. So we go from parity to about a $20,000 unfavorable comparison, from our point of view.

Under 1981's pre-ERTA law, given ideal circumstances (a 70 percent marginal rate, very low-basis property, little delay in enjoyment of the charitable deduction, brokerage commissions on sale, and a state or local capital gains tax), an outright contribution could produce a financial return superior to a sale. Reduction of maximum individual tax rates to 50 percent and corresponding reduction of maximum capital gains rates to 20 percent have ended the donee's ability to demonstrate parity of after-tax return. That's what the 1981 tax act rate change means in the outright gift situation.

Well, the picture is not a whole lot brighter with reference to the possibilities of a bargain sale. A modest example of what could happen in a bargain sale can be illustrated with a 1980 sale. The example is an unmarried taxpayer with an adjusted gross and taxable income of $75,000, owning property worth $50,000, purchased for $10,000. The basis, therefore, is $10,000. Now a 1980 sale, for comparison, with $6,000 offset for sale expenses, will produce a $34,000 long-term capital gain. That is subject to the capital gain deduction of 60 percent and then would be subject to tax to this particular taxpayer at 63 percent, a single person with income in roughly the $50,000 range. The taxpayer in this case would realize after tax a net of $35,432.

We're not entitled to use the full $10,000 basis to offset the gain on the sale part of this transaction.[4] We simply apportion the basis between the gift and the sale parts. Six thousand dollars of our basis goes to the sale part, giving us an amount realized of $30,000 and adjusted basis of $6,000. That means a $24,000 gain. (In a family transaction, however,

---

4. *Computing bargain sales.* When a taxpayer sells property to a charity at a bargain price, the gain in the property that is attributable to the "sale" portion must be recognized. The amount of the charitable deduction—the difference between the fair market value of the property and the sales price—is unaffected, but gain is required to be reported to the extent that the sale price exceeds that amount of the taxpayer's basis assigned to the sale portion by the special allocation-of-basis rule of Section 1011(b). The formula is as follows:

$$\frac{\text{Basis in sale portion}}{\text{Total basis}} = \frac{\text{Amount realized}}{\text{Fair market value}}$$

Mortgages or other liens to which the property is subject or which are assumed by the donee are considered amounts realized on the transfer.

you can use your whole basis. Only the charitable bargain sale is subject to this allocation rule.)

On the gift side of this transaction, we have a $20,000 contribution. The $20,000 contribution offsets the taxable income produced by the sale, which, after the capital gains deduction, was only $9,600. It produces an excess donation of $10,400, and that $10,400 excess produces a tax benefit of $5,720. When all is said and done then, the 1980 bargain sale at 60 percent of value produced a slightly better financial return than the outright sale would have produced. A large assumption there is the $6,000 commission, but there is going to be some transaction cost. I think this is a fairly realistic example of what could have been done in 1980.

Now let's look at the comparison.

1980 SALE

Amount realized	$44,000
Adjusted basis	− 10,000
Long-term capital gain	$34,000
Incremental taxable income	
(after 60% deduction)	13,600
Incremental tax (63% bracket)	8,568
Net after tax ($44,000 − $8,568)	$35,432

1980 BARGAIN SALE FOR $30,000

Amount realized	$30,000
Allocated basis	− 6,000
Long-term gain	$24,000
Incremental AGI and taxable income	9,600
Total return:	$35,720

Charitable contribution of $20,000 offsets taxable income produced by sale ($9,600) and provides additional $5,720 tax benefit (55 percent of $10,400).

Now consider the same choice for 1982.

1982 SALE

Amount realized	$44,000
Adjusted basis	− 10,000
Long-term capital gain	$34,000
Incremental taxable income	13,600
Incremental tax (50% bracket)	6,800
Net after tax	$37,200

1982 BARGAIN SALE FOR $30,000

Produces same incremental AGI
($9,600) as for 1980

Total return: $35,200

Charitable contribution of $20,000 offsets taxable income produced by sale and yields additional $5,200 tax benefit (50 percent of $10,400).

Bargain Sale Under Threat of Condemnation

There are several varieties of bargain sales that are not widely appreciated. There is a bargain sale that takes place in the context of an "involuntary conversion," otherwise known as a condemnation. Back in 1969 the Internal Revenue Service gave its benediction by published ruling to a sale under threat of condemnation to a private conservation organization. The facts of that ruling (69-303, the nature conservancy ruling) were that the property was subject to condemnation when the legitimate threat of condemnation existed. Often those threats, as you know, can be produced in a fairly amicable way. But the taxpayer, in apprehension of threat, sold to a private conservation organization, which took the property on an interim basis before public appropriations could be made to acquire it. That basic pattern has been used time and time again for condemnations.

You can use the condemnation in conjunction with a bargain sale. For example, let's assume that the condemning authority offers to pay appraised fair market value, as it's bound by law to do, of $250,000. Let's assume also that the taxpayer believes, perhaps on the basis of another appraisal, that the property is worth half a million dollars, $500,000. Now that's a large gulf, and it is probably worth arguing about. The drawbacks of argument are long delay, litigation expenses, and, of course, living with uncertainty of result for quite some time. In that case, the conservation organization has a role to play as an arbiter and can step in and negotiate an acquisition for a bargain price of $250,000. That's the price, of course, at which the property was valued by the authority to begin with. It may seem positively greedy for the taxpayer to say that a $250,000 deduction ought to go along with this. But if you think about it, there is really no inconsistency there. We hark back to the contribution "amount" as the price that a willing buyer would pay a willing seller with no duress. That amount is not the amount that the public agency appraises the property at; there's always a low end of the scale. That amount is the amount that will be established ultimately by reliable appraisal. Assuming that you have faith in your appraisal, you deserve a deduction for the $250,000 bargain element.

QUESTION: Considering most condemnations go to court, how reasonable is it to assume that the entity will accept your appraisal?

Hutton: The entity doesn't have to. That's the lovely part of it. Who has to accept the appraisal? The Internal Revenue Service. If it doesn't accept the appraisal, then of course you have the possibility of litigation. This, however, will be a less costly evidentiary proceeding in tax court. That's what usually happens.

There is a very interesting case involving the Rainier companies, the brewing company up in Seattle, which owned the old Seattle Stadium [Rainier Companies, Inc., 61T.C.68(1973)].

For years, the company wanted the city of Seattle to take it off its hands. Finally, after long negotiations, the city agreed to do so at a price of about $1 million, whereupon the company alleged for tax purposes that (1) the stadium had been voluntarily condemned by the city, and (2) it was worth more than a million dollars and that the company had therefore made a charitable contribution. There was quite a long history of unpleasantness behind this, and the tax court held against the company on both counts. The decision was based on the fact that there was no condemnation, it was an arm's-length negotiation, and that there was no charitable contribution because Rainier simply couldn't demonstrate they had the intent to make a gift. The evidence was probably pretty slim. But the case went up to the Ninth Circuit on appeal and was consequently sent back to the tax court for a finding on the charitable contribution count. The tax court, on remand, did find a relatively small ($100,000) contribution.

The significance of the case is that there is no suggestion in any of the proceedings that the government ever considered these things to be incompatible, that is, the involuntary conversion and the charitable contribution. So that's very hopeful authority and it's a very nice out. You might in some cases have a greater disparity than is evidenced here, particularly as to evaluations of California coastal properties. The condemning authority might come in at $200,000 and your private appraiser, who may make believe that the coastal commission is unconstitutional, will come in at $2 million, in which case you quite clearly are going to have a very large argument with the Internal Revenue Service.

A condemnation sale may be tax free. The Service clarified procedures this year by ruling that it doesn't matter to whom you make the sale. For example: A legitimately believes that the condemning authority is going to take his property (it's on a priority list). And the authority has the power to condemn. A sells the property to B (let's assume B is an exempt organization), and A alleges that this is at a bargain price. So A then has the benefit of what is Section 1033 of the Code. A can reinvest the sale proceeds. If he *reinvests the full proceeds,* he escapes the tax on the capital gain. Now B, the exempt organization, then may be taken out by the condemning authority. But if B were not an exempt organization, B similarly could sell that property at some point, maybe at a slightly higher price to C; and B can also use the provisions of Section 1033, since he meets the literal statute. There is no interpretation involved. It's just comforting that the Service agrees.

Bargain Sale at Below Market Interest

There is another variety of bargain sale that it seems to me you ought to be aware of and you may find somewhat surprising. Suppose you have the chance to get a loan at 7 percent interest, a five-year loan to underwrite a project. The lender may very well ask, "Won't I get a charitable contribution deduction for the difference between the lower rate and fair market rate interest?" The answer is no, you don't get a deduction for that because there has been no gift, no transfer of property. It's really a right to use money and that doesn't yield a deduction.

However, there are ways to give the donor that benefit through a charitable contribution. Suppose we have a *sale* at a rate of interest that is lower than market interest. This is descriptive of what is generously called "creative financing" in real estate today: The seller demands the price because he agrees to give very favorable terms. The lower than market rate of interest, however, cannot descend below 9 percent, because that is the level that the Internal Revenue Code and regulations now require to be provided on sales in order for no interest to be imputed. Section 483 of the Code says that if you sell property without providing any interest at all, then some of what you believe to be sale price, proceeds of the sale itself, or principal, are going to be turned into interest payments by the statute. If you don't provide any interest or you provide less than 9 percent, to the extent of the deficiency interest is going to be imputed at a rate of 10 percent compounded semiannually. You've got to provide 9 percent, but there's still a big gap between 9 percent and a commercial loan. Let's explore the potential for creating a charitable gift.

A seller transfers property with alleged fair market value of $100,000 to exempt organization buyer for $10,000 in cash and a $90,000, 9 percent note. The seller's amount realized through the sale is the amount of the cash plus the amount of the property received. You may not think of the note as property, but it is. A note is property. The note in this case is worth by assumption $70,000, because it is at low interest, with a big balloon payment at maturity in ten years, and consequently is worth substantially less than its face amount, maybe about $70,000. The seller has made a bargain sale, even though he may perfectly reasonably expect to be fully paid out at maturity. The seller is not getting the full $100,000 "price"; he is getting the present value, and that is $10,000 cash plus the note worth $70,000. The bargain element of $20,000 is a charitable contribution.[5] [See *Mason* vs. *Commissioner*, 513 F.2d 25 (7th Cir. 1975).] I shudder to think how many sellers who have given favorable rates of interest have not taken advantage of the charitable contribution.

QUESTION: How would we use this to our advantage because the example shows the land trust still paying full fair market value.

Hutton: No. The land trust *isn't* paying full market value. And in these inflationary times you must think in terms of present value. You have just got to train yourself to think that you are obligated to pay $80,000 for that land. Let me put it this way. You can choose to pay $100,000 now or choose to pay $100,000 with $10,000 down and 9 percent interest on the remainder with a big balloon payment of $90,000 in ten years. So you are not paying $100,000. You are paying $80,000, and that is why the charitable contribution of $20,000 is made.

QUESTION: When is the charitable contribution realized?
Hutton: When the closing occurs.

QUESTION: Doesn't that assume that the difference becomes 7 percent, and the real commercial rate is also constant the next ten years?

Hutton: Sure it does. You are entitled to measure that now and you can easily do that. Just measure it by what discount a solid, corporate obligation is subject to on the market. It's very easy in this case. The seller could simply take this note of the exempt organization down to the friendly savings and loan or commercial bank or three or four of them and get a price on it, assuming you could find somebody who is in the market for buying paper; you just price it and find out what the market will bring. If you don't want to go to that trouble, you can just pick up the *Wall Street Journal* and see what a AAA bond ten years out at 9 percent is going for and then maybe discount it a little further because you don't have AT&T.

---

5. Should he use the installment method of reporting gain, as he will be required to do unless he elects out per Section 453(d), consistency dictates that the basis for determining gross profit be derived under Section 1011(b); that is, that it be $8,000.

GIFTS IN TRUST

I think one of the things that has been both beneficial and burdensome in the environmental preservation movement is the fact that we are dealing with contributions of or interests in target properties. Since this has been our focus, there has been somewhat less creativity in general fund-raising development techniques. Hospitals and educational institutions that don't solicit contributions of medical paraphernalia, books, lecterns, and such, are way ahead of us in this regard. They have developed techniques for raising sustenance we have not thought about because our focus has been on land.

The charitable trust is something we ought to be thinking about. In 1969, Congress created the permissibility of certain limited kinds of gifts in trust that are intended to produce either a present or a deferred benefit to charity [Sec.170(f)(2), 664, 2055(c)(2), 2522(c)(2)]. Charitable remainder trusts are in some ways a little difficult to use in our context, but these provide an interim income interest for a term of years or for the lives of named persons, and then ultimately the charitable remainder interest comes to the charitable beneficiary. The other variety is just the opposite. In a charitable lead trust the charitable interest comes up front. Now let's take the 1982 estate and gift tax rates to illustrate how this works.

What we are attempting to do is to create income from a trust to go to an exempt organization for a period of years, after which the trust will terminate. What is left of the *corpus* will go to the individual, most likely children or grandchildren of the creator of the trust. Let's take a modest trust of $500,000, a charitable lead trust because the income interest "leads" off. We have to provide that the return to charity for a period of years is in the form either of an annuity (annuity is a fixed dollar amount that continues from year to year) or a percentage interest, a percentage of the fair market value of assets of the trust valued every year. Almost always these vehicles provide for an annuity interest because the trust *corpus* is expected to grow modestly, and the donor does not ordinarily want the exempt organization to benefit from that growth as much as the remainder beneficiaries, say his grandchildren. Now let's further assume that upon this contribution of $500,000 in trust, we provide for a 12 percent annuity, or $60,000 a year. The exempt organization income beneficiary gets $60,000 each year for twelve years, a total of $720,000.

There is no charitable income tax deduction, but any gift and/or estate tax liability is eliminated on acccount of this transfer. This transfer is first going to put $500,000 into the trust and then finally over to the grandchildren without any gift tax liability. How is it that we haven't made a gift to the grandchildren? By any reasonable economic construction of what's going on here, we have made two gifts. We have made a gift to the exempt organization of the present value of the right to receive $60,000 a year for twelve years, and we have made a gift of the difference between $500,000 and that amount to the grandchildren. But here we benefit from some anachronistic Treasury tables, because the Treasury tells us that we are only going to be able to produce a 6 percent return on the trust investments. The value of the remainder to the grandchildren is based upon the assumption of a 6 percent return. If we go out twelve years at 12 percent, there is no assumed value to the grandchildren's interest. So what we have done, in short, is to avoid any transfer tax. All of the gift to the exempt organization, which is deemed to be the whole $500,000, is free of gift tax because it is a charitable trust. This is only really workable when dealing with a fairly high-bracket taxpayer for estate and gift purposes.

We'll put this another way. Assume that we just invested $500,000, produced our roughly 14 percent yield, and that, after 50 percent income tax, the investment is going to give a 7 percent after-tax return every year. In twelve years that $500,000 will grow to approximately $1.2 million. Now assume that after that twelve-year period of time (which is the relevant measure point), the settlor dies and this property comes into the estate. What's left after estate tax, $600,000, goes to the grandchildren. That would be the nonlead trust setting. The grandchildren end up with $600,000 after twelve years, assuming we have not invaded any of these assets at all. In the charitable lead setting, we've not only been able to produce 12 percent to pay to the exempt organization, $60,000 per year, we've actually been able to see this trust *corpus* grow modestly. At that modest growth rate the remainder to the grandchildren is probably going to be worth about $600,000. So they get the same $600,000, and who benefits and who loses? It's obvious. No tax dollars paid and the exempt organization draws down its annuity for twelve years. There is, of course, a loss of revenue to the government—what otherwise would be $600,000 in estate taxes.

The property is out of the settlor's hands right now. It's gone, and it will eventually go to the grandchildren with no tax to pay. It's really a choice here of paying the government or paying your favorite exempt organization if you have the resources to do it. And many do. There isn't any limit as to the size of the trust, but these benefits really depend upon the assumption of a close to 50 percent gift/estate tax bracket. And now one reaches the top brackets really pretty quickly, about $2 million at present gift/estate tax rates.

I don't think we should lose sight of the fact that some of the development techniques that were pioneered elsewhere could very well be of interest to the kind of people we talk to, both for investment of liquid assets and securities and for real property. While real property is not frequently contributed to charitable remainder trusts, if the property is subject to no liability or if any liability can be satisfied prior to the contribution, funding a charitable remainder unitrust with substantially appreciated real property offers interesting possibilities.

Example: T owns undeveloped ranchland with a basis of $105,000 and a value of $1,650,000. Suppose that T contributes that property to a 6 percent unitrust [described in Sec. 664(d)(2)], making the "income only" and "makeup" elections available per Section 664(d)(3). Income interests are retained for T and his spouse, and succeeding interests to their three children, now ages 14, 11, and 6. The remainder interest is donated to a conservation organization, and T and his brother will serve as trustees.

1. *Tax-exempt vehicle.* For years in which it has no unrelated business taxable income per Section 512, the charitable remainder unitrust or annuity trust is *tax exempt*. Sale of the ranch to a person or persons not "disqualified" under Section 4946 will therefore produce a long-term capital gain of $1,500,000, none of which is subject to tax to the trust. Had T sold that land individually, the tax, at an effective rate of 20 percent, would be $300,000. The trustee's sale, therefore, effects a tax saving equal to 18.2 percent of the value of the contributed property.

2. *Charitable deduction.* The charitable deduction is a function of the percentage payout to the income beneficiaries (here, 6 percent), and the joint actuarial life expectancies of those beneficiaries (here, 75–80 years). The regulations' tables (Reg. 1.664-4) are based upon an income assumption of 6 percent; although it is possible to stipulate any payout percentage of 5 percent or more, stipulation of a percentage in excess of 6 percent creates the actuarial danger of exhausting *corpus* before the death

of the last income beneficiary. Where this danger amounts to more than a "remote possibility," the unitrust may not qualify on account of the lack of an allowable charitable deduction (see *Revenue Ruling* 77-374, 1977-2 C.B. 329). Accordingly, where the principal intent is to achieve Section 664(c) tax-exempt status for a trust with a very substantial (two or three generation) noncharitable interest, the payout should not exceed 6 percent.

Present value of the remainder interest is not required to constitute any minimum percentage of the initial fair market value of the trust *corpus*. (The framers of this 1969 reform act provision, in their determination to correlate the grantor's deduction with the charitable remainder donee's expectations, evidently completely overlooked this rather fundamental point.) So at a present value cost of perhaps 1 percent of value, D has saved $300,000 in capital gains tax on the trustee's sale to set the stage for diversification of the investment.

3. *Future income.* Income earned by the trust, in excess of that required to be paid to D and successor beneficiaries (6 percent of the value of trust assets valued annually) will accumulate tax free. The unitrust thus combines the tax-exemption feature of a qualified plan with the current return of a variable annuity.

4. *Investment policies.* The trustee's investment policies should take into account the present tax situation of the income beneficiaries without losing sight of the tax-free accumulation permitted the trust, the result of which will be to amplify future distributions (6 percent of an increasing *corpus*). In our example, consider the following strategies:

a. *Sell land for a long-term gain of $1,500,000 and buy highly rated corporate debentures yielding 15 percent.* Sale of the land will create $1,500,000 of "tier 3" income per Section 664(b)(2), but the ordinary interest income ($247,500 in the first year) takes precedence in characterizing the income paid to D and his spouse (approximately $106,000) [Reg. 1.664-3(a)(1)(iv)]. The trust *corpus* will grow under this policy at a predictable rate of 9 percent, doubling every eight years.

b. *Sell land and buy 9 percent municipal bonds.* Although this results in characterizing the income paid to D and his spouse as long-term capital gains, it substantially sacrifices the trust's growth potential and ought to be objected to by the remote income beneficiaries and, of course, the charitable remainder beneficiary (were it to know of the gift). [See also Reg. 1.664-1(a)(3).]

c. *Sell land and diversify into growth-oriented investments* yielding 3 percent (dividends). This balanced approach has the advantage of preserving the capital gain preference as to approximately half the income paid out while permitting the trust at least a reasonable opportunity to keep pace with inflation. Needless to say, the trustee's policy may change from time to time as beneficiaries' circumstances change, and future sales of appreciated trust assets, like the original diversification, will be tax free.

5. *Potential gift/estate tax liabilities* have often inhibited use of the unitrust in such circumstances, but with the 1981 act's amplification of Section 2010's credit, the unitrust may become a much more significant investment vehicle.

GIFTS OF PARTIAL INTEREST (NOT IN TRUST)

In 1969 Congress was concerned about certain perceived abuses involving gifts of partial interests in property, and the most obvious illustration is the gift of use [Sec. 170(f) (3)(A)]. Suppose you have a four-story office building and the rental value of each floor is $5,000 a year. Let's assume that it's all net leased and there are no expenses, so you can produce $20,000 of income. You rent out the lower two floors, which produce $10,000 of income, and we give the right to use of the upper two floors to appropriate exempt organizations. Now before 1969, that produced a deduction equal to fair rental value, and the net result, of course, was that you had a charitable contribution of $10,000. It was like allowing deductions for gifts of services. [Gifts of services that could be said to have coalesced into property (works of art) were indeed deductible. Artists painted their deductions at the end of every year, up to their percentage limitations. A lot of small museums benefited from them (there have been several attempts in the intervening years to restore that privilege). But pure gifts of services have never been allowed as a deduction under the regulations.]

Congress in 1969 carved out two categories of exception, and since then another very important one has been added. These categories cover gifts of remainder interests, gifts of undivided interests, and qualified conservation contributions.

REMAINDER INTERESTS

Gifts of remainder interests are limited to farms and personal residences, but those two categories are very broad [Sec. 170(f)(3)(B)(i)]. "Personal residence" doesn't have to be primary. The farm does not have to be a farm that the taxpayer himself or herself works; it can be a tenant farm [Reg. 1.170A(b)(3), (4)]. The problem with remainder interest gifts is that they aren't very attractive in terms of the tax benefits they produce. The remainder value, as with any remainder gift, is an actuarial determination. If you take a 58-year-old woman with a substantial estate that is a seasonal personal residence, a donation of the remainder interest in that residence would produce, actuarially, a deduction of roughly one-third. In other words, her life expectancy is deemed to consume two-thirds of the value, and the present value of the remainder is only going to be about one-third. Further, if there are any improvements, as there will be for personal residences and most farms, you also have to build in a reduction factor for depreciation [Sec. 170(f)(4); Reg. 1.170A-12]. Depending upon the size of the residence and its value relative to the land, you might come down to a deduction much smaller than one-third. For that, the taxpayer is giving up all rights of ownership after her death. For that reason, to a lot of people, the remainder interest donation just doesn't appear exceedingly attractive.

UNDIVIDED INTERESTS

The second exception, which unfortunately has been pretty much neglected, is the exception for undivided interests. Under the regulations (1.170A-7), an "undivided portion" of a donor's entire interest in property "must consist of a fraction or percentage of each and every substantial interest or right owned by the donor in such property and must extend over the entire term of the donor's interest." Where the prospective donor owns the fee, the donee must receive a fraction or percentage of that fee interest, i.e., must become a tenant in common. Where the donor's interest is for a term of years, the donee must take a coterminous interest (in tax jargon, a "vertical slice"). Note that gifts of undivided interests are present gifts; this exception may therefore cover transfers of fractional interests in tangible personal property, and, in fact, many donors of works of art thus secure current deductions while retaining undivided interests.

The donor and donee will typically execute a use agreement at the time of the gift. Occasionally it may be feasible to share all rights of access and exploitation equally, but much more common is an agreement that allocates use seasonally. The regulations sanction such a division, and a published ruling approves a transaction where the donor evidently reserved the most desirable (summer) season [Reg. 1.170A-7(b)(1)(i); *Revenue Ruling* 75-420, 1975-2 C.B. 78].

QUALIFIED CONSERVATION CONTRIBUTIONS

We come now to the third category, which is probably of paramount interest to many of you, the category covering qualified conservation contributions (P.L. 96-541, 12-17-80). Since the 1969 act it has been possible to take conservation easements, first under a rather illogical construction of the "undivided interest" exception. Then Congress, in 1976, created a separate statutory category for conservation easements. Under the 1976 legislation, it was possible to create such a creature for a thirty-year term. A year later, in 1977, the statute was amended to require the easement grant to be made in perpetuity.

There was a "sunset" date on the 1977 legislation, June 14, 1981, and about a year before that legislation was due to expire, the Treasury began to entertain lobbying for lifting the sunset date and for redefining conservation easements. The incentive for that redefinition, at the outset, was principally the problem of mineral interests. Now this never should have been a problem, as mineral interests are separate properties. In the view of the Internal Revenue Service, however, the mineral interest was part of the property and therefore donation of the fee subject to retained mineral interests was not permitted. The Service ruled in 1976 to that effect. There was considerable agitation over gifts, therefore, when donors wanted to retain mineral rights. That's how the legislation started. Of course it grew like Topsy, and what we got was an entirely new subsection of the Internal Revenue Code, Section 170(h), which is designed to define the kinds of interests that qualify as conservation contributions (see P.L. 96-541, 12-17-80). There are essentially three elements of this definition:

1. *"Qualified property interest."* The first has to do with the nature of the interest in property. Congress dealt with the mineral problem by providing that a gift with retained mineral rights will be deductible, provided that conservation purposes are protected. The principal protection is in the nature of the exploration and exploitation. Subsurface mining only is permitted and only to the extent that the integrity of the surface attributes is preserved. A gift of a "qualified property interest" also includes a remainder interest or a perpetual restriction on the use that may be made of the property.

2. *Qualified organizations.* Secondly, the donor organization must be either a public charity, a governmental entity, or an organization that is controlled by a public charity as a "satellite," that is, a Section 509(a)(3) organization.

3. *Conservation purposes.* Then there is the definition of "conservation purposes" protected in perpetuity. Any one or more of four categories of purposes satisfies the statute. Many of you are intensely interested in this, but the bounds of these categories are conjectural.

a. The first category contemplates public access for recreation or education of the public. That should create little difficulty, except perhaps where the use or access to the "public" would be severely limited. A typical easement does not provide for public access, is not intended to, and the positive rights of access are intended to be as they always were.

b. The second category covers "relatively natural habitat," an ecologically oriented category. This, too, except on the fringes of "relatively" natural land, should not create any problems. It may raise some interesting questions as to land that is not ecologically significant itself but that acts as a buffer to land which is.

c. Now the third category is indeed controversial, encompassing open space land, including specifically farmland and forest land. It is the first statutory recognition that the preservation of such properties may be a significant charitable purpose. The Internal Revenue Service does not apparently recognize as exempt an organization that has as its principal purpose the protection of open space or agricultural land. In Section 170, Congress has, implicitly at least, said that within the realm of charitability there is a place for open space preservation. To create such charitability, you need public benefit either through scenic enjoyment of the general public or through a clearly delineated governmental policy, productive of a "significant public benefit." It isn't the level of government we are concerned about; it's the means by which governmental policy is effectuated or declared. The legislative history serves as guidance. A mere declaration is said not to be enough. On the other hand, it isn't necessary to have a funded program.

If you have a funded program, it seems to me that ought to be sufficient. But we don't have regulations yet. I think that one of the significant lobbying efforts in the near future is going to be the development of governmental commitments on a more or less local level to further policies to preserve farmland.

d. Preservation of a historically important land area or a certified historic structure is also a qualified conservation purpose and is the fourth category under which a transfer may qualify.

The Service is apparently willing to issue private rulings as to the qualifications of easement contributions. That is by no means expeditious, and there are a good number of rulings that are pending. I am not aware of any yet issued, and the ones I am aware of were filed in the latter part of 1981.

QUESTION: What's the prognosis for a land trust accepting an easement contribution this year in absence of regulations?

Hutton: It depends on the property. Take the scenic category: If you have property that is largely or wholly visible from a fairly well-traveled highway and that you yourself believe is scenic and deserving of preservation, I really think that you could proceed on an opinion letter. I think it probably would be enough.

QUESTION: What do you mean by *opinion letter*?

Hutton: A letter of counsel. As to land qualifying pursuant to a so-called clearly delineated policy, I would be much more hesitant to say.

QUESTION: Are there problems with the donation of conservation easements and the retention of mineral rights by the donee? With the owners giving all the fee interest except the mineral rights?

Hutton: Literally, that is a statutory problem. One would hope the Treasury would not take the statute literally in that case. The surface rights are protected through the limitation to subsurface mining methods. The easement would qualify in one of these categories theoretically, but literally it may not meet the statute. That could be cured by regulations, and the Treasury has the authority to do it.

QUESTION: If somebody else owns and retains the mineral rights when the easement was given and granted, there is no problem, is that true?

Hutton: The real question here is whether you can assure the protection of the conservation purpose in perpetuity, and I believe you would have to have some sort of guarantee.

QUESTION: Can you artificially separate mineral rights from the land by giving them to your son?

Hutton: So that you set the stage for a gift? I am assuming that the regulations will bring those transactions together, and the facts you state indicate that the two steps ought to be "collapsed."

QUESTION: What about rejoining the easement to the fee interest if the conservation purposes can no longer be met because of external factors?

Hutton: The statute requires the protection by deed restrictions in perpetuity, and so you really have some prospects of awfully tangled land-use questions down the road. If the property no longer has ecological significance because it is no longer quality habitat, at least in theory you are not justified as the taker of that easement in effecting a merger of the easement and fee so that you can jointly sell the property and put that money in something more beneficial. You can't do it. Actually you will be able to do it, but it will take a court proceedings down the road somewhere.

QUESTION: Do you see any significant trends in the interpretation of easement law by Treasury in the current administration?

Hutton: No, I don't think so. The Treasury and the Internal Revenue Service, at least at the technical levels, are pretty well insulated from the political process. I don't think this question is political or that the regulations we are going to get are going to be reflective of any particular ideology.

QUESTION: If you are operating in a county, for example, which for some reason had officially declared itself a scenic place and had adopted a master plan to include a scenic preservation element, and which in fact had few means at its disposal to accomplish those goals, but felt that your work was helpful, would that be sufficient?

Hutton: I feel good about that. And if that involves any county budgetary implications, I would feel even better. I think you are quite a long ways along the road toward whatever the regulations will require. You may not be there but at least you've made a start.

ESTATE PLANNING and DEFERRED GIVING:
Recent Changes in the Law

Kingsbury Browne, Jr.

ESTATE PLANNING FOR LANDOWNERS

What do we have in mind when we talk about estate planning for landowners?

Estate planning is an overall response to a generally complicated problem that includes several elements that need to be identified with respect to the burdens of land ownership: maintenance, carrying costs such as property taxes, wealth transfer taxes, financial security (the widow's needs), the needs and desires of children, and ethical concerns, or land stewardship.

Estate planning identifies these burdens, then marshals a variety of techniques such as gifts, easements, trusts, and partnerships in an effort to meet and carry the many burdens of ownership without material change in land use.

Some of these techniques are designed to minimize property and wealth transfer taxes; others call on tax incentives to subsidize an estate planning solution. Estate planning is more than financial or land use planning.

Should Land Conservation Organizations Be Concerned with Estate Planning?

The subject is highly technical and traditionally thought to require experts—some lawyers, for example. Trained estate planners tend to focus on the content of their craft and neglect the delivery side. Although they meet together to figure out what the problems are, most tax lawyers seldom ask the basic question, "How do we deliver legal care?" On the other hand, the delivery of medical care in the United States is generally excellent—if cost is disregarded: Most communities or regions have a hospital with an emergency ward, laboratories, and trained staff. But in the less-developed countries, there may be a central hospital but no delivery system in the countryside. There are no clinics or midwives to deliver prenatal care; no means of first aid; no communication. The delivery of estate planning services to landowners in this country while better than the delivery of medical services in less-developed countries is still in the early stages of development.

There are several reasons for the inadequate delivery of estate-planning care:

1.   Until recently, the need was not perceived: Few, if any, estate-planning courses even now focus on the special problems of land.

2.   The literature is scant and often not available.

3.   The very nature of land ownership makes any planning for its future time-consuming and therefore very costly in terms of what the landowner must pay or in terms of the *pro bono* time the specialist must contribute.

4.   Traditional sources of estate planning assistance—law firms and banks, for example—are not perceived of as knowledgeable when it comes to land.

Given the present situation of mediocre delivery of estate planning assistance to landowners by traditional means, the land conservation organization (LCO) may well be the one emerging institution best equipped to deliver estate planning care to landowners. The LCO is out in the field, and, unlike law firms that simply practice law, the LCO can be a one-stop source of many services: After the LCO has provided forest management advice, it has the opportunity to bring up estate planning opportunities.

What Kind of Training Is Needed?
Given that the main problem is to equip LCOs to provide estate planning services, what materials would be useful? Do you need technical material? How would you go about talking with somebody in the field in a way that might tend to bring together these questions and some of the remedies? Much of what you have printed is good, but does not go deeply enough into planning.

How Does the Federal Tax System Relate to Estate Planning?
It imposes financial burdens that often affect the use of land—adversely from a conservationist's perspective: Developers close open space when the landowner is forced to sell to meet tax obligations. On the other hand, it offers means of financing land preservation: Tax incentives indirectly provide a federal subsidy.

What Are the Estate and Gift Tax Fundamentals
with Which LCOs Should Be Familiar?

1.   *Tax rate reduction.* Estate taxes have been at a maximum rate of 70 percent in 1981, and they will drop to 50 percent in 1983 for all transfers over $2,500. Certainly the tax rate is going to take some of the pressure off estates in terms of liquidity problems.

2.   *The unified credit.* After the gift or estate tax, that is, the wealth transfer tax, is computed, the unified credit is applied to reduce the tax payment. The unified credit increases from $47,000 for transfers in 1981 to $192,800 for transfers in 1987 and thereafter. For estate planning purposes, it is easier to think of the unified credit in terms of a portion of the landowner's estate that will be exempt from transfer tax: the so-called exemption equivalent (EE). In 1981, the EE is $175,000. The EE increases to $600,000 in 1987 and thereafter. The exemption equivalent is also sometimes called the *credit shelter.*

3. *Marital deduction.* After 1981, all transfers between spouses will be completely free of wealth transfer tax.

4. *Gift tax annual exclusion.* This exclusion, $3,000 in 1981, increases to $10,000 for gifts made in 1982 and thereafter. A spouse S-1 owning land worth $100,000 could transfer that land in 1982 to the spouse's five children without payment of transfer tax provided the other spouse S-2 consented to having half the gift treated as S-2's gift. In other words, by consenting, $50,000 is deemed to be the gift of each and since there are five children involved, each spouse has a $10,000 exclusion with respect to each child; so that this liberalization is going to make intrafamily transfers very attractive.

5. *The special valuation rules* applicable to farm properties have been liberalized. The present permissible deduction of $600,000 increases to $750,000 in 1983 and later years. The estate tax provisions permitting payment of estate tax over a fifteen-year period have also been liberalized.

Will These New Tax Benefits Reduce the Need for LCOs?

Given all these new tax benefits, do they reduce the need for conservation organizations? I have heard people suggest that there will be less inclination for charitable giving. Particularly in the estate tax area I think one has to conclude that the attractiveness of charitable gifts will have declined somewhat. When you look at the size of an estate that can now pass without transfer taxes, it is $1.2 million, properly structured. Those landowners may not be as inclined to use charitable deductions, but I don't think personally that reduces the needs for this kind of work by land conservation organizations. It seems to me that if I owned a piece of property that I wanted to keep in one piece, what I would want most to know, is not necessarily what would happen in the case of a charitable deduction, but how would I go about estate planning in such a way that the liquidity requirements at death would not destroy the property. I see a much stronger trend toward the *service function* by land conservation organizations as well as the traditional one of either accepting the land or facilitating its transfer. I guess that is a matter for the judgment of each of you, but I am not pessimistic about the effect of these tax liberalizations. I think they are going to help. The estate planning service role of the LCO is even more important as a result of complexities accompanying the new benefits. The LCOs cannot and should not replace lawyers. They should seek to assist them.

USE OF THE EXEMPTION EQUIVALENT AND
MARITAL DEDUCTION IN ESTATE PLANNING

In figure A, the rectangle is supposed to represent a $2,000,000 piece of land. In the first example, you see on the left-hand side, the unmarried decedent dies in 1981; you think of the estate tax, the transfer tax, as applying to $1,825,000 and the exemption equivalent as the small slice, $175,000. I compute the tax at $634,210. It is very large in this case because the example assumes no surviving spouse. (I think it was Mencken who said, "A spouse is an economic necessity.")

Then if you drop down to the second example, the unmarried decedent dies in 1987. (Really, one of the important estate planning recommendations is to stay alive. But lawyers are not legally competent to meddle in that area!) You have the same tract of land worth $2,000,000 and now the exemption equivalent carves out $600,000. And you've got a portion

ILLUSTRATIONS OF THE USE OF THE EE AND MD IN ESTATE PLANNING

Figure A. The Unmarried Landowner—$2,000,000 of land

The rectangle below represents the $2,000,000 of property.

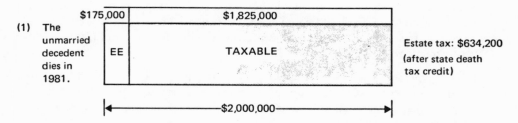

(1) The unmarried decedent dies in 1981.

$175,000	$1,825,000
EE	TAXABLE

Estate tax: $634,200 (after state death tax credit)

|←————————————$2,000,000————————————→|

EE = Exemption Equivalent or that part of the property that is not taxed because of the unified tax credit.

(2) The unmarried decedent dies in 1987.

$600,000	$1,400,000
EE	TAXABLE

Estate tax: $488,400

|←————————————$2,000,000 ————————————→|

The EE rises each year until 1987 when it amounts to $600,000.

of the $1,400,000 that is subject to transfer tax which I compute at $488,400. For the single taxpayer there is still a very substantial liquidity problem that requires you to look at one of the other tax areas for solutions.

The next diagram, figure B, deals schematically with the married landowner. Again the same $2,000,000 of land is involved. Since I have been instructed to take sex out of estate planning, S-1 is the first spouse to die and S-2 is the surviving spouse. In 1981, S-1, a married taxpayer, dies. There is an exemption equivalent of $175,000 of land not subject to transfer tax, assuming the maximum marital deduction in 1981, which is 50 percent. I know nothing really about community property; I think community property rules in California and the other eleven states produce maybe the same result, so that $1 million of that property is not subject to transfer tax at the death of the first spouse. The remaining taxable amount is $825,000 and the tax on that is $265,600; that is to be compared with the $634,200 in the case of the unmarried decedent dying in 1981.

Compare this now with the case in which the first to die, S-1, manages to stay alive another five years or six years when you have an exemption equivalent of $600,000 not subject to transfer tax. You have the same $1 million as above, and now that $400,000 on the right-hand side because of the new marital deduction rules is also free of transfer tax on the date of death of the first spouse.

Figure B. The Married Landowner—$2,000,000 of land: the death of the first spouse (S-1)

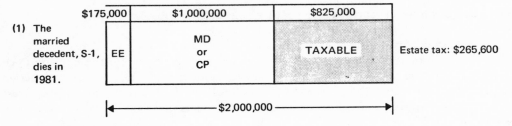

(1) The married decedent, S-1, dies in 1981.

$175,000	$1,000,000	$825,000
EE	MD or CP	TAXABLE

Estate tax: $265,600

←————————————— $2,000,000 —————————————→

MD = Marital deduction property
CP = Community property

(2) The married decedent, S-1, dies in 1987.

$600,000	$1,000,000	$400,000
EE	MD or CP	NEW MD

Estate tax: $0

←————————————— $2,000,000 —————————————→

The "old" marital deduction limited to 50 percent of the decedent's adjusted gross estate is now unlimited.

This example is typical of one form or one method of analysis. I think you can apply it to a larger estate and to smaller ones, but it is somewhat more dramatic at this level. Now to get that exemption equivalent, of $600,000 of real estate and $400,000 of marital deduction property, out from under transfer tax in the estate of the surviving spouse is the area that is preoccupying tax lawyers today. This simply represents a sort of result. It doesn't tell you anything about how to get there, and we have I think some quite interesting new concepts that are certainly going to require a great deal of redrafting of the instruments that we have used. You don't and you shouldn't think in terms of drafting instruments. I am perfectly prepared to defend the idea that you are not engaged in the unauthorized practice of law. But eventually some of this technical material simply has to come back to the hands of lawyers.

Creating a By-Pass Trust
If you wanted to expand on the B(1) illustration, you would indicate that the EE and the taxable portion went into a by-pass trust. In other words, in figure B(1) with the EE and the taxable portions, the net of taxes should by-pass the surviving spouse. There is no point in having constructed a tax-free transfer at this point simply to put it into the estate of the next to die. The tax reason for putting the exemption equivalent property into the by-pass trust is so that it doesn't show up in the surviving spouse's estate. If you just left it to the surviving spouse, it would then give rise to tax on S-2's death. What you are trying to do is to avoid trans-

fer tax on the exemption equivalent property in the first spouse's death and then again on the second spouse's death. So you use the by-pass, which simply says: The property can stay in one form of trust or similar arrangement for the benefit of the whole family, but we will do it in such a way that it won't get taxed at the death of the surviving spouse.

Death of Surviving Spouse

Now turn to the death of the surviving spouse; S-2 dies in 1981. See figure C(1). Assume that S-2 has no property other than what came from S-1's estate as marital deduction property. That amount is $1 million and was half of S-1's estate. The rest of the land is in trust to be passed on to the children. At S-2's death, $1 million is taxable. S-2's exemption equivalent exempts $175,000, leaving $825,000 to be taxed. I compute this tax at $265,600. That figure would be a great deal more if they had not used a formal by-pass arrangement, a simple demonstration of the utility of passing on property through an estate.

Figure C.   On Death of the Surviving Spouse, S-2

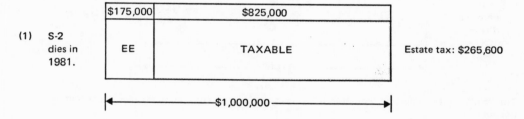

Assumption: S-2's estate consists solely of that part of S-1's estate consisting of CP or MD property.

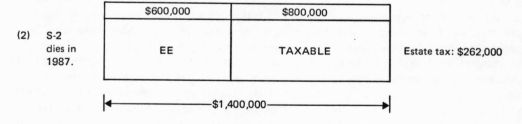

Assumption: S-2's estate consists solely of that part of S-1's estate consisting of CP or MD property.

COMBINED ESTATE TAXES	1981	1987
S-1	$265,600	No tax
S-2	$265,600	$262,000
Totals	$531,200	$262,000
Difference	$269,200	

What About Inflation in These Situations?

The exemption equivalent umbrella is not going to look as handsome in 1987 as it does today if inflation keeps up. As a general rule, rapidly appreciating property, whether by reason of inflation or real appreciation, should go into a by-pass trust. But you need to calculate the tax cost of doing it.

Dramatic Results of Changes in Law

The dramatic results of the new changes are shown in figure C. If S-2 dies in 1987, S-2 has a taxable estate of $1.4 million, and, you ask, why, if it is only $1 million in the first example, is it now $1.4 million? You must go back and look at the previous figure toward the bottom, where you will see that there was no estate tax in the estate of the first spouse to die because there was marital deduction from the property of $1 million, and we know that that comes into the surviving spouse's property, but there is an additional $400,000 that also comes in. The price of eliminating $1.4 million in the first spouse's estate from estate taxes is that it be includable in the estate of the surviving spouse. So here again we have an exemption equivalent in 1987 of $600,000, leaving $800,000 giving rise to tax of $262,000. What was previously not deductible becomes deductible so that your marital deduction applies to the entire transfer between the spouses. We now have $262,000 of estate tax payable in the estate of the second spouse, and if you compare what happens in 1981 with what happens in 1987 utilizing the new marital deduction rules and take advantage of the new exemption equivalent, the overall saving in estate taxes is $269,200.

Observations

1. The EE should not be left to the surviving spouse S-2 because it will then be subject to tax in S-2's estate: Leave it to children or in a by-pass trust for the benefit of S-2 and children.

2. The EE increases from $175,000 in 1981 to $600,000 in 1987, which means S-1's will, or testamentary trust, must contain a proper formula bequest to establish the tax-free EE.

3. Marital deduction (MD) property in 1981 is property that passes outright to S-2 or in a trust (marital deduction trust), the income of which is payable to S-2 and the principal of which at S-2's death will pass as S-2 may determine through the exercise of a general power of appointment.

4. MD property beginning in 1982 includes qualified terminable interest property (QTIP), in which S-2 has the right to income during S-2's life but no power at death to determine the disposition of the principal. The disposition of the QTIP property at S-2's death is determined by S-1.

Small Estates Need Planning

I do not want to suggest that these are problems only of very large estates. Families with estates not exceeding $1.2 million need not pay any estate tax either on the death of the first spouse or later on the death of the second. It is estimated by 1987 that only three-tenths of 1 percent of all decedents will be paying estate tax. The point to it is that even though there is no ultimate tax it requires very careful estate planning. I think that most plans drawn to date have got to be redrawn, or at least looked at very carefully. If the first spouse simply left everything to S-2 there would be no tax in the estate of the first spouse because any interspousal transfers after 1981 are not subject to transfer tax. But on S-2's death there would be a tremendous tax.

QTIP Trusts (Qualified Terminable Interest Property)

The QTIP trust provides an added marital deduction benefit without giving the surviving spouse control over the property. The QTIP trust has a serious disadvantage to it in an income tax sense. The QTIP trust income must be paid currently to the surviving spouse. If you have an estate of substantial size, that flow of taxable income over a long period of time through the surviving spouse's personal income tax return may prove to be more costly in terms of what is ultimately available to the children than if some tax had been paid on the death of the first spouse by foregoing the maximum marital deduction, again a matter of computation. The by-pass trust characteristically says that the income of that trust can be distributed by the trustee in such amounts and at such times as the trustee may determine to one or more members of the class consisting of the surviving spouse and children. And it provides *enormous* flexibility. The QTIP does not present that advantage.

Illustration of the Use of the Unlimited Marital Deduction,
the Unified Credit (Exemption Equivalent) and the New
$10,000 Exclusion in Lifetime Giving

In the first example (fig. A) S-1 owns land worth $630,000. There is no S-2. S-1 in 1987 gives the land to S-1's three children. There is no transfer, no gift, tax because of three exclusions of $10,000 each and an exemption equivalent of $600,000. In other words, the unified credit or exemption equivalent is available for both gift and estate tax purposes. So a very large lifetime gift can be made. There is no unified credit left at death because it has been used previously. The advantage is that it does get out of S-1's estate the appreciation that takes place after the gift and before S-1's death.

Now to take the same facts in that example except that there is an S-2 and the land is worth $1,260,000. If S-2 consents to having one-half of the gift being treated as made by S-2, then there is no transfer tax on a transfer of $1,260,000 of land. The figures work out that, by consenting, each spouse is deemed to have given $630,000 to their three children. Each is deemed to have made a transfer of $630,000. Each uses the exemption equivalent of $600,000 and each takes three $10,000 exclusions.

Should Spouses Acquiring Real Estate
After 1981 Take Title in Their Joint Names?

I don't know to what extent joint ownership is common in the West. It is very common in the East. We have had very complicated estate tax rules with respect to joint property. Historically, joint property simply meant that on the death of the first spouse the surviving spouse automatically assumed title to the property. The rule was that on the death of the first spouse to die, all of the property was includable in that spouse's estate, unless you could prove contribution by the surviving spouse. That became enormously complicated. It created all kinds of audit controversy. The law was amended to permit an election. If S-1 acquired the property and elected to have half of it treated as S-2's property, there was a taxable transfer at that time and then at death only half of the property was includable in the first spouse's estate. Rather a loose description of a complicated subject. The point is that after this new act, irrespective of who bought the property and paid for it, half will be deemed includable in the estate of each spouse.

There are some drawbacks to this new rule that relate to basis. One is that if there is any advantage to dying, it's the step up in basis you get for the property. Under this new rule, S-1's half of the property which S-1 is deemed to own, at death, gets a stepped-up basis in the hands of the surviving spouse. As to the other half, that is deemed owned by the surviving spouse; there is either no basis or it's some kind of carry-over basis from the time of origin of the ownership.

Under some circumstances, part of the family real estate should be divided between the spouses and not held jointly: the EE by-pass or credit shelter.

1. Suppose S-1 owns 100 acres of land worth $1,200 per acre jointly with S-2 (and no other property).

    a. If S-1 dies, there is no estate tax because of the unlimited marital deduction.

    b. When S-2 subsequently dies, S-2's EE eliminates 50 acres from tax but the other 50 are taxable and some must be sold, thereby reducing the acreage left to children.

    c. S-1 should have taken the 100 acres out of joint tenancy back into S-1's own name (no gift tax), left 50 acres outright to S-2 and 50 in a by-pass trust for S-2's benefit. There would be no estate tax on S-1's death. S-2's estate at death after 1986 would be limited to $600,000, and the EE would eliminate all tax.

2. If in the situation in 1(c), S-2 predeceased S-1, there is no estate tax on the land at S-2's death because S-1 owns the 100 acres. But on S-1's later death (after 1986), the $600,000 EE shelters 50 acres, but some of the remaining 50 acres have to be sold to pay S-1's estate taxes. S-1 should have given S-2 50 acres while they were both alive and each should have left 50 acres in a by-pass trust for the benefit of the other and children. In that event there would be no estate tax irrespective of the order of death.

3. A $600,000 EE can be worth more than $180,000 in tax savings, so proper planning is essential. An impecunious spouse can be worth $180,000 to the family!

GIFTS IN TRUST

I think that you probably want to rethink the use of short-term ten-year trusts. I am not sure that they are used much with land. Have any of you had any experience with short-term trusts of land as an estate planning device? It is usually used with high-income producing assets so that you can divert the cash flow to people in lower tax brackets, but it doesn't seem to me that ten-year trusts lend themselves that well to planning for land. I would be interested if anybody has had experience to the contrary.

CONSERVATION EASEMENTS

Charitable gifts of conservation easements have been very well covered elsewhere in this conference. The lawyer in the Chief Counsel's Office of the Internal Revenue Service in

Washington responsible for drafting the regulations is a man named Stephen Small. He is open to telephone calls (202-566-3238). He called me recently to say that next year the Form 990, the information return that is filed by an exempt organization, will have on it the question: "Did you accept any conservation easements; if so, please give us the taxpayer's identification number."

Reductions in Farm Valuations

The ability to value at current use instead of highest and best use at death is obviously under some circumstances a very valuable opportunity. There are limitations on the extent to which farming property may be reduced in value down to farm use value. Congress in 1981 says that the ceiling on that reduction is $600,000 but by 1983 it goes to $750,000. My guess is that some of the very technical language that loosens up the election will prove very helpful, but I just don't know. Conservation easement donations may also reduce the value to current use.

INCOME AND ESTATE TAX BENEFIT ANALYSIS

Unit 4 of TPL's land trust training program. This comparison demonstrates how to employ the estate preservation techniques of a conservation easement. In example A the ranch or farm has been appraised at its fair market value. By comparison, example B is the same property appraised for its agricultural value after the donation to a local land trust of a conservation easement. The property comprises 50 deeded acres, is both scenic and productive, has excellent water rights, and is traversed by a year-round stream.

ESTATE PRESERVATION CASE STUDY

	ESTATE VALUE EXAMPLE A	ESTATE VALUE RESULTING FROM DONATION OF CONSERVATION EASEMENT EXAMPLE B
Fair market value*	$20,000/acre	$5,000/acre
Decedent's gross estate	$1,000,000	$250,000
Debts, death expenses, legal	26,000	26,000
Adjusted gross estate	974,000	224,000
Marital deduction	0	0
Taxable estate	974,000	224,000
Federal estate tax	335,660	0
Federal tax credit	62,800	0
Federal estate tax liability	$ 272,860	$ 0

*The earning potential of the agricultural business remains the same, but the fair market value in property is reduced by the value of the conservation easement.

Beginning in 1982, a surviving spouse can inherit the deceased spouse's estate in its entirety, tax-free. The following summary compares the federal estate tax liabilities owed in examples A and B at the death of the second spouse for the respective years 1982–1987. By 1987 the full impact of the Economic Recovery Tax Act of 1981 on federal estate taxes will take effect. The comparison illustrates that estate taxes will still severely limit the heirs' ability to inherit large farm operations.

SUMMARY OF CASE STUDY FOR 1982–1984

	1982 A	1982 B	1983 A	1983 B	1984 A	1984 B
Federal estate tax	$335,660	$ 0	$335,660	$ 0	$335,660	$ 0
Federal tax credit	62,800	0	79,300	0	96,300	0
Federal tax liability	$272,860	$ 0	$256,360	$ 0	$239,360	$ 0

Excess of tax liability in example A over example B: 1982–$272,860; 1983–$256,360; 1984–$239,360.

SUMMARY OF CASE STUDY FOR 1985–1987

	1985 A	1985 B	1986 A	1986 B	1987 A	1987 B
Federal estate tax	$335,660	$ 0	$335,660	$ 0	$335,660	$ 0
Federal tax credit	121,800	0	155,800	0	192,800	0
Federal tax liability	$213,860	$ 0	$179,860	$ 0	$142,860	$ 0

Excess of tax liability in example A over example B: 1985–$213,860; 1986–$179,860; 1987–$142,860.

REPORTING CHARITABLE CONTRIBUTIONS

My guess is that many people who give gifts of conservation easements don't file a gift tax return. They will say, "This is to charity, I don't have to go through all this paper work." But that's wrong, you *must file a gift tax return* reporting the value of the gift and then claiming an offsetting charitable deduction. If you don't file the gift tax return and the gift turns out to be taxable, you may run into penalties for failure to file. There is now an overvaluation penalty. If the value as reported for charitable deduction purposes exceeds 150 percent of what is finally determined to be the value of the property, then there is a penalty that moves up in stages. That was designed, I think, for some of the extreme tax shelter situations involving manuscripts and graphics, but it would apply in theory in this area.

I think this means that land conservation organizations have got to take a harder look at what's happening in the valuation area. My view of the tax incentive is that it is really a subsidy to the land conservation groups; it's money put into your hands to attract charitable giving. And if that's true, then there may be much more of a responsibility in the valuation area than I think has been traditionally thought to be the case. I think overvaluations are going to hurt the land conservation movement. I think one reason that we have the new provisions affecting conservation easements is because of the Treasury's perceptions of aggressive appraisals.

Contemplation of Death

We do have new contemplation of death rules effective in 1982. Heretofore any gift by S-1 within three years of death automatically went back into the gross estate of S-1. Now the opposite is the rule. Gifts within three years of the death of the first to die are not brought back into the gross estate of the first spouse. The advantage is that appreciation after the date of the gift is no longer subject to transfer tax.

SIGN TACKED ON A DOOR AT THE U.S. TREASURY

"I know that you believe you understand what you think I said, but I'm not sure you realize that what you heard is not what I meant."

CONSERVATION EASEMENTS
Glenn F. Tiedt

ABSTRACT

The workshop began with a series of definitions of the different types of easements, followed by a discussion of how each conservation easement should be carefully designed for each individual situation. The monitoring of easements was mentioned only briefly, as this was the subject of an entire workshop (see "Management Implications of Land Stewardship"). Several case studies of organizations using easements to protect agricultural and open space lands were cited. Most of the discussion centered on the ramifications that the new draft federal regulations regarding easements will have on their use as tools for land preservation by non-profit organizations.

DEFINITIONS

What Is a Conservation Easement?

A conservation easement is a nonpossessory interest in real property granted by a landowner to another party. The easement usually is a voluntary grant by the landowner to a qualified government agency or charitable organization. The title to the property, however, remains in the landowner's name and the land may be sold on the open market, subject to the restrictions contained in the easement.

Easement Appurtenant vs. Easement in Gross

An *easement appurtenant* is one that benefits property adjacent to it. If you have an easement that prohibits your neighbor from developing his property in order to maintain your view, it is called an appurtenant easement.

If you don't own the adjoining property but have an easement, it would be an easement in gross, because there is no benefit to any property that you own in preventing someone from building on it. There has been a bias against easements in gross stemming from English common law, which frowned on them. In the early history of the law, records of land ownership were very sketchy. If a person bought a piece of property, there was no way of knowing whether or not there was an easement in gross on it. If there were an appurtenant easement, you could find

65

out about it from the neighbors. To this day, although record keeping is more reliable and most conservation easements are taken in gross, some states favor appurtenant easements.

Negative or Affirmative Easements

Conservation easements are generally negative. They prevent something—cutting down trees, subdivision, or altering the topography. An affirmative easement is one whereby you are granted certain rights in the property, such as easements that allow a certain amount of public access for hunting and fishing, a power or water line and right of way.

With or Without a Profit Attached

An easement with a profit attached is an affirmative easement that allows a commercial use such as grazing cattle or sheep or harvesting crops.

"In Perpetuity"

Conservation easements are generally donated "in perpetuity," a legal term that frightens many landowners. What it actually means is an interest of indefinite duration, as opposed to something that endures for a term of years. "In perpetuity" doesn't necessarily mean forever.

Conservation Easements Are in the Interest of the Future

Easements provide a unique opportunity to reconcile conflicts over property use by dividing up the ownership somewhat. A conservation easement on a piece of farmland can assure that the land stays in agricultural production, without resorting to public ownership and/or taking the land out of production.

DESIGNING EASEMENTS

Easements Should Be Tailor-Made for Each Situation

Easements can be written as simply or complicated as desired. Historic preservation easements can be very detailed, specifying the color of the paint on a facade, while an easement on a large ranch might be primarily a restriction on subdivision. But it is very important to thoroughly think through the things you *don't* want to have happen on a property. In Montana, the National Park Service purchased a conservation easement over the historic and scenic Grant-Kohrs Ranch, near Deer Lodge. The easement specified "agricultural use" but apparently did not prohibit the owner from turning the property into a feedlot, an "agricultural use" that would have destroyed the other values of the property. In this case, the Park Service had to purchase the property in order to prevent this development. Had they anticipated this problem and specified "no feedlot," this fee purchase might have been avoided.

To protect the Blackfoot River, in Montana, two different kinds of easements were taken by The Nature Conservancy and the State of Montana. The Conservancy's easements protect the river corridor, preserving it as a natural area from alteration of the shoreline and from having the trees cut down. The second layer of easements, taken by the State, covers the outdoor recreation on the land. The landowners were willing to have limited public outdoor recreation on their property, but they wanted to make sure it was properly administered and controlled. They were afraid to grant public use easements "in perpetuity" without evidence of acceptance of this responsibility, but were willing to donate easements "in perpetuity" to protect the river corridor. So the easements granted the State to administer public outdoor recreation started out in one-year periods and have now gone to five-year cycles, based on the landowners' satisfaction with how the public agencies are handling it.

Additional points to remember in regard to the creation of easement documents are that:

1. Conservation easements, in order to be enforceable in the legal sense, must be specific.

2. An easement may say, "Anything we don't like, we can proscribe," but then there is no evidence of *what actually has been given up* by the easement donor, so that the value is uncertain.

3. You must analyze the resources and what you are seeking to protect with an easement. That doesn't mean it has to be a complex *legal* document. Landowners are often put off by pages of complex legal language.

MONITORING OF EASEMENTS

Who polices easements, enforces their terms? The recipient of the easement has the right to enforce compliance with the terms of the easement. When land subject to an easement is sold or otherwise transferred, the future owners are bound by the easement's terms. Enforcement problems are more likely to develop with future owners than with the donors of the easement. Many land trusts require the donor of an easement to make a cash donation to help establish a stewardship or monitoring fund. Since you are providing the donor with a tax benefit, you are in a strong position to make such a request.

The new federal regulations will not require such a fund but will hold organizations accepting easements responsible for enforcing them. Each organization must ask itself two crucial questions:

1. How will it enforce the terms of an easement?

2. What will it do if conditions change so substantially that the easement no longer serves the purpose for which it was acquired in the first place?

In considering this subject, see also the paper "Management Implications of Land Stewardship."

REJOINDER OF EASEMENTS

While you may protect your property with an easement, what ultimately happens to it may be the result of factors outside the boundaries of the land itself. Easements can be extinguished by merger with the underlying fee. Some absurd situations may arise in the future when a land conservation organization may have to go to court to extinguish an easement that no longer has conservation value, faced with losing its 501(c)(3) status if it does not enforce the easement.

USING CONSERVATION EASEMENTS TO PROTECT
AGRICULTURAL LAND—CASE STUDIES

The Example of the Montana Land Reliance: According to Barbara Rusmore, board member and former staff coordinator of the Montana Land Reliance, conservation easements were one of the acceptable tools available to protect agricultural land in a basically conservative state, "where the flag everyone flies is 'it's my right to do what I want with my land.' " Conservation easements have been the means to put together a deal that meets the needs of both the Reliance and the landowners.

There are many different approaches you can take in working with easements. Overall, the MLR has presented itself as an organization interested in protecting farmland. It has put that word out through land transaction professionals such as lawyers, realtors, and CPAs. It has sponsored workshops on conservation law for those groups. It has gone into communities to talk to various groups and individuals about land conservation, the organization itself, and conservation easements. Generally, the MLR has found, as in all organizing, that it doesn't make sense to go into an area unless you have been invited.

Don't Be Discouraged by How Slowly Momentum Is Built

The MLR has been working in Montana for five years. Only in the last two has the network of supporters been strong enough to actually begin to get some returns. The numbers of easements pursued and lost has been very high. There are many reasons why easements won't work: conflicts with children, conflicts over present and future use. Often, though a landowner expresses a great desire to see the land stay as it is, when it gets down to the wire of using the actual legal language, he or she will back off, simply not being ready to make that kind of commitment. In some cases, an easement will work perfectly, but since the percentages are not high, an organization needs to be "out there," informing many people about what it is doing, building a constituency, and developing a strategy that works for the area in which it is operating. At the close of 1981, the MLR will have protected 22,000 acres with conservation easements. Of those 22,000, 16,000 were protected during the last year. Momentum builds slowly.

Jackson Hole: The newly formed Jackson Hole Land Trust is also working to protect agricultural land through conservation easements. Its purpose is also to protect wildlife habitat and scenic qualities found on these homestead ranches. The JHLT has three small projects going and is fortunate that people know about conservation easements through The Nature Conservancy, which took some easements in the Jackson area. Since Wyoming does not have conservation-easement-enabling legislation, the Conservancy has taken easements appurtenant. It acquired 1 acre of land for the express purpose of tying the easement to it. There are a surprising number of real ranchers and ranchland left in the Jackson area. It is their desire to continue ranching and to see the land protected in its current use.

San Mateo County—An Example of the Difficulties of Easement Use: Recently, the Mid-Peninsula Open Space Trust has been working on the coastal side of San Mateo County, trying to sell agricultural landowners on the idea of easements. The patterns of land ownership in San Mateo County make this a difficult task. One-third of the landowners are wealthy "hobby farmers" living on the land; one-third are wealthy individual and private investors, and one-third are the old landowners. The old-time farmers are hesitant to restrict the value of the land, since they haven't enough income from their farming operations. They cannot utilize the income tax deductions from the donation of easements. Even with the restricted value of property under an easement, the family may not be able to pay the high inheritance taxes. In addition, the county has down-zoned the area by 80 percent. Zoning land to a lower density, however, does not mean an easement cannot be placed over it. Zoning is a procedure highly subject to change. Easements offer longer-term protection. But land, even with restrictions on it, will still sell for $1,000 an acre for a 2,000-acre parcel. Local farmers simply cannot compete with this situation; they are used to leasing the land for $10 an acre.

PROBLEMS AND QUESTIONS WITH EASEMENTS

The foregoing case studies illustrate several of the problems with using conservation easements:

1.   Easements may actually enhance the value of land. Recently, a ranch in Montana sold for as much or more than a comparable ranch *without* an easement on it.

2.   They may be difficult to police (see "Management Implications of Land Stewardship").

3.   There are valuation problems. The IRS may not accept an appraisal that is deemed "aggressive."

4.   Because the desirability of easements stems from their tax deductibility, they often cannot help the land-rich, cash-poor landowners.

5.   How do you guarantee that placing a conservation easement on a property will maintain its present use, agriculture? Easements can preserve land; they can't guarantee productivity.

DRAFT FEDERAL REGULATIONS

Several discussion points were raised regarding the following section of the federal tax legislation on conservation easements:

(4) CONSERVATION PURPOSE DEFINED.
   (A) In General. For purposes of this subsection, the term "conservation purpose" means
      (i)   the preservation of land areas for outdoor recreation by, or the education of, the general public,
      (ii) the protection of a relatively natural habitat of fish, wildlife, or plants, or similar ecosystem,
      (iii) the preservation of open space (including farmland and forest land) where such preservation is
         (I)   for the scenic enjoyment of the general public, or
         (II) pursuant to a clearly delineated Federal, State, or local governmental conservation policy,
      and will yield a significant public benefit, or
      (iv) the preservation of an historically important land area or a certified historic structure.

Discussion Points

1.   "Significant public benefit" is a vague term. How do we know what qualifies and what doesn't without a private letter ruling from the IRS?

69

2.   How do you protect open space in the absence of a "clearly delineated Federal, State, or local governmental conservation policy"? Particularly in the West, there may be areas in need of protection where no such policy exists.

3.   What do you do if one of those conservation purposes cancels out another? If any of these purposes destroys another, the easement may not be valid. For instance, you can preserve a piece of farmland with an easement, but if you use a pesticide on it, you are destroying its natural value and the easement is no good. So it seems you have to consider all these points.

The Response to the Draft Regulations Is Very Important
Comments on the regulations should be made known at once to the regulations writers in the Treasury Department, as soon as possible after the draft regulations are published. Your comments can influence the final form the regulations take.

SELF-REGULATION
A concern raised by Kingsbury Browne is, How shall nonprofit organizations set professional standards for themselves so that the Treasury Department does not have to do it for them? Each profession has a means of regulating itself. Should the deductibility of easements be limited to organizations with a track record? Should the acceptance of all easements be subject to approval of state and local government? The consensual answer to the first question was, "No; how would new organizations ever get started?" An answer to both questions is that state attorney generals have de facto authority over nonprofit activities in their respective states. Still, the question of self-policing is one that deserves careful consideration by the staff and board of each land conservation organization.

WHAT'S WRONG with EASEMENTS?

Jon Roush

As tools for land protection, conservation easements have many advantages. Since they are voluntary agreements between the landowner and easement holder, they are very flexible. They can be negotiated where fee acquisition would be impossible. Because they usually do not change current land uses, they are politically popular. They can often be acquired at little or no costs. And finally, while easements can protect land in perpetuity, the landowner usually bears the ongoing costs of taking care of the land.

Less obvious are easements' many disadvantages. Because their problems are easy to overlook, conservation easements are rapidly becoming the most misused and overused tool for land protection in the United States.

Easements are unreliable. An easement's flexibility, while an advantage for negotiators, makes lawyers lose sleep. They have to draft a document that will unflinchingly protect the land forever but will also adapt to new owners, new ownership patterns, changes in the physical environment, urban growth and decay, new land use regulations, and every other unforeseen change. The cases in which this miracle is achieved are probably far fewer than we usually admit. Of course, the lawyers can include a clause allowing amendments. Then, however, they have to describe a process that will be fair forever and will not invite future landowners to try inappropriate changes. Moreover, if the easement is donated, an amendment clause could jeopardize the donation's deductibility, by giving the donor the power to take back what he has given. Even with such a clause, the most carefully drafted easements may not be proof against challenges to the original agreement as conditions and owners change.

Easements can be expensive. Legal challenges present the most dramatic problem for easement holders but by no means the only one. Simply monitoring the condition of the property can eat the easement holder's time and money. If the easements are numerous, far from each other, or hard to get to, the monitoring costs can be severe, but inadequate monitoring will only let the problems grow. Because two or more parties share responsibility for the land, monitoring an easement can actually be more difficult than watching over an area that is owned outright. And, of course, if a landowner does violate an easement, then the real expenses begin.

No organization should accept an easement unless it has a system for monitoring, the resolve and the legal resources to prosecute violations, and the money to pay for it all.

What Congress gives, Congress can take away. Easement holders are not the only ones with financial risks. The financial incentive that often makes an easement possible is an income tax deduction for the donor. Yet that incentive is no sure thing. The 1981 tax act, which reduced the top tax bracket from 70 percent to 50 percent, has already made donations less attractive to many of the wealthiest landowners. Other conceivable changes could redefine the kind of easements that qualify or limit the amount of deduction allowed. In short, the value of easements is determined not only by the market but also by the U.S. Congress, an uncertain ally. Both Congress and the IRS are watching easements closely, and they are likely to be even more vigilant as easements become more common.

If you like to gamble, you will love easement appraisals. An easement's value is the difference in the appraised values of the property before and after the easement is given. Yet appraisal is an art at best. It is the art of fiction, the story of a hypothetical willing buyer and willing seller who shake on a deal in the appraiser's well-informed imagination. And so far, imagination is about all the appraisers have had to go on when they determine the "after value" of most easements, because few properties have actually been sold with easements on them. In the absence of comparable sales, appraisers have used other methods to establish some sizable donation values for their clients. Future sales, however, could change all that. Real-life buyers might pay top price for some properties with easements, because of the amenities they offer. Then the IRS could reasonably question conventional appraisal methods and knock the wind out of many easement programs.

The valuation of easements, in short, is vulnerable to legal changes and to changes in IRS regulations as well as to normal market forces. Any organization that relies heavily on easement donations is equally vulnerable.

Other tools may work better. In many parts of the country, easements are relatively easy to acquire. For that reason, they are attractive to underfunded agencies and groups. As public and private sources of land acquisition funds dry up, easements will become even more popular. Many local land trusts already use easements as their sole protection tool. Yet easements are not right for all properties. Not all landowners are amenable to giving or even selling easements. Sometimes the answer is fee acquisition or a temporary agreement. If large or rapidly changing areas are involved, land use regulations might achieve more than easements and do it faster. Sometimes the owner merely needs technical or financial assistance to care for his land properly. Sometimes property can be protected by simply adding it to a state historical or natural-area registry. And sometimes a combination of such techniques can protect a place where none alone could.

Relying on any one tool to the exclusion of others will inevitably lead us to protect places that do not really deserve it and pass up places that do. When the tool is as easy to use as a conservation easement, we will fritter away precious resources in haphazard and often ineffective conservation.

CONSERVATION REAL ESTATE
Paul Brunner

ABSTRACT

Conservation real estate is a new field created by realtors such as Paul Brunner who sell properties, primarily those with high recreational amenities, to buyers who agree to preserve them undeveloped and unsubdivided. This is accomplished by placing conservation easements on the properties and by the realtor developing a strong reputation for this type of activity.

Through talking about his experience in Montana, Brunner explained the evolution of his own "rules of the game," why nonprofit organizations should work with brokers, potential problem areas, as well as case studies of some of the deals he has put together. The workshop ended with a call for new concepts in tax shelter legislation, since economic incentive must be the ultimate basis for the conservation movement.

Though we believe Brunner's experience has broad application in land conservation, these types of transactions might be limited to areas where properties with high recreational values are found.

A BRAND NEW FIELD

Conservation real estate, as exemplified in the career of Paul Brunner, of Eco Realty, Ovando, Montana, is a new field of action for the realtor who cares about land conservation and wise use of resources. Brunner has proven that selling Montana ranches only to conservation buyers—some 260,000 acres in ten years—can be financially workable as well as providing a deep sense of satisfaction for the conservation-conscious realtor.

Brunner first came to Montana from back East in 1968 and immediately fell in love with the country. While pursuing a degree in real estate at the university, he began selling houses, eventually getting a broker's license. As a dedicated hunter and fisherman, he realized that subdivision destroyed much wildlife habitat in the East and saw that the same thing would soon be happening in Montana. He became involved with local conservation groups, trying to point out the dangers of diminution of habitat. After speaking to a wildlife biology class on the need for land use planning, he was expelled from the local board of realtors for "unethical conduct" and was completely ostracized thereafter. Although the blacklisting bothered him,

73

he rented a small office and began Eco Realty. His first sale established his reputation early on: a ranch in Montana's Bitterroot Valley that was in danger of having a 1,000-unit trailer park developed on it. There were 7 miles of spring creek, blue heron, Canadian geese, and whitetail deer habitat on the ranch. Selling it to a conservation buyer was a widely recognized achievement.

RULES OF THE GAME

Brunner found that "conservation real estate" was not an established field, so he had to make up the rules as he went along. Some of the primary rules are:

1. Sell only property threatened by subdivision.

2. Sell only to conservation buyers. (This was difficult in pre-1976 Montana because there was no enabling legislation to allow conservation easement donations. So there was much risk taking trying to analyze buyers to determine if they really were conservation-oriented.)

3. Tax shelters are the primary incentive. No matter how conservation-minded people are, economics is a prime mover in buying these properties. Eco Realty uses the conservation easement as an incentive to buy a ranch from the very beginning. Information about easements goes out with every packet of information sent out by Eco Realty. Most people in this country still have not heard about them.

Brunner convinces sellers to list exclusively with him and to give him the right to screen potential buyers. When he advertises in the *Wall Street Journal,* a block-letter notice is posted in each ad reading "no developers." Now at least 50 percent of his buyers come from conservation groups, such as Montana Land Reliance, The Nature Conservancy, and Trout Unlimited.

REPUTATION AND PUBLIC IMAGE ARE KEY

There is good faith and risk taking involved in this business. The risk taking is particularly precarious. One subdivision on a ranch that Eco Realty sold could permanently ruin its reputation, and reputation is the key element in the business.

Brunner's public image is strongly antidevelopment. His bumper sticker "Keep Montana Beautiful—Shoot a Developer" is to be found all over the United States, and he claims he would do it if it were legal. Being an outspoken maverick and being in the public eye are good advertising, he says, and as in any other business, advertising is crucial for its success.

Another really important point: A broker *cannot* sell houses *and* also be a conservation realtor; there is no middle of the road. The credibility problem will be too great.

HOW CLIENTS ARE FOUND

Brunner is *always* selling real estate, whether in the office or on the trout stream, and most of his business is done in the woods, since people who are buying land in Montana are conservationists: hunters, fishermen, backpackers, photographers.

The properties are sold on the basis of three incentives:

1. A future investment—something to hand on to future generations

2.   Hunting and fishing properties

3.   Tax shelters

Most prospecting is done by word of mouth, working with conservation groups and some advertising. He makes it very clear that 10 percent of his gross commission goes to the conservation organization that sends him the buyer. (To give any *individual* more than 10 percent for referring a buyer is a problem under Montana law, unless the individual has a broker's license. This amount must also be called a consulting fee.) But it is made clear that this amount is a donation, *not* a commission.

DOCUMENTATION

In order to avoid problems with the IRS and other potential critics, every transaction should be very carefully documented, using good advisers, lawyers, and accountants.

It is important to use honest, competent appraisers, MAI (Member of Appraisal Institute) approved, who preferably have a long-standing relationship with the IRS so that they are willing to accept his or her judgment.

WHY USE BROKERS AT ALL?

If a land trust receives a gift of land, there is no problem. But if word gets out that a land trust is engaging in sales work, bringing in two or three wealthy people a year, selling them prime property, some real ill feelings will be created among realtors.

Utilizing local real estate talent is very good public relations and can be instrumental in saving some key ground. If a good broker comes up with a prime piece of property that really needs to be saved, he or she will probably come to the land trust first.

Few people in land trust organizations really have the expertise that a good broker has—knowledge of how to put a deal together, for instance. Transactions are something built up over the years through many experiences.

Negotiation and peacekeeping skills are important, being able to sit all parties to a transaction around a table with lawyers and accountants. Sessions can become very heated. The broker should be the peacekeeper because he/she is in the center of the transaction between buyer and seller.

Most brokers can do a better job of advertising the properties and coming up with the right buyers, also due to their greater experience.

In Montana, it is important that a broker know something about agriculture: carrying capacities, irrigation, water rights and water law, property boundaries, and drainages in areas. How many acres will support a cow in this particular valley? The biggest sales job is not selling the property—Montana ranches are so beautiful they sell themselves—but selling the rancher on using the broker's talents. Land trust staff are not always very familiar with agriculture.

Another reason for land trusts to use brokers is to take advantage of all their professional skills without having to pay for them unless a transaction is completed. Much money and time is "wasted" on deals that didn't go through.

POTENTIAL PROBLEMS

1.   The IRS could refuse to accept an appraisal, particularly if the easement appraisal were high and the appraiser unknown to the IRS.

2. A holder of an underlying mortgage could refuse the easement. Underwriters need to be sold on the idea of easements so they will go along with donating an easement over properties to which they have the mortgage title. Once they know what's involved, they will approve future transactions.

3. The diminution problem. In transactions where there is a low down payment and a high value to the conservation easement, donated immediately, the seller could be financially vulnerable if a buyer defaulted on a loan. The value of the ranch would be less than the original selling price and the down payment would not have covered the difference. This problem can be addressed by (a) getting top dollar for the seller; (b) requesting a financial statement from the buyer.

Easements Should Be Designed for the Long Run

1. Use the best appraiser.

2. Use the best conservation organization.

3. Use the best legal advice available.

CASE STUDIES

Two "Partnership" Ranches: A recent transaction involving Eco Realty illustrates a way in which tax shelters may be shared among several buyers. A professional in computer economics and accounting who specializes in financial partnerships had put together a group of seventeen buyers. Brunner sold this partnership a 4,000-acre deeded ranch with 12,000 acres of leased grazing adjoining the property. It is critical habitat for at least ten species of wildlife.

The intent of the seventeen buyers was not to have homesites, but to continue to run the ranch as a cattle operation, provide a tax shelter for themselves, and in the future, actually make some income from the place. None of the buyers were really wealthy. But the tax shelter would be massive because of the donated conservation easement and the depreciation that would ensue from running a regular ranch operation.

This year the same group is putting together another partnership to buy an adjoining ranch—with grazing complementary to the first—and run both ranches as a single operation.

The new ranch was purchased for $1.7 million or $400 an acre. There was an existing $1 million, 7 percent assumable contract with thirty-one years remaining on it. The buyers sat down and negotiated the financing. Brunner was in the unique position of wearing three hats: (1) representing the seller because he had the listing, (2) representing the buyers because they were his clients, (3) he was also a 5 percent partner.

Leasing out the grass on this ranch should produce $72,000 a year. This will be cut to $64,000 because one of the partners, a range management specialist, has developed a plan to gradually increase the resource base. Pasture fencing, pasture renovation, sagebrush burning, and ditch irrigation are the methods to be used. By 1991, the income should have increased to $114,000 a year, and the ranch should be better wildlife habitat as well.

With a $700,000 down payment spread over two years, a 10 percent owner would "come in" at $55,000 at the closing. That year, he would have a taxable income loss of $765, two months of depreciation. The tax benefit would be $383. The tax investment credit would be $1,000. This year net investment after tax would be $53,617; $28,750 will be the down payment next year, and each buyer will have to put in $12,300 more in additional operating capital for the large number of improvements that are planned as well as to make payments above and beyond the ranch's grazing income. Taxable income loss will be $1,400 because of depreciable assets. There will be a tax benefit of $7,700 and a $24,000 charitable contribution. Assuming a 50 percent income bracket, that's a $12,000 tax benefit. The following year there is no more capital contribution at all; the cash flow is only calculated at $3,100 per person with a taxable income loss of $10,400. The tax benefit is $5,200, and there is a $24,000 charitable contribution, or a $12,000 tax benefit. That year there will be $17,200 tax savings with a cash contribution of $3,100.

In 1986, a positive cash flow is predicted. Each person is going to start receiving an income. The charitable contribution will be used up, but the depreciation will still be taken although the new tax law will change the values of the depreciation considerably.

Brunner would like to do more of this type of transaction because it makes land available to those who are less wealthy; it opens the market to more people.

A Potential Conservation "Superdeal": This outline of a transaction that recently fell through for reasons unrelated to the deal itself illustrates great potential benefits for conservation. A 1,100 acre ranch on a trout stream backed by a wilderness area was for sale. A local conservation organization brought Brunner a buyer. The buyer would pay $800,000 for the ranch, donate an easement, and the conservation organization would receive a $20,000 donation from Brunner's commission and $20,000 donation from the buyer.

The buyer would donate the conservation easement and get a tax shelter of 50 percent. The party would have held the property for four years and then donated the property to the organization. Figuring on 25 percent a year appreciation, the property with an easement would be worth the original price, so that the buyer, after donating to the organization, would realize a tax shelter of $800,000. (These figures were carefully calculated based on preappraisals.)

Basically, this deal offers three things to a very wealthy person with tax problems: (1) the use of a beautiful ranch for four years; (2) a 150 percent tax shelter; (3) a strong feeling of satisfaction at having accomplished something for the conservation movement.

It is likely that the conservation organization would then have listed the property for sale through Brunner, who would have donated a percentage of his commission. They would have received the proceeds from the sale less the closing costs, $250,000–$300,000 in the beginning, and $70,000–$80,000 a year over a twenty-year period to help with their operation.

In addition, the buyer had agreed to a complete documentation of the tax consequences of the deal. This would have proven to be an invaluable tool in convincing others in the same tax bracket to arrange similar purchases. Brunner is still hoping to find another potential donor who will be interested in this same transaction: "This deal screams 'conservation' and 'tax shelter.'"

These transactions involve a certain amount of trust and risk taking because there are certain promises, such as the donation of a property within a certain time, that cannot be put in writing because of the tax consequences.

Partial Development in Jackson Hole: Although Brunner does not like the idea of partial development, he has become convinced that in Jackson Hole, this might be the only solution to some land use problems. Most of the land around Jackson is government owned, so what private land that exists will bring $12,000 an acre for condominium developments. The value of an easement on this type of property could be 70–80 percent.

Recently Brunner, together with the Jackson Hole Land Trust, has been arranging a transaction involving 400 acres of unimproved meadow and pine land at the base of a ski area near Jackson. The property listed at $7,250 an acre or $2.9 million. At those prices, no one person will pay simply to preserve the ground.

So a partial development was decided upon. The property will be marketed, with no advertising, to four buyers. Each of them will get a deed to a 20-acre tract (to comply with local zoning and subdivision laws) of the Land Trust's choice. They will actually have a deed released of 1 acre to build a house on, for financing purposes. They will buy the 400 acres together, probably in joint tenancy.

The Land Trust and cooperating planners and architects will be responsible for placing houses, roads, and all improvements, as well as have some aesthetic control over the building of the houses.

Each person will buy in with about $300,000 down. Each interest will be worth $750,000. A good 5-acre building tract near Jackson would be about $200,000. But these buyers, though they are paying more, will receive about $500,000 in conservation easement value off the top. They will get a joint tenancy in a 400-acre ranch that can produce a grazing income. The acreage is some of the most beautiful horseback-riding country around, borders Forest Service land, and is about fifteen minutes from a major ski area.

If this transaction is put together quickly and successfully, there will be fewer major subdivisions in Jackson Hole. Many of the directors of the Jackson Hole Land Trust are ranchers, and the word will spread. The planners will try to make sure that local ranchers get first shot at the grazing leases on these properties to build good PR.

The buyers will probably build their second homes, which Brunner doesn't necessarily like, but there don't seem to be alternatives.

Vail, Colorado: Roger Tilkermeir, a realtor, developer, and president of the Eagle County Land Conservancy, explained that he is putting together a transaction on a 2,000-acre ranch near Vail. The ranch operation runs 300 head of cattle. Thirty houses will be built around the irrigated hay meadows, and the ranch will continue to operate as an agricultural unit. Many older local residents of Vail will probably be among these buyers. They are wanting to get away from the congestion around Vail, something many of them moved to Vail to escape.

NEED FOR LEGISLATION

There is a strong need for land trusts to get to work in new land conservation tax shelter concepts. Economics is the basis of a growing conservation movement.

One Jackson Hole rancher said to Brunner, "I've got a ranch that's worth $12 million. I don't want to sell it, all I want to do is preserve the ground and keep on ranching. But I can't use a tax shelter." His idea was to donate an easement on his property worth $10 million and have a perpetual tax shelter that can be used against estate taxes and passed on for his children to chip away at.

In conclusion, says Brunner, if we really want to save agricultural land and life styles, we need to market better conservation ideas to the folks in Washington, D.C.

PARTIAL DEVELOPMENT OPTIONS
Davis Cherington

The term *partial development* actually refers to a process through which a land trust purchases a property and pays back its investment by selling off part of the land for development purposes. The concept has generated excitement in the conservation community because it solves a longstanding frustration. It allows the conservation entity to direct where building will occur, and it internalizes that conflict resolution in their hands. No more need for warring with developers. Robert Lemire pioneered the process in Lincoln, Massachusetts, and has written the handbook *Creative Land Development, Bridge to the Future,* a must read for anyone considering partial development.

ABSTRACT

This workshop centered around the efforts of the Massachusetts Farm and Conservation Lands Trust to apply this partial development concept to farmland preservation by a land trust. Their situation is somewhat more fortuitous than most, as is evident in the discussion of Massachusetts' Farmland Development Rights Acquisition Program, but the approach is sound and at the end of the workshop there was discussion about favorable applications in other situations. The write-up here follows the workshop format, beginning with background information on Massachusetts' situation and follows the development of a case example. Critical components for successful transactions are highlighted, and the process is transmitted step by step. This write-up concludes with limitations and problems of partial development and potentials for other applications. The resources and information sources needed by a trust undertaking a local partial development project are listed at the end.

PARTIAL DEVELOPMENT AND MASSACHUSETTS FARMLAND

Farmland in Massachusetts is a precious resource, and the people know it. The rapid industrialization and urbanization of the state since the 1930s has all but obliterated its once-agricultural economy. Concern for food self-sufficiency has grown with rising transportation prices and water shortages in the West and South. Now often surrounded by suburban development, the New England farm provides a local food resource as well as much appreciated open space.

PARTIAL DEVELOPMENT OPTIONS

Recognizing these values, the Massachusetts legislature in 1977 passed the Agricultural Preservation Restriction Act, providing for a voluntary application by a farmer to the Department of Agriculture to sell the farm's development rights. Once the development rights are acquired by the Department they are never exercised, and the farm is restricted in perpetuity. By 1979, the regulations had been written and for 1979, 1980, and 1981 the Legislature appropriated $5 million yearly for a total of $15 million for purchasing agricultural preservation restrictions. A gap soon appeared in the program. Many key property owners did not want to sell their development rights; they just wanted to sell and get out of farming altogether. The program needed a purchase and resale component.

To fill this need, the Massachusetts Farm and Conservation Lands Trust was formed in early 1980 as a private nonprofit organization. The role of the Trust was to purchase properties, apply for an APR (Agricultural Preservation Restriction), and then sell the property for the remainder fee to a farmer. For example, a purchase and sale agreement is reached on a $100,000 farm. An APR is applied for, appraised at $70,000, and granted; and the farm, now restricted, is sold to a farmer for $30,000. The Trust adds great flexibility and speed to the program by being able to acquire critical properties. This illustrates the main strength of private land trusts working in cooperation with a government program. Any state with a farmland purchase-of-development-rights program will need a private cooperating land trust to fill these functions.

The Trust also has the potential to lower the cost to the state of farmland preservation. Farmland is very expensive in Massachusetts. A property with good soils within 40 to 50 miles of downtown Boston, thereby close to markets and with the profit-making potential for roadside sales, might easily run $10,000 per acre for development purposes. A farmer acquiring the same property to enlarge his existing unit might be willing to pay $5,000 an acre, and an operator buying it as a self-sustaining unit could not pay more than $1,000. In such a situation, a partial development scheme becomes very attractive. A property could be acquired, a developable portion identified and sold, and the remainder restricted with an APR and sold to a farmer.

STEPS IN THE PROCESS

To undertake a partial development project, an organization must be willing and ready to take on a risky, time-consuming, and expensive real estate project. While the venture may pay for itself eventually, it requires significant front-end capital to secure options, pay for studies and consultants, and provide operating capital. The benefits are unique but do not come easily as the following process and case study illustrates.

This process assumes that a trust has located what appears to be a suitable property for a limited development project. The location and property characteristics are suitable, and there is a market for both the proposed type of development (residential, commercial, or recreational) and for farmland. The unique situations of each trust will lead them to different property selection criteria. These steps are based on the experience of the Massachusetts Farm and Conservation Lands Trust and follow the development of a case study.

The Project—Barton Estate: Barton Estate, a 77-acre farm for sale to highest bidder by the estate's lawyer. The property contains a variety of soil types and vegetation, much of it good farmland, some timber, a wetlands, and historic buildings. It is located in Sudbury, Massachusetts, and is surrounded by 1½-acre lots and an industrial park on one side. Sudbury had passed an open space acquisition bond several years ago and strongly supports farmland preservation for open space.

Identify Areas to Be Saved and Developed

A basic resource inventory is undertaken to identify the agricultural capabilities, wildlife habitats, and development limitations. Through a consultant, maps were prepared showing slopes, soils, wetlands, and limitations on septic systems. Most of this information was based on Soil Conservation Service studies and other publicly available documents with some field checking. Key open space qualities were identified with the town of Sudbury. Historical features also were identified and mapped with the aid of the local historical society.

Identify Development Potential

In order to bid effectively on the property and to select the most appropriate developable area, it is important to analyze the entire property as a developer would. Because this area had city water but no sewer, septic tank limitations were critical as were local zoning and building regulations. These factors will vary by area and parcel.

1. *Percolation tests.* A soils engineer was hired to carry out percolation tests over the entire property to accurately identify the septic tank limitations.

2. *Zoning and building regulations* were researched to determine potential lot size, frontage requirements, and other development standards.

3. *A preliminary site plan* involving a new road through the property was drafted based on this information and an assessment of the highest financial return. This is a full development plan, not what the Trust will propose. Knowledge of current real estate and development finance is crucial at this step.

Determine Price

At this point an appraisal becomes necessary. Only a development cost appraisal will provide useful information, so select the appraiser carefully and describe what you want. In the last step, a full development model was designed. Based on this information, an appraiser can evaluate the housing market for comparable sales, subtract the development costs (legal fees, marketing, engineering, cost of money), and come up with the price a developer would pay for the property.

Select a Developer

The selection of a developer with whom the Trust can work is essential. There must be a good basis for trust and open communication because although the land will be sold to the developer with a deed restriction to minimize the negative impact of development on the preserved property, a deed restriction is not a strong tool.

1. Solicit bids from developers.

2. Interview, look at previous projects, check credit.

3. Select developer and negotiate a bid on the developable portion of the property.

PARTIAL DEVELOPMENT OPTIONS

Design Trust's Plan for Land

Juggling the land use factors of farming, development, open space and historical preservation, along with the finances of the Trust, the APR program, the farmer, the Barton Estate, the developer, and the town of Sudbury, the MFCLT came up with a workable plan. No small feat. It involved the sale of fourteen lots to the builder and developer, the sale of a fourteen-acre parcel for open space conservation to the town of Sudbury, the sale of the development rights of over 37.8 acres to the Department of Agriculture and the town and the sale of the same restricted land (37.8 acres) to the farmer.

BARTON LIMITED DEVELOPMENT PROJECT
COMBINED FINANCIAL SUMMARY

EXPENSES

Purchase from Barton Estate	$537,500
Planning, survey, legal, and interest	28,625
MFCLT standard overhead (5 percent)	26,375
	$592,500

REVENUES

Sales to builder-developer (14 lots)	$271,000
Sale of conservation land to Sudbury	110,000
Sale of APR on 37.8 acres to coholders Commonwealth of Massachusetts Department of Agriculture and Sudbury*	188,894
Sale of 37.8 acres restricted farmland	22,606
	$592,500

*Commonwealth of Massachusetts and town of Sudbury will be coholders of APR.

In developing the concept of partial development the Trust had early-on selected 5 percent as its standard overhead fee. On this particular project, they will lose money at that percentage. However, when several projects occur simultaneously, this fee will be sufficient. For the sake of consistency and reliability in public relations, it is important for a trust to select a fee and stick with it.

Make a Bid

Throughout this process, the lawyer for the estate was kept informed of the Trust's intentions. There was another serious bidder on the property, a developer, and the lawyer was committed for estate reasons to selling to the highest bidder. The Trust pursued a policy of full disclosure negotiating with the lawyer, bringing him into the process early. This provided them with a favorable attitude from the lawyer, and he was willing to grant them the extra month or so that they needed to pull together their proposal.

After the appraisal was complete, the Trust basically knew what they would offer on the property. But prior to signing a purchase and sale agreement, they had to know exactly how they were going to sell the property and get their investment back. This involved lengthy and nerve-racking negotiations with all parties to finally reach a mutually agreeable deal.

Close the Deal

1. *Simultaneous closing.* For a deal like this to work, there needs to be a simultaneous closing, a meeting where everyone involved sits down, signs checks, and passes them around the table. This is a technique used by The Nature Conservancy, Trust for Public Lands, and in many other complex land transactions. It reduces the risk and the paranoia that often accompany such real estate deals.

2. *Line of credit.* The Trust, in order to have the situation covered in case any last minute difficulties arose, had arranged a line of credit through the American Farmland Trust.

LIMITATIONS AND PROBLEMS OF PARTIAL DEVELOPMENT

Before deciding that a partial development project is for you, it is important to undertake a cost-benefit analysis. The attractions of the project—its capability to effectively save land, encourage sound development, and pay its own way—are not an ensured end result. A few of the risk factors are identified here.

Partial development will not work everywhere. There must be a market for the type of development you are proposing. In today's building slump, it is a severely limited market. In many cases, the adjacent preserve land will be an amenity for the development and help to sell it, but there must be some market. Do a market analysis if uncertain.

High-risk enterprise. Real estate is always a risky business, and when you undertake a partial development project you are embroiled in a fairly risky venture. The front-end costs are high, and you must involve consultants from several fields. It is an unfamiliar concept, and people will be more suspicious than usual. There are many players in the game, and that makes it even more risky; they must all work together, and it is your responsibility to see that they do. There is something about land dealings that brings out the paranoia in people and partial development with all its unusual restrictions and contingencies is a perfect breeding ground for distrust.

Working with the public sector. Public purchase of the development rights is a great incentive for partial development. The common goal is achieved and everyone can come out ahead financially. If it is a part of your project, be aware that there are no guarantees. A purchase and sale agreement with a government entity is written completely in their favor. It is crucial to thoroughly understand the government program and develop a close working relationship with the administrators.

Working with developers. A good working relationship with the developer is critical. The long-term success of the project depends in large part on how well it works alongside of preserved ground, whether it be open space or agricultural land. While a trust can place deed restrictions in the contract with the developer to ensure correct future uses, they are only enforceable by going to court and arguing your case in front of a judge, an undesirable action.

Time-consuming. Working out so many different factors and with so many different people is an enormously time-consuming endeavor. To accomplish this project took weeks and weeks of fifteen-hour days, answering phone calls late at night and other Herculean efforts. Be prepared.

OTHER POTENTIALS FOR PARTIAL DEVELOPMENT

Like any new idea, the concept of partial development is evolving, and new forms are being constantly dreamed up. Combinations and permutations of the following suggestions might be just the answer for your program. The case study described in this write-up is predicated on the financial involvement of the Commonwealth of Massachusetts and the town of Sudbury. For organizations not having these types of development rights purchase options, they can still accomplish partial development by utilizing some of the following suggestions that either lower the necessary investment and/or increase the return.

Bargain sale. By working with the figures for this particular deal, it appears that a partial development project could have been accomplished without purchases by public entities if MFCLT had been able to arrange a bargain sale at about 50 percent. In other situations the figures would be different, but a bargain sale of the property is clearly an avenue for success.

Easement donation. It might be financially beneficial to use a conservation easement with either the developer donating an easement to shelter some of his gains or by passing through some of the benefits of an easement donation to the subsequent owners.

Homeowners' association. The developer could form a homeowners' association that could own all the property—even the restricted portion—and take advantage of an easement donation and/or lease the property to a farmer.

Leasing. If the Trust retains title to any of the property and can lease it either as housing or farming, so much the better. Leasing can provide a steady cash flow, and it allows the Trust control over the uses of the property.

Building for sale. Another way to generate more money from a partial development might be to build the development yourself and sell the completed homes. It is a higher risk venture and in today's market probably not worth it. But in better times or with the correct development, it might make sense.

RESOURCES FOR LOCAL ACTION

Partial development is clearly a project for professionals with a background in real estate and persuasive diplomatic skills. If you decide to pursue this possibility, your best source of information is other groups who have done similar work. Robert Lemire in Lincoln (his book of course, will be a big help), Davis Cherington, and Peter Stein of Trust for Public Lands Urban Program in New York would all be good starting points. Once you have begun a project, your real estate broker, consultants, financeers, lawyers, appraiser, developer, the federal agencies with information, local farmers, and many more people will all be useful and necessary for successfully completing a project.

AREAS of COOPERATION BETWEEN GOVERNMENT AGENCIES and NONPROFIT ORGANIZATIONS
Donald Rubenstein

ABSTRACT

Because government and nonprofit organizations are two different kinds of entities with different kinds of mandates and restrictions for their activities, there are several ways in which they can cooperate in achieving the same public good, in this case, land conservation.

The workshop began with brief definitions of several tools for cooperation between government and the nonprofit land conservation organization. Then each technique was described in detail, some with case studies to illustrate their applicability. While many of the examples were based on California, since Mr. Rubenstein's experience has been primarily with this state, there is no reason why these techniques cannot be applied anywhere there are similar conditions.

One technique that had been on the workshop agenda—development transfers—was not discussed due to its complexity and a time limitation.

THE TOOLS

Preacquisition

Preacquisition is the classic tool for cooperation between nonprofit organizations and government organizations. It consists of the acquisition, through a variety of different mechanisms and techniques, of a piece of property by a nonprofit organization and its resale to a governmental organization.

Brokering

Brokering, a sort of permutation of preacquisition, can be very effective. In this case, the nonprofit organization serves as a broker between the landowner and a state or other government organization that is interested in acquiring the property from a private landowner.

Option Sales

An option sale is another tool of the preacquisition game and involves the private nonprofit organization's acquiring an option to purchase property from a private landowner and either the sale of that option to a government organization *or* an exercise of that option and simultaneous sale of the full fee title to the property to the government organization.

A third variation is one in which the nonprofit organization buys a separate and distinct option to buy a piece of property, keeps that option, and sells a separate option to government so you actually have two options operating on the same piece of property. It is important to have the right timing on these, but there is no enormous complexity in setting them up.

Negotiating Trades

This is something that has fairly limited application, mostly because of the procedural problems in getting government organizations to trade property that they own. It can occur in a variety of ways. One way is for the nonprofit organization to get between a landowner and the government who owns property that the other wants to have. The nonprofit organization then negotiates the transaction. It can happen that a landowner is interested in taking another privately owned property. In this case too, the nonprofit organization can buy both pieces of private property and sell one to the government and one to the other party.

Development Transfers

This technique was not discussed due to time limitation but is one that people should become more familiar with.

Grants Through Other Entities

This is an extremely fruitful avenue to pursue. It operates on the assumption that most governmental organizations that have grant funding programs for land acquisition do not have the authority to give grants to nonprofit organizations; mostly they have the authority to give them to other governmental organizations.

In principle, there is nothing to prevent a qualified government recipient of a grant to contract with a land trust to carry out the acquisition or whatever land-related function is being grant-funded by a government source.

PREACQUISITION

There are two basic situations in which the preacquisition tool might be used.

1. A governmental organization wants a particular piece of property for conservation (or it could be for *any* purpose—development or redevelopment) but doesn't have the present funding capacity to make the acquisition. It could be that the property is on the market, that the opportunity will be lost if it is not acquired; or it could be that by the time the government has the money to do it, property values will have escalated sufficiently so that it is not cost-efficient for them to make the acquisition.

2. A nonprofit organization knows of a piece of property that belongs in government ownership, and wants to buy it, and feels confident they will be able to convince government to make the purchase.

Function

The nonprofit organization buys the property, using all the cost-saving tools in its bag of tricks, bargain sales, and so forth, and then resells the property to government for government purposes.

COOPERATION BETWEEN GOVERNMENT AGENCIES and NONPROFIT ORGANIZATIONS

The primary principle in operation is knowing, as a nonprofit organization, that the property is going to be bought by government. There can be a very substantial risk involved. If you buy a $100,000 piece of property for cash, you're stuck with a $100,000 piece of property; you may or may not be able to sell it. If you have to sell it to a nongovernment buyer, there could be a substantial impact on your reputation for selling a piece of property everyone knows ought to be in conservation ownership. You run the risk of losing money, even in such a resale. Perhaps you bought it in the face of tremendous development pressure, but it was rezoned for open space.

Ways to Minimize the Risk

1. Use options as much as possible, so that you pay a small fraction of the cost of the property—perhaps 5 percent or less—to secure the right of future purchase for you or your organization for a finite period of time. During that time, work with the government organization to make sure it will make the acquisition.

2. Get a prior commitment to purchase what is sufficient for your purposes. That sufficiency will vary according to the importance of the property. If it is an extraordinary piece of property, you are probably justified in taking a much greater risk.

3. Force the government agency to identify what contingencies exist to repurchase of the property. Are they dependent upon getting the legislature to make a specific appropriation to purchase that piece of ground? Or does the legislature approve capital funding monies for their program over which they then have discretionary use? If they have discretionary use of it, who makes the final decision to buy the property you own?

4. Be aware of what the government purchasing process is. What are the regulations? How do they proceed from step to step? Must there be an appraisal made? At what stage? Must the appraiser be employed by the state? What are the state bodies that have authority over an expenditure? Traditionally, in state and local government, an appropriation by the legislature does not guarantee the expenditure of funds. There are intervening bodies that must approve it.

These are risks. Know what they are. Most importantly, know how to control the risks. You may have to turn out some troops at a public hearing to make sure an appropriation is passed.

The Problem of Legal Agency

It is unfavorable for a nonprofit organization to find itself in the role of legal agent of the government organization that it is acquiring property for. One of the most onerous burdens of being in that role is having to comply with the uniform relocation laws. These laws were designed to protect owners and occupiers of land being acquired by government purchase. The easiest way to avoid becoming a legal agent is to have some modicum of risk in the transaction. It may be as simple as one state organization's needing approval from another in order to make the purchase. You may know that approval may almost certainly come, but if there is a possibility that approval might not be forthcoming, you are taking a risk and are protected from being an agent.

Advantages of Preacquisition

1.   Frequently, it is possible to acquire real estate much cheaper than it would be available to government. At the least, it comes to the government minus staff costs (which can be substantial) and at best, below fair market value.

2.   Frequently, it preserves opportunities to purchase land that would otherwise be lost.

3.   It extends the purchasing efforts of conservation or whatever other social benefit the acquisition seeks to advance. The more people involved in the effort, the better.

Risks

1.   Governmental agencies may not be able to buy you out. If that happens, and you don't have an option on the property, but have purchased the fee, you have two alternatives. You can go out and try to raise the money for the property and retain ownership for yourself or give it to government; or you can sell the property—or do a partial development—and basically relate to the property as an entrepreneur.

2.   A significant risk derives from how you develop your relationship with government. You have the right to give yourself a good deal, but you should pass along some benefits to government too in order to avoid creating ill will. Each organization has its own guidelines for passing on cost. The Trust for Public Land passes on property at 100 percent of fair market value, regardless of what it paid. The Nature Conservancy charges its direct costs in acquisition plus 3–5 percent of that figure as an indirect overhead. Mostly, you will be dealing with government appraisers so that you will be limited by what price government will pay. The Nature Conservancy has a standard formula of trying to purchase at 75 percent of appraised fair market value so that they have some leeway in negotiating.

In general, to avoid risks, be sure that the property you are buying is highly attractive to government. If you need to, be prepared to develop a constituency to bang on doors to protect land that should be protected.

Installment Sales

This is a special case of preacquisition that can be used to purchase a large piece of property over time when the seller wants to sell the land in this way. Government usually cannot make a commitment to pay over a period of years, since this would involve commitment of the funds of a future legislature by a present legislature and that is constitutionally impossible.

When you are stuck in circumstances where sellers insist on installment sales, the nonprofit organization can enter into an installment sale agreement with the owner, backing up each installment obligation with an option to the government.

If the property is worth $1 million and you're going to put $250,000 down and pay in $250,000 (plus interest) installments over the next three years, you make an immediate $250,000 sale to the government of $250,000 worth of the property. Then you give the government three options for the following three years. Those are each tied to the date by which you must make the installment payment to the owner. Each time you make a payment, the owner is required to release a piece of property free and clear, which you then pass through escrow to government. Government will not make payment without receipt of a clear title to real estate.

BROKERING

In California, every year the legislature passes on a list of specific properties to be acquired by the Department of Parks and Recreation, with specific purchase prices attached. So there is a fair certainty as to which properties will be available to the Department of Parks and Recreation in the following year.

In Los Angeles, there is an extremely effective and ingenious real estate broker who knows this political process well and follows it closely. He identifies which properties are likely to be approved by the state legislature. He then goes out as a private broker and negotiates acquisitions of these properties from the owners and presents completed negotiated packages to the state of California on July 1, the beginning of its fiscal year, for action by the Public Works Board at the end of July. At the very first availability of funds, this man is in the door. His compensation is a 10 percent brokerage commission. By July 30 of any given year, he has made all the money he needs to make for the next twelve months and has saved the state a tremendous amount of money because they have put no staff time into it. He uses forms identical to the state forms and knows exactly what is involved.

There is no reason that a nonprofit organization couldn't do that too. You simply have to make sure you are straight with the real estate broker's laws. You may have to become a broker. Whether this will work in any given jurisdiction will depend on: (1) the acquisition process in that jurisdiction. Is it predictable? and (2) the relationship that you structure with government. Don't appear to be trying to show them up or do their job better than they do.

Additional Benefits to Nonprofits Using This Technique

You can use bargain sales, putting you at an advantage with both seller and the government. In the right circumstances, you can negotiate on the basis of Sales under Threat of Condemnation, a provision of the Internal Revenue Code that gives landowners who sell property they believe to be threatened by condemnation several tax advantages. One is that they are able to defer capital gains tax altogether so long as the property sold is replaced with like-kind property of equal value within three years. Theoretically, using this provision, a landowner could sell a $1 million piece of property at bargain sale for $800,000, have that $800,000 to play around with for three years before reinvesting it, and in addition, have a charitable deduction of $200,000. To compound the benefit, the landowner could buy the new property with a down payment and debt financing, thereby retaining some of the original cash to use as he or she sees fit.

OPTION SALES

Another type of preacquisition technique is option sales. Using this model, the Coastal Conservancy is currently negotiating with the Big Sur Land Trust to go into a specific area and acquire options on pieces of property that the Coastal Conservancy has indicated it would like to have rights on. Once they get the options, the Big Sur Land Trust will sell them to the Coastal Conservancy. The Big Sur Land Trust would never be in the position of having to exercise their options speculatively and would never have to put capital out to close the transaction.

If the Big Sur Land Trust's option must be exercised by March 1, then the Coastal Conservancy's must be exercised by February 20. Closing on the two could come at the same time.

It's a handy device; it minimizes everybody's risk. The land trust is at risk for a short period of time, if at all. If they pay $5,000 for the option, the Conservancy will compensate them for it, so they are out the cash only for the time between their purchase of an option from the landowner and the Conservancy's purchase of an option from them. They are not an agent, because there is no guarantee that the Coastal Conservancy will ever exercise the option.

Problem. The price that government should pay under its option usually has to be confirmed by a government appraisal.

NEGOTIATING TRADES

At times, though it is complex, negotiating trades may be the only way to accomplish your goals. The attractiveness of a trade to a seller is that if a landowner trades like-kind property that has equal value, there is no tax effect. If the landowner sold the same property for cash, he or she would be liable for capital gains tax on it.

Sometimes trading is the only way to make a deal. That was the case with The Nature Conservancy in New Mexico, where the Conservancy acquired a 20,000-acre ranch for sale to the state of New Mexico. The owner of the ranch demanded that, as part of the compensation, another ranch be delivered to her. It was a nonnegotiable demand, and while the new ranch did not nearly reach the value of the old one, so that there was also cash compensation involved, the landowner had great personal compensation in not having to look for a new ranch herself.

Jackson Hole Case Study—Trade of Easement for Fee: In the Jackson Hole area, a transaction is being arranged whereby a landowner will trade an easement on his property to a federal agency in exchange for fee title to a piece of expendable federal land, which the landowner can then sell or use as he pleases. The Jackson Hole Land Trust has been involved in the discussions and stands ready to assist in the transaction if necessary.

Scenarios

1. Negotiating a trade could be useful in a situation where government is interested in a particular piece of property, but the landowner wants not cash but another piece of property. Frequently, governments don't have the program authority to go out and buy a piece of unrelated property for trade. A nonprofit organization can simply step in the middle of this transaction and basically, by using government's money, complete the transaction. All deals are negotiated in advance, so that if property A is the property that government wants and property B is the one the landowner wants to get in trade for property A, the nonprofit organization can go in and negotiate a contract for purchase of property A, and negotiate a contract for purchase of property B, contingent on the closing of each transaction. The nonprofit organization would then negotiate a contract for the sale of property A to the government. Then all these transactions would go into escrow, where money and property are thrown into the air at the same time and magically come down in their proper places. Government money flows into the escrow, which is then used to purchase property B. The land trust owns

for an instant property B and trades it to the landowner of property A. The nonprofit organization now owns property A free and clear and then conveys it to the state.

In this situation, it is critical to know government acquisition procedures, so that the whole deal doesn't collapse for want of one signature from a related government office.

2.   If you are able to work through government surplus lands processes, you can identify pieces of surplus government property. You can then ascertain their value, attractiveness, and marketability in the private market and negotiate conditional sales contracts on them. You can find an individual who has a piece of property that government does want, who is also interested in the property the government does own, and effect the trade yourself. In this case, the money comes from the sale of the surplus property. This requires four transactions: (a) transaction from government to you of the surplus property; (b) sale of surplus property to an interested (or unrelated) party; (c) purchase of property desirable to government; and (d) sale of property to the government. These are quite complex kinds of procedures.

Resources

There is a for-profit organization based in Arizona called FLEX, Federal Lands Exchange, that operates exclusively doing government land trades. This organization would be an important resource to turn to for advice and feedback, assuming that they feel themselves to be a part of a professional community and unthreatened by your activities.

GRANTS THROUGH OTHER ENTITIES

This technique is designed to avoid government's inability to give grants for acquisition or improvement of real estate to nonprofit organizations. Its success depends on: interest of qualified governmental recipients of that grant in completion of the project, whatever it might be; and government's own disinterest in actually implementing the project.

If the nonprofit organization is interested in implementing a program that the government organization would like to see accomplished, it can be done under a contract in which the governmental organization passes through funds it is qualified to receive to the nonprofit organization.

If the project involves land, it is unlikely that the land trust will end up with fee ownership. Ownership will go to the government, though the land trust could negotiate a long-term management contract on the property. If there were to be an income-producing activity on that property, the land trust could put itself somewhere in the chain of that income as a portion of its fee for services in carrying out the project. How likely all this is to occur depends on three things:

1.   The attractiveness of the project to government

2.   The constituency pressure for the project

3.   The specific relationship between the nonprofit organization and the government, which frequently boils down to personal relationships

CASE STUDY: The Humboldt North Coast Land Trust has worked in that capacity with the Coastal Conservancy, with the intermediary government agency being the city of

Trinidad. The city was interested in seeing coastal access trail improvements made on property within the community. The city has essentially no staff. It is an unincorporated community of less than 250 people with marginal government services. The Coastal Conservancy approached the city with the proposal that it give them a grant for trails improvement and that they contract with the Humboldt North Coast Land Trust. It has worked out easily and well.

Advantages

Though using grants is less attractive than a direct approach, they can be used. They can be used with land acquisition, for improvements, for community efforts. The Conservancy could, for instance, enter into a contract for the conduct of community workshops to try to reach consensus on how a project should be developed. Anything that grant funds are available for that are consistent with or compatible with the programs that nonprofit organizations can undertake is fair game.

Take a look at government grant funding programs to see if there is an opportunity that would be profitable for your organization.

REFINED WISDOM ON THE PROCESS OF DEALING WITH GOVERNMENT

1.   One of the most important things to remember is that bureaucrats are by and large sensitive to how they are perceived. If they feel themselves being shown up or outdistanced by your organization, you create an uphill battle for yourself. It is extremely important to represent yourself as a complementary force to government, not as one that does better than government. We are talking about men and women in state service whose reputations are on the line, who are frequently under attack in any case. It is not an attractive prospect to them to have somebody say, "I can buy property cheaper than you can and do a better job at what you're supposed to do and save the taxpayers money and maybe you'll lose your job."

Present yourself as being able to assist them in implementing their goals, in doing things they cannot do. Sell them on your capabilities and on the idea that *you* can *assist* them.

2.   Know who you are talking to. You will have to spend time talking to middle-level bureaucrats, selling them on the program. They will be the ones who will implement the relationship between yourselves and the government organization. They have to know what is going on. If they have a stake in and some sympathy for the process you are trying to get going, you stand a better chance. But be careful of investing too much time with them. They will not ultimately be the ones who decide whether to establish the relationship. It is not within the classic role for the middle-level bureaucrat to go to his or her boss and propose something creative and innovative. The sales job will have to be clinched at a higher level.

3.   Have your professional pitch together. Know what they need and what you have to offer. Be prepared with hypothetical or concrete examples; draw up a *pro forma* as to how the goals could be accomplished. Go in as if your career and your next paycheck depended on it.

4.   Be patient. Realize that government moves more slowly than we would like it to, particularly when we are talking about something creative that hasn't been done before.

5.   Know the process. Be sure you are not suggesting something that is impossible for a government organization to do. Don't suggest something they *have* to turn down.

6.   Be very sure you can deliver on what you are suggesting government entrust to you. Demonstrate a track record and be prepared to offer examples of other organizations that have operated successfully with other government entities.

PROTECTING FARMLAND and FARMING ENTERPRISE: Federal Tax Incentives

Edward Thompson, Jr.

ABSTRACT

If they are going to make a truly significant contribution to farmland and ranchland conservation, private land trusts must take a "great leap forward." Our current approach to the problem, using tax shelters to save farmland by acquiring easements, is so convoluted and offers so little incentive to the average farmer that it will never get the job done, except perhaps on a very localized, patchwork basis. A dramatic change is needed to make private sector conservation tools equal to the problem of saving 3 million acres of farmland per year (that is the current rate of loss), more than all the land protected by private conservation since World War II.

PROBLEM

The conversion of farm and ranchland to nonagricultural uses poses a double-edged threat to the nation's agricultural production capacity. The history of American agriculture has been one of the substitution of technology for land to increase yields to satisfy continually rising demands for food and other agricultural products. Our ability to continue on this course is cast into doubt, however, by the increasing costs of farm technology. These costs include both inputs to production, such as energy for fuel, irrigation, and fertilizer, and outputs (incidental effects), such as accelerating soil erosion. The historic trend of increasing crop yields is now leveling off, foreshadowing the possibility that we will have to reverse our course and again substitute land for technology in order to maintain production. Viewed against this backdrop, the conversion of farmland to nonagricultural uses represents a dangerous narrowing of our options.

But farmland conversion not only limits our ability to resubstitute land for technology, it *also* constricts our ability to employ new farm technology. Another cost of such technology is its effect on neighboring nonagricultural land users. Residential subdivisions, for example, are not compatible with modern agriculture when mixed together helter-skelter. Agricultural production usually results in odors, noise, dust, chemical spray drift, and other side effects that are offensive and sometimes harmful to neighboring landowners. These effects are multiplied as rural areas are more densely settled by people who are not engaged in agriculture. In areas where farmland conversion is significant and residential dwellings are scattered among working farms and ranches, increased governmental regulation of agricultural practices and private nuisance lawsuits against farmers and ranchers are threatening agricultural production by increasing its costs, reducing its efficiency, limiting its options for technological innovation, or curtailing it altogether. The "right to farm" movement among agricultural producers has been the result, and it is largely a reaction against the proliferating constraints on the use of modern agricultural technology.

Whether the future course of American agriculture will be to resubstitute land for technology, to rely even more heavily on new agricultural technology, or to do a combination of both, the conversion of farm and ranchlands to nonagricultural uses represents a threat to the nation's production capacity. To put it another way, agricultural land is a limiting factor in the production equation under any assumption about the relative contribution of technology, or so the "right to farm" movement seems to teach us. Protecting farming enterprise requires protecting farm and ranchlands against the encroachment of nonagricultural land uses and the conflicts they cause.

OBJECTIVES OF THE PROPOSAL

The basic objectives of the following proposal are to retain farm and ranchlands in agricultural production and, thus, to prevent expensive and debilitating conflicts between farm and ranch operations and neighboring nonagricultural land uses.

BASIC APPROACH

The basic approach of this proposal is to discourage the conversion of farm and ranchlands to nonagricultural uses within locally delineated Agricultural Enterprise Districts (AEDs). Federal tax incentives will be made available to farmers and ranchers who agree to prevent the conversion of their land to nonagricultural uses, in effect compensating them for choosing not to sell their land out of agriculture for the highest price.

TARGETING INCENTIVES

Only in certain areas of the United States is farmland conversion a significant problem. The solution should be tailored to the extent of the problem so as to avoid windfalls to landowners from the federal treasury and to maintain the present relative economic advantage of landowners. Therefore, federal tax incentives will be available to farmers and ranchers only in the following jurisdictions, which represent areas where farmland conversion and conflicts with nonagricultural land uses are significant:

1.   Counties (or other appropriate local units) located within or immediately adjacent to the Standard Metropolitan Statistical Areas (SMSAs) throughout the country. This will include the urban growth fringe around major cities. Farm and ranch production in these areas is very significant, representing about 50 percent of total farm income in the Northeast and Pacific states and 20 percent in the Corn Belt.

2.   Counties where population density is equal to or greater than that of 80 percent of all counties within the state. This will include the fringes of smaller cities and towns, generally in the South, Midwest and Mountain West regions.

3.   Counties where population growth during the last five consecutive years (continually advancing) is equal to or greater than that of 90 percent of the counties in the state. This will include rural areas, again generally in the Mountain West, where energy and mineral development has or will create boom towns.

AGRICULTURAL ENTERPRISE DISTRICTS

The key to the administration of the proposed tax incentives is the establishment of Agricultural Enterprise Districts by units of general purpose local government within the foregoing jurisdictions. AEDs should include all agricultural lands within the establishing jurisdiction, except those, generally adjacent to existing population centers, that are reasonably needed to accommodate nonagricultural development within a foreseeable planning horizon not to exceed ten years. It is crucial that the AEDs constitute discrete, contiguous agricultural areas of sufficient size to enable farming and ranching to take place without interference from nonagricultural land uses.

Within the AEDs, nonagricultural development should be generally discouraged by local public policy, and it should be prevented—not completely, but to the extent that it would tend to interfere with agricultural production using the latest technology. Generally, the extent of permissible nonagricultural development should be determined on the basis of a sensible density criterion, for example, 1 unit per 40 acres, or whatever figure makes sense in a particular local agricultural context. Such development should also be guided toward the least productive soils on any given ownership parcel.

Local jurisdictions should be free to adopt any effective means of discouraging and limiting nonagricultural development within AEDs. Their options range from the purchase of development rights at one end of the spectrum to agricultural zoning on the other, with an infinite number of combinations in between. Some 300 local jurisdictions have adopted some such program to date, and it is the intention of this proposal to accommodate all such efforts, if effective, and to encourage others where needed. Nothing would require a local jurisdiction to establish an AED or a program to carry out its intent.

Within AEDs, local jurisdictions should also avoid the regulation of agricultural practices, except in the interest of protecting agriculture (e.g., noxious weed control, soil conservation) and except where it can be justified for the protection of people and property outside the AEDs. Further, prospective nonagricultural residents of AEDs should be put on express notice that they must forego legal recourse to abate or interfere with customary agricultural practices that currently exist or may be developed through improved farm technology.

To ensure the effectiveness of local AED programs for discouraging nonagricultural development, there should be oversight by the states, preferably by state departments of agriculture, under criteria embodied in enabling legislation. To ensure that the purpose of the federal tax incentives is carried out and to guarantee even-handed application, the state enabling legislation should be subject to certification by the USDA under criteria embodied in federal legislation. The IRS would be involved only to the extent of determining questions of land valuation under the tax provisions. The entire oversight process would function like that under the national historic preservation districts program, keeping federal involvement to a minimum and stressing local control.

FEDERAL TAX INCENTIVES

The following federal tax benefits would serve as the principal incentive for the establishment of local AEDs and would further compensate farmers and ranchers for agreeing to prevent the conversion of their land to nonagricultural uses for protection of their mutual "right to farm."

The first federal tax incentive is exclusion of capital gains taxation of the proceeds of the sale of agricultural land to qualified farmers and ranchers. The intent is to ensure that the land is transferred to bona fide agricultural producers, individual or corporate. Qualification of transferees should be based on criteria similar to those defining "qualified heirs" and "material participation" under Internal Revenue Code Section 2032A, although the intent is not to be quite as restrictive. Local AED jurisdictions should apply these criteria, rather than the IRS, although there might be an oversight role for the latter.

This exclusion would also be available, regardless of the qualifications of the transferee, if an agricultural conservation easement (see below) is placed on the land prior to its sale. Since such an easement would restrict the use of the land to agricultural production, any transferee would presumably purchase the land for this purpose, dispensing with the need for qualification.

Once the capital gains exclusion provision is invoked with respect to a parcel of agricultural land, subsequent sales to unqualified transferees (except as noted above) should result in the treatment of the gain as ordinary income. The same treatment should occur if an AED is dissolved, although there might be some exception made in hardship circumstances, for example, where farming or ranching has become uneconomic or otherwise impossible due to reasons other than conflicts with nonagricultural land uses permitted within the AED. This feature is intended as a recapture provision to prevent abuses.

The exclusion of capital gains taxation of farmer-to-farmer transfers—which is analogous to and was inspired by the current homeowner roll-over provision of the Internal Revenue Code—would serve partially to compensate farm and ranch landowners for choosing not to sell their land for nonagricultural development at a price higher than what an agricultural producer would pay for it. The amount of compensation would be leveraged by the exclusion to the extent that landowners could accept a single lump-sum payment rather than installments that are now customary to spread out tax liability and invest the proceeds to generate additional income over what would be the installment period.

The second federal tax incentive is comprehensive credit against income, gift, and estate taxation equal to the value of an agricultural conservation easement donated or sold at less than market value (bargain sale or partial gift) to a qualified public or private charitable entity. The credit could be used against income tax liability, for example, ordinary farm or ranch income, or the income from investment of the proceeds of a sale of the property (above). It could also be used against gift taxation, for example, upon transfer of a farm or ranch to a son during the lifetime of the taxpayer. The remaining amount of the credit would further be carried over and could be applied against estate tax liability upon the death of the taxpayer.

This credit is similar to the current deduction for conservation easement donations permitted by Section 170 of the Internal Revenue Code. A farmer or rancher within an AED could elect the credit in lieu of the deduction, which would remain available outside of AEDs. The rationale for switching to a credit is that it would extend the incentive for easement donations to the "average" farmer or rancher, to whom tax deductions are generally not attractive.

Further, Section 170 should be amended to avoid the complications—and the chilling effect on easement donations—posed by the judgmental formula now used to determine whether farmland is worthy of protection as open space. The purpose here is not to preserve open space but to protect agricultural production capacity by maintaining the agricultural character of land. Hence, "conservation purposes" under Section 170 should include "preservation of the capacity of farm or ranchland for agricultural use."

The comprehensive tax credit would complement the foregoing capital gains exclusion, enabling farmers and ranchers within AEDs to recover most if not all of the difference between the fair market value of their land for nonagricultural development and the price it would bring from an agricultural producer. If an agricultural conservation easement on the land is donated prior to sale, the transferee need not qualify under the exclusion provision, and the credit would shelter income from investment of the proceeds of sale.

By taking advantage of both tax incentives, farmers and ranchers would have a wide variety of options for planning their financial affairs prior to and after retirement. They could earn substantially the same return after taxes by keeping their land in agricultural production—thus protecting neighbors' "right to farm"—as by selling it out of agriculture to the detriment of producers around them. These are the ultimate objectives that must be met if we are to protect farmland and farming enterprise where they are threatened by the conversion of land to nonagricultural uses and the resulting conflict of farm technology with unsympathetic nonfarming neighbors.

CRITIQUE BY WORKSHOP

The workshop participants critiqued the proposed law, bringing up general concerns as well as specific problems they saw for effective implementation. Their comments are summarized here, basically following the order given.

Regulation. Concern was raised that the proposal was too heavily weighted toward regulation. Asking a group of farmers to agree with a local government on an agricultural district would be difficult. The example of Wisconsin was used to counter this concern. A similar program has had excellent success there.

Boundaries. Some people felt that it shouldn't be restricted to areas near urban centers: Anywhere people want to preserve farmland, it should be encouraged.

Credits. The use of credits instead of deductions got solid support as an excellent approach.

"Qualified buyer." It was generally agreed that this definition would need more clarification.

Capital gains. It was pointed out that using a capital gains tax exclusion as an incentive might not be very stable due to the likelihood of congressional changes in the percentage taxed.

Conservation purpose. The clarification of farming as a conservation purpose received strong support.

Districts and easements. Combining these two actions could raise some valuation problems for conservation easements. If a property is already within an agricultural district, then what is an easement worth?

Carry-overs. There was strong support for extending tax benefit carry-overs through to heirs if necessary for full utilization.

Public lands. How would an agricultural district affect use of publicly owned land within its boundaries?

BRAINSTORMING SESSIONS: NEW and EXISTING TOOLS

UTILIZING PRIVATE CAPITAL for LAND PRESERVATION: Brainstorming Session

Paul Brunner, Davis Cherington, William Long, Jon Roush, Michael Swack, and Douglas Wheeler

ABSTRACT

The main purpose of this session was to identify the variety of ways that are currently being used to attract private capital to land preservation and to list new potential options. In the course of this work it was felt that various techniques might be identified that because of their potential warranted further discussion.

At the outset, two major types of land preservation were identified: (1) where a specific land use was to be preserved, for example, farmland or low-income housing; and (2) where the preservation of the natural condition of the land was to receive highest priority. The substantive difference here is that land uses have the potential to generate income and to create various tax deductions and credits while preservation generally does not. People with experience in attracting private capital for both these ventures were represented on the panel, and each was asked to give a short presentation on the successes or problems they had encountered. Then the floor was opened up for the audience to respond and suggest problems and potential techniques they would like to see addressed. One of these, the involvement of corporations in agricultural land preservation, was selected for further brainstorming by the panel.

The results of this brainstorming session provide an introduction into the functioning of the investment world and capital markets. The problems faced by land trusts in dealing with this world are reviewed as are the selling points unique to land preservation activities. While the list of financing techniques is extensive, only a handful have been successfully used. Attracting private investment and tax shelter money for land preservation is a relatively new concept, and we have just begun to tap the possibilities.

HOW MONEY WORKS—MICHAEL SWACK

Most nonprofit organizations have a common complaint: "If only we had more money we could. . . ." While they have a general sense that they need it and need it badly, they often do not have a specific plan for using or attracting capital. One of the cardinal rules of money is that once you know very clearly for what and how you will use it, attracting money becomes much simpler and perhaps a real possibility. If you think you need money, develop a financial plan.

A financial plan is your basic tool for attracting private capital. It is specific about what you plan to do, how you will do it, the benefits and risks involved, and why an investor would be interested. An organization can often find a sympathetic person, an accountant, lawyer, or financier, who can help them evaluate a project and draw up such a plan.

As a nonprofit organization you will most likely have to overcome prejudice when approaching financial institutions. At the worst many people perceive "nonprofit" as synonymous with charitable giving, shaky financial management, and certainly no place for an investment. At best, you are an unfamiliar type of organization with probably an unusual financing request. This is a serious problem in dealing with the financial community. The nature of the business is to invest in the tried and true; the unusual or unknown is to be avoided to reduce the potential risk. Keep this in mind while developing a financial plan and make it answer these concerns. The other way to address this problem is by getting to know your banker or other financial sources. As they become familiar with what you are doing, they will be much more willing to support it. For example, inviting high-ranking bankers, board members, or financiers to an introductory meeting on a beautiful property can be fun, informative, and help lay the groundwork for a later financial discussion. Generally they will be interested in attending: It's their business to know what is going on in the community; you may be asking them for a loan at some point in the future, and it is a lot more interesting than reading financial reports in the bank.

In developing and explaining your programs the issue of land ownership will certainly arise. Most land trusts originate in an attempt to deal with a couple of land-based dilemmas in our culture. Contrary to the real estate market, most trusts choose to value land not as a commodity to be bought and sold for speculative profit but rather as a heritage to be carefully stewarded. The high price of land and resulting difficulty of acquisition for most people has also led land trusts to look for alternative forms of ownership.

Most land trusts retain title to the land while providing for long-term, often inheritable, leases. A lessee can build equity by developing improvements on the property. Essentially all one is giving up is speculative profit. This unusual approach to land ownership can be a source of confusion on the part of lenders. The sensibility of a leasehold arrangement and the opportunity it offers makes a very persuasive argument that has been used successfully by land trusts in dealing with financial institutions.

Sources of Capital

There are several places that a nonprofit organization might approach for funding, but before selecting one, make sure that the form of the loan matches the use and objectives of the project. Often nonprofits think in terms of a grant when they need money. Many times a grant is the only appropriate source of support. But occasionally a grant might actually be better made as a loan if the interest rate can be low enough. The appropriate use of financing is very important. For example, if what you want is a long-term loan for property purchase, don't get a short-term loan and expect to refinance it later. Very often this sort of deal will fall apart, and at some point in the future the entire project will be jeopardized.

Banks. When most people think about where to get money, they think first of the banks, appropriately enough because most of the money is in the banks. However, for non-profit land conservation, banks may not be the place to start. They can be helpful, but you must be aware of what they are willing and not willing to do.

1. First off, banks do not like to make loans unless it is a less than 0 percent risk.

2. Banks need security such as a house, property, or another repossessible asset in case the loan payments are not made.

3. Will there be some money-producing use of the land? If so and if the cash flow has the capability to repay the loan at current interest rates, a bank may well be interested.

4. The language, terms, and concerns of bankers tend to be similar and predictable. Prior to approaching your bank, working with someone who understands bankers may significantly improve your proposal.

5. As mentioned, bankers tend to be prejudiced against the unfamiliar. Involve a high-level officer early in your project, well before you need a loan.

6. Banks are concerned about their reputation and if they become interested in the public benefit aspects of your project, their financial support may well help their public relations campaign.

If your project fits within these parameters, then a bank may be your source for capital. There are, however, several other sources to investigate.

Religious orders. Most religious orders have a substantial portfolio of investments from which they derive interest. This interest income is used for a variety of purposes, and part of it is generally given to charities. But most orders do not make loans to public interest projects, not because they do not have the capability but rather because no one has presented the possibility to them in appropriate terms.

Chuck Matthei has had good success in this field of "faith and finance" as he terms it. Several factors go together to produce a successful situation.

1. Investing in socially valuable programs is appealing to religious orders.

2. An argument can be made for low-interest and special-term loans because interest income is seen biblically as a sin. So a balance can be struck between maintaining the portfolio *corpus* and achieving maximum return in the interests of social good.

3. Religious orders tend to handle their investments on a local basis, not through a centralized system. This allows them to be very approachable and involved in the process. Centralization tends to kill innovation in financing.

4. Nuns tend to be more approachable than priests or brothers.

101

So if you have a religious community in your area that you think might be interested in your project, begin developing a relationship with them.

Members of your organization. We often tend to neglect what is closest to us for financial support, committed members of our organizations. In developing a financial plan, you should carefully evaluate your membership for potential support. While it is unlikely that anyone would have the capability to be your primary lender, they may be able to help by co-signing or otherwise assisting in getting a loan.

Leveraging capital. Suppose you were able to arrange a portion of your needed loan from one source, say, a member of your organization. You could take that loan and use it to leverage other capital sources, your bank or church contacts perhaps. In this manner you may be able to secure your full loan when it would otherwise appear impossible.

Financial Plan Summary

Your financial plan is your blueprint for your program. In the process of developing it and within the text of it as well, you must address your need for money in very specific and practical terms. What do you need it for? What are your potential sources? How will you approach them, including the potential for leveraging? What are your plans beyond the original venture? The success of your project rests on your capability to effectively interface your hopes for your project with the realities of the financial world.

PROGRAM RELATED INVESTMENTS—DOUG WHEELER

Foundations

The best source of private capital (and it's currently largely untapped) is foundations. Not grants, but program-related investments provide great opportunity for land conservation. If you have a project that fits a foundation's interests, there are several very attractive reasons for a foundation to consider a low-interest or special-term loan.

Recent changes in Treasury regulations provide that foundations need not pay out more than 5 percent of their *corpus* (total worth of the foundation's assets) in any one year. By making a loan or investment in a program, they can preserve their capital base. If the loan is to a project that fits their granting criteria and if the terms are "charitable," the loan will reduce the amount of the *corpus* subject to granting regulations.

We are speaking here about an investment, not a grant, and the ability to repay the investment is mandatory. This is an important point to make when developing your project and in negotiations with a foundation. Some of the past experience with program-related investments has been poor; the recipients of the loans have occasionally taken the attitude that because the investor was a foundation, they did not need their money returned. This approach has obviously made some foundations shy away from program-related investment but can be overcome with a responsible attitude and proposal for repayment.

You think you have a program that fits a foundation's interests; what investment terms will you need to negotiate with them?

1. *Interest rate.* A program-related investment has the potential to be offered at an interest rate lower than anywhere else on the market. An agreement will have to be

individually negotiated that will be workable both for your project and the foundation's needs.

2. *Repayment schedule.* As mentioned before, your realistic ability to repay the investment in a timely manner is crucial to negotiating a successful foundation investment.

3. *Performance schedule.* What are you planning to accomplish with this money and when? A foundation will be very interested in your capability to carry out your proposal.

4. *Timing of investment.* Will the loan be made in one lump sum at the beginning or in periodic steps based on the performance schedule?

5. *Form of the investment—loan or equity.* Most situations will probably be best handled by a low-interest, short-term loan. This is not always the case, and you may be able to negotiate a long-term loan. In some situations, an equity participation in the project is preferable, such as through "preferred shares."

All of these facets of a program-related investment are negotiable, so with your financial plan in hand, go in there and arrange a deal.

Insurance Companies

Insurance companies have been known to make subsidized loans for conservation purposes. While they do not have the financial impetus to make low-interest loans that the foundations do, the publicity value can be significant. If someone in an influential position in a corporation is interested in your program, you may have an opportunity to arrange a special loan.

WORKING IN THE CORPORATE WORLD—JON ROUSH

The success of the land conservation movement depends greatly on our success in dealing with the corporate world. They control a great deal of land, both agricultural and conservation properties, and will control more in the future. Something like the twenty-four largest land-holding corporations control a land area 1½ times the size of Texas. We must learn to deal well with the corporations; their centralization and concentration of power over farmland is a reality even if we do not like it.

Based on the experience of The Nature Conservancy, there are two strategies for financial dealing with the corporate world. One is to get capital from corporations; the other is to get into their game and generate money in a business venture.

Collaborative Action with Corporations

Especially for corporations with a natural resource base, land trusts can provide mutually beneficial opportunities for land conservation. The tax laws can encourage such actions through outright donations of conservation properties and other assets. They may also be interested in a land trust's expertise in good land management.

Many large corporations own a lot of land. Some of it they need for their work, some of it they don't; some of it gives them some real management headaches, some of it has public value. A land trust can offer corporations assistance to help resolve some of these conflicts over appropriate land use.

The concept of working with corporations is difficult to accept for many conservationists. It is likewise difficult for many corporate officers to imagine a friendly conversation with an "environmentalist," much less developing a working relationship. But there are common goals and symbiotic needs, and one can find a kindred spirit here and there. The conservation group that seeks out such situations and builds mutual trust opens the door to some of the greatest reserves of private capital.

Land donations.

1. *Problem properties.* A corporation may have a property that due to its location or natural qualities may be giving them problems with the public. Perhaps it's better suited as parkland or a nature preserve; or maybe it would be better as farmland than a mine site. A land trust can work in these situations often as a "neutral" party between a public interest advocacy group and the corporation. Combined with good statesmanship, the tax benefits of a charitable organization specializing in land transactions can resolve an apparently unresolvable situation.

2. *Dead assets.* These are properties that a corporation does not need for its work. Generally they do not have much ecological value nor economic value to the corporation. Such an asset can make a good candidate for donation to a land trust. Depending on the property, a land trust could sell or lease it and use the income for program support.

The situation must meet several criteria:

1. The corporation does not need the asset.

2. It is fully depreciated.

3. The capital gains taxes would be high if sold: It has low basis or has highly appreciated over time.

4. The corporation has sufficient taxable income to use the charitable contribution deduction created by the land gift.

If these factors are present, the donation might actually make them more money than a sale.

Looking a gift horse in the mouth. Being given a property can be wonderful, but it can also be a terrible liability. The Nature Conservancy, for instance, has been offered a toxic waste dump. Sometimes a donor will not even be aware of the potential problem.

1. *Merchantable property?* If you are given it, can you sell it or otherwise make a real economic gain? If not, don't accept someone else's headache.

2. *Legal problems?* Make sure the title is clear; easements, water rights, liens, leases, and a whole host of other legal problems can cloud a title, making the property undesirable.

3. *Publicity problems?* What is the history of ownership, neighbors, and public knowledge of the property? Are you getting into a situation that is politically sensitive now or in the future?

Do your homework on a "gift" of land; it may not be as great as it looks!

Corporations, land trusts, and farmland. In the past fifteen years many corporations diversified by buying agricultural land. For many of them it has posed problems because of the unfamiliarity of the enterprise. Land trusts with a primary focus on farmland preservation may find that they can help these corporations. While we do not have much experience now, the area holds great potential. Some suggestions for future work follow:

1. *Management.* Farm management is a very specialized field and to the dismay of corporate executives, a good factory manager is not necessarily a good farm manager. A local land trust might be able to offer its management skills to such a corporation. By overseeing the management of property, the trust could ensure sound management practices and find a local operator to handle the unit.

2. *Cash flow.* Some corporations bought agricultural land expecting to have a good annual cash return. Anyone who's involved in agriculture knows how foolish that expectation is. While it's hard to see how a land trust could help meet those expectations, perhaps their involvement could help make the reality of farming more acceptable in the corporate ledgers through, for example, a donation of an undivided leasehold in a property.

Money-Making Enterprises

While the previous discussion talked about attracting corporate money to support land trust activities, this section presents concepts for land trusts to make money in the corporate world.

Farming. Those of us involved in farmland preservation should be asking ourselves how we can make money in agriculture in a socially and environmentally responsible way. Not only might it create a needed cash flow but more importantly it would also help meet our goals.

Banking. We are in the capital intensive business of land transactions. Why not develop our own bank? There is some history here of special interest banks, for example, and while they have not always been a great success, we have learned some things and the potential for success is there. The primary purpose of the bank would be to make money; a secondary purpose would be provision of favorable loans to those members who formed the bank. The marvelous thing about banks is that it is difficult for them to lose money. For the safety of the banking public, banks are regulated to practically ensure that they will be a profit-making enterprise. What we could do is to pool lenders, spread the risk between several nonprofit organizations, and set up our own board.

Communications business. A field where things are changing rapidly is the communications industry, and in a changing situation there is always the possibility of making good money. Seriously though, if we are in the business of changing people's values about land, why don't we buy better media access? We could own our own television and radio stations, buy satellite time, run our own newspapers. There are Christian stations, why not land conservation stations?

Land banking. Perhaps there is a possibility of corporate backing of a land bank. For example, could a corporation provide a long-term loan to a land trust purchasing land, perhaps in an arrangement that passed through tax benefits but kept management control in the hands of the operator? Control Data Corporation (CDC) has a program called Rural Venture in which they purchase land and lease it out with an option to buy. The program is in operation in Minnesota and is designed primarily to work with a group of operators on producing and marketing cooperatively with the aid of CDC's computer system.

CONSERVATION BUYERS—PAUL BRUNNER

The land most critical to preserve is land that is for sale. A broker is in a unique position to see and screen a lot of properties and when he finds one that looks special and worth preserving, he can try to do something about it. Mr. Brunner generally tries to find a "conservation buyer": a person with a conservation ethic who wants to buy land in that area and does not want to develop it. While occasional properties might be suited for governmental acquisition, this is a slow and even more uncertain solution in the future.

Often when conservation buyers acquire a property, they will place a conservation easement over the property. Not only does it create a significant tax savings through the donation, but it also can provide an economic justification for keeping the property in agricultural use by reducing the basis and thereby improving the capitalization-to-income ratio. These economic incentives can also help rationalize the purchase of agricultural land that is otherwise primarily the fulfillment of an emotional desire.

How does one find a conservation buyer? The main source of clients is conservation organizations, who then are usually the recipient of the easement. Advertising is risky because a broker working in this field cannot afford any mistakes, cannot afford to sell a property to someone who turns out to have development schemes in mind. Working with buyers is always risky, however, because no one can require a donation of a conservation easement (then it would not be a donation).

There are other problems associated with conservation buyers. For instance, the typical buyer is a wealthy person from outside the area with another source of income. This can present some serious problems for the community through changes in management and access. Some of these can be alleviated by hiring a manager from the area.

INVESTMENT POOLS FOR CONSERVATION BUYERS—DAVIS CHERINGTON

Rather than spend time on the concept of limited development, which was discussed in a workshop, I would like to present a concept that had great promise but did not work out. We were intrigued with the conservation buyer concept and thought that it could be made more effective if a limited partnership were created for land purchase, donation of the easement, and then resale of the property for agricultural uses. If you were able to gather a group of investors into an investment pool and put the money out in sequential limited partnerships for this purpose for several properties, you would have a very effective land preservation tool. The dollars on the transactions came out all right, though one could still make more on other investments. The problem arose because of the nature and timing of the donation. It had to occur early on and without it, the finances were not appealing. Lawyers reviewing the proposal warned that the Internal Revenue Service would not approve because a donation would be expected, and if it is expected, then the charitability is suspect.

DONOR-ASSISTED MANAGEMENT PROGRAM—BILL LONG

The Reliance has developed a program that shows promise to protect land, to provide for research on ecologically sound management practices, and to improve access to an agricultural operation for a beginning operator. With the Donor-Assisted Management Program, the Reliance and investor form a partnership. The limited partner, an investor, purchases a property; and the Reliance, as general partner, arranges the management through a lease agreement that runs for 8–10 years. Toward the end of that time, the finances are such that the investor is encouraged to donate the property to the Reliance. The Reliance then continues to lease it out on a special management program lease. Again, there is risk involved because a donation cannot be expected or committed ahead of the actual time of the gift.

BRAINSTORMING ON PROBLEMS FOR DISCUSSION

After the presentations, the floor was opened to brainstorm a list of potential ways to involve private capital in land conservation. This list follows with brief explanations of each item.

Easement Donation by Seller: Pros and Cons

Seller can take advantage by sheltering capital gains and other assets.

It's easier to find tax advantages for buyer.

Land Banking

Saskatchewan Land Bank is backed by the provincial government. Could a corporation back a similar setup?

Alaskan Commercial Fisheries and Agriculture Bank makes loans at below-market interest rate.

Appalachian Regional Commission has just established a land trust/land bank with priorities to: (1) preserve land and (2) provide housing for low-income people.

Time Sharing of Recreational Properties

Management problems, for example, do hunting, agriculture, and preservation mix? Solvable with good land use and monitoring.

Corporate Retreat Centers

Acquisition of a preserve for location of a retreat or small conference ground.

Public Utilities

The Nature Conservancy has purchased water companies to protect water rights.

Rattlesnake Wilderness was possible because of a utility's willingness to make land trades.

Excess lands from completed utility projects.

Land Trades

Very complex deal but with the demise of land and water conservation funds, increasingly important. Examples: exchange federal land in fee title for conservation easements in an area of high public value, as in Jackson Hole; and acquire lands that a public agency wants, then trade the agency for land they want to get rid of, which the land trust can then sell.

Problems with land trade.

1.   Very time-consuming.

2.   May require several interagency dealings.

Needs.

1.   Technical help from private sector, lawyers, land planners, land dealers.

2.   Public and political support is needed to encourage public agencies to pursue land trades. The national park system has a draft policy giving trades for acquisitions a higher priority and suggesting a joint interagency land exchange board and land pool. Good concept, needs public support.

Lease of Rights for Renewable Resources
On acquisitions of preservation properties it may be possible to lease out various rights as a way to make income: water, grazing, selective timber harvest, solar and wind energy development potential.

Partial Development
Acquire a property and develop and sell or sell a portion for development, retaining the critical areas for preservation. Requires good organizational stability because it is high-risk and long, hard work; hard to achieve with a nonprofit organization.

Preservation Fund
Get money from developers of agricultural land for a land preservation fund. Example: Montana Sheepgrowers and Environmentalists Committee formed by two opposing factions able to agree on some similar goals and a way to work together on them.

Conservation Bonds

If there is strong public support for preservation of an area, a bond issue could be put on the ballot to raise the money.

CORPORATE OWNERSHIP OF AGRICULTURAL LAND

An attempt was made at this point to focus the discussion on one of the issues raised earlier: corporate involvement in agriculture and the potential for a land trust to work effectively for its goals with an entity often seen as arch villain. A synopsis of that discussion follows.

Is there workable common ground between corporations and land trusts? For starters, where do they have common goals? A major land trust goal is land preservation. While that certainly would not be a corporate objective, a corporation might have a desire to see stability in agriculture and, in fact, to see specific areas remain in agricultural production. Many corporations that have invested in agricultural land have done so as a long-term investment primarily because of its food production potential. With increasing population and decreasing available land for farming, they figure agricultural land to be a good investment. That goal is not too different than that held by many land trusts.

Land-holding corporations whose main enterprise is not agriculture, however, often find themselves with a problem they do not have the expertise to solve. Basically, they have an asset that they do not know how to manage. A land trust could provide that missing link by helping them develop a sound management plan and locating a good local operator to run the place. The potential exists for such a corporation to donate a conservation easement or to otherwise become further committed to land preservation. In following this scenario, some differences of strategy and tactics will arise depending on the land trust's objectives. Preservation of the land base as a species reservoir requires a different approach than the maintenance of sound farming practices with its attendant support community.

Many different techniques were discussed this afternoon, and a statement by one of the participants sums it up:

"This has been great to hear about all these techniques, and I agree we probably need them all and a few more; but when it comes right down to it, they're all the same. You put on your three-piece suit, if that's what the Romans are wearing, or you put on your cowboy boots if that's what the Romans are wearing, and you walk up to the folks and say, 'Hey, let's talk about it,' and that's where you start."

DEVELOPING a PROGRAM THAT WORKS for LOW- and MODERATE-INCOME LANDOWNERS: Brainstorming Session

Chuck Matthei, Joseph Brooks, Bill Gay, Thomas Mills, George Ballis, Steve Moody, and Jennie Gerard

ABSTRACT

The aim of the brainstorming session on developing a program for low- and moderate-income landowners was to address both the plight of the cash-poor landowner who wants to remain on the land *and* that of the nonlandowner who wants access to land that he or she cannot afford. As Jennie Gerard pointed out early in the session, so many land trusts are struggling to help landowners retain their land that access for nonlandowners is a question very seldom addressed. Participants heard from several organizations actively working in both these areas. After presentations by representatives from the Institute for Community Economics, the Emergency Land Fund, the Trust for Public Land, and National Land for People regarding their programs for low- and moderate-income people, Steve Moody, United States Trust, described his role as investment counselor for clients wishing to put their capital into programs that help to redistribute wealth equitably while providing a fair return for investment. Discussion following the presentations generally centered around the topic of land conservation and conservation organizations leasing land to young farmers and others without access to land or housing.

Though the ideal goal of the session was to generate some new thinking on these problems by bringing together people working on the cutting edge of the field, perhaps the most important function the session had was to underline the need for land conservation organizations (LCOs) *to become aware of the social consequences of their activities,* for indeed they exist. Land trust activity restructures economic value and has an impact on productivity. With this primary awareness comes the need for LCOs to build bridges with organizations working primarily with low- and moderate-income people and to extend themselves to these kinds of constituencies in the communities in which they work. From Pagosa Springs, Colorado, to the rural South, patterns of land ownership are changing, in turn disrupting the communities that live on the land. The urban poor are being displaced in a similar way. If this country is to continue to try to achieve the ideals of equality of opportunity, self-sufficiency, and independence that we all cherish, we must address ourselves to these social concerns at the same time as we work to preserve the land base. They go hand in hand.

SOCIAL AND ECONOMIC IMPLICATIONS OF THE CHOICES OF
LAND CONSERVATION ORGANIZATIONS—CHUCK MATTHEI

Why should land conservation organizations be concerned with these social problems?

1. *For their own survival.* In an era of shrinking resources, the public must understand the public benefit of land conservation activities. Land preservation must be marketed not only in terms of public image, but in the sense that LCOs must broaden their constituencies to include low- and moderate-income people if they are to survive the difficult political pressures of the 1980s.

2. *The inescapable moral necessity to confront the problem.* More and more people find themselves in real economic distress today, and this serious social need is too often ignored by land conservation organizations. The Institute for Community Economics has found families living in cardboard boxes in urban areas. They have found families that have had to give up their children for adoption simply to ensure a roof over their heads because they had no housing and there was no emergency housing available. An unofficial look at a never-released study by the city of Washington showed that within three or four years, 100,000 people—1/7th of the population—will be displaced from their homes with no provision for resettlement. When the Cambodian government started driving people into the countryside, George McGovern called for UN military intervention!

What are the issues that land conservation organizations need to be aware of in reaching out?

1. *Style.* Land conservation organizations must seek to be aware of the differences in personal and organizational styles that can exist between land conservation organizations and neighborhood and housing land trusts. Differences in vocabulary, dress, spending habits, and other areas can be barriers between these groups, and will affect the perception of land conservation organizations by low-income people, for whom their styles are not habitual or even possible.

2. *Group process.* Land conservation organizations should develop a sensitivity to people's history and experience of group process—their confidence in themselves and ability to participate. Sometimes in attempting to institute democratic reforms, organizations have become less representative in fact.

3. *Local control.* Who and how many in the local community are making the critical decisions that are going to affect the nature of land and its use in the community?

4. *Marketing.* How broad is our concept of marketing and to what extent does it include a good-faith outreach to constituencies who traditionally would not either have contact with a local LCO or be the recipients of conventional professional marketing efforts.

5. *Choice of land.* When we look at land and target it for acquisition, do we also keep in mind social needs and the importance of meeting both social and environmental agendas over time?

6. *Financing source and terms.* A number of organizations have undertaken historic preservation projects that are ultimately not affordable for the people already living in the project areas. There may be times when an LCO might take an opportunity loss on a partial development to make sure that land is made available to low- and moderate-income groups. The social benefits might outweigh economic costs in many instances.

7. *Specific land tenure and protection techniques.* What is going to be the cost of transfer when land changes hands? If we are going to make land available to low- and moderate-income people in times like these, what are the land tenure techniques that will enable us to do this? How are we going to make land available to people with little access to capital?

8. *Meaning of ownership is changing.* Some of the techniques that many of our land trust and conservation groups use are becoming more common: restrictions in ownership and partial interest, private developer-land trusts, shared appreciation mortgages, some joint purchase agreements. All of these developments, in both private and public, in the nonprofit and for-profit sectors, are radically changing the meaning of ownership, as it will be available to future Americans.

There are going to be changes in our legal relationship to land and our traditional property rights. The critical questions will be not whether these changes occur but rather *who* will control them.

9. *The social agenda of an organization could determine its future success.* Recently, in a midwestern city in which the Institute for Community Economics was working, a local neighborhood land trust in a low-income neighborhood joined with other neighborhood groups to go to the neighborhood advisory committee (part of city government) to block the effort of the local historic preservation trust to expand the historic district. The historic preservation board chairman was appalled and said to Matthei, "We have been blocked in the last two neighborhoods where we've tried to expand the historic district by an unholy alliance of business community people—who want no limits on development—and low-income groups who say we're gentrifying the neighborhood. They fight with each other but unite against us." Here is a case in which the historic district, had it made an effort to address the concerns of the low-income groups, could potentially have developed a good-faith partnership and succeeded in reaching its goal.

STEMMING BLACK LAND LOSS IN THE SOUTH—JOE BROOKS
The Emergency Land Fund is an organization created to help keep land in the hands of black landowners. Ninety-seven percent of all black land ownership is in the South, so ELF operates in eight southern states. Loss of black-owned land is staggering, half a million acres per year from a base of 4.7 million acres reported by the 1979 census of agriculture.

Land is being converted to other uses in the South at a faster rate than in any other region. Blacks depend on farming more exclusively than other groups, yet there are only fifty-seven operating black farm units left that are making $2,500 in gross sales per year. The federal farm policy that said "bigger is better" had a disproportionately negative effect on blacks.

Black Land Loss

Blacks lose land for many reasons. Often, they do not write wills, and scattered family members with partial interests may be bought out. The person who buys interest may then demand that the land be sold. Failure to pay taxes is another cause of loss of land. Many black people are also isolated, still dependent on white people; the plantation economy and psychology continue. Many black people still cannot read or write. Many have limited access to institutional support, such as the FHA. The FHA often discriminates outright; they do not seem to believe that black people need to own land. During the civil rights campaigns, much of the bail money was raised by black landowners. Fear of too much black independence continues to be an undercurrent in today's bureaucracies.

Solutions

The solution to this problem has many aspects: educational, financial, and legal. The ELF saw from the beginning that this problem is a public policy issue: that it is in the best interests of America not to allow blacks to be permanently severed from agriculture and rural life.

Although ELF has been a lending source of last resort, its backbone is legal assistance. It has worked with 6,000 individual farm families in eight southern states. It is a highly decentralized operation, because each local area is different; in some areas conditions vary from county to county because each plantation was set up differently. In many instances, ELF augments the extension service, advising people on the best use for their land, rethinking their farm plans to stretch out income opportunities over the year so as not to be dependent on only one crop.

The basic work is done by volunteers—called county contacts—of which there are 72 operating in 125 black counties stretching from Mississippi to the Carolinas.

Association of Black Landowners

ELF is most proud of its assistance in organizing a membership group of 2,000 black farmers and landowners across the South. Much black agricultural land is out of production, so this organization consists of everyone from farmers to little old ladies without as much as a home garden. ELF serves as the technical assistant or agent for these people. In the final analysis, these landowners are facing a political problem. They must take on and control these public and private institutions in their own communities that have everything to do with who ends up owning the land.

ELF is also part of a consortium providing training—both in-classroom and on-site—to help small farmers increase their income with resources they have. The organization also has a $1 million line of credit with a life insurance company as an intermediate financing for the purchase of prime agricultural land.

ELF also lobbied for a bill passed in Alabama whereby relatives are given first chance at buying a partial interest in family-owned property. According to this law, the court now appoints an appraiser to set fair market value. This law has minimized the loss of black land through the partition suit, in which land was sold at auction if no will was left by the deceased landowner. To enhance this situation, ELF would like to see a program enacted like those in Georgia and South Carolina whereby the state creates a pool of money so that heirs can borrow from it on convenient terms.

As a result of participating in a federal study, ELF believes there are close to 11.5 million acres of black-owned lands. As part of its educational work, ELF has developed primers on various aspects of the problem of black land loss, targeted for the black communities where the land is being lost.

DEVELOPMENT IMPACTS ON TRADITIONAL COLORADO AGRICULTURAL COMMUNITIES—BILL GAY

Bill described the negative impact that the beauty of western Colorado has had on traditional ranching communities in that state. He is a field representative for TPL's Land Trust Programs, working with local groups responding to the pressures of second-home development and energy development on the productive hay meadows of ranching operations in this area.

Maintaining Agricultural Production Is Key

The way to keep the integrity of rural communities is to keep the land in agricultural production. Second-home development, urban sprawl, and energy development upset the balance and continuity of these communities that have been developed over the past 100 years.

The new community, consisting of outsiders, really doesn't have much continuity, and at the same time as it disrupts the old rural community, it destroys open space and wildlife habitat and production from the land in that community.

TPL has helped develop local land trusts in three western Colorado communities: Eagle County, Mesa County, and Pagosa Springs. Care is taken to see that local residents develop their own organizations.

Conservation Easements, a Tool: Pagosa Springs

One of the tools that these land trusts are working with is the conservation easement, which may be used to remove the potential threat of development and subdivision from those areas where people want to keep the land in production and move it on to future generations. For example, there is a 500-acre ranch along the road to the Piedra Wilderness Area near scenic Pagosa Peak, which rises right above the ranch house. If this property were subdivided for condominiums, it would ruin the view and much of the area as well as being a defeat for this family, who want to keep ranching a family operation.

Agricultural Economics Root of Problem

An easement in this case is very appropriate, but it cannot address the real roots of the family's problem: agricultural economics. If current market trends of 60 cents per pound for steer calves continue, and your cost of producing them is 75 cents per pound, and you must borrow operating capital at 18 percent interest, this family could easily decide that they couldn't make a living in the cattle business. When they start to look for potential buyers, they will find that neighboring cattlemen are in the same financial situation, so they won't be able to expand their operations either. So the buyer will of necessity have to be an outsider. And if you are an investor looking for a cattle ranch, wouldn't you rather buy a 100-cow, 500-acre ranch near the San Juan River in beautiful southwestern Colorado than a 500-cow operation next to the air force base at Minot, North Dakota? If you are going to lose money on a 100-cow operation, you'll merely lose more on 500 head. You might as well have the scenery, skiing, hunting, and other amenities of the Colorado ranch. So this ranch is not going to sell for its agricultural value, but someone will still pay $1 million for it. Furthermore, outsiders who come in and sell their steers at 60 cents per pound and write the loss off their taxes, are competing against families who have no other source of income. The newcomers can still afford a new tractor and can still build new homes. This situation causes a real rift in the community.

STEPS IN DEVELOPING A PROGRAM TO PROVIDE ACCESS TO LAND FOR LOW-INCOME GROUPS—TOM MILLS

The Trust for Public Land's Urban Program shows community based organizations how to acquire land for uses for low- and moderate-income people.

The Trust for Public Land works either on a consultant basis or under a matching fee basis to impart information on how to acquire land for the community, using the vehicle of a nonprofit corporation. Since TPL is also primarily interested in capacity building, it seeks to make organizations self-sufficient for the tasks they want to accomplish.

What are the steps for laying the foundation for a program that can be effective in providing access to land for low- and moderate-income nonlandowners?

Organize

The first step is organizing. You must look at the critical issue before people are reacting to a situation rather than acting. Many times people wait until they're being displaced by a redevelopment project before they begin to grapple with issues that should have been examined earlier.

Identify Resources

The next step is to be able to identify resources. For instance, in Santa Ana, where TPL is helping to coordinate an owner-built housing program, there was an opportunity to work with a number of different groups that wouldn't ordinarily have worked together effectively. Individuals from lending institutions and government were included in an advisory capacity rather than being approached right away as financial resources. Involving them in the planning process initially makes it more likely that they will also provide some financial support later on. You also need to spend time identifying the available capital resources. By careful planning early on, chances of success will be maximized.

Analyze the Data and Build the Program

Next you need to analyze the available data. Look at ownership patterns, land values, and economic trends in a very systematic way. If, for instance, you want to work in a particular area, unless you have done your homework you may find that property values are beyond your financial capability.

Building the program itself requires three elements:

1. Careful planning. Look at various strategies after you have set up your objectives. A lot of nonprofit organizations overlook the opportunities for syndications, joint ventures, or negotiated developments, or leveraging available capital and labor. In TPL's Santa Ana program, the "sweat equity" approach is being utilized, in which owners will be involved in building the houses they will live in. In the pilot project, using this approach, one-half of the construction costs were saved.

2. Based on good information, a certain amount of experimentation and risk taking can pay off.

3. In management, one should strive for an enabling model rather than a dependency model. If you or your organization do all the work without involving the recipients in the process, you run the risk that you will be stuck using all your resources to maintain the program. Or, if you let it go, you may see it fail because the recipients don't know how to run it, and the project cannot stand on its own.

Summary

Organizations that are working in this area must reach out more fully to other groups, must instill the idea of working in a pro-active rather than a reactive way, and must look at ways of being more flexible and adapting those things that have been done in the private and for-profit sector to benefit those without access to land.

LAND, PEOPLE, AND FOOD PRODUCTION ARE INTERRELATED—GEORGE BALLIS

According to George Ballis, terms glibly used in agricultural economics such as "the efficiency of size" only justify the "preexisting outrage." It is important to remember that many of the land tenure patterns existing in California are the result of who slept with the Queen of Spain 250 years ago or of who bought off the U.S. senators from California in 1860 (the Southern Pacific Railroad).

The Southern Pacific Railroad, the largest private landowner in California, received its land free 100 years ago for building a railroad, part of which was never completed. The understanding behind this land grant was that the railroad would sell railroad tickets and land to the settlers. But soon after, Southern Pacific stopped selling the land. They hung onto it and were excused from the obligation to sell by various public and private dispensations from the government that "they owned."

In the twentieth century, large landowners are now after water. Beginning in 1956, National Land for People grew out of an effort to stop violations of the Reclamation Act by large landowners in California. The Reclamation Act states specifically that you must live on or near the land to receive water from federally subsidized projects, and you cannot have more than 160 acres worth of that water. NLP became a corporation in 1974 when it decided to take violators to court. It won all the cases, but "nothing happened."

Everything Is Connected

So the organizers decided that there was more involved and have since discovered—through several steps widening their scope of activity—that everything is ultimately connected. They decided to form an organization to help farm workers get on the land. Their first success came from 6 acres of cherry tomatoes, farmed by several migrant farm-worker families, which is now producing a $64,000 crop annually. The Bank of America's computer initially told them they could not make money, but they have proven the computer was in error.

Alternative Marketing, Nonchemical Growing, and Independence

Through this experience, it became clear that an alternative marketing system was necessary. So NLP began doing experiments with marketing, including producing a yearly map of local growers.

It was also clear that *how* people grow crops is predetermined—by what people do at the University of California. NLP has become committed to growing without the large amount of chemical input usually required.

People also needed to become unhooked from the system. NLP does not take government money. So in the last year, as a fund raiser, they have begun to cater meals. The menu is a political one, and each entree is explained. The meals are always vegetarian, and they try to use foods from NLP's farm. Also listed are foods *not* included on the menu. Coffee is on top of the list, being representative of a food that is good neither for the body nor for sane economics—it produces only dependency for both growers and consumers. What you eat is what you vote.

All these steps are tied together. And the final step is actually having your own hands in the dirt, so that you become a warrior, protecting *your* land, rather than an advocate. Wendell Berry says, "What I believe in is what I stand on." To really be effective in conserving land, it has to be *our* land, and we have to be willing to fight for it.

CASE STUDIES

The Institute for Community Economics has worked with several groups of indigenous, low-income, landless people. Many of them came from families whose land has been sold or lost within the last twenty or thirty years.

HOME (Home Workers Organized for More Employment): Hancock County, Maine, lost two-thirds of its family farms in the 1960s. It is an area characterized by small, rocky farms, fishing fleets, and seasonal work. Most farms were lost to second-home development and urban immigrants who have taken the land out of production.

To attack unemployment, a Carmelite nun organized 100 local farm women to do piecework from a local shoe factory in the home. Eventually, when the factory pulled out, they organized a craft co-op to market whatever they could make at home. Though there was no master plan, one thing led to another. The need for craft skills gave impetus to a training program, which in turn brought to light the serious problem of adult illiteracy. A learning program was developed to meet this need, as well as a day-care center, newspapers, and seminars on agricultural skills to meet other needs that arose. They work with Heifer Projects International, providing free heifers in exchange for the first-born females. The co-op also leases or borrows hay lands on five- or ten-year leases and then sells hay to members at one-third market cost. A special services project does basically anything for anybody: transportation to the doctor or store, food, clothing, shelter, assistance in emergencies of different kinds.

The need for housing in this area is acute, particularly for low-income people. Tarpaper shacks will rent for $150 a month. The Institute for Community Economics worked with HOME to set up a small community land trust. The two greatest problems were financing and local policies, which were designed to prevent local development but which were also used to prevent development for and by the poor.

What HOME has done to solve this problem is to develop a combination community land trust and low-income housing construction company with volunteer labor, to keep the costs down. A 1,200-square-foot, two-story house with a solar greenhouse and enclosed garage on 12 acres of land was constructed for $18,500. Through low-interest financing, such a home was made affordable for one family whose monthly income was $350!

Clairfield, Tennessee: In this valley, 90–95 percent of the land was owned by the America Company, a British corporation. When Marie Cirillo, a long-time valley resident, helped organize the resources to create a medical clinic, no land could be found on which to construct the clinic because it was all being held for investment by the company. This group is now developing a program similar to HOME. They have acquired two tracts of land and have received some financing commitment for low-income housing.

New Hampshire Forests Management Pool: Most forest land in New England is in small privately held tracts, too small for any one of the landowners to be able to afford a management program. So either the land is not being harvested or it is being decimated by fly-by-night loggers.

The Institute is working with the Society for the Preservation of New Hampshire Forests and a community land trust to organize a demonstration forest management program. Twenty-five landowners, with a total of 4,000–5,000 acres, have put their land into a management pool. The local land trust is acting as manager and will conduct a timber inventory and an analysis of management and economic development. A fifteen-year projection of what this program will do for the landowners and other members of the community who have no land will be prepared. Ideally, this program will not only help preserve the land but create a job base for skilled and unskilled labor while utilizing available resources wisely and efficiently.

INVESTING IN PROGRAMS FOR LOW- AND MODERATE-INCOME PEOPLE—STEVE MOODY

Steve Moody is vice president of investments, United States Trust, Boston. A portion of the United States Trust clientele are interested in seeing some compatibility between social and ethical values and their investment programs. Some loans are being made to low-income groups such as HOME (see case studies).

The most important thing to realize when you engage in any kind of land trust activity is that you are creating, changing, and restructuring economic value. At some future point, that value is going to be recaptured in some way.

The clients involved in this program are most interested in whether or not that economic value contributes to the restructuring and the democratic distribution of wealth and income in this country. Loans to suitable organizations and groups are one way of accomplishing that.

A bench mark in making loans of this kind is trying to make sure that the capital doesn't disappear and that there is some recognition of the level of risk involved in a loan, which means interest rates similar to those of corporate entities.

Tax shelters are another tool that can be used to recapture economic values—including depreciation and investment tax credit—ordinarily not captured by loans. Tax shelters can be set up so that they dissolve themselves through donation to a tax-exempt entity once most of those economic values have been recaptured. Syndications are a possibility for tax-exempt organizations, and they should give more attention to the possibility of using them.

The most important obstacle to further work of this kind is that there aren't more good community organizers around. Also, a nonprofit or profit-making entity should be established to do syndicating work with nonprofit organizations. Investment managers themselves would like to stay out of structuring syndications, but so far they have had to be involved in the syndication process itself because no one else had the technical expertise to set them up.

DAMP Program

The Montana Land Reliance has been developing a program (DAMP—Donor Assisted Management Program—see the paper beginning on page 99) whereby a nonprofit entity could be established to carry out the leasing activity as the general partner in a partnership. The limited partners could be investors that could hold the property until they had recaptured most of the tax benefits. The limited partners can then donate the property to the nonprofit entity, permitting them to take the normal tax deduction for a charitable contribution.

One problem is that the donor cannot commit him/herself in writing ahead of time to making a donation, since the IRS would then consider the donation to have been made at the time the whole tax shelter was set up. But the general partner (land trust) would have control over the management of the partnership. To work, this program requires that all parties trust each other. The Land Reliance is now looking for a suitable property and lessees to test this program out with a concrete example.

COMMENTS AND DISCUSSION

Most of the discussion following centered around leasing as a method of entry to young farmers. The following points were made.

1. Many elderly agriculturalists have donated their land to institutions, such as the University of California, that have not treated the land very well. Land trusts should develop a program to receive, hold, and manage the land, perhaps making it available to new entry farmers.

2. One of the obvious bridges between low-income groups and land conservation organizations is leasing. The land trust can hold the land, leasing it to people who need land. This kind of program suits the skills of land trusts, but must be carried out while fulfilling the charitable purposes of the organization.

3. Typically, in the HOME example, such a program is set up so that the trust holds fee interest in the land but distinguishes between the land and improvements, so that the leaseholder has a lifetime inheritable use right to the land but actually owns and has equity in the improvements. In the event of sale, the improvements are offered first to the trust.

LEASING VS. OWNERSHIP

Is ownership preferable to leasing? Yes, for psychological and symbolic reasons, and because it gives incentives to future generations. If, however, the land is sold, rather than held in trust, one always runs the risk that the next owners will not buy it for production. One way to counteract that situation is to sell it with a reverter clause so that it goes back to the land trust if it is not kept in production.

Also, the young farmer could be one of the partners in a syndication so he has some equity share in the management.

The approach of the Institute for Community Economics is to separate ownership of land and improvements. "Land is finite in quantity, infinite in existence, and its value is largely not derived from the effort of the individual." With improvements, the situation is the exact opposite. But whether a legal document is a lease or a deed, people bring a psychological background to each term. If the term is lease or rent, the background is short-term security and a for-profit situation with entirely separate landlords and tenants with often conflicting interests and no interest in improvements. Likewise, people associate the potential for speculative gain with ownership. It seems clear:

1.   That if we are to keep land in agriculture and make it accessible to low- and moderate-income people, we must do something to limit the full market value transfer of land.

2.   That the traditional rental situation is completely unacceptable. People have a right to long-term security, the possibility of inheritance, and to work and build equity.

We are almost at the point where it doesn't matter if we use a lease or a deed. Either instrument can be used to craft the mixture of rights and limitations for the given situation. It is easier to get agreement on what each party *wants* than to begin by discussing whether a lease or deed should be used.

Leasing is a very appropriate avenue for getting started in farming. It offers the advantage of having the time to find out if you really want to do it or not and to see whether or not you are successful before having to make the commitment of purchasing the land.

Paying Taxes on Leased Land

The land trust is a community based organization. It would be a bad move to ask for exemption from paying property taxes. It is a quick way to sour the attitude of the community toward your activities.

However, rental income from these properties is not usually reported as unrelated income, therefore not subject to income tax, since these arrangements are a part of the charitable activities of the land trust. For these purposes, the kind of tenant is important: leasing to young, struggling farmers rather than any farmer who came along may protect your tax-exempt status.

If the original purpose under which you were granted the exemption does not include charitable purposes of the kind discussed here, there is a risk of infringing on your exemption. If you do have this charitable purpose and are screening applicants and can demonstrate that the community would otherwise not have access to the land, you should not have any difficulty with the IRS in carrying out such a program.

1981 NATIONAL CONSULTATION: LOCAL LAND CONSERVATION ORGANIZATIONS

LAND TRUST EXCHANGE

On October 14, 15, and 16, the National Consultation on Local Land Conservation convened in Cambridge, Massachusetts. Many who participated have since expressed the feeling that this meeting will be remembered as a landmark in the evolution of local private land saving in America. This report is an effort to capture the substance of that meeting and to share its spirit with the hundreds of individuals across the country who constitute the essence of this movement.

Following a brief review of the Consultation itself, this report includes: a selection of thoughts of the conference participants; and a set of short papers prepared by the participants and others for the Consultation.

SETTING the STAGE

The local land-saving movement is made up of a great variety of organizations, each with its unique combination of motives, priorities, and strategies. Their unifying characteristic is a commitment to the preservation of land resources through private effort. They are charitable groups serving what each conceives to be a public interest in the protection of properties of special natural, aesthetic, cultural, economic, or social value.

Although the focus of attention of most of these groups is at the community and regional levels, they have national concerns in common. The most serious of these shared problems is an uncertain public perception of their aims and motives. Changes in the 1981 federal Tax Code critically heighten this issue of public attitudes. The Tax Code amendments challenge whether or not the preservation of values in land serves a broad social purpose. Local land conservation organizations are being forced to substantiate their credentials as legitimate charitable enterprises. In view of this challenge, it is imperative that organizations carefully and precisely define their objectives and the public benefits that these objectives are intended to secure.

An important aspect of this task is the orderly analysis of the distinctions between private conservation action and government responsibility. Local land-saving activity can and should complement government efforts and should concentrate on opportunities that government units cannot, or will not, efficiently pursue. Not only should local conservation organizations be accepted as an integral part of community structure, but they should be recognized as contributing significantly to strengthening community self-reliance and local control.

NATIONAL CONSULTATION on LOCAL LAND CONSERVATION: A Review

Alan D. Spader, Leonard Wilson, and Terry Bremer

THE CONSULTATION

For three days in mid-October, 1981, forty people met in Cambridge, Massachusetts, for an intensive discussion of land conservation by local, private organizations. The participants came from all over the United States at the invitation of the Lincoln Institute of Land Policy.

The majority of the participants were individuals serving in staff positions with local or regional land trusts. The group also included volunteer local leaders from five states and professionals who, either as individuals or as staff to national organizations, provide direct technical support to local organizations. They met to exchange information and share some kind of sustaining relationship within the local land conservation community.

Prior to the October meeting, each participant was asked to prepare at least two papers addressing his or her personal observations on, first, the issues facing private land-saving efforts and, second, on one or more agreed-upon subjects. These papers, along with the inventory described later, served as significant ingredients to the Consultation, and, in various published forms, provide a unique perspective on the current substance and problems of private local land conservation in the United States.

BEGINNINGS OF LAND SAVING

Charles Eliot, in creating in 1890 what is now the Trustees of Reservations in Massachusetts, wrote that "several bits of scenery which possess uncommon beauty and unusual refreshing power are in daily danger of destruction." The following year, a citizen organization was incorporated and empowered by law to hold and maintain for the public "beautiful and historical places and tracts of land."

Ninety years later, not only "bits of scenery" are endangered, but huge tracts of prairie and range land, miles of stream bank and lakeshore, and whole areas of productive farm and forest land have been heedlessly and very often needlessly lost to unprecedented and unplanned effects of man's "progress." The relentless desecration of the American countryside proceeds at an incalculable cost in degraded natural resources, deteriorating landscapes, and shrinking open space. The public is evermore deprived of that "unusual refreshing power" provided by access to natural beauty.

THE INVENTORY

Increased awareness of those lost resources and concern about new threats posed by the potential erosion of traditional sources of support were among several impulses that led to the gathering in Cambridge. The Consultation was the product of more than eight months of discussions, review, and refinement by a number of leaders from the land conservation community.

To lay the foundation for the meeting, a nationwide survey was conducted by two interns from the Environmental Intern Program. First, they identified groups that are private local land conservation organizations. Then a questionnaire was mailed to each group, seeking information on budgets, staffing, activities, and achievements. The questionnaire data were computerized and published as the *1981 National Directory of Local Land Conservation Organizations*. This directory describes over 400 local land-saving groups and includes the following data: name, address, principal officers, date of founding, total budget, types of land, modes of transactional activity, and number of acres protected. Nonprivate and other supporting organizations are also listed. The directory provides a tangible valuable resource to all local land trusts, fostering communication and increased sharing of information, experience, and expertise.

A preliminary review of the questionnaire data points to a movement with deep historical roots as well as a sense of dynamic newness, a movement that, collectively, is making a significant, tangible contribution to the protection of land resources. While the greatest concentration of groups is in the Northeast, there are organizations in all sections of the country. Three-quarters of the organizations have been created within the last seventeen years. About 50 percent have annual budgets over $5,000. More than a quarter have budgets over $20,000, and an equal number have some kind of paid staff. Volunteer forces—their initiative, spirit, driving energy and dogged hard work—continue to provide fundamental support for the overwhelming majority of local land conservation organizations.

Nearly 95 percent of the reporting groups have successfully protected some acreage of land, most through outright purchase or gift. The use of less-than-fee techniques varies considerably in different regions and is proportionately most widely used in the West. Those organizations responding report that their efforts have resulted in the protection of more than 670,000 acres.

What is coming to be called the local land conservation "movement" has in fact been a growing number of diverse and relatively autonomous local responses to threats to specific local land resources. While the number and scope of these local efforts have been growing over the past two decades, only in the past five or six years has the sense of "movement" begun to be perceived. Many groups still operate in isolation, forced to reinvent techniques and strategies others have already put into practice. Until recently, there have been few available sources of advice and reassurance in times of stress. Participants at the Cambridge meeting repeatedly expressed their conviction that the time has come to seek out colleagues, find out what other groups are doing and how, and explore the possibilities of exchanging information and cooperating to influence public policy in some organized fashion.

TAX POLICY CONCERNS

In a narrow but very significant sense, the issue of the validity of land-saving objectives is being raised in the context of national tax policy. Wording in the 1980 amendments to the Internal Revenue Code casts doubt that gifts of conservation easements and restrictions will be treated as charitable donations eligible for tax deductions. Some see the shift in public policy as apparently attributable both to perceived past abuses in evaluation of such gifts and, more substantially, to a questioning by federal officials of the real benefits derived by the public from land conservation transactions of this type. However, there is also a growing sense that key national public policies, while theoretically sympathetic to private sector initiatives, are being formulated without regard to unique problems of local private land conservation efforts.

Because the use of easements has become an increasingly important tool for landscape protection, local land conservationists recognize an urgent need to unite in a concerted effort to amend the federal government's perception of local land conservation work. They must persuade the Internal Revenue Service to adopt regulations so that gifts of easements and restrictions can be treated as charitable gifts when they are made to organizations whose objectives are to provide demonstrable public benefit through land conservation activities.

The Cambridge meeting recognized the tax treatment of easement donations as an issue demanding immediate collective attention. Moreover, the 1980 Internal Revenue Code amendments may adversely affect the private land-saving movement in other respects. As charitable organizations, local land trusts have depended on gifts and bequests of money and property. At the meeting, several expressed concern that changes in tax rates and inheritance tax liability levels will sharply reduce the monetary incentives of the wealthy to be charitable.

LAND TRUST PROFILE

One of the functions of the Consultation was to explore the common ground that is shared by this diverse group of local organizations, which are called "trusts," "conservancies," "foundations," and "reliances." In basic terms, they share a common focus on transactions involving specific parcels of land and operate at a local, regional, or state level. Some are uniquely concerned with acquisition and management of property. A small but growing number of local land trusts work with developers and public jurisdictions to make project plan approval conditional on the protection of natural areas and open space. Perhaps because of differences in scale, national conservation organizations tend to focus on the protection of specific types of land objectives—watershed and wetland protection, historic preservation, scenic and recreational lands and rights of way for hiking, as well as wildlife and plant habitat, neighborhood open spaces, and farmland and timberland protection.

Examples abound of local land trusts with differing approaches and areas of emphasis. The Montana Land Reliance, a pioneer in the use of easements, is combining farmland and scenic lands preservation. The Trustees of Reservations in Massachusetts has created an auxiliary organization that serves as a middleman in the purchase of farms and development rights under a state-sponsored agricultural land protection program. Responding to a state-sponsored planning effort in Colorado, a new group is forming, backed by corporate money, to secure buffer zones of open space between the sprawling urban areas along the Front Range of the Rockies. Dairy farmers in Marin County, California, are pioneering new methods for securing land in agricultural production. Over seventy local groups in Connecticut form an important grass-roots element of land-saving efforts in that state. The work of the Maine Coast Heritage Trust has led to the protection of more than 20,000 acres of coastal lands, while the Brandywine Conservancy focuses its energies on the protection of watersheds in southeastern Pennsylvania.

A number of conservation organizations concentrate on protecting and developing open space in urban areas, from downtown pocket parks to extensive linear parks along city streams and rivers. Community land trusts, created as self-help organizations for economically disadvantaged groups, undertake land conservation projects to provide neighborhood amenities and recreational opportunities in impoverished urban and rural communities.

A third of the responding organizations include in their goals the preservation of historic and archaeological sites, demonstrating increased understanding of the mutual dependence of historic preservation and open space protection in urban and rural areas. Conservation of the rural landscape is now seen to include protection of countryside settings as well as preservation of buildings and villages of cultural significance.

A newcomer to this field is particularly struck by the inherent contradiction that appears in land trusts, on one hand as individualism, self-reliance, and diversity of individual local land conservation efforts, and, on the other hand, as a need of many of these diverse and autonomous programs to be related in some way to a larger whole. Initially as well as perpetually, the creativity of each local land trust and its ability to inspire individidual initiative and to draw out private resources is directly tied to its freedom from external bureaucratic agendas and interference. Volunteer skills, while absolutely essential, are as widely variable and diverse as the many individuals involved. And local programs find themselves heavily reliant on both a complex combination of transactional techniques and a fragile body of public legislative and regulatory actions. It was in the context of this dynamic situation that the National Consultation on Local Land Conservation was conceived; no doubt, this will ultimately test the strengths and weaknesses of the private land-saving movement.

COLLECTIVE ACTION

The conference papers and discussions at the Consultation give increasing evidence that, beyond the need for informational and professional interchange, some form of collective action should be undertaken based upon those areas of common ground. The need for collective action is expressed in several areas. Many participants point to the importance of articulating and communicating the conceptual premises of private land saving to the public at large and to public agencies in particular. Others seek collective performance in the refinement of land-saving techniques used by local programs. Yet others give priority to coalescing some form of practical political action that addresses public policies essential to the success of local programs.

TECHNIQUES AND STRATEGIES

The discussions of land-saving techniques and strategies ranged across the entire spectrum of approaches now being employed by land trusts in the country. Inflation and cutbacks in public land conservation funding are severely dampening the traditional techniques of purchase and donation. Therefore, most of the discussion focused on the alternative land-saving techniques of easements, limited development, transferable development rights, and land exchange.

Easements

Because of the tax issue, easements were given extraordinary attention. While there was general agreement that less-than-fee acquisitions were a vital conservation method, there were words of caution about relying too heavily on this approach rather than developing a diversified strategy. Although easements are becoming a widely used tool in many areas, actual experience in the long-term effectiveness of this approach is still fragmentary. Most local programs are only now beginning to address the problems of long-term easement management, and few have been able to set forth formal easement management plans or strategies.

It was also noted that easements seem to have limited utility in urban settings. The problem of valuing easements both in terms of initial appraisals and assessment of property taxes was raised at several points during the proceedings and pointed to as a subject for more systematic investigation.

Limited Development

It was reported that a small but growing number of local land conservation organizations are experimenting in negotiating limited development transactions in which certain areas of a building development project are covered by restrictive agreements. In some instances, land trusts have been given easements as a condition of the developer's land use permit. In others, property has been purchased by the trust—or given to it—and has then been sold with restrictions on its development. A common technique is to persuade or to have local authorities oblige land subdividers to assure protection of certain areas and amenities through covenants with lot purchasers.

Participants were warned of the danger of jeopardizing the credibility of the trust by not giving enough care in the selection of the developer or other entrepreneur.

The technique of limited development always involves compromise and some loss of open space. If used indiscriminately, it can actually promote intrusion of development in agricultural, range, coastal, and desert areas where development should not be permitted at all. By allowing some development where previously there had been none, more is invited. However, when development cannot be avoided, negotiated restriction may be the only way to protect natural areas and scenic quality.

Transferable Development Rights

The topic of transferable development rights seems to arise whenever land-oriented persons meet. While limited experiments have been successful, this strategy—once thought to be a land-saving panacea—has not proven to be widely applicable. Such issues as the evaluation of use rights separated from land and establishing the rationale by which some areas will be selected for high-density development have proven to be both intellectually and politically complex. However, some hope was expressed that transferable development rights strategies can be developed that will at least be functional within single jurisdictions.

Land Exchanges

There were differing views on the utility of land exchanges as a land-saving tool. At best, it is cumbersome. Its greatest potential seems to be in the West in dealing with federal lands.

LAND MANAGEMENT

A perennial question for land trusts is whether or not to hold and manage lands. Particularly where there is pressure for recreational use, the problems of ownership and management can be very difficult and costly. Unless there are overriding considerations of preservation, the total exclusion of the public is unacceptable. Controlling public use requires manpower and facilities. While most local organizations do not now envision themselves as land managers, land management is certainly going to become a more significant land trust function in the future. In the discussions focusing on the subject of public access, those involved in farmland preservation pointed to serious problems arising: the potential conflicts between farming and recreation objectives.

Another management problem troubling conservation organizations is the monitoring of easements. If unattended, property under easements may be misused and the organization holding the restriction placed in legal jeopardy as well as losing credibility in the eyes of the public. Trusts that acquire easements must be prepared to monitor them. To cover the costs of easement management, some trusts require that easement rights given them be accompanied by an endowment.

While the need for more formal land selection criteria was generally acknowledged, most felt the achievement of community acceptance on a case-by-case basis was more relevant and practically achievable at this time.

INSTITUTION BUILDING

In the wrap-up session of the Consultation, it was noted that the participants seemed much more comfortable talking about land-saving techniques than they did discussing questions of institution building, that is, administration, membership, funding, professional development, lobbying, and the building of community support. While the specifics of real estate transactions, tax regulations, easements, and land management will continue to dominate their day-to-day work, it is becoming increasingly evident that greater attention must be paid to strengthening the organizational foundation—the institutional capacity—of each local program, large and small. Cutbacks in government support for land protection are further highlighting these institutional questions. Public cutbacks are not only challenging private programs to take up the slack in actual conservation efforts, but they are also adding major new dimensions to the competition for the private financial resources upon which many local groups have come to depend.

For more than three-quarters of the nearly 400 local land conservation organizations so far identified in the Lincoln directory, local institutional capacity must be considered minimal when measured in terms of staff and budget. No more than 120 local programs are funded sufficiently to employ even part-time staff and fewer than 50 have full-time professional staff support. To be sure, there are numerous examples of successful land-saving programs being carried out essentially by volunteer effort and, indeed, the grass-roots essence of this movement includes a major volunteer component. Nevertheless, professional and financial constraints limit the ability of most local land-saving programs to undertake not only complex land transactions but also the challenge of long-term management. The provision of external professional-technical support and the building of local financial self-sufficiency are essential ingredients of the future viability of many local programs.

POLITICAL ACTION

Political action is a difficult subject among those active in local land conservation efforts. Some see influencing public policy as vital to protecting land resources while others regard government as an ineffective and unreliable agent in land protection. There is also fear in some areas that possible association with the more extreme forms of environmental advocacy will frighten away potential donors, cooperators, and members.

While there is almost unanimous agreement that collective action is needed to overcome recent changes in federal tax legislations and regulations that threaten some major land-saving tools, there is much less agreement as to the specific tactics or strategies for such action. This is where basic differences among the participants are most pronounced, indicating the need for patient molding of a broadly based consensus combined with effective lobbying. In the past, joint lobbying efforts by a few of the major local organizations have proven relatively ineffective for a variety of reasons.

SELLING THE CONCEPT

There was an almost universal conviction among the participants at the Cambridge meeting that the land-saving movement was not getting its message across to the public. The constantly recurring themes of the sessions were communication, education, marketing, and public relations.

Because local land trusts must raise money, attract property donations, seek membership, inspire volunteers, address local fears of tax loss, promote sound government land-use policies, fight for favorable tax treatment of their transactions, and otherwise influence public opinion, communication is a critically important factor in land trust operations. Most of the Cambridge participants view public relations as the least well-performed activity of local land conservation organizations. As one participant put it:

> Let's not kid ourselves. We are in trouble politically. With the loss of the Land and Water Conservation Fund and the tax ruling on easements, we suffered major losses last year. Yet, this is not a game; the demand to save land goes on. The forces that created our individual programs have not gone away. We need to work harder to get beyond our image as a bunch of dilettantes just playing do-gooder games.

The budget and time limitations of most local groups require that their education and marketing strategies be very skillfully crafted and that priorities be carefully considered. Key audiences must be identified, starting with the organization's own directors, staff, members, and volunteers. It is essential that they understand and be able to convey to others the mission and objectives of the operation. As a prerequisite, the leadership of each organization must define its purposes, scope, priorities, and procedures, an often neglected imperative.

Organizations must build community acceptance and support. Local government officials should be informed of policies and programs and, where possible, actually be involved in the planning activities of the organization. In order to overcome community fears and hostilities, local land trusts need to be as open as the nature of their transactions permit.

There are a number of key groups in every community whose support can greatly assist local conservation efforts, while their suspicion and enmity can frustrate the most carefully laid plans. Among them are lawyers, bankers, real estate brokers, and certified public accountants. The most important of them are the developers. Developers should be courted as potential allies who stand to profit from good community planning and the retention of amenities and environmental quality in a growing community.

The Cambridge participants were divided over the degree to which local land trusts should advertise their achievements, particularly when the result was removal of property from tax rolls or from the potential for lucrative development. While acknowledging the need for prudence, most felt that success stories were important to build support and confidence. It is critical that the public benefits of a good transaction be carefully analyzed and displayed.

The participants at the Consultation recognized the need to combine their resources with other local and national organizations in promoting the basic concept of private land saving and the role of local conservation groups in particular. There was a sense that the currents of public opinion were toward favoring less government activism and greater private sector responsibility in conservation as well as in other areas. It was felt that there was an expanding opportunity to attract corporate support for well-packaged programs and projects. There was also a strong sentiment that the federal establishment must be persuaded that tax policies should be designed to encourage rather than deter potential donors of easements and other protective restrictions.

Among the specific actions taken in Cambridge was the initiation of a working group to study the problems of evaluation for tax purposes of easements and restrictions, with the objective of recommending to the Internal Revenue Service a standard process of appraising partial interest in land that the IRS could accept as validating gift evaluations.

NATIONAL/LOCAL RELATIONSHIPS

Throughout the Consultation, participants made reference to the important roles played by several national organizations in developing and advancing the concept of private land conservation. The Nature Conservancy and the National Trust for Historic Preservation were singled out for their major contributions in their respective areas of preservation. The participants also noted the unique role of the Trust for Public Land in its efforts to support locally based land saving in both urban and rural settings. The emerging contribution of the American Farmland Trust in the preservation of agricultural land resources was acknowledged, as were the land-saving efforts of other national groups such as the National Audubon Society and the Isaac Walton League. Finally, the role of various governmental agencies in support of local land trusts was discussed, particularly the technical assistance services of the National Park Service.

The discussants clearly indicated the debt owed by virtually every local program to one or more of these national programs either in terms of tangible support or by example. Moreover, despite cautionary notes about the dangers of being subsumed in "someone else's national agenda," most of the participants agreed on the need to build reciprocal and mutually beneficial alliances between national, regional, and local groups wherever possible.

NEXT STEPS

A significant aspect of the discussions in Cambridge about techniques and strategies was the recurring conclusion that the really important need was to find ways for local land conservation organizations to exchange information and experience on a regular basis. The participants continually expressed their conviction that the groups had to work together to make sure that they were not repeating each others' mistakes and were not wasting time and effort inventing techniques that were already in use by other organizations. This impulse to associate was reinforced by the realization that strength in numbers was imperative to market the land trust concept and to promote supportive tax policy.

There was strong sentiment opposing the creation of another national conservation organization with an overburden of staff, committees, surveys, reports, and conferences. There was also little support for asking an existing organization to become an umbrella for the local trusts, although it was felt that existing national groups in the land-saving field were an important resource.

There was widely felt concern among most of the participants about the potential loss of individuality and creativity that could be threatened by the creation of a national organization. The words "service," "fellowship," "Quaker meeting," "town meeting," and "grass roots" characterize the unmistakable feeling that permeated the commitment of the participants to pursue some next steps. In keeping with the self-help roots of the local land conservation community, the concept of a mutual support network was clearly on the minds of the participants. While acknowledging the important role played by existing national conservation organizations, both in carrying out their own land-saving programs and in providing specific types of support to local groups, there was a nearly unanimous feeling that it would not serve the needs of local groups to look to existing national organizations for umbrella support or affiliation. As one participant put it, "We are not uniting against anyone, nor are we seeking a spokesman for local land trusts. If we are to succeed, we must speak and act for ourselves—with all the help we can get from our friends."

Personal interaction is absolutely necessary for growth and mutual support—politically, personally, and professionally. Peer learning and peer support were terms often used to express this feeling. In the words of another participant:

> It's easier to take risks when you know someone else has already blazed the trail. It's easier to sell a new idea to your board if you can point to a specific experience of another trust. It works even better to share experiences with an actual participant in another trust situation.

It was suggested at several points during the meeting that much could be gained from uniting the experience and tradition of the established organizations with the enthusiasm and willingness to experiment found in the newer organizations. Another proposal along this line involved having the larger established organizations share their experiences and technical skills, and, in some instances, their credibility with fledgling groups that are popping up in all parts of the country. Parenthetically, this meeting seemed to demonstrate beyond any doubt that whatever the regional differences that might exist between local programs across the country they were more than compensated for by a common commitment to preserving land resources on a local level.

What was wanted was some sort of service bureau that would be the focal point of coordination and would serve as an information clearinghouse, would organize joint action on public policy matters, and might begin to design a national public awareness program.

At the request of the group, Allan Spader agreed to accept, as an interim assignment, the role of catalyst for moving the concept of interorganizational communication and alliance toward concrete realization. In turn, several members of the group accepted responsibility for exploring sources of funding for the support of a continuing program.

The meeting concluded with a visit to properties of the Trustees of Reservations and, appropriate to what was said to be a richly rewarding experience, finished with a feast of clams and lobsters.

SELECTED THOUGHTS

Rusmore. We need to find the context for land conservation—who are we? We need a national structure which does not stifle local initiative and local energy.

Miller. When some of us went to Washington last year we were referred to as a bunch of amateurs. One definition of an amateur is one who does something for love. If we succeed, it won't be because we put all land under easement, but, rather, whether we influence how people perceive and treat the land.

Rusmore. Here in the northern Rockies, we are working hard at protecting properties, mainly ranches with recreation amenities, and we are headed toward making a real impact in several stream valleys. The impact is occurring partially because of the strong interest and support these actions are generating in the area. Before long we will need new tools and approaches.

Cirillo. The task ahead is for local citizens to learn how to rebuild a community with a plan that includes reverence for and care of the land that is their "place." I see the community land trust as an act of reconciliation between mankind and land. It is a peaceful solution to rebuilding an industrially destroyed community.

Rusmore. What could make all this stronger? More money always helps. However, more importantly and more universally available is tapping into the wellspring of people's enthusiasm and desire to make a difference. When people are encouraged to act on something they believe in, the results can be astounding. The potential has yet to be reached because of the newness of the movement and subsequent floundering about in search of workable goals, strategies, and techniques. Solving this is largely a matter of time if the basic techniques remain intact and are strengthened. If conservancies could not play the tax game, it would be extremely difficult to accomplish much.

Johnson. A new spirit of cooperation is essential among nonprofits and in many cases a consolidation of organizations to provide needed professional services may be warranted.

Carbin. A change in the land ethic will have to start at the community level. There is no single approach that will accomplish this. We try to involve the public in as many of our decisions as possible. It's very tempting for a private organization to keep quiet about its activities, particularly in something like land acquisition.

Vilms. Change in public attitudes has to start at the grass roots. The public will react negatively to any kind of change that is perceived as coming from above, especially when it is something as deeply ingrained as land.

Emory. Organizations able to do so should make it a priority to share technical knowledge, experience, and even capital resources. Fortunately, needed networks are developing to exchange information on successful techniques, federal tax developments, and the like. Witness expanding national links between many of the best-known and professionally staffed organizations and at least regional links between smaller, mostly volunteer organizations. We must continue to build and learn from these networks.

Allmaras. Our little conservancy is stuck without a consensus within our county about the value of agricultural lands. We must find ways to quantify those values and to demonstrate the need for a balance between farmland and development.

McClure. Certainly, there are occasional strictly altruistic situations, but by and large resource protection must be economical for it to work. And if we, the professionals, are going to be able to sell our ideas, we must prove their economic value.

Dennis. We must organize to assure the development of a permanent cooperative structure. Ideally, this structure will evolve into a focal point of information exchange, political action, and technical assistance. We must work together to build public awareness of the national context within which the local efforts go forward. Even some of "us" don't appreciate the depth, breadth, and competence of the land conservation movement.

Tiedt. Although local land conservation has become a movement, it hasn't yet become a system. Each organization independently addresses the problems it was created to resolve, and each has developed its own approach to the solutions. This diversity is one of the basic strengths of the movement, but there is little or no understanding of the relationships between the activities of one local organization and those of another and the environment as a whole. What is needed is an ecology of the land conservation movement to develop a comprehensive understanding of what is happening. Such an ecology would provide a theoretical framework for the future of the movement.

Dennis. It seems obvious that the local land conservation movement faces a somewhat tumultuous future due to recent changes in federal tax laws. At the same time Congress is beginning to look seriously at alternatives to fee acquisition of property as a means of preserving public values in the land. The landscape conservation community must organize itself to make the best of such an opportunity.

Abbott. We are the best-kept secret in Massachusetts. The question is, who do we want to understand what we do? The land owner? The general public? The user? The board member? With limited resources we need to be selective about who we are trying to reach.

Neuhauser. The appointment of James Watt may qualify as one of those catastrophic events necessary to stimulate citizen involvement. Whether it is or is not, we can't sit idly by, for some of the other active ingredients to initiate involvement are both within our control and within our responsibility as leaders. Improving the education of the general public to be aware and appreciative of our efforts is critical. We need, in sum, to concentrate on marketing.

Spader. The relatively spontaneous accomplishments and growth of the local land trust movement seem to me unique in a world where success is measured in terms of media hype, professional constituency, or a government program grant.

Wilkins. Building local, professional support capability, particularly legal, is a critical element in building a local program.

Emory. In some areas there is concern about the long-term viability of local organizations. Donors and others are sometimes nervous about the stability of the trust. Priorities change, for example, when personnel changes. One response is to build layers of protection, that is, involve other organizations in the project. We need some research into more effective ways of reinforcing organizational stability.

Augsburger. To be effective, local organizations must have a strong governing body, capable of developing community support, at least part-time professional staff, and the potential to build a solid financial base. Primary responsibilities include communications of the conservation message to landowners and influencing public policy to reflect conservation and recreation concerns. Land organizations should be seen as the advocate of those landowners who are practicing good stewardship at their own expense.

Dunham. We communicate our message to landowners by aggressively pursuing opportunities. Any major threat to land or water or the local economy or style of life will make people in a given locale ripe to listen to you and to act.

Emory. Conserving land requires diverse knowledge and skills. Recent tax law changes have proven the need for in-depth knowledge of both lobbying and relevant tax law. Raising funds is an obvious area of required competence. We may be less awake to the need for developing greater skill in public relations.

Vilms. Get help! If you are not confident of your skills in a particular situation, rather than play it badly, don't play it at all. Major mistakes in land transaction situations will come back to haunt you.

Rubenstein. Our experience points to the conclusion that where the private land-saving movement is going depends in part on the availability of technical services. In the absence of appropriate assistance, some local projects would not have been undertaken and, in some cases, land trusts may have foundered in the confusion that surrounds the process of transforming the inspiration of a few individuals into organizational structure and programs.

Ackelson. Success of private nonprofit corporations will be largely dependent upon the availability of professional expertise, particularly in fund raising, law, public relations, and social and political sciences. Based on our experiences, there is a growing need for an informational exchange and/or a technical assistance group to provide professional consultation to local private land conservation organizations during their organization, infancy, and development stages.

Sellers. Land conservation has to be run as a business, but unlike many businesses, it has to deliver a hand-tailored product, and it may take years to develop a project. It requires professional staffing with a business-type approach, but also requires continuity of personal contacts because success requires a level of trust beyond that of many businesses.

Vilms. Diversification. This one word describes both where the local land trust movement is going and how it can be strengthened. Diversification of land-saving activities; developing and using a complete vocabulary of land acquisition tools; expanding the trust's scope of services; expanding project activity to include the full spectrum of natural and managed resource lands; and build bridges between private land conservation and public planning policy. Diversification of sources on income, charitable contributions, and revenue generating projects. Diversification of support services: financial, educational, and administrative techniques.

Johnson. Local organizations tend to spring up to meet a specific challenge or threat to a specific piece of land. These motives are often primarily defensive and once specific action has been taken, the organization looks for new challenges. If the challenges and funds are found, the organization begins to shift from volunteer to professionally staffed status. The shift often creates conflicts. As public funds dry up, many have not developed self-sufficient strategies. To strengthen those organizations that can demonstrate long-term potential, there needs to be a new orientation including: professional staffing, program orientation, a sound financial plan leading toward self-sufficiency.

Ackelson. In the rush to establish new nonprofit programs—while all may be well-meaning—many will lack specific direction or an understanding of fundamentals and thus we will undoubtedly see an increase in the failure rate.

Dunham. Young groups have to be ad hoc by definition. They have to focus on what will work in their area just to gain credibility.

Vilms. Maybe we don't need to raise public consciousness about each individual land trust but rather about private land saving in general. How about a national marketing project of some sort, a film or TV series?

Wilkins. Most local trust people already have access to support from the business and corporate community. The problem is teaching them how to use these contacts.

Cook. We have to educate corporate givers to the values of local land conservation and the self-help nature of the movement. Foundations are not sophisticated in nurturing self-sufficiency. They tend to encourage dependency and like to stick to the tried and tested.

Ackelson. Farm people seem to place more faith in the corporate sector than they do government. We are therefore trying to get greater land consciousness into corporate advertising.

Abbott. Land conservation organizations should place a greater emphasis on telling people about their contributions to the quality of life in the state or community and thus to its business climate. European conservationists are way ahead of us in explaining the economic advantages of land conservation.

Dennis. Land saving has to be a community activity. Our experience indicates that if one landowner really wants to do something with his land and it's valid, the surrounding landowners will help provide the critical mass.

Sellers. It is relatively easy to get money to acquire land and relatively difficult to get anyone to appreciate the costs and problems associated with long-term protection.

Johnson. Our uniqueness lies in our willingness to become a manager of lands. Nobody else seems to want to do this. Many have said stay out of land management, yet we think we can and should do it.

Miller. Our problems are going to increasingly be how well do we manage the land we already have. In ten years our problems will really begin, when the heirs get in the act. Yet, at this point, we don't have enough experience to anticipate the conditions that might make us want to, for example, change an easement agreement.

Maxwell. The local land trust has considerable potential to act as a contract land manager for federal and state-owned lands, particularly in the current political climate. Nonprofits can be politically more acceptable in this role than a for-profit corporation. Such a role can be a sound money maker for the trust and can help reinforce the credibility of the local trust as a sound businesslike operation. You will, however, have to be prepared for criticism.

Stein. Easements don't seem to work as well in urban settings. Lenders have problems with clouds on the title. We are looking at other less-than-fee techniques. The undivided-interest route is useful but not as a permanent solution.

Emory. There is a very real danger in overselling the easement tool. We need some more definitive standards as to when this tool should and should not be used.

Gerard. The potential viability of an acquisition or easement program depends on having initial goals clearly thought through. There are basic differences between having formal criteria for land selection and the development of a general community consensus on the viability of a particular land-saving objective.

Dennis. Public access supervised by landowners is a tradition in Virginia, for hunting, riding, hiking, etc. Few organizations have the capability to manage public access. Management is the only option in many cases. Nevertheless, as a practical matter, the owner must have the right to restrict public access. If he doesn't have the right to throw people off his property, he won't give the easement.

Dunham. Four years of initial efforts have driven home to us the lesson of the absolute necessity of land preservation groups actually getting "points on the scoreboard," actually preserving pieces of land. This is now our major daily focus and is also the key to continued fund-raising success and the survival of this organization.

Allmaras. We are having success with our efforts to place more emphasis on helping the farmer make a living on his land and thus help keep him on the land.

Cirillo. People need to be able to see alternative ways of using land in terms that they can understand and relate to—more than in the abstract. This is the value of demonstration projects.

Rubenstein. All land trusts and other private local land conservation organizations have need of similar information. When they are just beginning, they need to know how to secure funds, etc. Once they are operating, they need technical assistance on more discrete matters: structuring real estate transactions, meeting the Internal Revenue Code, negotiating strategies, etc.

Hurchalla. If you come too soon with technical assistance, you run the risk of smothering a new program. Wait until they have at least one acquisition under their belts.

Maxwell. While it is necessary for the land trust to be sensitive to community conservation issues, it is important to maintain a role of nonadvocacy in the formation of land use policy. The reason, of course, is that a land trust must maintain credibility with diverse interests throughout the community as a fair and professional organization with which to do business.

Allmaras. We avoid direct confrontation with public policy whenever it is possible, but there are instances where we have individually initiated suits in favor of wise land use planning. Mostly, we try to influence public policy through informal conversation with elected officials, but we recognize the need for a consensus that retaining land in agricultural production is an important goal.

Sellers. The question of geographical scope or interest is an important one because of the single fact that, up to this point in the development of the movement and probably for some time into the future, one cannot build a strong, professional, effective, and well-financed organization if the geographic scope is too narrowly focused to be really effective on its own; and many large organizations cannot manage programs over large areas without local assistance. New relationships between the two need to be developed.

Miller. A statewide trust cannot protect all lands. Its resources are inadequate, and many valuable lands do not have statewide significance. Local land trusts can be custom-made to serve their communities and mobilize the enthusiasm, energy, and ingenuity of their people. They can get to the people where they live.

Horne. We are seeking opportunities for cooperative actions to replace adversarial situations. You have to somehow demonstrate the kinds of changes you want to happen.

Emory. Despite the problems, there is tremendous potential in working cooperatively with the public sector.

Schmidt. There is a potential conflict between the "let's do it ourselves" approach and building long-term cooperation with public agencies. Working with government is a very exhausting and frustrating process. Cooperative action is going to turn off those individuals who get turned on by doing deals.

Browne. When Congress and the Treasury added new tax restrictions in 1980 they were responding to several concerns, the most revealing of which doubted the capacity of many land trusts to choose wisely among proffered easements and to monitor and enforce them on a perpetual basis: Poor choice and unpredictable protection was not sufficient consideration for the indirect monetary subsidy provided by the charitable tax deduction. If there is no response to this skepticism, easement programs will languish in many areas.

Dennis. The politicians and bureaucrats in Washington don't think badly of land trusts. The problem is that they don't think about us at all. We are very, very low on the priority list relative to all of the others now scratching for survival at the public trough.

Zeller. During the 1970s several states became actively involved in land-related issues. Now the pendulum seems to be swinging the other way toward less government involvement altogether. However, some states have recently begun to show interest in the private alternative.

Peters. We are fortunate that the governor of the state, the county, and the city have nurtured this organization and endorsed the concept. We have discovered that the governments will generally not take the initiative, and citizens' groups must be the organizations out front. Our shore experience demonstrates that each organization must start from ground zero and do a lot of spade work to grasp the dimensions of the project. The assistance of local government planning staffs has been an indispensable requisite to developing a plan.

Maxwell. The land trust's ability to deal with state government can be substantially enhanced by developing working alliances with other organizations which are in more regular contact with state agencies and the legislature.

Morris. Gaining support from the state is a question of selling your product. Your state legislator is often the most accessible and helpful point of contact with state government.

Stockdale. Be careful not to dismiss local public agencies because of the problems and failures of the federal government. We depend a great deal on the support and cooperation of local governments and have had success telling our story to local officials through their various state associations.

SELECTED THOUGHTS

Watson. We must be aware of public agendas versus private agendas. While you must focus on your own opportunities and needs, don't blind-side others who are working alongside you in the same arena.

Matthei. Community groups and traditional land groups need to have more communication. There is great potential for diverse and creative interaction and cooperation. Active understanding will be increasingly critical to success on both sides.

Maxwell. We might look to the professional real estate community for ideas about how to build more cooperative relationships among land trusts. The real estate community consists of a large number of small, highly competitive organizations which have also achieved high levels of cooperation.

Neuhauser. While diversity often lends stability to ecosystems, the same may not be true for organizations in the land conservation effort. The inherent costs of organizational maintenance may be too high, especially when a growing number of programs are on shaky financial grounds now. Some degree of consolidation might facilitate our collective efforts. If territorial imperatives make that difficult to accomplish, then at least more cooperation and sharing of skills seems in order.

Browne. It might be possible to structure some form of joint responsibility between an established land trust and the new entry into the land trust field, a bond that would dissolve with the passage of time and a record of achievement. Given such an approach, government agencies (i.e., the Treasury) might more readily entrust private organizations with the hard decisions that involve determinations of "public benefit."

Dunham. Two of the support services most beneficial to local organizations are regional or national seminars on techniques and a national newsletter. Both can serve to keep local organizations abreast of new changes in laws and techniques, strategies, and successes and problems encountered by other groups.

Vilms. Regional programs are important for (1) regular professional interchange, (2) board people, for reinforcement of commitment, and (3) outside people for education.

Hocker. We cannot let the setbacks of past years keep us from finding new ways to make our case more effectively.

Hocker. The recent national Consultation was a real milestone for those of us involved in private land conservation efforts. It was the first time, I believe, that those of us in the West had the opportunity to sit down with our eastern colleagues to examine our common needs, goals, and directions and to share ideas. A real strengthening of the private land conservation movement began to emerge during those two days.

Brenneman. The Consultation has been an outstanding exhibition of peer learning. We do not need an organization but, rather, a concept of how to reach toward a higher level of competence amongst ourselves.

Rubenstein. The more I reflect on the Consultation, the more pleased I become. We achieved some very important things: the coalescence of the beginnings of a community, probably the single most important thing we could have hoped for; and recognition of the needs for (1) professionalization, (2) communication, (3) taking unified positions on matters that affect us all, and (4) marketing ourselves to the general public as a positive social tool.

Emory. The meeting greatly expanded the existing information exchange network, and it enabled us to begin planning future cooperative endeavors which strengthen all our programs. I am very excited by the fact that almost certainly the Lincoln Institute meeting was not a one-time event but, rather, the initiation of much closer coordination in the future.

Gerard. This has been a great chance to recharge my batteries. It is important to remember the many people who are important to this movement who are not here. We must guard against becoming an "in-group."

Wheeler. Our presence at the Consultation has afforded us with a clearer and more practical understanding of how [American Farmland Trust] can work cooperatively with local groups by helping to fill some of their program and financial voids. I believe that it is incumbent upon the national organizations at this time to respond with substance to the momentum that your good efforts have generated.

Peters. I felt like a sponge absorbing tremendous amounts of information from people well qualified in the field. I came away with some solid ideas for direction of our Greenway.

Augsburger. In a sense, one might compare this meeting to an old-fashioned revival meeting. Here we had a group of "circuit riders" from all over the country, coming together to refresh, reinspire, and reeducate each other. The result was indeed electric.

WHAT IS OPEN SPACE and HOW SHOULD IT BE PRESERVED? HOW SHOULD PUBLIC INTEREST BE DEFINED?

Russell L. Brenneman

As a young reporter, I was taught to supply in the lead to all news stories answers to the questions "Who?" "What?" "When?" and "Where?", as well as, wherever appropriate, the questions "Why?" and "How?". A purpose of this Consultation, as I understand it, is to address those questions from the standpoint of local land conservation. You certainly are not going to answer them definitively, nor is it even necessary to do so in the abstract sense. You are going to share with one another how you individually and organizationally arrive at answers that work for you, and along the way, discover, perhaps, useful commonalties and areas of shared needs. Since the essence of grass-roots land saving is its response to particular local needs and the pragmatic diversity which has emerged from that response, we should not urge upon one another the necessity to reach consensus on all the answers to any of these questions, least of all the definition of "open space."

How do you define *open space?* You have your own personal definitions. The vest-pocket neighborhood park may be significant open space in San Francisco. A Montana mountain range is open space. Habitat for a rare species may be what a Louisiana natural area preservationist means by open space. The rich farms of southern Illinois may mean open space to someone protecting agricultural land. Open space may be unsullied by human users or trafficked by campers and hikers. There is, can be, and should be no all-purpose definition of open space. *Open space* is in the eye of the beholder.

Who are the *beholders?* For the purpose of this gathering, they are organizations engaged in the conservation of open space at the local level. While they are diverse, they also share one transcendent characteristic. They are all organizations carrying on their work as charities, in the traditional sense. Charities are specially favored by a variety of legal and tax rules because they are perceived to act in the general interest to further socially valuable objectives. Organizations protecting natural resources historically have fallen within this favored category at common law. And contemporary tax law recognizes them as being properly engaged in tax-exempt charitable, educational, and scientific activities, according to their nature.

It is not surprising that organizations with such a broad charter perceive open space differently. What is important is that the special nature of the beholder as a charity is recognized and understood. It is no more necessary to arrive at a general definition in the case of land conservation than it is, for example, in the case of museums. There is no philosophical or intellectual requirement that every entity which calls itself a museum collect and exhibit the same kinds of things and pursue their affairs in exactly the same way; yet they are all museums. The key is the nature of the beholder.

Failure to see and apply this rationale leads to the remarkable problems that now beset both charitable organizations and federal tax administrators as a result of the amendment of the Internal Revenue Code adopted in December of 1980 affecting deductions for charitable gifts of conservation easements and restrictions. As a result, it is now not solely the character of the recipient organization that determines deductibility and gift tax liability but also whether or not the transaction itself meets standards set forth in the law that are unique to these types of gifts. Among the transactional criteria for an eligible contribution is the preservation of *open space,* a term undefined by the Tax Code. The ensuing debate on the meaning of open space would be unnecessary had Congress stuck to the touchstone that governs the deductibility of other charitable contributions, that is, does something of value pass to an eligible organization and is the transaction a gift?

Why should there have been a failure to see and apply a rationale so obvious to land savers? This question may come as close to stating the reason for this Consultation as any other. The answer lies in the circumstance that while each organization has a subjective definition of open space which works for it and land-saving organizations collectively have no doubt of their charitable purpose and identity, the community outside the land-saving movement has a blurred perception. The movement becomes authentic and credible when it becomes clear that it is pursuing an orderly and explicit process which is primarily directed toward some generally perceived public good. To establish authenticity and credibility, obviously persuasive communication with those who are not members of the land-saving community is needed.

HOW SHOULD PUBLIC INTEREST BE DEFINED?

We emerge from this maze when we concentrate as much on our behavior as charities as upon the resources we seek to safeguard. As we serve society as a whole, so we must publicly demonstrate the public benefits that flow from our efforts. The notion of bestowing a public benefit is the pillar of all charitable enterprise, yet it is an inexact concept. It embraces the sense of promoting values that are communal rather than private, general rather than individual, and lasting rather than transitory. The preservation of open space surely qualifies as a charitable activity and does confer numerous public benefits. But that cannot be considered a self-evident proposition.

A local land trust must develop a statement of its charitable purposes and faces a special urgency in doing so as there is no public ordering of open space upon which to rely. Yet how to proceed? We cannot compute the public interest with mathematical certainty; we cannot determine with irrefutable objectivity that a certain parcel merits preservation or does not. Any allocation of resources to the end of conservation is a judgment. It is a judgment as to how best to promote the welfare of given human and natural communities. Our concern is not so much with the substance of that judgment as with how it becomes a legitimate charitable transaction.

Every land trust is entitled to its own conclusion as to what it preserves and why. But each trust must reach those conclusions by an orderly analytical process. For example, two trusts survey the land within their geographical boundaries; they classify those lands according to stated ecological principles; and they examine the conservation needs of the affected communities. Based explicitly on these investigations, they draw up a charter, draft by-laws, begin operations, and conduct a public education program. One devotes itself to saving farmland through a purchase and lease-back program to stabilize the region's agricultural base and runs tours of working farms. The second purchases parcels on nearby mountain tops to promote the study of their boreal flora and restricts access to certified scientific researchers.

Under the rubric of preserving open space, each trust concentrates on different types of land, each pursues different public benefits, each engages in different land acquisition and management practices, and each faces different problems of public persuasion. Both are compelling as charitable endeavors because of the open, orderly examination of public purpose they undertook and then anchored their actual operations to. The process then is paramount in making legitimate specific judgments as to the reasons why and manner of preserving open space.

Emphasis on the process must never, though, corrupt the definition and establishment of public benefit into a formality. The integrity of the land-saving movement rests upon its ability to understand and convey its charitable purpose. Without that reasoned discipline, we cannot garner widespread public support or survive the scrutiny of governmental agencies associated with our efforts. Without it, we may, indeed, finally fall prey to the view that local land trusts are composed either of romantics who would shelter every shady hollow willy-nilly or of cynics who would pay for their private suburban green belts with U.S. Treasury funds.

ONCE WE EMBARK ON THE PROCESS OF DEFINING PUBLIC BENEFITS . . .

How should open space be preserved? As this Consultation itself will abundantly demonstrate, that depends upon the nature of the open space and what is to be accomplished by its preservation. The "how" includes critical components, one of which is "by whom" and the other of which is "in what manner." Open space may be preserved by units of government, by land saving charities, and by private owners. It may be preserved through ownership of the entire fee or through less-than-fee arrangements such as promises in respect to the present and future use of the property in the form of restrictions or easements. (Controlling the future of real estate does not require ownership of the fee.) There being an array of organizations as well as an array of methods, it becomes critical to define precisely the objective sought to be served by preserving the open space and the general benefit that those interested in preserving it wish to create.

IS the PRIVATE LOCAL LAND-SAVING MOVEMENT SUCCESSFUL?

Donald Rubenstein

Measuring the success of anything requires criteria, and to the extent that we are considering private conservation organizations, it is tempting to use the activities of government as some standard. With a few exceptions, it has been government that has preserved our natural lands. Some private owners, through design or inadvertence, have served this end, but by and large it is federal, state, and local parks and conservation agencies that save land, so much so that relatively few people have developed an understanding that any other quarter is capable of doing it. There are dangers in using government as too strict a standard, but it is a constructive point of comparison.

Three general questions can be addressed in this comparison: Are private local land conservation organizations doing things that government does not traditionally do? Are they doing things traditionally done by government but doing them somehow better? Are they doing things government has traditionally done but can no longer do?

My knowledge of specifics in answer to these questions is limited to my experience in California, although I am generally aware of organizations elsewhere in the country that measure up to one degree or another in these areas.

On one level all organizations compare favorably under the first question. Regardless of what they do, they are doing something not traditionally done by government because they are doing it privately. However, specific land trust projects illustrate how the actual function of local private efforts also goes beyond government's traditional province. In 1979 the Big Sur Land Trust preserved a 3,200-acre coastal tract by buying it from a development-oriented owner and selling it to a private conservationist. The project was completed at no capital cost to the Big Sur Land Trust, and in the process of resale it reserved sufficient interest in the property to assure that the land will be preserved regardless of the will of any subsequent owner. Government simply does not do that.

The Humboldt North Coast Land Trust (HNCLT) is an example of a California nonprofit that is doing a traditional governmental task more effectively than government, and it is doing it because it demanded the opportunity to do so and mustered enough political support to make its demand stick in the Statehouse. HNCLT represents a small community, and it was formed as an alternative to the imminent purchase and development of a state park in the heart

145

of a small fishing town that would have been changed forever. Asserting that scenic and natural preservation and the provision of coastal public access can be undertaken through private community efforts, HNCLT won the support of the Legislature for a bill that rescinded $1.3 million in parks acquisition funds. The bill also appropriated $100,000 to the State Coastal Conservancy for land acquisition grants to HNCLT. The trust board devised a preservation program and soon began soliciting gifts of key parcels and conservation easements. It also determined which parcels were important enough to buy and commenced negotiating bargain sales on them, relying for capital upon the $100,000 available in grants from the Coastal Conservancy. HNCLT has now exhausted those funds, but it has acquired property valued in excess of $500,.000 for the $100,000 it has received. Additionally, it is actively implementing the government's coastal access plan for the area with capital funds coming in the form of modest grants from the Conservancy's coastal access program.

Had the state pursued its plans, it would have spent $1.3 million, permanently altered the character of a unique commercial fishing town, and displaced more than 100 local residents. HNCLT has now completed more than a dozen transactions, expending only $100,000 for property (fee and conservation easements) worth upwards of $1 million. Further, it has secured and improved many of the coastal trails originally envisioned for the park. It is tempting to conclude that HNCLT outperformed government in government's own domain.

It is difficult to determine whether local private conservation efforts are doing in California what government is no longer able to do. The effects of Proposition 13 are only now being driven hard against state and local agencies, and the dust of the new federal administration has not yet settled. It is likely, however, that governmental conservation priorities will tighten around areas of greater national significance, leaving local, regional, and even some statewide needs unfulfilled. There will be an opportunity for private local groups to fill that void. Likely, too, the demand for private efforts will exceed many communities' abilities. Setting priorities will be a difficult but extremely important job.

Even if private, local land saving does compare well with what government does and does not do, is it successful? Is that a matter of how many acres are saved or of how many projects are completed? I think not; the standard is broader than a mere numbers game because private efforts contribute not only to the collective mass of saved land, but they serve as an important educational vehicle as well. These activities have an impact on communities and on private landowners and that too needs to be measured in assessing success.

I mentioned earlier that relatively few people perceive any alternatives to government when land needs to be saved. Broader public knowledge of examples of successful local private efforts will wean the public from that provincial attitude. Projects such as those described here and the dozens more in other areas are clear demonstrations of a new tool that can be used when government's services are unwanted or unavailable. However, more comes from this demonstration than the simple awareness of a new tool; communities are educated to their own possibilities. Self-reliance is fostered by the realization that a community can provide for itself services for which it historically depended on some external source.

Are private local land-saving efforts increasing communities' self-reliance? Are they a source of encouragement in the increasingly popular interest of communities in mastering their own destinies, in exercising local control?

Another important area in this evaluation is the impact of local land-saving efforts on the private owners of resource lands. Government efforts at purchasing land frequently run afoul of entrenched resistance of landowners to what is perceived as the public's insatiable appetite for real estate. Most owners find it hard to identify personally with the projects for which government wants their land. Private local purchasers have an excellent opportunity not only to discharge this traditional animosity but to redirect an owner's attitude. Such groups are free of government's taint; they are small and somehow more comprehensible and more approachable; their purposes are clear, and their motivation is public spirited. These elements can coalesce to give a landowner the sense that a private local purchase is something that he or she actually wants to be a part of—not something to resent or resist.

Are private local land-saving efforts helping to reeducate owners of resource lands? Are those owners developing a sense of community pride in local projects and are they beginning to think of protecting the resources that they own as a positive alternative?

The measure of success for private local land-saving efforts extends into other areas of analysis as well: the internal structure of organizations, their access to funding sources, and their relationship to government, to name a few. These areas will be explored in other papers. I have chosen to limit myself to community based criteria because the organizations of concern here are community based groups. Their success in this sense is not just a function of the size, number, and quality of their projects but of the contribution they make to their community's sense of itself.

DIVERSITY
of APPROACH

The local land trust concept had its origins in the desire to preserve natural amenities against the tides of metropolitan sprawl. Late in the nineteenth century, the advent of mechanized transportation opened the prospect of bedroom communities sheltered from downtown commerce and industry. The invasion of the countryside by these new suburbs began to close off opportunities for city dwellers to find easy access to recreation and aesthetic enjoyment in natural settings.

Loss of open space and degradation of natural areas remain the dominant concerns of local conservation activists. However, local land trusts vary greatly in their objectives, some being highly specialized and others having a broad array of interests. Some have been organized to preserve specific islands, marshes, shorelines, forests, hiking trails, river corridors, or scenic areas. There are groups whose mission is to secure land in rural poverty areas and in city slums. Other groups are concerned with scientific and ecological aims. There are many groups with a range of purposes that may include historic preservation, recreation, renewable resource productivity, landscape protection, and wildlife propagation. The geographic focus of land trusts extends from inner-city neighborhoods to remote wilderness.

good quote

In recent years, rapidly accelerating dispersal of residential, commercial, and industrial development into rural areas beyond the urban fringe has created a growing awareness that a substantial amount of productive agricultural land is threatened with irreversible conversion. The retention of farmland has been added to the agenda of existing land-saving organizations and has prompted the creation of new, specialized farmland preservation trusts.

Different regions of the country have different land conservation problems. While agricultural land conversion is a serious problem in the East and far West, in the Midwest the expansion and intensification of agriculture is creating a critical need for conservation action. In the farm-belt states, current cultivation practices are causing serious soil erosion, surface and ground-water depletion, wetland drainage, wildlife habitat loss, and the destruction of the remnants of native prairie and woodlands. Farther west in the Rockies, coal, oil and oil-shale prospectors, in a headlong rush to exploit energy resources, are diverting scarce water from essential irrigation use, stripping prime farmland and building instant cities on the open range.

Not only do the regions of the nation have differing problems, they also have quite different political climates that must be taken into account in land-saving strategies. In the East, the conservation tradition is strongly rooted; the local land trust movement has a long history, and its objectives are widely accepted. In the Midwest and Mountain West, the myths of boundless space and inexhaustible natural resources still persist.

The geographic setting and the political climate and perceptions of community constituencies dictate the approach conservation groups adopt in pursuing their goals. Strategies for local land-saving organizations vary according to their diverse objectives and the types of problems they attempt to solve. Full ownership of property may be acquired or only those rights needed to secure the values sought to be preserved. Acquisition may be by purchase or donation. The property may be passed through to public ownership or the organization may assume responsibility for management. Some organizations serve primarily in a brokerage role, matching sellers or donors with recipients committed to conservation. For many local land-saving organizations, raising public awareness, influencing public opinion, and working for changes in government policies are dominant activities.

An increasing number of conservation groups are trying to develop the capacity to operate with complex and innovative strategic approaches to enable them to respond to a variety of opportunities and challenges. These organizations are developing a high degree of professionalism with staffs competent in real estate negotiation, property management, tax consulting, land use planning, public relations, and dispute mediation. Local, state, and government agencies have learned to utilize the transactional skills of these conservation professionals who are free of the political, bureaucratic, and jurisdictional constraints that often prevent timely and effective action in the public sector.

A good working relationship with government is by no means a universal characteristic of local land-saving organizations. For many, the relationship is necessarily adversarial. However, in the present climate of fiscal austerity, federal program elimination, and hostility to government intervention, there is a growing awareness that conservation responsibilities heretofore regarded as belonging in the public sector are being shifted, by default, to private agencies. Not only is there need to develop cooperation between government and private groups, these conservation groups themselves must overcome differing perspectives and operational isolation to develop creative relationships among themselves.

HISTORIC ORIGINS
Gordon Abbott, Jr.

Awareness of the importance and meaning of the natural world comes easy for Massachusetts, home of William Cullen Bryant, Emerson, Thoreau, and F. L. Olmstead. And it was a young landscape architect, schooled in these traditions, who in 1891 gave the world its first land trust. His name was Charles Eliot, and his idea was to establish an organization with a board of trustees that would have "power to hold lands free of taxes in any part of the Commonwealth for the use and enjoyment of the public." The concept of *the trustees of reservations* (originally the Trustees of Public Reservations; the word *public* was removed in 1954 because the organization was confused with public resource agencies) soon spread throughout the world, first to Great Britain, where The National Trust was founded in 1894, then to Scotland, in 1934, and in 1939 to the United States. Today, there are national trusts in Bermuda, the Bahamas, New Zealand, India, New South Wales, Australia, Ireland, Canada, and similar organizations throughout Europe. All owe their beginnings—and in many cases the wording in their charters—to The Trustees of Reservations right here in Massachusetts.

It's interesting to look back and to see what gave rise to the concerns that established the trust movement. They were not concerns that involved the scientific understanding of the physical environment we have today. They were concerns that related to a rural country which was rapidly becoming urbanized. Between 1870 and 1900, the population of the United States was to double from 38 million to 76 million, and a third of its people were to live in cities. It was an era marked by the end of the dirt road and the horse and buggy, of the family farm, especially in New England, and a simpler way of life in tune with the seasons and the weather. Immediately ahead was the arrival of the gasoline-powered automobile and a revolution in living that would sweep the nation.

Eliot and other planners and architects, social scientists and historians watched with concern as people with a rural background and traditions migrated to the cities. Planning was at a minimum. Indeed, as suburbs grew, conflicting interests and desires delayed the construction of such basic services as sewers until a scandal all but forced the Commonwealth to establish a metropolitan drainage commission. Acquiring open space was a low priority and, as Eliot wrote, "Boston, like New York, may yet be compelled to tear down whole blocks of buildings to provide herself with the needed oasis of light and air."

City squares and parks (such as the Boston Common and the Public Gardens in Massachusetts) had existed since Roman times. But Eliot declared "a crowded population thirsts occasionally at least for something very different from the square, public garden or ballfield. The railroads," he continued, "and new electric street railways which radiate from the Hub, carry many thousands every pleasant Sunday through the suburbs to the real country, and hundreds out of these thousands make the journey *for the refreshment which an occasional hour or two spent in the country brings to them.*"

Again, he emphasized the psychological and physical importance of association with scenic landscapes: "Within ten miles of the State House, there still remain several bits of scenery which possess uncommon beauty and more than unusual refreshing power. . . . Each of these scenes is, in its way, characteristic of the primitive wilderness of New England, of which, indeed, they are surviving fragments." The importance of preserving these "special bits of scenery" for the benefits they bring to spirit, the mind, and body is illustrated in all of Eliot's early writing.

The statement of reasons why The Trustees of Reservations should be established begins, "It is everywhere agreed that it is important to the education, health, and happiness of crowded populations that they should not be deprived of opportunities of beholding beautiful natural scenery." Light and air offered by the countryside were also vital considerations in cities where houses were heated and industries run by coal.

At the end of the nineteenth century, there was, of course, a real awareness of the need to conserve the nation's resources. The first national park had been established. And here in New England, the Appalachian Mountain Club, the Massachusetts Horticultural Society, the Massachusetts Historical Society, and the Arnold Arboretum were small but flourishing. But few people were paying much attention to preserving country parks. The Trustees of Reservations won easy legislative approval. With a government much smaller and simpler, the members of its governing board or standing committee began to work for a public agency to establish and maintain regional parks. The result was the Metropolitan Parks Commission, the first of its kind in the nation, founded in 1893.

Today, Massachusetts can be pardoned if it looks with some pride and pleasure upon what began here 90 years ago: using private initiative to accomplish public purposes in the field of land conservation.

We've grown considerably more sophisticated, of course, with knowledge about the importance of wetlands and the floodplain, soils, wildlife, vegetation, and clean air and water as well as the desire and need for recreation, but throughout the world there seems to be still, as Charles Eliot declared, universal agreement about "the particular pleasure and refreshment which the contemplation of natural scenery alone affords" for us all.

THE TRADITION of LOCAL PRIVATE ACTIVITY in the EAST
H. William Sellers

Private land conservation[1] in the East has few ivy-encrusted traditions. For one thing, most local land conservation groups are less than twenty years old, and many had few, if any, contacts with groups outside of their own states until the last five years.

Although some local land conservation organizations can trace their origins back thirty or forty years, the majority, at least in numbers, are creations of the last two decades, born of an age of affluence, interstates, massive suburban growth, high federal taxes, and attractive charitable deduction tax laws. In Pennsylvania, in Maryland, Delaware, Virginia, New Jersey, Connecticut, Maine, Massachusetts, and other states, the rural estates of the rich and relict agricultural enclaves on the outskirts of metropolises, coastal islands, marshes and wetlands, and remote historic villages were suddenly awakened in the 1960s by interstates or plans for such, mobs of new home buyers or vacationers, and plans for jetports, industries, regional malls, and mammoth land developments.

While these trends occurred in all sections of the country, the East had ample ex-

---

1. The author excludes from this discussion local groups that are creations of national organizations such as The Nature Conservancy and Audubon.

amples of past problems with destruction of historic sites and natural areas, the various types of pollution that follow urbanization, and overuse of important resources. Appreciated land values and attractive tax benefits made charitable gifts of land interests more attractive to those facing large income, gift, and estate tax problems. It is important also to note that to many wealthy Eastern families, land ownership has been the result of wealth and not the producer of wealth. Consequently, tax planning has been directed to protecting cash assets or wealth-producing assets by donating land assets. Such gifts have the added benefits of preserving hallowed family ground and maintaining long-term friendships with neighbors.

Most of the land conservation organizations formed in the last twenty years were the creations of single individuals or small coteries of close friends who recognized the problems and the conservation possibilities of the areas that they knew quite well and that were under imminent threat of some major change. Although many of these organizations enlarged their geographical areas of interest over the years, quite a large number have remained totally focused on small areas and those that have expanded have often created local affiliates or provided affiliation arrangements to local groups.

Many of the groups committed principally to protecting areas proximate to their principal residences have tended to downplay the need for staffs skilled in land transactions and land management and have relied instead on volunteer professionals for those staff needs. Staffing in such groups has been directed to fund-raising, education, and community action purposes. All too frequently, this reliance of locally organized groups on land preservation assistance from volunteers has resulted in underachievement of land preservation goals that might have been met with assistance from paid professionals skilled in conservation *and* real estate matters.

The land conservation goals of the private groups have included among others: natural areas and/or historic site preservation and protection; acquisition of hunting or nature preserves, parklands, trail systems, and other recreational areas for state or local governments; control of densities or uses in ecologically sensitive or scenic areas; protection of land areas critical to water resources; and more recently, agricultural land preservation.

Although the record varies, private groups formed by landowners exclusively to preserve or protect particular areas where they live year-round or seasonally (e.g., Nantucket) have tended to avoid major land interest transfers to government. In contrast, groups with regional or statewide support bases have focused more on "roll-over" transactions or fostering landowner-to-government donations. Recent trends in federal support for land acquisition as well as poor experiences with government management of land are resulting in some organizations reconsidering roll-overs and building land management and income-generating skills in order to retain ownership.

In the absence of an established interorganizational communications structure (excepting New England Natural Resources Center and Open Space Institute projects), most land conservation groups have sought inspiration and guidance from several esteemed spokesmen of land protection methods and analytical techniques as well as from other successful organizations. Whyte, Browne, Brenneman, and McHarg have been widely read and followed.[2] Most

---

2. William H. Whyte's *Last Landscape* and *Securing Open Space for Urban America: Conservation Easements* have inspired many easement programs. Kingsbury Browne's editorial guidance and contributions to *Case Studies in Land Conservation* as well as his continuing advisory services have had major impacts. Russell L. Brenneman's *Private Approaches to the Preservation of Open Land* (1967) is a standard reference.

organizations to this point have focused on charitable donations or purchases of land interests and have avoided mixing conservation objectives with development or commercial objectives. Ottauquechee, the Philadelphia Conservationists, Society for the Protection of New Hampshire Forests, Brandywine Conservancy, and several others have strayed from orthodoxy, and Robert Lemire has contributed a publication that provides several alternatives to more conventional approaches.[3]

Many larger land conservation organizations in the East have other conservation objectives and programs. Some of these programs as well as others are also provided by a multitude of small environmental and cultural organizations. Nature centers, historical societies, antipollution groups, and other single and multipurpose groups are profusely distributed across the Boston-to-Washington land corridor. While some competition (for funding or land donations) may exist between these groups and those with major land acquisition goals, many mutually supportive relationships have been established. More are necessary, however, because the lack of land transaction and management skills, particularly in the enviro-cultural groups, has resulted in many lost opportunities for land conservation and a number of notable failures.

THE TRADITION of PRIVATE LAND SAVING in the EAST

David Moore

Private philanthropy has played a key role in the preservation of parks and natural areas in the eastern United States. Prior to the 1960s, most parks and reservations were acquired by donation.

In New Jersey, although some land purchases were made to *add* to donated parcels earlier, it was not until 1953 that any major land acquisitions were made in the nation's most crowded state. Island Beach State Park, a 10-mile natural barrier beach, was purchased that year by the state of New Jersey; Wharton State Forest, a 100,000-acre reserve in the Pine Barrens, was added the following year. Both acquisitions resulted from special legislative appropriations.

---

3. Robert Lemire, *Creative Land Development: Bridge to the Future.*

State and local parkland acquisition in New Jersey started in earnest in 1961, with passage of a $60-million bond issue called Green Acres. Similar programs in a few other eastern states, such as Project 70 in Pennsylvania, followed, as did federal programs like Mission 66 and the Land and Water Conservation Fund.

Cooperative ventures between the public and private sectors emerged, the Maryland Environmental Trust in the mid-1960s and the New Jersey Natural Lands Trust in 1968.

In the meantime, local land trusts, established at the municipal level in New England states, took advantage of land donation possibilities, sometimes combining such gifts with public land acquisition. The Nature Conservancy got its start in 1951. The New Jersey Conservation Foundation began in 1959 as an issue-oriented group, organized to save the Great Swamp of Morris County, New Jersey.

Many of the same kinds of groups that emerged in the 1960s at state and local levels played the role of matchmaker, putting individuals concerned about preservation of their own lands in touch with groups and agencies whose business was open land management.

During all of this time, there was an underlying presumption that the private sector had a role to play, but not in a steady state. Private actions have their ups and downs in the public mind. The presumption of private involvement was at its lowest ebb in the early 1970s, at least in New Jersey: It seemed that the willingness of the people of the state to preserve whatever needed to be preserved by public land acquisition and management knew no bounds. Such public commitments are still strong, but not as powerful as they once were, given the slowdown of growth and the subsequent waning of commercial and residential demands for vast amounts of farmland and open space.

The tradition of involvement by the private sector as experimenters with new land-saving techniques, as gap fillers when the public sector has hesitated, and as matchmakers has been and remains viable. For example, work with conservation easements, with the exception of early attempts by the National Park Service, has fallen primarily to the private sector.

The impetus for new legislation promoting open space preservation has also come from the private sector. All four of New Jersey's Green Acres bond acts were encouraged and promoted by private-sector groups. The same is true of the current $50-million Farmland Preservation Bond Act now awaiting a November vote in New Jersey.

It is also clear that government hasn't the long-range planning capability to carry forward multiyear projects or those that cut across political jurisdictions. The Appalachian Trail is a good example. Even now, the Heritage Conservation and Recreation Service, which did have some responsibility for ensuring the trail's protection, has disappeared into whatever heaven there is for such agencies. In time the private trail groups will be responsible for long-term protection. The same is true for watershed projects of more local but nevertheless multijurisdictional nature. That tradition is likely to continue, because of vagaries of government with its four-year philosophical seesaws on the executive level, which are currently painfully obvious.

The private sector thus will be a critical factor in open space preservation: in planning for the future, in experimenting with new ideas of pairing opportunity with agency, and in influencing the direction the land preservation movement takes.

CONSERVATION ISSUES in the MIDWEST
Mark C. Ackelson

The midwestern agricultural states are under resource pressures somewhat unique to this region. There has been little population growth during the last census period and consequently little development pressure outside of the periphery of some major cities. Even so the losses of natural resources are still staggering, and the rates of loss are increasing. In Iowa, for example, the population grew less than 1 percent between 1970 and 1980, but approximately 25,000–40,000 acres of forest lands are lost annually; and the rate of loss is increasing. This has reduced the 7 million acres of forest at the time of settlement to less than 1.5 million acres today. Only 3,000 acres remain of the prairie that once covered 85 percent of the state. Seven million acres of wetland have been reduced to 60,000 acres. In addition, 5,000 miles of streams have been lost and our rich top soil has been reduced by erosion to less than half of its thickness in less than 150 years.

"The Remnants"

No living man will see again the long-grass prairie, where a sea of prairie flowers lapped at the stirrups of the pioneer. We shall do well to find a forty here and there on which the prairie plants can be kept alive as species.

Aldo Leopold, *A Sand County Almanac*

Most of these losses have been to tremendous gains in agriculture. But as agriculture pressure moves into natural lands (and other marginal agricultural land) and reduces fence rows and other edge conditions, not only is there a reduction in habitat but also ever-increasing losses to wind and water erosion and subsequent impact on water quality. Underground water supplies are depleted by consumptive uses and its quality impacted. Plans for massive water diversions are being developed.

Additional factors impact heavily on the natural resources in the Midwest. The competitive attitude of the family farmer is becoming keener as they feel the economic pinch and are encouraged by national policies that encourage vast surpluses. Secondly, many farms are not being passed through families but instead sold to absentee landowners or those without strong

156

ties to the land. Lower profit margins require consolidation of farm units into large ownerships. As a consequence, short-term production and gain become paramount. The wilderness attitude still prevails and is emphasized by a "this land is mine, to be conquered" philosophy.

In Iowa, these resource losses have persisted despite the state's production of national conservation leaders such as Herbert Hoover, Ding Darling, and Aldo Leopold.

General public awareness becomes a major need while at the same time efforts must continue in working with those landowners and agencies concerned with natural resource conservation. Negativism provides no encouragement. A positive program that recognizes good land stewards and works to ensure continuation of their efforts becomes a major thrust.

Conservation in the Midwest, therefore, includes a variety of major issues and concerns requiring a broad perspective. Private conservation efforts must emphasize the economic impacts as well as the natural, aesthetic, and recreational values and strive to maintain a balanced contingency.

CORLANDS
Judith M. Stockdale

CorLands was established in 1978 in direct response to the felt needs of public land managers in the Chicago metropolitan region: The land market was moving too fast for their slow bureaucracies to allow them to be financially competitive land purchasers. It is often easier for such agencies to purchase over a period of time, but hard to find sellers willing to commit themselves to such agreements. Since its inception CorLands has stood as the middleman in the purchase and transfer of over 400 acres of land. It has also accepted conservation easements on several parcels of land. It is not CorLands' intention to hold parcels of land in perpetuity; we aim to pass them on to a local land-holding agency for the use of the public. We have worked in close partnership with public (or quasi-public) agencies, realizing that our relationship with our "take-out" agency is vital. Because of this we have not approached an agency with a "deal" in hand unless we are sure that it is a land parcel that fits into their plan. Generally, the public agency has approached us for help.

During our first years we have striven for good contact with land acquisition agencies and to let the greater public know of CorLands' existence and its services, but we do not attempt to influence public policies affecting land conservation. It has been our feeling that a land-holding agency should avoid confrontational situations simply to protect the land assets that it holds at any one time. However, CorLands was created by Open Lands Project and is an affiliate corporation. The Project is an educational organization that addresses public land policy.

In order to purchase land CorLands has borrowed commercially. When CorLands began, after discussions with the major Chicago banks, it was decided that a small capital fund ($300,000) would be necessary to serve as a collateral pool. This has been largely established, and we use it to bridge on a loan until title and survey are cleared and the bank is willing to use the land alone as collateral. The capital fund has been invested throughout and, while it has seen some growth, we realize we may have to increase its size when CorLands' scope increases. However, our main financial problem currently is being at the mercy of high interest rates. Local agencies may want CorLands' services, but since we pass through our direct costs, they think twice about paying 20 percent (even if the costs are spread over a number of years on a lease-back agreement) and are now frequently pulling their horns in, letting some lands go by the board. We feel that the development of below market rate financing schemes is a vital area of consideration for the future of local land purchasing.

Another problem is, of course, achieving wide recognition of local land conservation groups' existence and encouraging more and more agencies to use their services. As I have noted, CorLands has developed good relationships with public agencies. Rather harder to develop, in view of constantly changing personnel, is a relationship with the estate planning community in banks and the larger law firms. We are currently conducting a series of seminars with senior personnel at the major institutions and firms but are interested in other programs that are used or being considered.

CorLands is run by a voluntary board of directors, all business people involved in land development, law, or banking, and the group is active. However, we have found the need for a small professional staff (one land resource professional, one lawyer) as well as administrative support. In addition, having recently received a grant to ascertain CorLands' role as a private land bank of inner-city lands, we have added the services of an urban planning consultant for the next six months and are eager to discuss the experiences of other organizations with urban lands.

THE DEVELOPMENT of a STATEWIDE CONSERVATION PROGRAM in OHIO

Robert Currie

The Ohio Conservation Foundation (OCF) was founded in 1969 to foster wise land use in the state of Ohio. Since moving to Cleveland in 1973 OCF has undertaken a number of projects designed to enhance the land conservation efforts of both public and private sectors. OCF produces information materials and conducts meetings, seminars, and conferences to educate Ohioans on land use issues. Some of OCF's activities between 1974 and 1980 included the following: land use attitude survey of Ohio; documentary film on land use attitudes in Ohio; land use workshops; two statewide assemblies on land use; local programs in land use and the humanities; restoration of the Stephen Frazee House; Cuyahoga Valley Perimeter Protection Project; and a growth policy assistance program.

During the period from 1974 to 1980, the collection of OCF's activities was determined more by opportunity than by precise design. This is probably not uncommon; however, it makes the task of communicating a coherent programmatic approach more difficult. An important factor has been the "personalities" of OCF's principal sources of funds. OCF has received a majority of its funds from two sources. Recently, one has taken a more regionalistic posture and, as a result, OCF has taken on more projects in northeastern Ohio than it might have.

OCF's interest in direct land conservation has not really expressed itself. In 1975 OCF produced an information brochure on conservation easements; however, few attempts were made to secure easements. The Cuyahoga Valley Perimeter Protection Project was designed to encourage landowners near the recreation area to donate easements; this phase of the project did not commence until 1981. For 1981 OCF has a project underway to prepare a plan and program for using conservation easements in the Cleveland area. OCF's articles of incorporation were amended in May 1981 to allow acquisition of land or any partial interest in land. Conservation of land resources through acquisition in some form will be a growing part of OCF's work in the next couple of years.

THE FUTURE OF THE OHIO CONSERVATION FOUNDATION

In 1981 OCF has worked mainly in three areas. The Land Use Information and Action Project, which is an extension of past efforts to encourage support for legislative improvements in land use and land use planning, is designed to develop, with the assistance of key land use decision makers, specific legislative proposals that could be widely supported. OCF is also preparing a plan and program for using conservation easements in the Cleveland area. Third, OCF assisted the city and township of Perrysburg, Ohio, to develop a growth management plan. In planning programs for the latter half of 1981 and for 1982 our emphasis is shifting from state-level matters such as legislation toward activities that will assist communities or individuals to conserve land. We hope to develop a somewhat more unified programmatic approach, a more even geographical distribution of activity, and a more balanced funding base. Three interrelated programs will form the core of OCF activity. They are: (1) OCF will assist communities in development of growth management plans; (2) OCF will assist community conservation efforts by conducting workshops, providing technical assistance to community groups and landowners, and by directly initiating land conservation activity; and (3) OCF will work to preserve Ohio farmland by preparing booklets, hosting a conference, conducting workshops, and by providing technical assistance to farmers and local farmland conservation groups.

Establishing a more even distribution of activity and broadening our funding base are closely related goals. In order to build a reputation as an effective statewide land conservation organization we must be active throughout the state. In order to be active throughout the state we must develop funding from members, corporations, and foundations in all major cities.

A COMMUNITY LAND TRUST EXPERIENCE in TENNESSEE
Marie Cirillo

My experience has allowed me some fifteen years of living in a small unincorporated community where over 85 percent of the land is owned by absentee land companies. Coal rights have been leased for strip mining since the mid-1940s and for deep mining since the late 1800s. At its peak, the Clairfield mail route served 12,000 people. In the years when there was a slump in the coal business (some thirty years) the population was close to 1,200 people. People from Clairfield experienced, and continue to experience, rural and urban poverty. Migration is part of their life. It is hard and uncertain.

A conspicuous part of the poverty of Clairfield has been experienced in the loss of its natural wealth. Water is polluted, top soil destroyed, trees are dead, rocks are cracked. Wildlife, wild greens, fish and nuts are gone. Heavy rains wash clay and shale and rock and debris into the creek beds. Floods leave a crusted substance over garden and pasture lands. Foundations mildew. The human body is plagued with fear and tension, and bones creak with arthritis. Hepatitis and parasites play havoc with the young and old. With practically no tax base (the companies pay very little tax on their large holdings), the county water, sewer, sanitation, health, road, and education systems are totally inadequate.

It is no wonder that over 3 million Appalachians left their land in the 1950s and 1960s to work in Detroit auto factories, Cincinnati formica companies, and Chicago's maze of industries. In Appalachia democracy was not working. The vote had no way of directing its power on the absentee landowners. Life as a whole was not working—no jobs, no services, no protection of land or life.

The option to run from the rural place is no longer timely. People are now running from urban places. But is that really a livable option, always running from that which is not working? Or must people come to grips with the problems of a sustainable planet? If there are only places to run from, there will soon be fewer places to run to. We must look at *place* in new ways. For *place* is the physical world upon which society (whether urban, rural, or suburban) must be built.

In 1969 Bob Swann visited some community workers in Appalachia. His concept of a community land trust was right—but the time was not right. People had their sights on coal. It was the problem, and (ironically enough) it offered a solution. For many communities it provided the only jobs, while at the same time destroying its future.

In 1977 massive floods washed thousands of homes away. While the floods could have been attributed to the mining, the fact was that the sites where homes had been were now in flood plains. Overnight there were thousands of people in search of land. Only then did they realize their vulnerability in the midst of corporate land control.

I made the 5-hour car trip back to Clairfield after a citizen meeting held in Williamson, West Virginia, and in that period of time I decided it was time for citizens of my community to think about a community land trust. What might happen if we would form a nonprofit organization that had no agenda but to reacquire land for the community?

The step was taken in 1978 by three incorporators of a community land trust. By 1979 we had a board of seven and many knowledgeable neighbors. Today the group has 60 acres of land. The task ahead is for local citizens to learn how to rebuild a community with a plan that includes reverence for and care of the land that is their place.

I see the Community Land Trust as an act of reconciliation between mankind and land. It is a peaceful solution to rebuilding an industrially destroyed community.

AGRICULTURAL LAND CONVERSION: Mesa County, Colorado

Herman C. Allmaras

THE SETTING AND THE PROBLEM

Nowhere can the land conversion process be more vividly seen than in the region where prime agricultural land is relatively scarce. In Mesa County, Colorado, midway between Denver and Salt Lake City, the fertile irrigated acres on the floor of the Colorado River Valley are also blessed with a long growing season. The green color of the orchards, alfalfa fields, and gardens stands out from April through October as a precious jewel surrounded by the brown colors of the surrounding hillsides. At higher elevations the rugged slopes are forested, providing a watershed and recreational opportunities.

This agricultural jewel is flawed by the tremendous coal, gas, oil, and oil shale deposits that surround the valley. Because of the energy impact, food is transported into the county in ever-increasing amounts as farmland is converted to urban sprawl of the worst kind. The county, claiming insolvency, is asking for a new tax on November 2. This is a 2 percent sales tax, another burden, to be added to the already high cost for agricultural production. The hillsides remain undeveloped, and the sprawl on the valley floor is not paying its own way.

Actually the hillsides are being converted too. The ranching operations, faced with declining markets, loss of ranch hands to city jobs, increased taxes, and higher costs for equipment, are selling their land as 40-acre ranchettes, thus effectively removing the land from production.

Without irrigation water the valley floor would be a desert. While the city of Denver has transmountain diversion of western slope water, the states of Arizona and California with the country of Mexico draw on the downstream water. Now we find that the energy companies are deploying and are seeking to buy water rights from every source possible.

MESA COUNTY LAND CONSERVANCY, INC.

The Mesa County Land Conservancy board has operated by consensus from its inception nearly a year ago. With the invaluable assistance of the Trust for Public Land we charted a new course through somewhat hostile territory. There is no room for misdirection or weakness in the image projected to the public or to our potential clients. The idea of land conservation is fragile, and it must grow at a deliberate pace. All of the board is new at this sort of endeavor, and our clients are very independent people located in a very conservative community.

We avoid direct confrontation with public policy whenever it is possible, but there are instances where we have individually initiated suits in favor of wise land use planning. Mostly we try to influence public policy through informal conversation with the elected officials, but we recognize the need for a consensus that retaining land in agricultural production is an important local goal.

Our activities to date have been organizational, educational, and probing the opposition. There are five projects for the transfer of development rights, and once completed they will launch us into a higher level of activity.

GETTING IT TOGETHER in COLORADO
Martin Zeller

The following is a brief description of efforts to establish a corporately funded, non-profit foundation designed to address the dramatic and accelerating decline in open space in Colorado, particularly along the Front Range due to rapid growth. The need for an open space entity is highlighted by the following considerations:

Colorado is growing at three times the national growth rate. Eighty percent of Colorado's population is concentrated in the thirteen counties comprising the Front Range. The equivalent of one-half of all the development that has taken more than a hundred years to evolve in the Front Range will be added in just twenty more years.

Governor Lamm's Colorado Front Range Project, launched two years ago as a broadly based citizens' effort to prioritize critical issues facing Colorado in the next twenty years has identified the funding and acquisition of open space, particularly buffers between communities, as the number one priority.

The major decline in federal and state land acquisition funds has led to the virtual cessation of land acquisition programs.

While there are a variety of groups addressing various aspects of land preservation, in total they lack the resources, are too narrowly focused, or individually lack the expertise to make a significant difference.

In response to these concerns, the Colorado Forum, a socially motivated business advocacy group comprised of twenty-three chief executive officers from major Colorado corporations set up an open space subcommittee to determine if there was an appropriate role that they could initiate. After investigating resources available in Colorado and other land preservation organizations with similar backgrounds, such as the Iowa Natural Heritage Foundation, it was recently decided to develop a full-blown proposal for funding an organization to be acted upon by the full Forum membership at the beginning of December. Don Walker, author of the Boulder open space program, and I have been chosen to design the program.

As currently conceived, the proposal we will present to the Forum will call for a small, professional staff with an aggressive deal-making, project orientation. The nonprofit corporation, which will be functionally independent of the Forum, would provide a catalytic and intermediary public-private service in facilitating and packaging locally identified open space preservation priorities. The initial credibility of the nonprofit would ideally be established through the completion of several key land preservation projects. These "hides on the wall" would provide the basis for the nonprofit to expand and modify its initial demonstration role. The Forum would commit to funding the operational budget of the nonprofit for one year, and its continued livelihood would be contingent upon its initial success. Specific project funding would be presented to the Forum and the larger public-private community on a case-by-case basis. The nonprofit would operate on the principle of maximizing the leverage of limited private resources for carrying out open space preservation strategies. The activity of the nonprofit would be overseen by a board of directors balanced with respect to public, private, and political affiliation and would be assisted by a board of advisers, combining a mix of local and national talent.

While most of the ingredients necessary for success of this kind of program appear to be in place, there are several that we will have to carefully ascertain. The first concerns whether the general commitment to the idea of open space preservation can be turned into a potent financial commitment. Until now the Forum has restricted its role to advocacy, and the establishment of an open space entity represents a significant departure from previous activities. Secondly, it is clear that effective business leadership will have to emerge from the process if the organization is to be effective.

PRIVATE LAND SAVING in the WEST and ALONG the YAKIMA RIVER in PARTICULAR
Douglas D. Peters

The West includes Oregon, Washington, Hawaii, Alaska, Idaho, and Montana (California and the Southwest states must fend for themselves). Urbanization of the West is in full progress. However, there are vast areas of the West with relatively small populations (exhibit A gives the 1980 population by state), and there are tremendous opportunities in the West for the preservation of open space.

EXHIBIT A 1980 POPULATION		EXHIBIT B FEDERALLY OWNED LAND (FIGURES IN ACRES)	
Alaska	400,481	Alaska	359,134,000
Hawaii	965,000	Hawaii	661,000
Idaho	943,935	Idaho	33,760,000
Montana	786,690	Montana	27,741,000
Oregon	2,632,663	Oregon	32,314,000
Washington	4,130,163	Washington	331,157

Much open space is presently publicly owned. The "sagebrush rebellion" has disclosed the figures of federally owned acreage, shown in exhibit B.

Even though there are great opportunities in the West for acquisition of property, there is an inverse relationship concerning the ability to purchase those properties. The Nature Conservancy has found that their greatest source of funding for purchasing property in the West is from out of the area. This is because of the fewer people of substantial wealth in the West and the "sagebrush rebellion philosophy."

Source information acknowledged from Elliot Marks of the Washington chapter, The Nature Conservancy, and Joel Kuperberg, vice president, Northwestern region, Trust for Public Land.

The sagebrush rebellion philosophy is a generalized feeling that there is already too much land in public ownership. For example, counties in the state of Washington receive tax funds from timber cuts. Large timber holdings in public ownership that are not available for cutting reduce potential revenue to counties. Washington currently has areas considered for wilderness designation under the RARE II study. A lake area close to Goose Prairie (home of the late Justice William O. Douglas) is an area proposed for wilderness designation. The matter has been pending in Congress for about twenty years.

Most of the public lands are being administered by public agencies for multiple-use purposes. Tension between timber interests, recreationers, snowmobilers, hunters, and hikers over the proper administration of "public use" areas adds to the general public unhappiness with public administration.

By state, a brief synopsis would indicate that in Alaska there is great unrest, particularly with unresolved issues of Indian claims and state claims. In Hawaii, it is difficult to purchase lands. The lands are either owned by native Hawaiians, large corporate holdings, or effectively administered by land use planning, not requiring private ownership for protection purposes. In Idaho and Montana, there are tremendous opportunities but few local financial resources who see the need to preserve these lands.

Public awareness in the states of Oregon and Washington is somewhat similar. The populations of these two states seem to recognize the importance of preservation and are "on guard" for the intrusion of development in the loss of open space and agricultural lands.

My presidency of the Yakima River Regional Greenway Foundation has allowed me to focus on the development of a large 3,600-acre park called the Yakima Greenway along the Yakima River and its associated wetlands. This area is immediately adjacent to the city of Yakima, having a metropolitan area population of approximately 87,000 persons. This river has been neglected and generally intruded upon in a negative way since World War II. The Yakima Valley is a desert area, except for intensive irrigation from sources in the Cascade Mountains developed in the early part of the twentieth century. In contrast to earlier statements I have made on a regional basis, I have found tremendous public support for the concept of the Greenway. In Yakima, water, its preservation, and uses have high visibility in the community and are respected by all. The difficulty and challenge has been to show progress that will retain and develop public confidence. The particular Greenway has been an idea from approximately 1950, but only in 1979 has momentum occurred. Keeping this momentum is the critical issue for the next few years. Visible progress at the river rather than do-gooder rhetoric is our highest priority.

ISSUES of PRIVATE LAND SAVING in the WEST
Joan Vilms

My private land-saving experience is derived from land trust consulting in four contiguous northern California counties, Sonoma, Napa, Marin, and Lake. While these counties have certain physical traits in common, the political, economic, and environmental values vary considerably, thus affording a much wider perspective than their limited geographical area might suggest.

Located north of San Francisco Bay, a steady drift of conservation and development pressures emanates from the south. For years the Bay Area has been under intense pressure to urbanize. Major development opportunities in the South Bay have been virtually exhausted. The situation in Marin follows suit, and land prices soar as these areas approach their development limits. Looking for fresh opportunities and lower prices, developers head north to Sonoma and Napa counties, with some spillover farther north into Mendocino and Lake. Speculation precedes development, heating up local real estate markets and generating expectations for quick profits, both of which undermine long-term resource management decisions.

Economic uncertainty is another destructive force. Some landowners cash out while the market is hot. Others consider their land a hedge against inflation and want to maximize, not limit, their development options.

While more people agree that we must maintain a healthy balance between developed and undeveloped lands, few can agree where to draw the line, and fewer still are ready to set an example by voluntarily restricting their own lands.

What are issues unique to land saving in the West? The following cause-and-effect format attempts to delineate the inconsistencies and contradictions that characterize the politics and practice of private land saving in northern California.

Beneficial and adverse impacts on land conservation are identified by plus (+) and minus (−) signs.

1. *Massive migration to rural counties*

   (−) People fleeing urban areas bring urban problems (crime, congestion, air pollution) and values (increased demand for services) with them.

(+) Urban refugees include among their ranks many environmental activists and conservationists.

(−) Large landowners split off and sell hobby ranches and rural estates, often resulting in irreconcilable land use conflicts, typically between rural, residential, and agricultural forces.

(+) Coalitions are being built between farmers and conservationists to protect agriculture and related resource lands.

(−) Breaking down of large land holdings into smaller and smaller units increases the difficulty of assembling and securing large tracts of resource lands.

(+) Increasing parcelization increases the significance of the large tracts remaining and, sometimes, kindles a sense of stewardship and public trust among large landowners remaining.

2. *Highly inflated land values*

(−) Intense pressures to convert resource lands to other uses. Great temptation to sell out for big bucks to developer/speculator.

(−) When resource landowners begin thinking like developers, land management declines and long-term investment decisions are postponed.

(−) If one landowner subdivides, surrounding landowners feel pressure to do the same, caused partly by inflated land values and partly by the fallout from residential intrusion: roads, traffic, dogs, fences, vandalism, and so forth.

(+) High value of "development rights" provides economic incentive for gifts of land and conservation easements by people in high tax brackets with conservation motives.

3. *Economics of scarcity applies to jobs and housing*

(−) Frontier mentality and myth of wide open spaces persist despite rapid rate of urban expansion and rural development.

(−) Cities pay lip service to "infilling" and "compact growth" but expand their boundaries opportunistically (and short-sightedly), citing more jobs and housing as the justification for paving over prime ag land.

(+) Resource management tends to be labor intensive.

(−) Favors "technological fixes" and short-term exploitation of land and resources over conservation ethic and long-term quality of life.

4. *Physical hazards: Earthquakes, landslides, fire storms, floods, water scarcity*

(+) Inspire respect for nature's destructive power.

(+) Public support for development limitations in these areas.

(−) Challenge engineers to seek technological solutions.

(−) Relatively low market value inspires unscrupulous developers to buy cheaply and press for development approvals.

(+) Low development potential enhances appeal of conservation options, especially where land values are inflated by frequent sales at increasing prices.

5. *Dramatic landforms, beautiful scenery*

(−) Prompt in-migration and development to such an extent that it becomes increasingly difficult to maintain a healthy resource base.

(+) Inspire land-saving ethic among newcomers and old-timers alike.

(+) Are the basis for a healthy tourist industry that depends on protecting, not destroying, scenic resources.

6. *Public land use planning and regulation*

($\pm$) As political mood and climate change, so do planning policies.

(+) Protecting agricultural land by creating buffer zones and reducing rural residential intrusion is now in vogue.

($\pm$) Development trade-offs becoming more frequent: requiring grant of restrictive easement as condition of development approval.

(−) Land use policy favoring conservation is always subject to challenge by opposing forces and requires constant vigilance.

(−) Development approvals are subject to challenge for a limited period of time. Once built, a project's impact is permanent and irreversible.

(+) The temporary and regulatory aspects of public planning policy are strong selling points for permanent, voluntary, private sector land saving.

BUILDING NEW RELATIONSHIPS BETWEEN CONSERVANCY TRUSTS and COMMUNITY LAND TRUSTS

Chuck Matthei

Many of the same economic and political trends that today pose new and greater dangers to environmental protection and preservation efforts have also increased the difficulties and sufferings of individual families and local communities. At the heart of many environmental *and* social problems is land, and both have given rise to local land trust initiatives. Long-established conservancy trusts are growing and new ones developing in many communities, and the relatively newer community land trust (CLT) movement is experiencing unprecedented growth in numbers, geography, and diversity of purposes. One might well assume that conservancy trusts and CLTs would be natural allies, would seek out and support one another. There certainly are many good reasons why this should be the case, but it often is not, and an active commitment is needed now to build new bridges between these two land trust families.

The organizational structures and land acquisition techniques of conservancy trusts and CLTs are largely similar. Their obvious and principal difference lies in the stated goals of their respective land acquisition programs and the uses to which the acquired lands are put. With the federal commitment to preservation much diminished and public appropriations at all levels reduced, conservancy trusts will undoubtedly play an even more singular and critical role in preservation of wild lands and wildlife and conservation of natural resources. As the traditional dream of home and land ownership—of security, equity, and a legacy for future generations—fades for most Americans as a result of continuing inflation, high interest rates, and speculation, CLTs are focused primarily on land for housing and productive uses. CLTs in rural areas are working to provide access to land and decent housing for low-income people, preserve family farms and farmland, and facilitate sound, long-term timber management. Urban CLTs have formed to combat speculation and gentrification, preserve and develop low- and moderate-income housing, and maintain useful urban open spaces.

These various purposes are surely not mutually exclusive and should be complementary. Conservancy lands offer recreational, educational, and psychological benefits to local residents and often protect water supplies and other vital resources. CLTs frequently do set aside or protect conservation lands and work to develop economically viable land use plans to protect both social and natural characteristics of local communities. But there are some differences—

both real and perceived—of orientation and strategy, and these differences are partially responsible for a prevalent lack of communication between the various trust organizations.

Another difference between many conservancy trusts and CLTs, although there are a number of notable exceptions, lies in the social and economic characteristics of their memberships. Conservancy efforts are often associated (whether in fact or in the public mind) with middle- and upper-class communities and concerns, while many (though by no means all) CLTs are based in low-income communities whose members have no conventional access to security and equity through landownership. These differences of background and personal circumstances are manifested in differences of style, vocabulary, perspectives, and priorities. The groups frequently have different skills, resources, and access to resources (technical, financial, and political) as well.

Once again, these differences *need* not be a barrier to communication or a cause of tension between conservancy trusts and CLTs, but at times they do prevent a sharing of resources and formation of effective partnerships. Recently, in a low-income, inner-city neighborhood of a large midwestern city, CLT members joined other community residents in opposing an application by the local historic preservation organization to expand the historic district boundaries. The application was denied. The members of the preservation group, whose intentions were certainly positive, were disappointed and also confused. The president of their board explained that they had met an unexpected and "unholy" alliance of business interests (resisting any restrictions on future development) and low-income community groups (concerned that preservation would mean gentrification and displacement for neighborhood residents).

The historic preservation group had recognized the fears of residents in a neighborhood that had experienced considerable demolition for highway construction in the early 1970s and currently faces gentrification. For this reason, the preservation group had primarily purchased vacant buildings, believing they would thus avoid displacement. Nevertheless, suspicion and opposition prevailed and grew.

Community residents expressed a number of continuing concerns. They contended that there had been little real consultation between the preservation group and neighborhood residents (rehab costs and financing barriers made the historic housing inaccessible to these people, and the preservation group had made little use of phased rehab, alternative financing, or mixed-income development techniques to provide lower-cost housing), no process for social integration of the new higher-income residents, and no controls on future resale prices and speculation.

Neighborhood residents and organizations (including the CLT and its members) did not object to historic preservation and development per se, but in the absence of an evident commitment on the part of the preservation group to meet the pressing physical and social needs of a low-income community, they felt that opposition was a necessary act of self-defense. While parallel conflicts in rural communities are often less intense, the confrontations less direct and personal, the same issues do arise in some rural conservation efforts. Without adequate communication or representation, some community residents may perceive a conservation organization's attention to "wilderness" as conscious neglect or disregard of human needs; others are concerned about the impact of conservation acquisitions on property values and taxes.

Such conflicts and failures in communication are similar to those encountered by other environmental and alternative energy advocates. But increasingly, environmentalists, low-income community groups, organized labor, and other constituencies are beginning to find common ground in their concerns, and some important new alliances are beginning to emerge.

Conservancy trusts and CLTs do have a strong basis for relationship and common effort, and each has resources that can be critically useful to the other.

With current economic problems so often used to justify environmental compromises, and budget reductions reducing the pool of available public funding for conservation efforts, environmentalists need a broader grass-roots base of public and political support, in local communities as well as on the state and national levels. Conservancy trusts and historic preservation organizations will need support from growing numbers of community residents. On the other hand, as the same economic problems raise traditional financial and access barriers even higher for low- and moderate-income people (whose problem has often been more lack of credit than poverty itself), these community residents, and their local CLTs, will need the typically greater technical skills and financial resources of the conservancy trusts.

The proliferation and growth of both conservancy trusts and CLTs is likely to continue and increase, often within the same communities or regions. As this occurs, and economic and political pressures continue to mount, their relationships (or nonrelationships) to one another will not likely remain static, but will tend toward greater cooperation or conflict. There is every reason, both principled and practical, for conservancy and community trusts to make conscious and constructive efforts to bridge communication gaps where they do exist, to introduce themselves to one another, and to form an active, mutually supportive alliance to address both environmental and social problems.

RURAL CONSERVATION:
Historic Preservationists in the Rural Landscape

A. Elizabeth Watson

With historic preservationists popularly viewed as other-worldly elitists or as little old ladies in tennis shoes throwing themselves before bulldozers and wrecking balls, who hold dear their genealogies, antiques, and stuffy house museums, why does historic preservation deserve a hearing in a forum for those involved in land conservation? In fact, preservation has moved far beyond saving buildings as house museums and last-ditch, save-it-at-any-cost efforts that polarize all groups with an interest in development decisions. Today, preservationists concern themselves with a broad range of land use, economic, and social issues, aiming for the improvement of environmental quality. In rural areas, where historic preservation has received little attention, land conservation organizations are needed to advocate preservation values alongside goals for environmental protection.

Why preserve? Old buildings, structures, and sites—such as the Old North Church, the Golden Gate Bridge, and the trail of the Pony Express—are our roots. They tell us who we are and where we have been as a nation and society, as much as our writings and oral traditions. This insight is basic to the *historic* in historic preservation; preservationists know it as "sense of place."

There are, however, additional motivations for preservation. In many cases, it costs less to preserve through rehabilitation or adaptive use than to build anew, a helpful economic argument that grew out of the inflation of the past decade and came into full bloom with the tax incentives provided by the Economic Recovery Tax Act passed in July, 1981. Related to this argument, old buildings constitute "reserves" of energy and natural resources. It takes energy to convert natural resources such as stone, iron, and wood into building materials, to transport those materials, and to construct the buildings themselves. New buildings require duplicating those energy expenditures, discarding building materials, and additional energy for demolition. The waste involved in unwise new development should be an especially appealing argument to those working to protect the natural environment.

Finally, old buildings are a source of visual splendor and delight. In fact, the aesthetic appeal of old buildings often provides the first attraction for the new historic preservationist, who later learns the arguments cited above. Aesthetic appeal is the basis for the historic preservationist's emphasis on design standards for rehabilitation and adaptive use that respects original designs. It surprises many to learn that preservationists are not necessarily antipathetic to new buildings, even in designated historic areas, but advocate sensitive designs and will welcome imaginative, modern solutions to the problems of constructing new buildings in older surroundings. Adoption of design standards for old and new buildings often relies on the successful articulation of the economic benefits of protecting property values, of which aesthetics are a part.

In rural areas, historic resources are inseparable from their setting. The location and growth of farms, villages, and other rural development generally were determined by the availability of natural resources: prime farmland or timber, minerals, water bodies suitable for transportation or power. Indigenous building materials, climate, topography, and the availability of water contributed to the design, construction, and siting of rural structures. The functional and harmonious relationship between early rural structures and their surroundings evolved over the decades; it is part of the meaning to be found in rural historic resources.

Thus, we come to rural conservation, a specialized branch of preservation planning that advances well beyond traditional historic preservation to encompass activities that protect the settings of rural structures, such as agricultural preservation, natural resources inventories, scenic (visual) analysis, open space protection, and land use management. Put another way, rural conservation, in the historic preservationist's lexicon, is land use planning with emphasis on historic preservation values along with more commonly perceived environmental values.

Historical and cultural influences in the rural landscape are important factors in perceptions of scenic quality. The strength of the appeal of these influences should not be underestimated in determining the motivation of those who support land conservation in their rural communities. Because traditional perceptions of historic preservation are limited in scope, it is easy to overlook historic preservation values when they are to be found in more general perceptions of environmental quality. Yet, it is also easy to imagine the impact of the loss of locally valued cultural resources, still in use and thus not perceived as historic: a barn along the road lost to fire, a farmstead surrounded by housing tracts, a village hemmed in by commercial strips. Linking these values to the goals of a land conservation organization may broaden the appeal of the organization's activities, gaining it useful allies and acknowledging a subconscious need in the community.

The land conservation organization can make use of a variety of preservation planning tools:

Surveys of historic resources, to identify them and plan appropriate protection

Nominations to the National Register of Historic Places, which protects historic places—including open land—from adverse federal or federally funded actions

Local ordinances designed to protect historic resources through local land development codes, which, unlike listing in the National Register, provide controls over the actions of private property owners

Conservation easement programs extended to protect buildings and historic open space

Acquisition and development activities that directly preserve rural buildings and promote sensitive design

With these tools listed, it is necessary to add a *caveat* for organizations active in rural areas: Historic preservationists are only beginning to learn how to transfer to rural areas the lessons of fifty years of successful urban preservation activities. Few rural surveys have been performed by or for the responsible state agencies, and rural historic resources are vastly underrepresented in the National Register, so that procedures for successful nominations of large land areas (as distinguished from nominations of individual buildings) are not well established in many states. Few rural communities have employed a comprehensive, rural conservation approach, historic district ordinances, or acquisition of properties for preservation and development to achieve historic preservation goals.

As a result, the National Trust for Historic Preservation established the special four-year Rural Project in 1979. The project's objectives are twofold: (1) to develop comprehensive rural conservation programs in two communities (Oley township, Pennsylvania, near Reading; and the town of Cazenovia, New York, near Syracuse) as examples for other communities. In the process, staff members and others cooperating in this work are refining preservation techniques for use in rural areas and researching protection techniques in related fields such as farmland retention, land use management, and the designation of scenic areas; and (2) to develop educational programs to disseminate the experience and knowledge gained through its research and demonstration work, using publications, conferences, workshops, and field assistance from the Rural Project and the Trust's six regional offices (in Washington, D.C., Boston, Charleston, Chicago, Oklahoma City, and San Francisco). When appropriate, collaboration with and referral to organizations with related environmental goals, such as the Trust for Public Land, the American Farmland Trust, and The Nature Conservancy, are part of this work.

For the organization willing to expand its role in protecting the rural environment to include historic preservation, then, one source of assistance is the National Trust. In addition, the land conservation organization can turn for advice to the state historic preservation officer (similar in function to the state liaison officer for the Land and Water Conservation Fund); a statewide private nonprofit preservation organization, if available; and local preservation groups. Planning agencies and redevelopment authorities at the local and regional levels may have one or more staff members familiar with preservation; and knowledgeable architects, attorneys, and other professional consultants are increasingly available. National Trust regional offices, in addition to providing direct assistance, can guide the organization in determining what sources of financial assistance and technical advice are available in the organization's area.

In conclusion, there are land conservation organizations that have incorporated an emphasis on historic preservation into their programs. Among these are the Trustees of Reservations in Massachusetts; the Berks County Conservancy, the Brandywine Conservancy, the Bucks County Conservancy, and the French and Pickering Creeks Conservation Trust, all in Pennsylvania; the Two Rivers Ottauquechee Regional Planning Commission in Vermont; and the Piedmont Environmental Commission in Virginia. Only a few such organizations exist, however; more, many more, are needed.

GREENING of the CITY
Peter R. Stein

Land is an enduring resource—or is it? This truism is challenged daily in cities across America. Trash piles up on vacant lots. Empty buildings collect the scars of vandals' sport. Neighborhoods decline. Land values depreciate. Local governments can do little to arrest this process. Nobody seems to care.

To the low- and moderate-income residents of inner-city neighborhoods, however, these urban wastelands mark their economic limits. To these people falls the burden of rescue, and many of them are gladly picking it up.

Since 1975 the Trust for Public Land (TPL), a nonprofit organization, has drawn on techniques and experiences used in the land conservation field to help local organizations rescue their neighborhoods. Hundreds of community gardens, tot lots, playgrounds and landscaped sitting areas tell of residents' hard-won success in surmounting lack of funding, community apathy, and bureaucratic torpor to create green spaces for their own pleasure and the beautification of their neighborhoods.

Just prior to World War II, a private developer purchased a portion of an old DuPont family estate in what is now the south ward of Newark. Thirty-one wood-frame, single-family homes were constructed along a short street, subsequently named White Terrace after the developer. Most of the homes have been continuously occupied for the last thirty years. In the wake of Newark's riots, the residents of White Terrace organized a block association to protect their block from becoming a "slum and a ghetto." Their first efforts focused on code enforcement, home maintenance, and sidewalk landscaping.

Maud Carroll, president of the White Terrace Block Association, first heard of the Trust for Public Land while taking a community gardening course at Rutgers University. A house at the end of her block had been burned and abandoned, and she called the Trust. Beginning with that first call to TPL in the fall of 1976, White Terrace residents began the battle to reclaim a small portion of their neighborhood.

Gathering support from neighbors, politicians, and a local foundation, the burnt-out building was demolished and the land recycled through "sweat equity" into a neighborhood recreation space. Many hours of donated labor plus thousands of dollars of donated equipment from local corporations and legal and technical assistance from TPL have produced a playground and sitting area for the White Terrace community that has been well kept and well used.

To protect the community's investment of time, money, and energy in such projects, TPL helps residents to secure legal control over the land they improve. Restoring the neighborhood landscape and establishing a land trust taps a reservoir of community spirit and builds pride.

"After acquiring the land, working together, cleaning it up and preparing the soil for planting, we saw something happen in the Stonehurst neighborhood that has never happened before," says June Norman, a member of the Stonehurst Land Trust in Oakland, California. "We were able as a community to turn a liability into an asset."

What is a land trust? It is a state and locally approved, nonprofit, tax-exempt corporation, formed by members of a community as a way to acquire, own, and manage land in common. The land trust's tax-exempt status enables the group to offer tax benefits to donors in return for land, buildings, equipment, and money.

The land trust is not a new concept. Begun in New England more than a century ago, land trusts have served as effective land preservation tools for rural and suburban communities. Modeled after the "town commons," land trusts enable citizens to pass the benefits of their collective action from generation to generation.

TPL has helped transform this experience into a handy modern tool for urban revitalization, one that satisfies local residents' need to own community property and reinforces the cooperative spirit indispensable for citizen action. The sense of shared responsibility and community stewardship are key ingredients in the land trust corporate structure and are part of the corporation's legal purposes.

Through TPL, citizens receive training in land recycling, acquisition, and conservation techniques while working in the field on actual projects. Experienced members of the community, armed with techniques to ensure community control and responsibility for the reclaimed areas, can then seek out new projects and provide stable, long-term management support. Based on its project experience, TPL has expanded its regional technical-assistance program to assist growing numbers of community organizations around the country.

Staffed by TPL-trained land acquisition experts, the technical-assistance program attempts to equip residents of inner-city neighborhoods with the skills to manage their surroundings.

The technical-assistance program represents a commitment by TPL to provide expanded resources to low- and moderate-income neighborhood organizations. This aid is directed toward helping these residents preserve important neighborhood amenities and develop a sense of competency and self-reliance as a springboard for further neighborhood landscape revitalization.

Says Tom Libby, a participant in TPL's Boston Training Program: "Land trusts provide the only mechanism to achieve long-term concrete results in the positive conversion of vacant lots by block clubs. TPL's training has provided for a transfer of skills to block-club organizers from various Boston neighborhoods who in turn can work with their own groups to apply the information to get results."

What began a short time ago as an experiment by the Trust for Public Land has blossomed. Neighborhood land trusts are being used throughout the country to assure long-term community responsibility for the protection of neighborhood green spaces. These projects are an integral part of community revitalization. Housing, jobs, and educational opportunities all need a livable environment, and neighborhood land trusts can help make cities livable.

A REVIEW of the 1981 NATIONAL SURVEY of LOCAL LAND CONSERVATION ORGANIZATIONS
Terry Bremer

Documentation of the growing land conservation achievements by private local groups is in hand. The first National Survey of Local Land Conservation Organizations (LLCO) verifies that 400 groups representing over 250,000 members are committed to using primarily volunteer initiative and private funds in forty-one states to preserve over 675,000 acres of valuable resource lands. Their numbers demonstrate a twelvefold increase from 36 groups in 1950 to 400 by the end of 1981. The movement is clearly more established in the New England and Middle Atlantic states, where over 240 groups have protected over 60 percent of the national total of 675,000 acres. Organizing at a national rate of 20 per year since 1975, the West Coast, Rocky Mountain and Plains states have shown the most dramatic increase in organizations since then.

Defined now by the first systematic survey of their activities, LLCOs form a multi-faceted group. The land's ability to sustain diversity in nature is being mirrored in the diversity of those 400 groups dedicated to its conservation. LLCOs preserve land for food and shelter; land for wildlife, plants, and people; land for water quality, soil conservation, and water quantity; land to satisfy visual sensibilities and physical needs; land to learn from, to play on, and land to dream on—prairies, dunes, deserts, and coastlines, marshes, rivers, and flood plains; land for folks rich and poor, urban, suburban, and rural; and land for land's sake.

The diversity of LLCOs is their greatest strength because that diversity arises from the special local conditions of the land that surrounds each group. While safeguarding natural resources for the future, LLCOs can monitor land resources and can creatively and flexibly organize local action when a threat to the environment is perceived. Forming in response to just such local needs, data in the survey demonstrates that groups most often preserve land for wildlife habitat; scenic and recreational enjoyment; and wetland, watershed, and coastal areas. Preserving dwindling farmland has been highlighted more recently and is a priority of more than a third of the groups responding to the survey.

Financial difficulties were cited as the principal problem for LLCOs by a three-to-one margin. More than half the LLCOs have budgets of $5,000 or less and have saved less than 11 percent of the total acreage preserved by all LLCOs. This confirms the finding of the Consultation that development of organizational capacity is a critical need for these groups. Most respondents to the questionnaire simply cited lack of money as the problem, but a few pointed to specific causes of distress like the demise of the Land and Water Conservation Fund, or the skyrocketing price of land in coastal zones and certain areas of the West, or the general state of the economy. Often noted was the pressure of reconciling large goals with limited time and resources—"We're just doing the best we can in our small area, with no resources to speak of." A common attitude was that without money you can't save land; many were not aware of alternative land protection techniques. It is astonishing that many do not now actively solicit donations of land.

LLCOs indicated that many had tried a variety of money-making ventures, ranging from annual dinners, bird-a-thons, and boat races to bluegrass concerts and pig roasts. T-shirt sales have been surprisingly lucrative, as have native plant and shrub sales. An adopt-a-tree program in Alabama raised $12,000 in six weeks to pay the down payment on a threatened property. Direct solicitation, limited development schemes, sale of publications, technical services, and promotional films to present their stories have raised substantial funds. A mail-order business of desert ceramics and jewelry netted the Desert Tortoise Preserve $59,000. All of the above demonstrate an ability to use local customs and needs to raise enough money to maintain self-sufficiency, but, in general, lack the high return that might be expected from more professionally assisted and planned efforts.

Many sounded overworked in their battle to preserve land. Frustrated by the lack of continuing administrative staff and yearning for even greater volunteer participation, the all-volunteer groups were discouraged by their inability to afford paid staff. This again corroborates the Consultation findings on the need to build organizational capacity. Perhaps because board members tend to volunteer for other causes, some groups expressed a need for more education of their boards on complex land conservation issues. As one New Hampshire group put it, "All-volunteer organizations need a hard-charging driver." Although embattled, there was frequent attestation to their overriding enthusiasm, conviction, and willingness to persevere.

The indifference and, occasionally, the hostility of the public to land conservation efforts were a problem for many. The public's general lack of understanding of the values of land preservation as well as its failure to grasp the specific tax benefits seemed to frustrate a number of groups. This underscores the Consultation's awareness that a more effective public information delivery system is needed. For some, interaction with "short-sighted," "bickering" local officials and their "love affair with developers" has been more difficult than relationships with state and federal representatives. Apart from current tax issues, however, federal policy can be a problem for local conservation, for example, in Louisiana, where flood plains and wetlands are reclaimed; and in Alaska, where control of much land by native corporations and the federal government are described as hampering local efforts.

General development pressures, inability to compete with developers, and a shrinking supply of available open space seem of special concern to groups in areas of high population concentration in states such as California, Connecticut, Illinois, New Jersey, and New York. Surprisingly, only a few LLCOs mentioned specific land management problems such as vandalism or control of erosion.

In sum, then, lack of money, staff, and support from the public and local officials were the four most common problems, summarized by a Pennsylvania group as "money, apathy, staffing—same old thing."

Comments received during the survey revealed that most LLCOs were surprised and heartened to discover so many other similar organizations operating near their own area and across the country. While many had been assisted by national conservation groups, including The Nature Conservancy, the Trust for Public Land, the National Trust, and Audubon societies, many were unaware of activities by many smaller and medium-sized LLCOs.

In all, over 1,000 organizations were polled in the survey conducted by telephone and questionnaire by two interns from the Environmental Intern Program.[1] By the end of 1981, 660 had responded, reflecting a healthy rate of response. Based on follow-up phone inquiries and polling of an additional 400 secondary sources, it is estimated that the 400 LLCOs confirmed so far constitute at least four-fifths of those that exist. Documentation of LLCOs is continuing; another 50 "good leads" presently await confirmation at presstime.

---

1. The survey, funded by the Lincoln Institute of Land Policy and others, was made during the summer of 1981 by Russell Cohen and Terry Bremer, interns in the Environmental Intern Program. (EIP places college graduates and upper-level undergraduates in energy and environmental projects for sponsors in the private, public, and nonprofit sectors.) Results of the survey are in the *1981 National Directory of Local Land Conservation Organizations,* published by the Land Trust Exchange.

GROWTH OF LOCAL LAND CONSERVATION ORGANIZATIONS

Through 1964 (95 groups).

1965 through 1975 (173 groups).

1976 through 1981 (136 groups).

All confirmed groups as of 1/1/1982 (404).

STRATEGIES
and TACTICS

High interest rates, sustained inflation, loss of federal sources of funding and changing national tax policies are causing considerable uncertainty regarding a number of aspects of local land-saving activity. The situation presents new opportunities at the same time that it threatens the land trust movement. The only certainty is that land conservation organizations must recognize that changes are taking place and adjust and respond to them.

Land has become a favored investment for individuals and corporations seeking alternatives to the volatile money market and the stagnant securities market. In many parts of the country, agricultural and forest lands are selling to speculators at well above their resource value. On the other hand, there is a buyer's market for land in some areas as large tract owners find potential purchasers scarce. For land trusts seeking to compete with speculators or capitalize on bargains, the problem is the same: finding funds.

For organizations that have depended either on their own use of Land and Water Conservation Fund grants or on public agency use of LWCF money, the loss of this federal source is crippling. The fiscal condition of many state and local governments has left them unable to buy conservation and recreation lands. Borrowing by private trusts often adds prohibitive costs to property purchases. In this situation, the development of innovative financing strategies is a vital concern of land-saving organizations.

In the longer run, the impact of federal income and estate tax reductions is in question. On the one hand, tax benefit incentives for charitable gifts by the affluent has been greatly reduced, but, on the other hand, they have more disposable income to donate. Property gifts and bequests will definitely be less financially beneficial when the full tax cut program takes effect.

However, for those who wish to see their properties preserved in perpetuity, the expectation of purchase and management by either a public or private entity is becoming increasingly unrealistic. Not only are recipient organizations obliged to insist on the property being donated, but many also require that management be provided. Land management is costly and management expenses must be taken into consideration when a land trust intends to acquire property to hold permanently. The clash of public uses and preservation objectives must be dealt with by some form of control and enforcement. Unless adequate professional staff and financial resources are available, trusts accept management responsibility at great risk.

As the costs and problems of acquiring and managing properties escalate, land trusts are seeking alternative ways of preserving land resources and environmental value. Securing protective restrictions in lieu of outright purchase achieves conservation objectives at lower initial cost and at minimal or at least greatly reduced management expense, although monitoring for compliance with easement conditions is essential. When such restrictions are donated, the property owner retains use and enjoyment of his property and reaps tax benefits. However, current uncertainty over the federal tax treatment of gifts of easements has clouded the future prospects of this important source of open space protection.

Conservation groups are becoming increasingly alert to opportunities to preserve significant natural and scenic areas through influencing public bodies to require developers to leave such areas undisturbed as a condition of planning or zoning approval. In some cases, organizations are negotiating directly with developers to work out plans that assure that projects will meet both economic and environmental objectives. Groups are also offering planning and management assistance to local governments that lack professional staffs competent to protect natural assets and environmental quality.

In the community, generating awareness of the need for conservation action and building confidence among community leaders is imperative. Cooperation with local officials, lawyers, real estate dealers, and bankers must be cultivated. If agricultural land retention is a principal objective, the farming community must be persuaded that its interests are served. Compelling economic arguments for preserving amenity, environmental, and other open space values must be convincingly developed.

While it is essential for local land-saving organizations to clearly articulate their purposes, policies, and procedures, they must also have the ability to respond to changing realities, new opportunities, and sudden crises. Experience may dictate a modification of objectives and criteria. The flexibility to be opportunistic in the face of unexpected events is essential. The mechanics for adaptation to change must be provided in organizational procedures.

CHANGING ECONOMICS of LAND CONSERVATION
Thomas Schmidt

The most significant recent economic change for Western Pennsylvania Conservancy has been the effective abolition of the federal government's Land and Water Conservation Fund (LWCF), the main source of the "take-out" money for our revolving land purchase fund. As we are unwilling to spend land purchase revolving funds unless there is an assured take-out, our direct land acquisition will be limited to small natural areas and purchases for those state agencies that can reimburse us from hunting and fishing license fees and oil and gas royalties.

Because of inflation and high interest rates, there now exists a buyer's market in real estate, especially in large tracts of land (exceptions in this area are purchases for oil, gas, coal, and timber). At the same time, inflation continues to eat away at our land purchase and endowment funds at a rate of more than 10 percent per year. Consequently, our finance committee is considering taking a portion of these funds, which would normally be invested in bonds, and purchasing one or more large scenic tracts suitable for recreation near population centers at their current, depressed market prices. These tracts can be held until interest rates decline and pent-up demand for housing and real estate again becomes effective, perhaps in several years. At this point if government take-out funds are available, the land can be permanently dedicated to scenic and recreational uses. Otherwise, it can be sold and the proceeds devoted to conservation purposes.

"Cheap" ways of acquiring and holding land, given the lack of LWCF take-out funds, are being utilized. We may rely increasingly on easements and deed restrictions. New regulations that penalize donors of easements for making valuation overstatements will discourage some gifts. However, somewhat to our surprise, we have found that local governments are willing to "adopt" some of our easement programs into their own "clearly delineated conservation policies," thus making deductions more easily available for the preservation of open space.

We feel that land exchanges will become more useful given the changing economics of land conservation. Swaps enable companies to exchange, without tax, nonproductive real estate that has conservation value for economically productive land. Recently, Western Pennsylvania Conservancy gained extensive scenic river frontage in exchange for selective timber cutting rights for a seventy-five-year term on Conservancy property located outside the scenic river corridor. Another example, where this Conservancy has a role, is the exchange between a national forest and a major timber company involving 25,000 acres of timber lands. This exchange will permit the national forest to consolidate its holdings for better management. The main problem is the 2 percent Pennsylvania real estate transfer tax on the $12 million of value, which amounts to $240,000. We are working in the Legislature to amend the law to exempt government or nonprofit parties where the exchange is for conservation purposes.

We are working with oil, gas, coal, and mineral companies to obtain natural surface lands for public recreation. When natural gas is deregulated, gas company profits should soar. Donations of surface for public recreation will then be useful to them for tax credits, particularly since the Economic Recovery Act of 1981 increases the ceiling for deductions for charitable purposes from 5 percent of taxable corporate income to 10 percent.

Another possibility we are investigating is the preservation of farmland in scenic easement areas. Individuals with money available for investment have approached us saying that they would be willing to buy working farms and subject them to permanent agricultural easements. They feel that the tax deduction coupled with future appreciation in the value of farmland, together with the reservation of several home sites, will provide a profitable investment as well as conservation benefits.

The changing economics of land conservation are thus forcing us to seek cheaper ways to acquire and hold land. In the meantime, the funds that we would normally revolve with LWCF take-out money will be invested. Some of the income must be reinvested to counteract the effects of inflation. We plan to spend some of the balance in areas that will only indirectly affect land conservation. Three of these areas are computerization of natural area inventories, environmental education, and mediation. We have been requested to mediate land disputes between government and industry because we have maintained credibility in each camp. To the extent that we can do more of this for a fee, we feel that we can further the wise use of land without depleting our hard-raised land revolving funds.

Another area where the economics of land conservation is changing is fund raising. We have put more effort into increasing membership this year. Sales of conservation-related literature and clothing merchandise with a conservation message have also increased in our gift shop. We are not sure how tax rate reductions will affect contributions. People should have more income to spend, but with the highest bracket being reduced from 70 percent to 50 percent there may be less incentive for higher-bracket taxpayers to give. Perhaps the biggest negative impact of the tax changes will be in estate planning, where there will be less incentive for gifts of land to reduce estate taxes. However, despite a difficult economy, we have received increasing income from our year-end fund drive in each of the past four years. With the interest and concern for the best of our natural heritage, we expect that land conservation will remain a popular charitable cause in this area for the foreseeable future.

ECONOMIC PERSPECTIVES on LAND CONSERVATION
Barbara Rusmore

Before talking about the economics of land conservation, one must have a sense of the economic functions of primarily undeveloped land. It is often said about land that they aren't making any more of it. The market is currently responding to this ageless maxim as it does with scarce commodities. The price is rising above that justified by the cash-flow productivity of the property, and people are buying land for speculation, betting on continuing appreciation. It is a gamble, and the land price bubble has popped before, but for now people seem to think that land speculation, particularly in undeveloped land, is one of the better games in town. In the last ten years, appreciation rates in agricultural land have certainly supported this position.

Who are the people buying land? They either have substantial wealth and/or a favorable borrowing capacity. Often they are interested in its investment value. Sometimes they are major corporations diversifying their investments. Agricultural operators wishing to expand their farms can often refinance their old places incorporating or spreading the debt of the new places over the old, thereby lowering the per acre carrying cost to an affordable level.

This brings up the point of who can afford to own land of any substantial size. At the risk of being obvious, one must either have outside income to support the land debt load and operating financing or be able to make enough from a productive land-based enterprise. With today's high finance rates and low agricultural commodity prices, landowners can frequently find themselves between a rock and a hard place. What this all means is that if you haven't got land already and you don't have substantial wealth, you most likely will not be able to buy land.

The land conservation movement is also aware that this land base is all we have but is responding with a fundamentally different perspective. Rather than seeing land as a speculative commodity to be bought and sold, for the conservationist land has intrinsic value. The joy, the awe, and the mystery of the natural world do not translate easily into today's marketplace. Stewardship and renewable productivity are concepts that can be approached in economic terms, but they do not compare favorably with the finances of most other land uses. The marketplace is just not set up to encourage land conservation; but nobody said it was going to be any easy task.

Dismal as the picture may seem, the public does recognize conservation values. Parks are established and national forest management plans consider conservation values. The government recognizes conservation groups as working in the public good and grants them nonprofit status. Donations of land for conservation purposes are considered as charitable gifts and can create sizable tax savings for landowners. Furthermore, many of the people who own or buy land do so because they appreciate its intrinsic amenity value as well as the financial benefits. By working with these people, the land conservation movement builds a bridge between their goals and the marketplace, over which much has been done in the last fifty years to preserve our national heritage.

The economics of land conservation are currently undergoing some changes. In the past, much of the activity in land conservation centered on moving land from the private sector into governmental ownership and on classifying public lands into protected status (national parks, wilderness and primitive areas, monuments, etc.). In the present state of tightening public budgets, money for land acquisition is rapidly drying up and resource development of public lands is receiving federal encouragement. Leaving the issue of struggle over public land management aside, the strategies of the land conservation movement are adapting accordingly as they look increasingly to the private sector for support and action.

The private sector is proving to be a formidable ally. Most of the land in the United States is in private hands, and given the moral inclination and encouraged by tax incentives, some of these owners are committing their properties to conservation purposes. We are just beginning to see the potential of this approach. National organizations such as The Nature Conservancy and the Trust for Public Land have been leaders in this field. The small local organizations are beginning to successfully adapt some of these techniques, such as conservation easements and partial development to their low-budget operations. Some of the newer directions are incorporating the speculative buyers of land into land conservation transactions and being able to offer them tax incentives in return for lower returns on their investment. As creative minds in the financial, real estate, tax, and conservation fields explore the potentials of private action for land conservation, more techniques will begin to evolve. It is a sometimes tenuous business to draw together private enterprise financial goals and land conservation values, but it is a challenge for the conservationist with great rewards.

RESOURCE CONSERVATION:
Make It Economical
Jan W. McClure

Our best teacher is often history. Turning to the Forest Society's "history book," a publication called *New Hampshire Everlasting and Unfallen*, I found an apt quote. In a caption to a faded picture of a Congregationalist minister and staunch Forest Society supporter in the early part of the century, the author quotes the aging character, "It is easy to see, on mere economical grounds, that the destruction of forests has been the ruin of many a nation which did not have wisdom enough to keep them."

The economics of resource protection in all its aspects are perhaps even more important today than they were eighty years ago when my organization was in its infancy. The driving force behind the Forest Society's beginnings was protection of the White Mountains, which were systematically being stripped of all their timber by six lumber companies. With the passage of the Weeks Act in 1911, the White Mountain National Forest was established, and the Forest Society redirected its energies to fire protection, establishment of a state forestry department and nursery, and legislation providing equitable forest land taxation.

Notable scenic landmarks like Mount Monadnock, Crawford Notch, a dramatic gorge, and a stand of primeval pines were acquired in the early years. Land protection, legislative, and educational efforts have continued and expanded, ranging from conservation camps for teenagers and teachers to twenty-year-long negotiations to keep an interstate out of scenic and historic Franconia Notch.

The common thread of all these efforts and the reason for their success, I believe, has been a commitment to wise and *economic* use of our natural resources. Certainly, there are occasional strictly altruistic situations, but by and large resource protection must be economical for it to work. And if we, the professionals, are going to be able to sell our ideas, we must prove their economic value.

Federal tax incentives have been a tremendous help, but there are other economic advantages worth publicizing. For example, protected undeveloped areas do not require increased community services and can increase the value of adjacent lands; both results enhance the local tax climate.

There are some other more fundamental advantages. Protecting farmland and forest land for long-term management makes economic sense, in two more immediate ways. First, resource management is a source of income for the landowner who donates his/her time, money, and energy; and second, the fruits of his/her labor are food, fiber, energy, social and economic health, recreational opportunities, and scenic beauty for society—the average John Doe on the street.

We are not "saving land for its useless beauty"; we are protecting resources on which our very life depends.

Lest we become a "ruined nation" lacking the wisdom to keep our resources, as the minister in my history book warned, conservation work must continue to develop and promote protection techniques that make economic as well as social and environmental sense.

HOW ARE LAND-SAVING DECISIONS MADE?
Establishing Criteria, Keeping Priorities
Samuel W. Morris

Quite commonly land conservation organizations originate out of a crisis—some particular piece of open space is about to be lost to development or a historic site is on the verge of being demolished. So it was in the case of our French and Pickering Trust. In 1967, a 100-acre farm adjacent to French Creek was about to be sold to a developer and peopled with houses. This became the catalyst that started the Trust.

This crisis was overcome and the land saved, not without considerable effort. The Trust purchased the farm with help from the Philadelphia Conservationists and a number of local donors, plus a purchase money mortgage from the sympathetic owner on generous terms. Then we realized that if the organization was to become more than just a one-project affair, plans had to be made for extending and enlarging its program. Purposes and goals had to be defined, an area of operations delimited, and methods or techniques developed for achieving the goals that had been adopted.

Within the year we were helped on our way by another crisis. Another 100 acres on French Creek, this time adjoining a county park, came on the market. The county park board wanted the land, but the county government could not move quickly enough, so upon request by some members of the park board we moved in. Again, the owner was sympathetic, but he did want cash. The Trust's purchase was finalized over the telephone for the same amount offered by developers just ten minutes before they arrived with a check for the down money.

We then set out to raise the funds to complete settlement, in which we were again successful because of generous loans from the Philadelphia Conservationists and The Nature Conservancy, a gift from one kind supporter and a loan from another. We have never forgotten the help we got on this occasion.

My reason for dwelling on the experiences of our own organization is that they are concrete examples of the points I am trying to make about planning and priorities, how they are developed, and the direction an organization's goals may take.

After our first purchase, we worked out our basic objectives and the conservation techniques we hoped to use. We wanted to establish green belts in the watersheds of our two creeks, thus preserving water quality and quantity by saving the flood plains and wooded hillsides. At the same time scenic panoramas and farmlands could also be preserved. We decided to fill in the areas of our concern as best we could with separate acquisitions by purchase or gift of properties in fee simple and by open space easements. These were the primary techniques we agreed on.

Since part of the area is highly significant historically, being the seat of much of the colonial Pennsylvania iron industry, historical preservation became another of our objectives. Our technique for this aspect of the work was to catalogue as many historic structures in the area as possible and to register these on the state and national registers.

Our easement program was started with a large conference in 1974 that resulted in an opportunity to work out plans for open space conservation with several individual landowners in the Pickering Valley. This effort was subsequently expanded by the publication of a preservation report addressed to all landowners within three townships in the Pickering watershed and also to the governing bodies of those townships. Over the succeeding years this report has helped to preserve many acres in the Pickering.

We have had numerous other crises on both creeks like the first two with key properties coming on the market, some requiring purchases at public auction, and struggles to finance these acquisitions. We early came to realize that these crises were actually opportunities. Each one not only helped to fill in the green belt concept, but increased our experience and capability in dealing with private and governmental financial sources and creative financing in general. These events also brought us into contact with more and more of the people of our area, for whom we were really working, and with helpful government officials. Even more important, each experience raised our confidence and increased our faith and our courage to take financial risks before having complete assurance that funding would be forthcoming.

Therefore, I would submit that while establishing criteria and setting priorities is extremely important in the land-saving "business," it is really the area of operations itself, plus the crises or opportunities that arise, that provide the way and shape the directions a conservation organization must take. In our case the existence of public parks—the Chester County Park already mentioned, Hopewell Village National Historic Site and French Creek State Park at the western end of French Creek, and Valley Forge Park to the east of our area—provided limits or anchors to which our work could be attached. At the same time they have provided us with some of our great opportunities. Since the first 100 acres was added to our county park, we have been responsible for transferring an additional 135 acres to areas held by the county park, and we are well along to establishing a 9-mile hiking and riding trail along French Creek with both public and private support (the latter through gifts of scenic and right of way easements). At the moment we are participating in a 500-acre addition to French Creek State Park.

There are other factors, too, that help shape conservation planning, criteria, and priorities. I have mentioned the preservation desires of individual landowners. Financing needs in general also provide a planning stimulus. Without a coherent general plan and the establishment of some definite plan of action, together with criteria and priorities, it is difficult to gain support. However, "nothing succeeds like success," and the crisis properties acquired fill in the gaps and provide shape to the general picture of an organization's endeavors, thus inspiring public confidence.

Another factor that is important in shaping the general conservation plans of an organization is to be found in the interests of the individual people and groups with which it works. We have numerous examples. The fishermen who use French Creek have been most helpful. Without the support of trail riders' and hikers' organizations our present efforts could not have been so successful. This factor works both ways. Each of these groups has helped to shape our priorities and each in itself was a target of opportunity. The same is true of the historical aspect of our work. The historic significance of the Trust's area of operation plus the historical bent of its founders led to the addition of historical preservation as a Trust objective. This aspect of our work has led to a whole constituency of devoted history buffs and the recruiting of an army of volunteers to help in the work of cataloguing and registering historic sites, as well as considerable financial support, from both private and public sources.

To sum up then, by all means make plans, set criteria and priorities—a conservation program must have form. But never let that form become hidebound. Keep in mind that it is the crises that bring the opportunities. Also never forget that once the land is lost, it is lost forever.

THE GROWING IMPORTANCE of PRIVATE LOCAL ACTIVITY in FARMLAND PRESERVATION

Jennie Gerard

Farmland preservation wouldn't happen without private local activity. It's as important and as simple as that.

Private and *local* are words close to the heart and soul of the American farmer. For the most part, land-based farmers will be suspicious of institutions or persons that appear to be meddling in their affairs.

THE GROWING IMPORTANCE of PRIVATE LOCAL ACTIVITY in FARMLAND PRESERVATION

Farmers need each other and a local and regional service network for their economic survival. If the farmer down the road goes under, then that's one less customer for the tractor repair service, one less member of the farm bureau, and so on. If the agricultural services move out of the area, the farmer is handicapped—sooner or later his costs will go up too far because of it. They can't depend on advertising or a marketing strategy to bail them out—they depend on each other.

In preservation of agricultural land, it is this farm community that must be dealt with. There is no such thing as dealing with just one farmer. If the agricultural base of a valley is threatened, it will take the cooperation of all the landowners.

In December of 1978 when the Trust for Public Land's agricultural land trust efforts were just beginning, a dairy wife and a conservationist from Marin County, California, came to talk to me about preserving the dairy ranches in west Marin. Marin County has a reputation for peacock feathers and hot tubs to many, but the western part of the county is rural in character with dairy ranches spread out across the gently rolling coastal hills. A. P. Giannini opened one of the early offices of the Bank of Italy, later known as the Bank of America, in Tomales in west Marin to serve the farmers there.

Ellen Straus is herself a rancher or a ranch wife as she might be likely to say, who had the foresight to recognize the threat of urban encroachment in west Marin and its effect on the dairy industry. Her partner in concern was Phyllis Faber, a biologist and prime mover behind the Marin Conservation League. They wanted to establish a land trust and came complete with a recommended list for its initial board of directors that included every notable, liberal lawyer and progressive pursuer of the public interest that could be found in Marin. Their approach was a logical place to begin. Certainly that kind of support and endorsement is characteristic of, and in many cases necessary to, other successful preservation efforts. But I had to tell them that for what they wanted to do, it wouldn't work. They needed involvement and support of the dairy ranchers whose land they wanted to save. They needed dedicated volunteers from the agricultural community who were willing to serve and *work* on the board of directors: individuals who were willing to struggle with a new concept, educate themselves on how to make it work for them, and see it through the process of incorporation to a successful land trust.

They went back and they got them: the endorsement of the Marin County Farm Bureau. I am pleased to say that the Marin County Land Trust was incorporated last year.

In June of 1981 I ran into Hank Korda, the newly elected president of the Marin County Farm Bureau, who had an exciting story to tell me. It was about Marin County's new agricultural land trust. To me this was symbolic of success. It signified that the Marin County farmers had embraced the idea as their own, and from their enthusiasm had created the land trust. The Marin County Land Trust is now negotiating its first projects.

This kind of private and local participation and endorsement is essential. Agricultural preservation will not come about without protecting the farming community, their interests, and economy. The farmers themselves can do this better than anyone, and therefore their involvement and support of preservation efforts will ensure its success.

LAND-SAVING DECISIONS in SONOMA and NAPA COUNTIES, CALIFORNIA
Joan Vilms

LAND-SAVING CRITERIA

Local land trusts are able to maintain close contact with the communities they serve and the resources they protect. This "keeping in touch" enables them to move quickly and to keep their policies flexible.

Most land-saving decisions are made on a case-by-case basis, using three fundamental criteria: (1) local resource value, (2) long-term public benefit, and (3) tangible community support. Other considerations include: practicability, revenue generating prospects, expansion potential, and clear title.

Typically, projects come to our attention either directly through landowner contact or indirectly through referrals from a variety of sources. Most projects that meet the above criteria make it to the "active" file. Of those, the few that reach the "resolution of acceptance" stage in any given year are generally accepted.

Often the exception is more instructive than the rule. Consider this synopsis of a rejected project: In 1978, Sonoma Land Trust was offered a gift of 11 acres of riparian corridor and beach frontage along the Russian River. The land had significant resource value, definite public value, and resource expansion potential across the river. After considerable debate, the board of trustees refused the offer for the following reasons: lack of financial or volunteer support from neighborhood associations, lack of endowment from owners, and "attractive nuisance" liability (drownings, diving injuries). Being on insecure financial footing at the time, the trustees didn't want to risk accepting a project that appeared to be a financial and administrative burden. Although the land could have benefited from habitat enhancement, it was a bit of a hot potato, having achieved notoriety in local and Bay Area newspapers as a nude beach.

LAND-SAVING DILEMMA

The land-saving decisions currently generating the most controversy are those involving (1) partial development—conservation restrictions plus limited development potential—and (2) development trade-offs—major subdivision, usually cluster-type, granted go-ahead in exchange for easement dedication.

LAND-SAVING DECISIONS in SONOMA and NAPA COUNTIES, CALIFORNIA

An Example of Partial Development, Napa County:

Scenario: Wealthy landowner wants to subdivide 420-acre parcel and place conservation easement. (CE) over ridgeland forest and meadows. Has requested Napa County Land Trust to approve CE concept and configuration of 3-lot subdivision (negotiated downward from 5 lots) before proceeding with subdivision application.

Total acreage: 420

Proposed CE: 260 acres total

    1. 150-acre parcel with 1 potential home site.
    2. 60 acres of 100-acre parcel, no home sites on easement, some off.
    3. 50 acres of 170-acre parcel, no home sites on easement, some off.

Land is located on uplands of municipal reservoir (Lake Hennesey) and has wildlife, watershed, and scenic resource value. Easement could be divided into a maximum of 3 ownerships, with 1 potential home site on total easement area. Trustees concerned about future development on land not encumbered by easement. They recognize resource value but don't want to be seen as setting aside private enclaves for the rich. Should they vote to accept or reject?

An Example of Development Trade-offs, Sonoma County:

Scenario: First landowner divides 167-acre parcel into 4 parcels (25, 28, 95, 19 acres). He sells 25-acre parcel, keeps others. Then he applies for 3-lot subdivision on 28-acre parcel. Neighbors object and hire attorney. Attorney suggests mitigating scenic impacts and limiting future development by granting restrictive easements to Sonoma Land Trust.

Development proposal: Subdivide 28-acre parcel into 3 lots.

Mitigation: 1. CE for scenic purposes over 28-acre upland parcel, with 3 home sites.
    2. 20-year open space easement over 95-acre ranch parcel, with 1 home.
    3. CE over 19-acre river and marshland parcel, no development.
       (Note: In California CEs must be granted in perpetuity; open space easements may be granted for a term of years.)

Land is located on highly visible slope of rolling grasslands, surrounded by ranches, with cattle grazing and oat hay cultivation predominant land use. Even small amount of development has heavy impact on relatively undeveloped resource lands. Since neighbors, county board of supervisors, and landowner all agreed to mitigation, Sonoma Land Trust accepted easements.

A Hypothetical Example of Development Trade-offs:

Proposal: 525 acres total. (Surrounded by agricultural preserve.)
34 units clustered on 125 acres.
Restrictive easement over 400-acre residual with provisions for main house, guest house, outbuildings, vineyard, and horse ranch.

County approves project after much public controversy. Landowner wants to grant easement to Land Trust before selling to developer.

Land trust concerns: 1. That landowner will try to claim charitable deduction even though there is strong evidence of *quid pro quo* transaction.
2. That LT will be criticized for participating in project considered by many to be more destructive of resources than protective.
3. That if LT doesn't cooperate, easement will go to county and, according to state law, be subject to challenge by petition for abandonment sometime in the future.
4. That, in some cases, trading off development now for permanent future protection has merit.
5. That, in other cases, such trade-offs might well result in more harm than good by introducing development pressures and residential conflicts into relatively undeveloped resource areas.

To date, both Sonoma Land Trust and Napa County Land Trust have accepted easements involving partial development. Only Sonoma has accepted easements involving "small-scale" development trade-offs, as previously cited.

Will both land trusts continue to stay behind the scenes and play it "safe"? Or will they be forced, either by public pressure or their own principles, to take a stand in the brewing controversy?

CONSERVATION EASEMENTS:
Two Problems Needing Attention
Benjamin R. Emory

Two critical conservation easement problems in Maine, and almost certainly elsewhere, are (1) weak public support for easements and (2) ineffective monitoring of properties protected by easements.

WEAK PUBLIC SUPPORT

There is real need for better public education about the benefits and technicalities of conservation easements. Not only should easement programs do all they can in their home territories, but a coordinated, national education effort should be considered.

The public finds conservation easements difficult to understand. Misconceptions have significantly contributed to widespread public apathy and opposition. Even in the absence of misconceptions, the public benefits of conservation easements can be subtle. Many people believe that unless an easement authorizes public use of the property, there is no public benefit.

Local control and individual rights are strong traditions in New England and elsewhere, and some people view conservation easements as contrary to these traditions. A town may not take kindly to having a state or federal agency gain a say in the amount of development allowed on a particular property, and many people believe that it is unfair for a landowner to tie the hands of future owners.

Most frequently at the root of opposition to conservation easements has been the fear of erosion of the property tax base. If one taxpayer's taxes are reduced everyone else must make up the difference. The person with nothing extra resents the assumed additional tax burden.

Public apathy and opposition discourage landowners and intimidate recipient agencies, particularly governmental ones. Landowners and bureaucrats alike shy from initiating controversy, and too many bureaucrats lack the vision to comprehend what can be accomplished with conservation easements.

INEFFECTIVE MONITORING

Ineffective monitoring of existing easements could prove to be the Achilles heel that nullifies all the effort to date. Recently, a major conservation organization has learned from a midwestern landowner that a timber company, without the owner's knowledge and in violation of an easement held by the conservation organization, has stripped the timber off 400 acres of a 1,200-acre property. The conservation organization's current staff did not even know about the easement.

To find out the status of monitoring in Maine, Maine Coast Heritage Trust in 1980 mailed a questionnaire to all agencies holding conservation easements. All four federal and state agencies indicated that they have monitoring programs. Only three of the nine towns and two of the five nonprofit organizations responding said that they have a monitoring program.

The effectiveness of some monitoring programs seems questionable. A federal agency with a monitoring program never noticed in the eight years after an easement was granted that the easement failed to list among the existing and permitted structures on the property a guest-house that has stood for many years.

Supposedly, conservation easements run in perpetuity. Failure to monitor and enforce an easement could cause a court to rule it legally abandoned. Conservation easement programs must devote more attention to assuring as well as possible that effective monitoring will be maintained as years and generations go by.

DONATED EASEMENTS:
Problems and Possible Solutions
Robert T. Dennis

As this is written, there is one central obstacle threatening the future of programs built around the donated conservation easement. That obstacle, of course, is the absence of even draft regulations by which 1980 changes in the federal Tax Code will be implemented—as well as uncertainty about the nature of the final regulations. Already, in my own state of Virginia, easements granting protection to 11,000 acres are stuck in the pipeline. Clearly, regulatory problems could virtually eliminate the donated easement as a landscape conservation tool.

Leaks and rumors of the moment suggest that, under the new regulations, it will no longer be left to easement-accepting organizations and agencies to determine which easements are and are not in the public interest. In the worst case, such determination will be made by the Treasury Department on an individual basis. Probably the best we can hope for is certification by some federal or state resource agency (e.g., Secretary Watt's Department of the Interior) that easements in a particular geographic area or under a particular program are in the public interest—and therefore assuredly tax-deductible. In either case, we will need to develop new strategies for justifying easements and for maintaining the confidence of would-be donors.

Beyond that—until new regulations are issued, at least in draft form—it is almost presumptuous to discuss issues relating to donated easements.

However, assuming our ultimate success in handling the regulatory situation, it seems likely that we will still be left to deal with the basic problems that roused the Treasury's concern in the first place. Other than the question of "tax expenditures," which is a philosophical issue related to the whole U.S. tax structure and not a topic of discussion here, there appear to be three such problems: (1) easement administration and enforcement, (2) evaluation of easements, and (3) equity.

ADMINISTRATION/ENFORCEMENT

As the easement concept has gained acceptance, and as easement programs have proliferated, it is both logical and proper that people not familiar with either the concept or the programs question how easements are supervised and enforced. In short, do donors and subsequent owners of the property really—over the long run—respect the restrictions for which tax benefits were claimed?

I cannot fairly give an affirmative answer to that question even for my own neighborhood, simply because an answer probably requires fifty years hindsight with respect to both donor and successors, and donee and successors. And I confess to having read an easement or two donated outside Virginia that left me wondering about enforceability. At any rate, there are at least four short-run responses to the enforcement question.

1.   Every easement-accepting organization should adopt formal written policy and procedures for monitoring its easements, including annual visits, use of air photos, and the like. To make a clear record, it may be desirable that each easement document include information on monitoring techniques.

2.   Easements that clearly restrict subdivision of property are to a great extent self-enforcing. Inappropriate land uses are less likely on large tracts, and the title search will scare off those who would purchase a parcel for such uses.

3.   We should stress that in the usual case of easements being sought on a block of properties owned by different people, each easement is monitored by adjacent owners. For example, when one Virginia donor began deep-tilling easement-covered land preparatory to installing a vineyard, a neighbor quickly telephoned the donee Virginia Outdoors Foundation to report a "strip mine"—of course a nonpermitted use.

4.   Effort should be made to keep out of easements restrictions on actions that can only be detected by full-time presence on the covered property, for example, prohibition against trail bikes or snowmobiles. In short, provisions in one easement document that cannot readily be monitored or enforced can lead to questions about the validity of an entire program.

EVALUATION

Probably the most difficult issue we face, the issue perhaps at the root of Treasury/IRS concern about easements, is that of easement valuation. My own feeling is that Congress might best set an evaluation policy to carry us until we have the benefit of more of the hindsight factor.

We all know that certain federal resource managing agencies—the Forest Service and National Park Service—purchase conservation easements from private landowners in congressionally designated areas (e.g., Sawtooth National Recreation Area, St. Croix National Scenic Riverway, Appalachian Trail). Appraisal practices for purchased easements are fairly uniform, and often demonstrate values falling in the range of 60-30 percent of fair market value of the land. In the case of donated easements, however, the Internal Revenue Service appears likely to challenge appraisals at that level. During 1980, for example, the IRS argued for a time that two easement donations in Virginia had no value at all, even though they were similar in terms to nearby Appalachian Trail easements purchased by the National Park Service. The result has been to create economic uncertainties for potential easement donors and consequently to hamper easement projects that rely on voluntary participation by landowners.

Below is a graph that presents my own theory about the problems inherent in appraising partial rights in land.

Explanation of Graph

1. The first person in an "easement project area" to donate or sell an easement gives up a large percent of the value of his land. No one else may follow his lead, and he may end up holding an almost unmarketable property. He has reduced his land to its use value. National Park Service and U.S. Forest Service appraisal policies (reinforced by court actions?) almost require that easements be appraised at point A, which accounts for easement purchases in the range of 60-80 percent of fair market value.

But, as soon as A's neighbor gives or sells an easement, the value of A's land is somewhat enhanced. The neighbor's easement is "less valuable" than A's.

2. By the time several owners have given or sold easements so as to form a "cluster," they have created a scarce resource—properties in a "protected zone." In the area of point B, easement-protected properties totally surrounded by other protected properties may even be more valuable than nearby unencumbered properties. (In the nor-

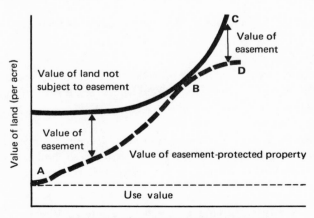

Percentage of land area subject to protection

mal scheme of things, some land developers accomplish a similar result by selling houses subject to covenants.) I believe the IRS tends to look at point B when it evaluates appraisals of tax deductions on *donated easements.*

I'm not aware of any easement project area that has progressed beyond point B. Clearly, however, as less and less unrestricted property remains, its value increases. And probably the value of restricted property diminishes as more than enough becomes available to meet the demands of willing buyers.

3.   The last person to sell or give up his development rights in a protection area ("the last potential condominium site surrounded by Jackson Hole perpetual ranches") relinquishes an enormous value.

4.   It is even conceivable that once all properties are protected, their values have again declined substantially toward use value.

Perhaps the solution to the evaluation dilemma would be to establish an arbitrary easement evaluation floor (50 percent of preproject fair market value, excluding structures and building sites, unless the landowner can demonstrate high values?) until research provides a better handle.

EQUITY

The equity issue has been cited by Treasury as a criticism of easement programs, but it has more to do with the ultimate success of the landscape conservation effort. Simply stated, can tax policy offer benefits to "lesser-income" donors that are commensurate to benefits available to donors in upper-income brackets? If not, we will continue to find it difficult to attract a large group of landowners to our programs.

No doubt we should wait to learn the effect on our programs of the 1981 income tax overhaul. But at some point it will probably be desirable that we approach Congress about further changes in the Tax Code to:

allow easement donors to claim tax credits as an alternative to deductions.

permit spreading of the value of a donation until the full value has been claimed.

NOTES IN CLOSING

As observed at the outset, regulations under the 1980 tax amendments could virtually eliminate the donated easement as a tool for conserving rural landscapes. If that unhappy situation does materialize, we are left with perhaps three options:

1.   Go back to Congress for what I believe would be a difficult, but eventually successful, struggle to reverse the 1980 action. What we should seek, however, would be a comprehensive conservation easement policy package that addresses the concerns discussed above.

2.   Ask Congress to designate specific geographic areas (e.g., Virginia Piedmont, Maine Coast) as worthy of preservation for rural uses, and within which tax benefits

for donated easements would without question be available to all donors at or above an assured valuation level.

3. Figure out how to make the transferable development rights concept work.

Finally, the landscape conservation community might do well to work toward these three objectives even if the 1980 regulations turn out to be entirely favorable.

ACQUISITION and RESALE:
A Case Study
Richard W. Carbin

Last spring a group of concerned neighbors in East Barnard, Vermont, approached the Ottauquechee Regional Land Trust (ORLT) seeking advice. An 800-acre parcel of farm and forest land in that community was for sale. A developer was negotiating to purchase the property. The East Barnard residents did not want to see the land lost to major development.

Since neither the seller nor the developer was willing to agree to limit development, there was only one option left to those who wanted to protect the land: Buy it themselves. They asked the ORLT to help them do this.

If the land were to be purchased, it could only be done at development prices. The sales price was fixed at $1.85 million ($2,300 per acre). As with most local conservation organizations, the ORLT does not have such resources available. The source of financing would have to come from elsewhere.

In discussions with the East Barnard community it became clear that it would not be possible to raise any substantial amounts through cash contributions. However, the borrowing capacity among enough concerned people did exist. A number of residents were prepared to borrow funds, but not without reasonable assurance that they would not lose money in the end.

Prior to purchase, therefore, the ORLT undertook an extensive land use study and analyzed financial alternatives. (In many cases the need to act quickly precludes such a planning process until after acquisition, clearly a riskier venture.)

A land use plan resulted that would protect all of the productive timberland and farmland through the use of conservation restrictions. Twenty home sites were designated. A financial plan that would cover costs was then developed based on a combination of tax-deductible gifts of conservation restriction and resale of the developable land. With these recommendations in hand the East Barnard residents entered into an agreement to purchase the property. The purchase will be financed by a local bank.

In this case the acquisition of the land was necessary if the community were to gain control of what would happen on the land. Because of the high cost of the purchase the only way to accomplish both the conservation and financial objectives involved was through allowing limited development. There remains the risk that through resale not all costs will be met. The group who agreed to purchase had to be prepared to absorb any losses. Without this ultimate commitment there would have been no chance to conserve this land.

MARKETING LAND PRESERVATION, with an EMPHASIS on CONSERVATION EASEMENTS
William H. Dunham

The principles that determine success in this field are the same as those in any other kind of outside sales, with minor adaptations. First, you need a salesman who is effective with your type of clients. Since they are primarily wealthy businessmen or agriculturalists who are conservative, pragmatic, and tough-minded, you need a salesman who is likeable, down-to-earth, but also well-educated, comfortable dealing with the wealthy as an equal, a businessman with proven sales experience and a very strong environmental commitment. Your point man must be able to talk the businessman's language and to wheel and deal. He must be backed up by a highly competent staff that can carry out the land transaction expertly and on schedule.

Utilizing the following techniques and principles intensely for the past five months, our staff of 1½ positions is presently taking conservation easements on 16,000 acres in Montana. The key is to implement these ideas persistently and very aggressively, with strong determination, enthusiasm, positive mental attitude, and an in-depth knowledge of your product.

Set specific goals. Establish a challenging but realistic one- and five-year acreage goal; then work toward it with everything you have. Without these goals, you are like a ship leaving harbor without a destination, and you won't end up getting anywhere. Goals focus your energy and efforts. Ordinary sunlight when focused through a magnifying glass can create a fire; focused even more intensely as a laser beam, light can cut through anything. Focus on your goal and every day do the things you need to do to achieve it. If you do, eventually you'll arrive at your destination.

Become a GOYA (get off your ass) person. Get out of your office several days every month and *see the people.* As Pete Rose's T-shirt proclaims, "Hustle made it happen." Get out there and aggressively, enthusiastically tell your story to as many people as possible month after month. We fail because we don't make enough high-quality presentations per year to give the law of averages an opportunity to go to work for us. The proverbs "Seek and ye shall find" and "Knock and it shall be opened unto you" are truths, but you must seek and knock persistently and well. Few people realize that Babe Ruth not only held the record for the most home runs, he also held the record for having struck out the most! But what made him great was that even when things weren't going well, he never slackened his all-out effort when he came to bat. He believed, correctly, that "the ol' law of averages will hold as true for me as for everyone else if I just keep on swinging and swinging hard."

Leads. Every good pool player concentrates as much on positioning the cue ball for the next shot as he does on sinking the ball he's presently after. It's essential that you do the same thing: Pull at least six good leads from *every* strong contact you meet, especially from easement givers and your financial supporters. Qualify your leads and run the best ones first. In six months you can create two years of work. Meet with landowners concerned with impending logging, subdivisions, watershed damage, mining, road building; fish and game personnel; agricultural groups; local planning groups. Write or encourage articles on easements for your newspapers and various special interest group newsletters, such as *Trout Unlimited,* or *Farmer Stockman.* Remember, your audience is interested in what you can do for *them.* Show how you can help them and they'll listen.

Create your own volunteer sales force. In each geographic area you wish to work, carefully select a few conservation-minded, successful attorneys, CPAs, and realtors. Show them how easements can bring them business and better help them serve their clients. Every time you locate a good one, ask him to recommend a couple of others. Remember, these are the professionals that landowners turn to for advice. We win them to our cause not only via one-on-one contact but also by conducting conservation law seminars to educate them on the financial and legal workings of conservation easements and other forms of charitable conservation conveyances. It doesn't take long to form a statewide sales force that will bring you business.

Create a bandwagon effect using reverse psychology. OK, you've been out there beating the bushes for six months, you've gotten a few easements and now the serious inquiries are really starting to roll in. You've got momentum. Now is the time to start using reverse psychology. Inform your prospects that you are booked solid for the rest of the year and are accepting applications for next year and that even those spots are filling up fast. "If you want your tax break for next year I'd suggest you get things going soon. Well, if you *have* to have it this year, maybe we could squeeze you in, but only if we hire extra staff and that's going to cost money." Don't overdo it, but make them realize all the shrewd people are catching on; make them hungry. You'll close them faster and get a better deal when they are anxious not to miss the boat.

Benefits, knowledge, and efficiency. People buy *benefits*, not features. Keep stressing what easements can do for them and their family. Because these deals involve a lot of money, you must project an image of expertise, authority, and solidness. You must be able to field any question smoothly. If you don't know the answer, don't lie, but don't let this happen very often. Your staff, attorney, and tax consultant must likewise be expert and efficient. If you do a fine job on schedule, you'll soon get a lot of referral business and can also use your past clients as references. Do a poor job, and you won't last long.

Perfect your presentation and close. Both are critical and each is a book in itself. As an expert salesman you should be an acute practical psychologist who knows the laws of human behavior and how to make people *want* to do what you want them to do. You must be keenly aware of your prospect's beliefs, interests, life style, and concerns and must be constantly monitoring the feedback you're getting. You must also be aware of the vibes you're sending out and what effect they are having. Are your appearance, speech, and mannerisms creating like and trust? Learn everything you can about selling, apply what you learn, and correct your mistakes. With concentrated study and hard work, you can greatly improve your average. Remember, they will feel exactly what you feel, so you have to feel strongly and communicate that intense feeling. You have to reach their hearts as well as their heads.

Negotiating. On money and easement restrictions *always* deal directly with the landowner, not a manager or underling no matter how high on the ladder. Be honest and forthright about the costs fairly early in the game. These two tips will save you a lot of misunderstanding, hard feelings, and wasted time. In accepting an easement you're doing them a big favor because you're saving them a lot of money. They know there's no free lunch. I like to play the role of being caught in the middle between my desire to save the property and a board of directors who are tough about the terms and the properties they will accept. Hammer out an initial agreement with the prospect; then say, "I'll do my very best to sell the board on what you want, but they may insist on such and such . . . and if they do, what shall I do then?" He'll give better terms, and you've got them. It's a very effective position to wheel and deal from.

In summary, keep seeing the people and selling your message to everyone you meet. Keep pushing 110 percent. O. J. Simpson and the world champion bull rider both agree that their extremely rough sports are actually 90 percent mental concentration and determination and only 10 percent physical. "You have to have that rank bull whipped in your mind before you ever leave the chute." If you don't have your client sold in your mind before you ever leave the office, you're dead in the saddle and you don't even know it. Enthusiasm is the number one factor in selling. Combine it with knowledge and sustained hard work, and you'll be surprised at what your team can accomplish.

MARKETING LAND TRUSTS
Benjamin R. Emory

Land trusts may be paying insufficient attention to the marketing aspects of their mission. They must convince landowners, public officials, and the general public of the desirability of conserving land, and "selling" the concept of protecting land is akin in many ways to selling toothpaste, computer services, or any other product. Should not the same skills and techniques be applied?

My concern about marketing stems from my own experience at Maine Coast Heritage Trust. I believe that we should have been able to convince more landowners and to generate more public approval than we have. I suspect that similar potential for improvement in marketing land conservation exists at other land trusts too.

We would eagerly participate in an organized effort to exchange and analyze information about the marketing approaches of land trusts and the lessons learned. The analysis should help land trusts spot weaknesses in their own marketing programs, and it should determine whether professional marketing consultants might markedly increase the amount of land protected by land trusts.

We would like to share information on the following aspects of land trust marketing efforts:

1. Types of personal characteristics, skills, experience, and training needed by land trust staff members

2. Degree of marketing knowledge and experience present on board of directors

3. Target audiences

4. Demographics of landowners who have acted to conserve their land

5. Types of marketing communications and messages that have been tried and degree of success with each

6. Utilization of marketing consultants and whether such utilization has proved beneficial

7. Image problems and their solutions

8. Whatever thoughts land trust professionals may have on the subject of marketing

Is there an organization or an individual willing to spearhead this first step in helping land trusts to do a better job of selling their product and, consequently, to conserve more land?

LONG-TERM MANAGEMENT:
Problems and Opportunities
Gordon Abbott, Jr.

The Trustees of Reservations has long maintained that there are two steps involved in land conservation: first, the immediate step of acquiring or preserving; and second, the too-often-neglected concern of providing the structures and mechanism to continue that preservation. We call that *management*, and we believe it is every bit as important as protecting land in the first place.

Management of conservation land has been part and parcel of the Trustees of Reservations since its establishment in 1891. Its charter calls for it to "acquire, hold and maintain . . . beautiful and historical places and tracts of land open to the public under suitable regulations." Its very name *Trustees* indicates that it holds its properties in *trust* for the enjoyment of this and future generations. This fiduciary obligation—its role as a *trustee*—is where its concept of management begins. And this extends itself logically to the management of other resources given or acquired in trust, such as the funds in its endowment portfolio which now total some $9.6 million.

Another concept of management policy is that *preservation* is the organization's *primary* responsibility and that where preservation and use collide, preservation has preference. This has tended, where recreation is involved, to lead it toward activities of a passive nature; whereas the managers of public resource lands generally find themselves dealing more with the pressures of active recreation. Indeed, we work closely with public agencies to reinforce this role, feeling in general, that camping, the use of snowmobiles and other recreational vehicles, and the establishment of major facilities for visitors are better left in the hands of managers of public resources who may have to compromise somewhat more and offer "all things to all people" because of the political process. We are still *private property* although open to the public, and it's the phrase "under suitable regulations" that is the core of continuing management.

We arrive at these regulations, as most every resource manager does, with a system that we call *master planning*. This involves simply the identification of the resources we're preserving, both natural and cultural, and the establishment of policies that best protect those resources. What's fascinating about this process at the Trustees is that each of our now sixty-seven properties is so very different. Our management responsibilities range from agriculture and forestry to museum houses, prints, pictures, and the decorative arts, recreation (most passive but some active, such as the ice-skating program at Rocky Woods Reservation), the sale of food and other refreshments (now grossing $77,000 a year at Crane Beach) and—in conjunction with our affiliate, the Castle Hill Foundation at the Crane Reservations, Ipswich—the care, feeding, and presentation of a thirty-four piece baroque orchestra that performs during the summer months for audiences of up to 5,000 persons.

Management thus not only involves people, it involves landscapes and buildings and, most important, it involves money. The operating budget of the Trustees totals $1.3 million. Ninety percent of this goes to management. Of our 40 full-time employees and 135 part-time, almost all, with the exception of those assigned to the office of land conservation and the office of development, are involved in managing land and its related resources.

As we look ahead at the effect of continuing inflation on overhead, including salaries, some 62 percent of our budget, we are obviously concerned. Today, we generally take no new properties that can't pay their way. Although we reserve the right—and cherish it—to make an unbusinesslike decision to preserve something exquisite. This, after all, is why we're a charity.

We're also fortunate that user demand enables us to raise 35 percent of our operating income from admission fees and that these can be adjusted within reason to catch up with inflation. We're great believers in the fairness of users paying their way. But we also recognize that use fees generally about meet the cost of opening properties to the public—providing the rangers, hostesses and guides, and other services necessary. Fees do not generally provide for contributions to a depreciation reserve to continue to preserve the essential features of a property whether they be the Great House—we've just replaced the roof at Naumkeag, a magnificent Stanford White house in Stockbridge, for $85,000—or the tree-lined drives at World's End, Hingham, originally planted by F. L. Olmstead. These kinds of things must be taken care of by endowments or by special fund-raising campaigns.

Looking ahead, we are hoping to increase the number of cooperative management projects: We now manage Great Point, Nantucket, as agent for the U.S. Fish and Wildlife Service. It borders our Coskata-Coatue Wildlife Refuge, some 987 acres. And we have cooperative relationships, formal and informal, where other properties border lands of the National Park Service, the Massachusetts Department of Environmental Management, and the State's Division of Fish and Wildlife. We're involved with the Appalachian Mountain Club in a pilot program that grants public funds to private conservation organizations to accomplish planning and management tasks on public lands. Its theory is that the private sector can accomplish the job more efficiently and effectively with trail systems in national forests and with the Appalachian Trail.

Three final points. First, because of changing financial structures, the traditional acquisition of endowed properties we believe will slow down and we'll be concentrating on ways to help preserve land that may not be open to the public using conservation easements (but we can't forget these have major management responsibilities in their inspection and enforcement which is often overlooked), farmland preservation, limited development projects, and so forth, the same kind of thing that our new affiliate the Massachusetts Farm and Conservation Lands Trust is engaged in now.

Second, it may be time to revive the idea of establishing a private, nonprofit corporation that would manage public land on contract. And, third, it may also be time to consider in greater depth how even mergers of nonprofits that have land management responsibilities might reduce costs (especially overhead) and add efficiency, all to the benefit of the public.

THE CHALLENGES
of LONG-TERM MANAGEMENT
Andrew Johnson

The nonprofit sector, supported by the backpacker set, appears willing to sit on the for long-term management of projects. The exceptions have been mainly limited to endowed properties on an individual parcel basis. Once transferred to government, the nonprofit sector has played a "watchdog" role with limited authority and funding. The private sector has generally not been viewed as the proper vehicle to hold land in perpetuity despite the successes of conservation easements. Easements have generally been used in isolated cases and seldom are utilized except between existing landowners looking for tax relief through contribution credits or reductions in inheritance taxes.

A fundamental aspect of any discussion regarding long-term management is that the costs of management for projects are seldom recognized initially and rarely funded to necessary levels. Also, vandalism and misuse have dramatically increased as access to natural areas has become easily available.

The ethic regarding natural areas that all those who fostered open space acquisition assumed would follow has not materialized; if anything, the demands are for more parking lots, "modern" camping facilities, snowmobile and minibike trails, and launching sites for motorboats. This conflict will continue to expand and demand professional management of a new dimension.

The nonprofit sector, supported by the backpacker set, appears willing to sit on the sidelines and criticize government management practices every time an abuse occurs.

The current reduction in funding and the increased demands may provide many new management opportunities for the nonprofit sector. However, these opportunities will require nonprofits to develop management capabilities far beyond the "naturalist" on the nature trail concept so prevalent. I can envision nonprofits taking over underfunded parks, charging admission fees, and serving as concessionaires to reach a new equilibrium between demand and cost. Most institutions of higher learning pay lip service to training persons equipped to manage open space areas, but the skills are "quasi-scientific" and students do not possess experience in practical skills so necessary to manage parks. Training programs must include: law enforcement, business management, fire protection, road maintenance, and public relations.

The demand for new land management capabilities may come from many sources. In our work, we are currently providing interim management services for: (1) elderly owners who wish to remain on their land but can no longer manage their properties, (2) corporations who are holding land as an investment and will eventually develop portions of the land, (3) developers who have included open space areas in their development plan but have little interest in managing these areas, and (4) local governments who own natural areas but whose management capability is stretched by the maintenance of active recreational areas.

We have promoted a new concept over the past few years that is now beginning to receive more attention at the federal level of government. The concept is to allow a nonprofit to acquire an entire project (in this case a 4,000-acre estuary) and then sell a conservation easement over the entire project to the government. The guidelines for management would be jointly agreed to for the project between the purchasing agency and the nonprofit; however, the management responsibility would remain with the nonprofit. This would allow for less cost for the government both in acquisition and, we are convinced, management expenses.

The nonprofit sector has an exciting array of potential management responsibilities in the future. This potential will continue to expand as the rising costs of management by government agencies and conflicting demands for varied outdoor experiences collide. The conflicts between the backpacker seeking wilderness preservation and the macho motor-home owner driving out into the open spaces trailing all the latest gadgets for "conquering" the wilderness have just begun!

ADAPTING the BRITISH COUNTRYSIDE COMMISSION IDEA

David Moore

Rural and remote areas the world over are feeling the pressures of more and more people seeking a day's or week's respite from urban life.

It has become quite common to hear farmers and rural landowners complain that they are increasingly plagued by uninvited visitors randomly trespassing and, more troublesome, committing vandalism. Farmers tell of constantly having to chase intruders off their land and of finding broken fences, gates off hinges, damaged farm equipment, and general litter.

One Pine Barrens farmer describes this "invasion" as almost continual, whether in the form of people wandering up from a nearby river to nose around a little vacation cabin or entire convoys of four-wheel-drive vehicles zooming around his bogs and wreaking havoc.

Vandalism from these visitors ranges from simple disappearance of signs to deliberate wrecking of farm machinery and tampering with bog gates.

These complaints and problems probably sound frustratingly familiar to any landowner whose land looks inviting and attracts a steady outpouring of city and suburban folk seeking a "day in the great outdoors."

Visitors in search of recreation and nature are clearly overwhelming the existing rivers, trails, lakes, and camping spots in areas like the Pine Barrens, mainly because there are not enough accessible facilities.

What are farmers to do? They can try, as they have in the past, to erect even more signs signaling what is their property and telling people to "keep off," spending more time and money policing their land or organizing to get better patrols by the state. Or they can try to persuade the state to buy more land for recreation and open more public land.

The first strategy has been tried with little success. One farmer and his workers cannot keep track of what happens on thousands of acres. The second calls upon a state government that is already stretched thin.

The New Jersey Conservation Foundation has proposed an innovative solution that not only expands recreational facilities by financially rewarding landowners who allow some access to their land for hiking, camping, swimming, and picnicking, but also shifts responsibility for these sites to a local warden.

Based on an English agency known as the Countryside Commission, this concept has proven popular because it eases the city-country conflict and has benefits for all concerned. Farmers get new income, as well as someone else to take charge of whatever facilities are established. Not only is this arrangement far cheaper than actual acquisition, it leaves the lands in the hands of the farmers.

In England, the government-funded Countryside Commission has concentrated in recent years on defusing the problems of city people coming to the country to get away from it all.

"We recognize that no invisible hand can be relied upon to harmonize the interests of the rural community on the one side and their uninvited and not always welcome visitors on the other," stated one Countryside report, "but we are also convinced that points of conflict have been much exaggerated by misunderstanding, and that with goodwill on both sides mutual adjustment should be possible."

The Countryside Commission believes that channeling hikers, campers, and other visitors into designated trails, picnic spots, and campgrounds goes a long way toward easing existing problems.

Rather than buy up necessary land and run these many facilities on its own, the Countryside Commission instead seeks wherever possible to encourage private farmers and landowners to allow access across their land for trails and also to develop for-profit campsites and snack bars.

Not only are the farmers paid for allowing trails, but a local warden with a great deal of autonomy then takes responsibility for setting up the hiking paths and maintaining them. Each farmer has an individual contract with the Commission, usually for one or two years' duration, specifying where access can take place and freeing the farmer of liability.

The Commission also seeks to protect such charming rural landmarks as historic structures and special views, again by helping to maintain them or by, say, compensating a farmer to renovate an old wooden barn that otherwise would be replaced by a more economic but less attractive tin structure.

There were also significant financial incentives to preserve such visual charms as small groves of trees or the traditional hedges or a particular view, as well as to develop small campsites and similar facilities to cater to visitors.

"Our experiments in countryside management have shown that something practical and effective can be done to resolve the conflict between the visitor and farmer. . . . Such practical help to the economy of agriculture is comparable to a new production technique or a more effective marketing arrangement," reported the Commission.

The approach is really quite simple. Each district has an appointed warden with a great deal of autonomy to proceed as he (or she) thinks necessary. Working closely in concert with local farmers and community leaders, the warden selects the paths—be they hiking trails for people, bridleways for horses, or dirt tracks for jeeps or motorbikes—and makes sure they are properly marked and maintained and that appropriate facilities are available along the way. The warden is really the crucial element in the success or failure of the enterprise.

Working this way, district by district, the Countryside Commission has encouraged the preservation of many lovely groves and the planting of yet more. Little parking lots have been installed, and campsites or swimming spots opened. Local farm groups have sponsored visiting days. Hundreds of miles of trails and routes have been established, many of which follow footpaths known as "ancient ways" that were major transportation routes much earlier and had fallen into disuse.

In addition to promoting rural conservation and recreation, the Commission has also tried to establish basic standards of behavior for visiting city folk with a list of dos and don'ts called the Countryside Code. It is distributed at nature centers, erected along trails, periodically published in magazines and newspapers, and, most important, taught to schoolchildren.

Its tenets are: Guard against all risk of fire; fasten all gates; keep dogs under proper control; keep to the paths across farmland; avoid damaging fences, hedges, and walls; leave no litter; safeguard water supplies; protect wildlife, wild plants and trees; go carefully on country roads; and respect the life of the countryside.

Many people in this country believe "The British are different. Their land setup is different and their ways and attitudes are different." Yet the Appalachian Trail, running from Georgia to Maine, has been around for decades and crosses public and private land. It is also maintained and run by what are basically volunteer wardens—members of local trail clubs.

The Batona (for Back to Nature) Trail in New Jersey is a local example of a comparable success. Started in 1961 by an outdoors group based in Philadelphia, the trail was laid out by volunteers and continues to be maintained by local trail clubs. This is not to say there are not problems, but a spirit of cooperation and responsibility has prevailed.

Among landowners large and small, there is real interest in a Countryside Commission type of program. But in all cases, there is also concern about its ramifications for them.

As is natural in a society as litigious as ours, one of the first worries is liability. Yet under New Jersey law, any property owner who allows his land to be used for recreational purposes by the public is shielded from all liability. The New Jersey Conservation Foundation, which over the years has held thousands of acres that have been kept open to the public, has never experienced any difficulties with litigation.

Then owners say, "What if it doesn't work out? Am I stuck?" In England, all agreements are quite short-term, running one or two years. Similar arrangements would certainly make sense here.

There are a number of major differences between the United States and England when it comes to land use and people. The first and most important is the fact that British law guarantees access to the long-distance footpaths known as "ancient ways." However, these paths are as good as closed without the good will and cooperation of farmers, and it is this situation that the Countryside Commission has worked to change.

(Interestingly, it is the experience of the Appalachian Trail people here that many property owners who are quite amenable to allowing the trail through their property on a voluntary, cooperative basis are quite averse to actually selling the land to the government. They prefer the friendly agreement.)

The common understanding with the American right-of-way law is that any path or street in continuous use for twenty years becomes a public way. Many property owners make sure this does not happen by blocking off whatever trails or roads run through their property every twenty years for a day or so. But because the thrust of government trails programs thus far has been acquisition, there has been very little testing of the twenty-year rule.

In any case, the Countryside Commission's role is not to try to force access on unwilling owners, but to defuse the trespass problem by funneling visitors into places geared to handle them. As Mr. Hookway of the Commission noted: "Its main success derives from the informal, unbureaucratic, short-term, identifiable and, one might say, opportunistic nature of the approach."

It is worth noting that an arrangement similar to England's Countryside Commission has been flourishing in New Zealand, where land use patterns and attitudes are closer to ours. Known as the New Zealand Walkways Act and in effect since 1975, it has produced thirty-five long-distance trails totaling thousands of miles. As in England, individual contracts are drawn up with each landowner and compensation takes the form of both payments and, in a New Zealand variation, tax deductions. A code similar to the Countryside Code has been promulgated.

The Countryside Commission concept is a new and innovative approach to solving city-country conflicts, while opening more areas for recreation. It yields benefits for both land-owners and hikers as well as others who enjoy the outdoors.

There is widespread dissatisfaction with the current state of affairs, for there is no reason farmers and other open-space landowners should bear the brunt of an unprecedented outpouring from the cities and suburbs. Something should be done, and the Open Lands Management Program, like the British Countryside Commission, offers a cooperative approach based on good will and widespread local involvement. We have entered an era when we now acknowledge that government cannot best solve all our problems and that solutions that draw on the private sector will offer greater economic efficiencies and flexibility. That is the beauty of the proposed program. The concept has worked in England; it can work here.

LAND MANAGEMENT: Easements
David P. Miller

All land must be managed. We have been so concerned about preserving land that we haven't prepared ourselves adequately to take care of land once we have it.

Even wilderness areas must be managed, because surrounding land uses and people affect the wilderness itself. Fire, trespass, erosion, storms, disease and infestations, taxes, and tenants require us to manage land.

Local land trusts are uniquely placed to oversee easement sites. Proximity, familiarity with local land, people, and customs, and their enthusiasm contribute to a more efficient, consistent, and effective surveillance of land.

Others here may address the problems of managing natural areas and farmland. We are setting *perpetual* restrictions on the use of land and should anticipate as much as possible the problems our successors may face on our easement sites. Although my remarks should be addressed to rural lands, here I wish to consider only open land under easement that is part of developed land: the typical residential "subdivision" made up of single-family residences on separate lots, or apartments, clusters, or rowhouses with "open space" for flood plains, steep slopes, recreational use, buffering, or future development. The local subdivision ordinance usually requires the developer to set aside a certain portion of his land for such uses, either in fee or under a conservation easement. Ownership usually resides in the developer, the community organization of the subdivision, or all of the property owners if it is a cooperative or condominium-type of ownership. Local government usually will not want any responsibility for such land because it does not want the expense and day-to-day responsibility of managing the land or enforcing an easement. Such lands present three kinds of problems for the long-range future:

1. As adjacent land uses change, the optimal use of such restricted sites may change significantly. Who should decide if the use of "open space" may be changed to a more intensive, or less intensive, use?

2. Undeveloped land of the subdivision itself may not serve its prescribed purposes. Who, if anyone, may make decisions to adapt to unexpected conditions?

3. The owners of the land in fee, that is, the developer or the community association, may find more profitable uses of the land that may conflict with the prescribed purposes of the easement. Who, if anyone, may decide what changes, if any, may be allowed?

I assume that a dominant American attitude about land will persist for a very long time, that is: It is natural and desirable to develop land and unnatural and undesirable to leave land alone. Consequently, every group will have internal pressure to translate land into dollars. A memorial ornamental garden of a church, for example, may be looked upon as "unproductive land" by people within the institution itself.

Historically, courts (and certainly many lawyers) do not favor easements because they restrict freedom. Courts may tend to be hostile to easements, especially if they are perpetual, and, if they find purposes of a conservation easement are no longer served by the deed of easement, may choose to nullify the easement instead of adapting it to new circumstances. Also, any citizen has the right to petition a court of equity to test whether the purposes of an easement are being honored. I am sure that someday some disgruntled heir or assign of easement grantors will attempt to have a court of equity nullify some of our easements. Consequently, a deed of easement should be drafted to allow the following:

1. Amendment of the easement:

   a. During the lifetime of the Grantor

   b. After the lifetime of the Grantor

2. Amendment of the easement:

   a. To allow land uses or activities that were not anticipated by grantor and grantee but that are consistent with the purposes of the easement

   b. To adapt practices to help carry out the purposes of the easement

NEGOTIATED LAND DEVELOPMENT TECHNIQUES

Peter R. Stein

Increased fiscal, regulatory, and environmental constraints prevalent in American real estate markets have persuaded land developers to explore methods of closer cooperation with community groups and public interest organizations. In this light, land conservation organizations are provided a unique opportunity to play a decisive role in land use and land management issues facing local communities. Negotiated land development strategies represent a vehicle for land conservation organizations to use in working out compromise solutions to land use and land use intensity conflicts. Typically, negotiated land development includes a process for resolving conflict over land development when normal decision making is stalemated, difficult, unpredictable, or outside the control of public regulatory agencies. Land conservation organizations can be in a prime position to initiate negotiated land development projects based upon their extensive understanding of land resource values and their ability to communicate a strong sense of "public benefit" as part of the negotiated process.

It is now an accepted maxim that planned growth makes sense in economic and social terms for both the community and the developer. Unfortunately, current public planning and regulatory functions provided local government do not guarantee that growth will actually be planned.

Time has shown that growth and development just for the sake of growth and development is both unwise and unprofitable. Surplus school buildings, underrented shopping centers, and poor community facilities demonstrate a desperate need for land planning techniques and innovative development projects that better reflect the community values we all cherish and that can be leveraged to sustain proper and sensitive real estate development projects.

However, many small- to medium-sized real estate developers are unequipped to navigate through the relatively uncharted waters of state and local environmental regulations. Such inexperience, coupled with an inability to formulate creative solutions on their own, have resulted in construction delays and higher housing costs to the consumer. The tax advantages that nonprofit land conservation organizations can offer combined with environmentally sensitive planning guidelines can serve to generate a land development scheme that is financially viable for the real estate sector and provides meaningful public benefits in the form of accessible open space or protected conservation lands.

NEGOTIATED LAND DEVELOPMENT TECHNIQUES

The chart below describes in generic terms the course of events surrounding a negotiated land development project:

Typical Series of Events for a Negotiated Development Project

1	INITIATION	• Land to be conserved • Regulation to be enforced • Development proposed	Community action, administrative decision, or a development proposal provides the impetus for negotiations.
2	INFORMATION GATHERING	• Environmental analysis • Financial analysis • Sociopolitical analysis	Investigation of a broad array of characteristics provides a common data base for negotiations.

3	DISCUSSIONS	• Timing
		• Financial resources
		• Community benefits:
		    environmental
		    social
		    financial
			Preliminary discussions reveal bargaining positions and indicate potential options for resolving conflict.

4	NEGOTIATIONS	• Trade-offs
		• Concessions
		• Permit process
		• Management agreements
		• Legal arrangements
		• Land transfers:
		    fee
		    less than fee
			Options are brought to the bargaining table and, through negotiations, are eliminated or reshaped. Implementation and enforcement mechanisms are discussed.

5	COMPROMISE	• Site plan approvals • Bonding • Restrictive covenants • Recorded land use agreements • Conveyance of land and/or property interests	The compromise development option and appropriate enforcement mechanisms are put into place.

Land conservation organizations can begin to couple their knowledge of land protection issues with the planning requirements of development projects and hopefully meet their eleemosynary goals at the same time that they add to the effectiveness and the efficiency of the local planning effort. A case in point is the work of the Ottauquechee Regional Land Trust in Woodstock, Vermont, which has worked to provide for sensitive new residential and commercial development while at the same time retaining prime agricultural land.

In heavily regulated real estate markets, developers may not be in a position to move their projects forward without meeting complex permit approval requirements or providing community amenities as part of their development scheme. Both the General Development Corporation of Port Charlotte, Florida, and the Amboy Road Company of Staten Island, New York, demonstrate the positive results of a working partnership between land conservation organizations such as the Trust for Public Land and real estate developers to achieve a unique degree of site planning sensitivity, natural resource protection, and provision of important community amenities. The tax benefits that accrue to the developer demonstrated in both of these cases reinforce the positive financial aspects of entering into a negotiated land development project—both for the developer and for the nonprofit land conservation organization.

THE GROWING IMPORTANCE of PRIVATE LOCAL ACTIVITY in FARMLAND PRESERVATION

Herman C. Allmaras

The family farm community that produces a surplus is under attack from many directions. It is increasingly important for everyone to understand the issue and for them to act favorably to preserve the land, the very basis of life-sustaining food. That private local activity is of growing importance is an understatement with respect to farmland preservation. I believe that the situation is critical and has been for some time in many areas of this country. The issue is complex, but I pull out four distinctions by which private local community activity is best suited to bring positive results in farmland preservation.

Expectations. The family farm community has several parts, each with its own dependent expectation. The farms themselves, the marketing aspect, and the support services each have vested interests and have more to lose than any other group or political body. They can speak more clearly and convincingly as to the benefits generated by farmland preservation because of their commitment. Any other entity will have only indirect concern in any decision-making process and will, relative to farmland preservation, have conflicts. As an example, consider how the expectations of an agricultural community can be reversed by the placement of an interstate exit ramp or a shopping center or a school between two urban areas on farmland. The landowner now in many instances becomes a speculator holding the land for an inflated price retirement sale. Mixed expectations destroy the farmland preservation by bits and pieces so that strong and permanent measures must be used to maintain the desired expectation.

Farm economics. Agriculture Secretary John Block recently said, "Net farm income dropped 40 percent in 1980 alone, and if you figure inflation this is the lowest since the 1930s." Increased activity in the area of direct marketing can increase the net farm income. Direct marketing is clearly a private local alternative and can be a key factor in the farmland preservation issue.

Continuity of ownership. The farm family, expecting profit and rewards for its labor, can transfer the farm ownership from one generation to the next. A community of such families develops an identity and generally will support one another. By increasing the use of the estate and the gift tax laws along with deed restrictions, the various types of land and water conversions might be minimized.

Community activity. It is increasingly important that the farm communities have activities that promote themselves. Meetings that shape marketing strategies, endorse political candidates, educate on new farm techniques, and socialize all will help offset the external and internal forces of land conversion. Land conversion becomes the concern of each community member.

PUBLIC/PRIVATE
RELATIONSHIPS

For local land trusts, the most urgent current problem relating to government is federal tax policy. The deductibility of charitable gifts of easements for open space protection is no longer certain. The decision to curtail tax incentives for conservation efforts apparently reflects Treasury concern with "tax expenditures" and with recurring abuses in the form of inflated appraisals of property donations.

The uncertainty concerning tax benefits for grants of easements is discouraging contributions of this important preservation instrument. In an effort to restore the tax incentive, land conservation organizations may have to establish their willingness to assure both that conservation donations provide demonstrable public benefit and that they are fairly appraised. A possible basis for remedial legislation is the assignment of these responsibilities to qualified organizations as a basis for allowing tax deductions.

Taxation issues also exist at the local level. Local land trusts are subject to hostility from those who regard them as taking property off the tax rolls causing other landowners to pay compensating property tax increases. Another common charge is that conservation groups seek amenity values for an elite at the cost of community growth and taxable development of general benefit.

The local land-saving organization is being increasingly pressed to provide convincing evidence of the broad public benefits of its conservation efforts. Some are striving to be accepted as an integral part of community institutional structure by offering cooperation and services to local government and to other levels of government in their local operations. Private groups can assist government agencies in mediating disputes, in negotiating property acquisitions, in education and training activities, in generating support for government conservation programs, and in providing professional consultation.

The curtailment of government land acquisition programs in the current economic and political climate provides a special challenge to the local land-saving movement. At the federal level, there is a substantial danger that critical inholdings and contiguous properties in areas of national parks, wildlife sanctuaries, and other federal lands will be sold for development because the government purchase alternative is apparently foreclosed. At the state and local levels, with Land and Water Conservation Fund grants no longer available, similar losses can be anticipated. It is beyond the capacity of private-sector groups to begin to fill the gap through an outright purchase program. However, using the kinds of innovative land-saving techniques they have pioneered, local groups in partnership with government agencies can significantly contain the threatened damage to these critical areas.

Conservation groups can make an important contribution by demonstrating alternatives to public ownership when critical areas are threatened. Public agencies have much to learn about new approaches to land use planning and control, land swapping, less-than-fee acquisition, negotiated development restriction, and public-private cooperative management of sensitive areas. Well-informed conservation professionals can play a vital role in the public sector in education and cooperative action.

PROBLEMS of FEDERAL TAX POLICY and PRIVATE-SECTOR EFFORTS to CONSERVE LAND

Kingsbury Browne, Jr.

Federal tax policy support through tax incentives for the conservation of land has diminished in recent years. The Internal Revenue Service now refuses to grant tax-exempt status to organizations engaged solely in the protection of farmlands without some demonstration of ecological significance. In the 1960s and 1970s, charitable gifts of easements for the protection of "open space" were deductible. "Open space" embraced many innovative programs ranging from forest management to water resource protection. The deductibility of such gifts now requires proof of several qualities, among them unique habitat or scenic qualities or the presence of clearly delineated federal, state, or local governmental conservation policies plus significant public benefit. The decision to cut back the availability of tax incentives for private-sector efforts to conserve land has halted many programs across the country by contributing landowners.

The reasons for this policy change are obscure but probably include Treasury concern with tax expenditures generally and a sense of pervasive abuse, especially in the use of inflated appraisals.

As a first step to restoring for the 1980s the tax incentives available in the 1960s and 1970s and to provide a broader working relationship with Treasury, land conservation organizations might try to look at tax incentives as a source of funds with which they acquire land. To expand the notion, if a land conservation organization paid a landowner up to 70 percent of the fair market value of the contributed land, the acquisition would be a bargain purchase. If the organization could draw directly on Treasury for the funds with which to make such payment, the transaction could be characterized as a Treasury-financed, private-sector bargain purchase. Land conservation organizations do not, of course, have direct access to Treasury funds, but indirectly they do. The net effect of allowing a landowner a charitable contribution for the fair market value of contributed land is in terms of payment the same as if the land conservation organization had drawn directly on Treasury funds and then reimbursed the contributor a percentage of the fair market value of the land determined by the contributor's marginal tax bracket.

If a land conservation organization will regard tax incentives as a means of financing the acquisition of land, some provocative questions will follow. Does the use of federal funds impose some responsibility on the land conservation organization to police appraisals—perhaps by seeking its own appraisal, which then becomes part of the public record? The notion that the organization should acquire land at the least possible cost to itself and to Treasury is not hard to accept. In the same vein, should the new organization having no track record be as eligible for indirect federal financing as the established organization? In 1969, the Congress chose to provide a greater degree of tax incentive support to public as opposed to private foundations.

Remedial tax legislation is probably needed, in which case the approach suggested, which focuses on the responsibilities of the land conservation organization, could eliminate many of the present complexities. It would lodge in the qualified land conservation organization instead of Treasury the responsibility for determining whether a given piece of land offers scenic, unique habitat or other resource qualities deserving of preservation.

WORKING with PUBLIC OFFICIALS
Benjamin R. Emory

Land trusts will protect more land in the long run if they establish working relationships with government. At Maine Coast Heritage Trust we have worked effectively with some public officials while encountering maddening frustration dealing with others. Much has depended on the interests and capabilities of the individuals holding particular government jobs.

Land trusts can cooperate with public officials in varied ways and at all levels of government. For example, in Maine we have negotiated donations of land and conservation easements to federal and state agencies and to towns. With Maine's Bureau of Taxation we co-sponsored a for-credit workshop for professional assessors on the effects of conservation easements on property taxes. Under contract from the state planning office, we authored a booklet on voluntary land conservation techniques. We have lobbied in the state legislature and in Congress on bills affecting land conservation. We conducted workshops for municipal officials on the fiscal effects of residential subdivision and open space conservation. Regularly, state agencies consult us for information about particular properties and their owners.

Most difficult in Maine has been developing effective working relationships with town officials. We have had good successes in a few towns, but in general, we have failed in trying to generate demand for our advisory services from towns. Some town officials have a quite limited perspective on the world, but, regardless of that, immediate crises, not long-term programs, tend to take up the time that town officials can devote to town affairs. Also of real hindrance are the widely shared beliefs that land conservation only benefits an elite few and the fear that preserving land erodes the tax base and forces up property taxes.

Developing and maintaining linkages with the public sector demands constant effort. Land trusts must expect to meet public officials more than half-way, particularly when the latter lack interest, initiative, or time. Often public jobs experience relatively rapid turnover, and personnel changes usually require starting all over in establishing working relationships. In addition to making a constant effort, land trusts must develop a reputation for professionalism, expertise, and objectivity and get to know personally the public officials with whom a land trust should be working.

PUBLIC/PRIVATE RELATIONSHIPS:
Land Saving by a Quasi-Public Agency
David P. Miller

The Maryland General Assembly established the Maryland Environmental Trust in 1967 to "conserve, stimulate, improve, and perpetuate the natural, scenic, and cultural qualities and welfare of the environment of Maryland." Its mandate (Section 3-201 of the Natural Resources Article) includes authorization to acquire property or interests in property to this purpose.

Since 1972, the Trust has been given 56 conservation easements restricting 13,287 acres of farmland, woodland, natural areas, waterfront, scenic corridors, and other open spaces. The Trust has a paid staff of four, with many volunteers.

The Trust's activities are defined and governed by a fifteen-person board of trustees made up of twelve volunteers and three *ex officio* members (the governor, the speaker of the House, and the president of the Senate). The governor in 1967 appointed the original twelve volunteer members; since then, the board of trustees has selected its own replacements according to its own by-laws.

There is an urgent need for the local land trusts, for two principal reasons:

1.   A state trust's resources are inadequate (and probably will remain so) to deal with the number of sites in need of special protection.

2. Many valuable sites within the state are not of statewide significance; either because of small area or composition, many areas proposed for conservation easements do not qualify for the Environmental Trust's program.

The constitutional nature of the Maryland Environmental Trust can be a model for land protection agencies where neither a public agency, such as a state department of natural resources, nor a private land trust is acceptable to the public. Such a quasi-public entity can foster confidence that specific conservation goals will be honored because such a trust is not "just another government bureau" or is not private, and therefore somewhat mysterious and suspect.

A local land trust with a board of directors independent of both local government and private firms could be chartered by local government to oversee the open space of subdivisions and rule on future uses of such lands in perpetuity. The California Coastal Commission has proposed such an idea for managing lands that connect public roads with the shore itself. Recognizing that neither the state government nor the local government wanted the responsibility of managing such "hot potatoes," the staff of the California Coastal Commission seized on the constitutional structure of the environmental trust as a prototype for managing areas of crucial public significance.

In Maryland, for example, local subdivision ordinances require developers to set aside a significant amount of land as "open space." Usually developers retain title to such land or dedicate it to the community association of the fledgling subdivision (local governments usually will not accept title to such land even if it is offered). Such lands, as the years pass, are subject to neglect, manipulation, or misuse by the titleholders. Today's "open space," often "undevelopable" by present standards, may become a tempting site for concentrated development by latter-day techniques.

Being quasi-public is no guarantee of wisdom or success, but I believe the success of such entities is a good omen for such an experiment.

LAND TRUSTS and GOVERNMENT:
A Case of Distrust

Maggy Hurchalla

On the surface local, state, and national governments work with land trusts in coalitions touted by our press releases as the best of the public and private sectors. Hopefully it is the best, but it happens only as a result of tact, time, and enlightened self-interest. Like the prefeminist bride, the lion's share of tact has to come from the land trust. When all is happily accomplished, we forget that there is a basic distrust on both sides.

The attitude of government toward trusts is not unlike the police toward the heroic private detective. As all good mystery readers know, the policeman distrusts the more agile detective, suspects him of both vanity and incompetence, and eventually charges him with murder if at all possible. Our hero, the detective, is quite sure that all policemen are both vain and incompetent and suspects that they are also corrupt. The reason for the friction is obvious. They are both after the same criminal.

It takes no long search to find the basic reasons for distrust where private and public groups deal with the land. America has been a poor steward of its land at all levels of government. Somewhere between Teddy Roosevelt and James Watt the Industrial Revolution won out over the purple mountains' majesty. Land trusts are largely an answer to government failure. As a result, they are an accusation.

Like our hero the detective, we in the land trusts think of ourselves as more agile and more committed. If in place of the lovely and innocent client, we have a land about to be raped, then the land trust is often the last refuge of the innocent.

The conflict deals with power and territory. There is no way to eradicate it, and it is dangerous to pretend that it does not exist. It is a happy monument to patience and hard work that it surfaces less often.

More than tact and patience are required to resolve conflict. The simplest way to convince any opponent is enlightened self-interest. Luckily, land trusts have a variety of benefits that they can offer to government and government officials. If power is threatened by the very existence of trusts, it can be vastly expanded also. A single-purpose effort outside the red tape we so fondly call "checks and balances" can achieve government goals without government cost. A trust can expand resources in terms of people, time, dedication, and money. Government is particularly impressed by the money. Because government wrests money from both corporations and citizens in the name of taxes, few are eager to make donations to government. That wonderful American instinct to help save the true, the beautiful, and the underdog, has trouble identifying with government at any level. In a similar vein, the property owner with a penchant for preserving his land, is unlikely to deal with the agencies that promulgate zoning law. Wherever trusts can save governments money, there is a real basis for overcoming whatever doubts and jealousies exist. As Proposition 13 spreads to the White House, power and territory that have no funds become an albatross to all levels of government.

Backing off from broad generalities, let's make up some concrete examples of war and truce. Stand with me in the shoes of a local official where a trust has been created.

First, let's take the worst case. There I am chewing on a cigar and trying to stay elected. I pick up the paper and read that for years my district has been a horrible slum. Government is accused of neglecting the whole neighborhood and of especially neglecting a particularly odious vacant lot full of broken glass and winos. A national conservation group interested in land trusts has come to the rescue. The Continental Whoozits Corp. has donated the lot. A neighborhood land trust has been set up. The lot is now clean and sparkling. It is planted with vegetables and swing sets. All the winos are sober.

After reading that glowing account, your politician is unhappy. Not only did I not get credit, there was a suggestion that I might be at fault. Making the best of a bad situation, I put down my cigar and call the trust. I offer a good friend for the job of director. They tell me that it doesn't work that way, and there is no paid director. I decide it is all a communist plot.

Now let's take a best case. There I am in a California valley watching the grapes grow and chewing on a granola bar. My only worry is getting elected again and keeping housing developments (full of people who might not vote for me) from replacing the grapes. I pick up the paper and read that a land trust has formed in the valley. Local wine growers have donated scenic easements and development rights that will guarantee the preservation of the valley. I run out and join the trust.

Both examples point up the fact that the politician's interest, both real and perceived, will determine his attitude. If he isn't helped out with his perceptions, the result may cause hostility.

In the real world conflicts are less stereotyped and less amusing. I am a local politician and a local land trust member. We almost lost state acquisition funds for a wilderness purchase because local government distrusted the trust. They reacted violently to a "secret private group" being granted power that might be theirs. The state reacted equally violently to the idea of controversy in any form. At the last minute some genius came up with wording that meant appropriately different things to appropriately different people. A truce was reached, and a lesson was learned.

That lesson goes beyond the thought that good public relations are necessary. It comes back to why I've dwelt on the negative side of distrust when land trusts are so clearly good and wonderful.

More than good communications and a good heart are needed. When you are dressed in a gorilla costume and people start waving guns, you are likely to communicate like crazy. When you are dressed in shining armor, you forget that it is necessary. Trusts need to recognize that their shining armor can be frightening, even if you are not a dragon.

CUTBACKS in PUBLIC LAND ACQUISITION:
Opportunities for Innovation
Jean Hocker

Throughout its history, the United States has been both an acquirer and a disposer of vast amounts of land.

Between 1781 and 1867, the federal government acquired over 2 billion acres of land, beginning with cessions from the original states and ending with the purchase of Alaska from Russia. At the same time, federal policy encouraged transfer of public lands into private or state ownership; in the end, nearly two-thirds of the public domain lands were sold or given away to homesteaders, railroads, mining and timber interests, states, and various others.

In 1872, Congress, recognizing the need to assure continued federal ownership of some land "as a public park or pleasuring ground for enjoyment and benefit of the people," established Yellowstone National Park and ordered the "preservation from injury or spoilation of all timber, mineral deposits, natural curiosities or wonders within said park and their retention in their natural condition." In subsequent decades, several other national parks were reserved from the public domain lands, but not until well into the twentieth century did the federal government begin to acquire (or reacquire) private lands in order to protect their natural and scenic resources.

Since 1965, federal land acquisition has been largely financed by the Land and Water Conservation Fund (LWCF). The Fund's income, most of which comes from off-shore oil leasing revenues, is supposed to be "not less than" $900 million. Since its beginning, the Fund has protected nearly 2.8 million acres of nationally significant scenery, wildlife habitat, and recreational lands. New national parks and refuges have been created and private lands within and adjacent to existing reserves have been purchased and added to the federal systems. In addition, states have acquired another 2 million acres of land for recreational purposes, using money from LWCF.

Now, federal appropriations for land acquisitions are being scaled back dramatically. This is partly a function of general belt-tightening and partly the result of an apparent philosophy in the present administration, and among some members of Congress, that further federal land ownership is undesirable or at least unnecessary. The administration has recommended a LWCF appropriation of $45 million for the coming fiscal year, a sum hardly likely to cover even emergency acquisitions where national resources are severely and immediately threatened by changes in land use.

Perhaps we must learn to live with this. No doubt, we must accept, at least for the short run, a significant reduction in federal land acquisition.

What does this cutback mean for future protection of our nation's land resources? What responsibilities does it place on private land conservation efforts? What new opportunities and challenges does it present?

The immediate effects of drastic reductions in federal land acquisition money are becoming clear. For example, an 800-acre forest inholding, which is important moose and elk habitat and a gateway to Grand Teton National Park, will probably be sold to a developer. The owner wanted to sell to the Forest Service, which would have restricted development. Several hundred acres of private land inside the National Elk Refuge boundaries may also be plotted for subdivision; the Fish and Wildlife Service will not likely be able to purchase the property.

Private lands within our national parks are also vulnerable and can be subdivided for residential or commercial use if there are no federal dollars to acquire them. Furthermore, many recent additions to the national park system, already authorized by Congress, may never be acquired. Although these lands were deemed worthy of federal protection, many will be bought instead by private interests seeking to develop or exploit them.

Can local land conservation efforts compensate for this cutback? Not directly or entirely. It is unrealistic to expect local and/or private groups to protect land inside our national parks, forests, and wildlife refuges or to create major new national reserves. Critical wildlife habitat, outstanding scenic areas, and important recreation lands are certain to be lost or diminished because funds are not readily available to purchase them.

Reductions in federal acquisition money may, however, stimulate private land protection efforts, encourage innovation, and foster new public-private partnerships. Some of this is already happening. For example, as hope faded for federal acquisition of conservation easements on private ranchlands next to Grand Teton Park and the National Elk Refuge, residents of Jackson Hole, Wyoming, organized a local land trust. By the end of 1981, after only a few months' existence, the Trust will have received easements over nearly 300 acres of land—a small but promising beginning.

In addition to encouraging formation of new private-sector groups, lack of federal dollars ought to stimulate development of new public policies and laws to provide other incentives for land protection. Three examples follow.

1. *Income tax incentives.*

   a. Allow a tax *credit* for donations of land and easements for conservation purposes.

   b. Extend or eliminate the five-year carry-over period for conservation gift deduction, so the value of a major gift of land can be used up.

   c. For gifts of conservation land and easements, raise the amount of adjusted gross income, which can be deducted annually from 30 percent to 50 percent (without the necessity for reducing the value of the gift).

2. *Estate tax incentives.* Recent changes in estate tax laws will ease pressures on many heirs of agricultural land and open space. But in areas of great development

pressure, a farm or ranch may be valued at millions of dollars in an estate, still posing enormous estate tax problems. At least in some locations, estate tax credits could be granted for the donation of a conservation easement. In effect, an owner could "prepay" his heirs' estate taxes, or the heirs themselves could pay the estate taxes by donating a conservation easement.

3. *Land exchanges.* Particularly in the West, where much of the land is still in federal ownership, there are opportunities to transfer some public land of little conservation value but of high development value for private land or easements on land with high conservation value. There are many problems with current land trade authorities and practices that should be addressed to make exchanges work smoothly and achieve conservation goals.

The National Park Service is now studying several areas of national interest to determine how various alternatives to federal fee acquisition might be used. If these studies, scheduled for completion in early 1982, actually result in new policies and laws, benefits could extend far beyond the specific study areas to locations that would perhaps never receive direct federal dollars for acquisition, even were they available.

Federal land acquisition is certainly not the total answer, nor necessarily the best, for protecting our nation's open land and natural resources. It can be slow, expensive, inflexible, and for some people, threatening. It is always limited, even in the best of times. But federal acquisition has protected millions of acres of critical wildlife habitat, breathtaking scenery, and outstanding natural areas. It has been a fine complement to the long tradition of private land conservation in this country.

The years ahead, when federal dollars will be fewer, should be a period of growth and creativity for the land conservation movement. Necessity should be the catalyst to stimulate a range of new ideas and actions: expanded networks among private land conservation groups; new coalitions between private and public agencies; new ties between business and financial institutions and land conservation organizations; and new incentives from the federal side, as described previously.

Federal acquisition remains a powerful and appropriate tool for protecting our country's great natural and historic areas and for undertaking protection projects that are simply too large for the private sector or other levels of government. The Land and Water Conservation Fund should be used for the purposes for which it was intended and for which funds are earmarked.

Nevertheless, we must deal with reality. If we use the time of fiscal austerity well, to think creatively and to develop new skills and tools, we can emerge with land conservation programs at the private and local level stronger and more successful than ever before. Perhaps then we may even have reason to thank the federal budget-cutters for giving us the unmistakable nudge!

REDUCED PUBLIC FUNDING
and a NEW ROLE for NONPROFITS
Glenn F. Tiedt

The sharp reduction in appropriations from the Land and Water Conservation Fund not only will have an impact on federal, state, and local agencies, it will also have an impact on nonprofit organizations. Many such organizations have been acquiring lands by gift or bargain sale for later resale to public agencies. The price paid by the public agency was always more than that paid by the nonprofit organization, and in some cases the additional amount covered little more than the nonprofit organization's costs for handling the transaction. In others, the nonprofit split the gift with the public agency and increased its own treasury in order to give it greater flexibility to act in the future. If the public funds dry up, however, the nonprofit organizations will have no market for resales, and without the revenues generated by this activity may have to reduce their staffs in the same way public agencies are being forced to reduce theirs.

The emphasis for public agencies today is shifting from land acquisition to land protection. Land protection takes a wide variety of forms from zoning to restrictive covenants to conservation easements. It can even take the form of fee acquisition, but fee acquisition will be the last resort rather than the first option.

The emphasis for nonprofit organizations likewise will have to shift from land acquisition to land protection. But nonprofits have a big advantage over public agencies; they are used to accomplishing great things with limited resources. While federal agencies are being severely criticized by the Government Accounting Office for failing to make effective use of less-than-fee acquisition techniques, some nonprofit organizations are using these techniques as the backbone of their programs.

It is in the area of less-than-fee acquisition that the public agencies have a great deal to learn from the nonprofit organizations. It is also in this area that I see a substantial opportunity for innovation. One of the reasons public agencies have tended to purchase fee simple rather than less-than-fee even when their own plans called for less-than-fee acquisition on particular properties has been the offer by the landowner to sell the fee. The landowner frequently wants out, and he is not interested in selling less than his entire interest to anyone. Since the public agencies like to work with willing sellers, they find it easy to acquire the entire interest and forget the plans that call for something else.

The diminishing flow of public funds will increase the pressure on public agencies to acquire less-than-fee where appropriate. It will not, however, decrease the landowner's desire to sell his entire interest, and here is where the nonprofit organizations might begin to play a significant new role in land protections. The nonprofit organizations could acquire the properties in fee, impose restrictions in accord with agency plans, sell the property subject to the restrictions, and be reimbursed by the public agency for the costs of the restrictions plus administrative overhead. This approach to land protection offers nonprofit organizations the opportunity to continue to generate some revenue through purchases and resales. It offers public agencies the opportunity to acquire partial interests through negotiated purchase in situations where this was formerly impossible, and it offers the general public the best buy in land protection because the restricted interest would be sold in the marketplace. The value of the restriction would be determined by a willing buyer and a willing seller rather than an appraiser.

Conservation easements will become the cornerstone of public agency land protection programs. Nonprofit organizations have the experience and knowledge to continue to make a significant contribution to the land protection efforts, and the reduced public funding for land acquisition will make nonprofit activities more important today than they have ever been in the past.

PRIVATE LAND CONSERVATION and LOCAL REGULATION in VERMONT
Richard W. Carbin

A high percentage of towns in Vermont now have comprehensive land use (or development) plans and some form of zoning regulations. The number of towns that have other types of regulations, such as subdivision regulations or capital investment programs, are decidedly fewer (particularly those with any kind of capital program). The quality of these regulatory activities is, from a land conservation point of view, poor.

Under Vermont law, local land use regulations (zoning and subdivision regulations) cannot be put into permanent effect unless the town has adopted a master plan. A town plan can be adopted by the local legislative body (the board of selectmen). Regulations implementing the town plan must be voted upon in all communities under 2,500 people (most towns in Vermont). Regulations adopted must follow the recommendations of the town plan.

Generally speaking, because the political process is easier in adopting a town plan, these documents are more thorough in their considerations and recommendations with regard to natural resources. Even though in theory land use regulations are supposed to parallel town plan recommendations, in practice they generally are much watered-down versions. This is because at the local level in Vermont there is a strong resistance to any regulatory control. Only minimal levels of development control have any chance to be voted upon favorably. The effect of local regulations is often further weakened by poor administration, political pressure on local boards, and a lack of public understanding of the regulatory process.

For these reasons it can be stated honestly that no local land use regulation can be relied upon to protect Vermont's natural resources. Vermont does have a state Land Use and Development Law (Act 250), which requires comprehensive review of many proposed developments, including consideration of the impact on natural resources. This provides better-quality control of major development, but the law administers development on a piecemeal basis and cannot assure conservation of natural resources in any comprehensive way.

These aspects of the public land use regulatory process in Vermont both help and hurt local land conservation efforts. On the negative side, once even the most inadequate regulations are put into place, there is a sense of security that sufficient environmental protection exists. This often makes it difficult to convince people that more remains to be done and that one alternative is to support local private initiatives to conserve resources. On the other hand, the inability of local regulations to deal effectively with land conservation issues, can strengthen the resolve of those in the community who do see a problem to supplement the public regulatory process through private action.

In Vermont it turns out that both the public planning and regulatory process and the private conservation effort can work together. Since town plans are generally more comprehensive in dealing with conservation concerns, these documents can often help local conservation organizations identify protection priorities and justify the public purposes behind private land conservation efforts. This kind of relationship can provide a community with a set of regulations that can control at least the most basic land use abuses while at the same time establishing a broader context of community conservation needs that the private conservation organization can address directly.

PUBLIC LAND ACQUISITION as LEVERAGE for COOPERATIVE LAND MANAGEMENT

Hans Neuhauser

The hostility of the present administration and certain members of Congress to the appropriation of monies for public land acquisition is neither a new phenomenon nor an unexpected one on the political scene. While few of us have been willing to articulate it, the fact remains that government, at whatever level, cannot afford to buy all the land and natural resources of this country that need to be protected and conserved. Much as we might like to, our government can't afford to buy all the remaining undeveloped barrier islands, river swamps, prairie potholes, mountain wildernesses, and urban open space. The money just isn't there.

One alternative to ownership is government regulation. The environmental impact statement process, the Section 404 permit requirements, the Endangered Species Act, and others all help; but they are not adequate to do the job at hand. And even in their inadequate form, these and other regulations are threatened with their own extinction.

Obviously, alternatives to government ownership and regulation must be found. A number are being tried, some successfully: creative development, transfer of development rights, acquisition of scenic or other easements among them. One that has not received much attention and yet may offer significant benefits is cooperative management.

Cooperative management is the control of an ecosystem or other resource through the active and combined efforts of a variety of different parties in such ways that the interests and actions of the different parties are at least compatible and are hopefully mutually reinforcing each other. In other words, cooperative management consists of the public and private sectors joining together in the management of an area in ways that do not create any "big losers."

Last November the Georgia Conservancy hosted a workshop on cooperative management of coastal ecosystems. The intent of the workshop was to assess the nationwide experience of managing large ecosystems on a cooperative basis rather than relying upon purchase in fee simple or in part. If the assessment demonstrated that these systems could be managed cooperatively, then what were the common threads—if any—that contributed to their success, and what—if any—were the pitfalls?

The ecosystems we evaluated were large, diverse ecologically, and owned or controlled by multiple public agencies and private individuals and corporations. Among the areas examined were the Adirondack State Park, New York; the New Jersey Pine Barrens; Appalachicola Bay, Florida; Grays Harbor, Washington; and Coos Bay, Oregon. Although most of the areas examined were coastal, the lessons learned have broad applicability to noncoastal situations.

While the proceedings[1] of the workshop are still in preparation, a summary of the conclusions and some noteworthy observations can be provided.

The process by which a cooperative management program is developed requires the most attention, for the success of the venture depends primarily on the voluntary agreements of the participants. If one interest is angered or ignored, they could walk out and take their marbles with them.

The process has to revolve around a clearly defined resource unit; the boundaries have to be defined and agreed upon.

The process needs to have a simple-to-understand goal, something that can be clearly expressed on the back of a business card or during a thirty-second interview on television. Details are, of course, necessary, but you need to be able to express the central objective clearly and concisely.

Disagreements are likely to arise in the development and operation of the management program. Traditionally, disagreements have been dealt with by: (1) ignoring them and hoping they'll go away or solve themselves, (2) refusing to let the dissenter participate in the process, or (3) putting off the argument until later. Sometimes these techniques work, but they're not often successful in a cooperative management program. A more satisfactory mechanism is to have as an integral part of the process a dispute-resolution procedure. The participation of an environmental mediator may be necessary to resolve fundamental disagreements.

Evaluation is also necessary to foster success. It, too, should be an integral part of the process, so that everyone understands why the evaluation is taking place, when it will be done and how. No one, and particularly the management team, will have to feel defensive about the review.

The conclusion emerged from the workshop that cooperative management could work if the following steps were taken:

1. Identify the resource unit to be managed.

2. Obtain funds for management and, if necessary, for key land acquisitions from government and nongovernment sources.

3. Establish a policy committee that would call the shots.

4. Establish a technical committee to provide information and advice to the policy committee.

5. Define the goals, objectives, and policies for management.

6. Use mediation as a conflict resolution mechanism.

7. Develop a compact to provide both a blueprint for the future and predictability.

---

1. H. Neuhauser and J. Clark, eds. *Proceedings of the Workshop on Cooperative Management of Coastal Ecosystems,* forthcoming. For further information, write The Georgia Conservancy, 4405 Paulsen St., Savannah, Georgia 31405.

8. Build procedures for review, revision, and evaluation into the process.

9. Establish a management team.

The unit to be managed can be as small as an estuary or as large as a watershed. Regardless of its size, however, there are probably one or more areas that must be protected in order for the whole idea to work. These areas, whether they be a wetland or a boat-launching spot or a scenic vista, may have to be purchased in fee simple and possibly with public funds. The acquisition of a key area can be used as both focal point and leverage for the implementation of a cooperative management program.

THE IMPACTS of PUBLIC REGULATORY ACTIVITY on LOCAL PRIVATE LAND CONSERVATION EFFORTS
Judith M. Stockdale

Of all the forms of public regulatory activity that directly and indirectly affect land and land use (planning, zoning, subdivision and building codes, and the gamut of environmental regulations, such as air and water quality standards), I have separated environmental regulations from the rest, because there is a fundamental distinction. Environmental regulations are uniform across the nation because they have been reinforced by federal law and, while states are at liberty to impose more stringent measures, the federal influence does establish a minimum standard. However, although there are some exceptions, for example, the Flood Insurance Acts and some lip service in the Clean Water Act Amendments, for the most part environmental regulations have not yet directly affected land use. Long established as the very essence of American rights and bound into the law, land use control is the domain of the states, not the federal government, and generally the states give way to the local jurisdiction and, very often, the local entity is swayed by the individual. Only a few states have instituted state zoning or land use initiatives; several have tried and reneged.

ENVIRONMENTAL REGULATIONS
While environmental regulations have done little as yet directly to affect land use, they have helped in this last decade of their effectiveness to raise environmental consciousness and to establish an environmental professionalism. These phenomena have, I believe, had an effect on the establishment of private land conservation organizations in two ways: They have created a

climate in which environmentalism in all its forms has been viewed favorably by private funding sources; and they have caused the realization that the private sector has a role in land conservation in the face of limited public control. In the recent years of increased environmental bureaucracy, we have even seen private organizations faring well by being able to offer often more direct solutions with less red tape. So, to date, environmental regulations may have had a considerable indirect effect on the inception of local private land conservation groups but little direct impact on their activities of land acquisition and transfer.

The future may see more direct effects: The Clean Water Act offers an example. In northeastern Illinois we are starting to see the 208 plans come into effect (Sec. 208 of the Clean Water Act, requiring regional waste-water treatment plans to be drawn up). Areas of land that are currently unserved by waste-water treatment facilities and that fall outside treatment area boundaries lose development potential. In this instance local decision is backed by federal law. Continued urban sprawl and rising land values may well be checked by court decision, leaving in the wake land for which private conservation techniques may be suitable. (If, however, standards and regulations are subjected to the kind of review that the current administration has indicated, the future effects of environmental regulations on land may be no more direct than in the past.)

PLANNING, ZONING, AND CODES

These activities have a much more direct effect on land, its value and its use. Because of this it seems to me imperative that local land conservation groups not only need a thorough grasp of local regulatory agencies, politics, and procedures but also should develop good relationships with them.

Ideally a land use plan is built from the capacity of natural resources. Those lands for which conservation is most appropriate are so allocated and compatible zoning reinforces the intent of the plan. When this is the case a local conservation organization can work very effectively with a local (or state) regulatory agency. A group of communities in suburban Chicago have worked through a council of governments to produce a joint plan for their region. Wetlands areas are designated as open space (for conservation and to prevent flood damages) and, working with local land conservation organizations, these lands are being preserved through private action.

Unfortunately, many locally laid plans are not based on the natural resources; wetlands, prime agricultural lands, and aquifer recharge areas, for example, may often be considered "buildable." In those cases, local land conservation organizations are working against considerable odds; not only is the plan endangering the land resource itself but the value of lands unsuitable for development is artificially raised and landowners have unrealistic expectations. Here the role of the private conservation group becomes educational—often a long-term effort. Planning commissioners and members of appeals boards are voluntary; one group may have been "conservationally educated" when election or appointment time rolls around and all the characters change. But with patience, attitudes can be altered.

To conclude, the regulatory activities that have the most impact on local private land conservation efforts are local zoning and planning decisions. The local land conservation group must be in the position to work closely with the local public agencies and must encourage the type of plan that will uphold zoning appeals. Where possible techniques beyond traditional zoning (transfer of development rights, cluster zoning, land banking) should be explored by public agencies in conjunction with local private groups.

ORGANIZATIONAL
PERFORMANCE

The mettle of the local land-saving movement will be severely tested in the immediate future. At the same time that government at all levels is having to back away from land acquisition and protection, federal government policies are making operating funds for private organizations increasingly difficult to secure. To meet the challenge of doing more with less, local conservation groups are going to have to become more professional in their management, more aggressive and sophisticated in securing financial support, and more committed to working together to build collective strength and competence.

Leadership is the key to effective organization performance. A strong and influential board of directors inspired by the organization's mission is the critical leadership factor. The board must define the role of the enterprise, set its objectives, choose its staff, and evaluate its accomplishments. Members of the board must be emissaries to the community and promoters of the organization's goals. Of most importance, directors must assume responsibility for securing and allocating the financial resources needed to achieve the group's objectives.

Particularly in the early stages of development, committed leadership is crucial. Prior to launching any public fund-raising or operational efforts, the direction and scope of the group's program must be determined and the overall strategy with the highest possibility of success selected. This process should include consultation throughout the community and with organizations elsewhere that have experience to lend. Only when a definite course and mode of operation has been determined and articulated is it time to seek funding. Initial financial resources should be used to achieve early successes on which further solicitation for operating funds and, eventually—as these successes mount—for endowment funds, can be based.

The financial needs of the organization will be determined by the nature of its programs and the relative importance given acquisition, property management, information and education, technical services, and public advocacy. The interrelationships among these activities must be analyzed in terms of budget impacts. Opportunities for generating income from transactions and services need careful consideration.

Management capability is vital. The investment in professional skills is essential for organizations buying, selling, brokering, or managing property. The risks are great and the price of mistakes can far outweigh the cost of competent support. Not only should there be professional capacity in the legal, financial, and land management areas, but an effective organization should also have institutional management capability comparable to modern business establishments.

There is an urgent need for outside help for local land-saving groups that are trying to get started or trying to improve their effectiveness. This has been recognized by several national organizations that have begun to offer information and technical assistance. The Trust for Public Land has established its Western Land Trust Program and The Nature Conservancy has sponsored a pilot project in Connecticut, the Land Trust Service Bureau. The American Farmland Trust now offers a range of technical and financial services to groups concerned with farmland retention. The National Park Service provides information and technical assistance to both public and private groups through publications, workshops, and direct consultation.

Much can be accomplished through sharing of experience and strategies among the many groups across the nation with land-saving objectives. With a minimum of staff and structural formality, the member groups can establish a communications network and put together some working committees to deal with far-ranging problems of mutual concern. Such an effort will require some outside funding and a great deal of effort by the practicing members of the local land conservation movement.

GOVERNING BOARDS, PROFESSIONAL STAFF, and VOLUNTEERS CAN BUILD CONTINUITY
Robert Augsburger

To build for the future and provide long-term continuity requires leadership, leadership, and more leadership.

Whether volunteer or professionally staffed, the most critical element is the make-up of the governing board. Only those organizations with a strong, committed, and influential board are likely to succeed. Board members must define the organization's purpose and must develop the policies to implement the purpose. The board is primarily responsible for community relations and interpretation. It is responsible for the *procurement* and allocation of financial resources. The board is accountable for the results of the organization. The primary criteria for board selection are the potential member's *ability* and *influence* to help achieve the organization's mission. One wag has summarized board-member qualifications as work, wisdom, wealth, and wallop.

It is the unusual organization that can achieve success today in the absence of professional staff. That staff may be only one person—full- or part-time—to provide information to and coordinate the efforts of board members and other volunteers. Size and background of staff is dependent upon the mission, the time frame, and funding sources. An organization operating in an urban area may require a different quality and type of individual than one operating in an essentially rural community. The availability of volunteer talent will also influence the nature of any staff.

No single kind of background training and experience seems essential for staff positions. Whether a planner, a fund raiser, a land manager, a businessman, a lawyer, or environmental scientist depends upon the nature of the organization, its mission, and the availability of candidates. What is important is the person's ability to function as a generalist, to communicate, and to work well with a wide variety of people. Where there is evidence of long-term staff commitment, opportunities for special training in some of the above areas should be a part of the compensation package.

The first step in building a volunteer corps is the creation of a relatively large advisory council. Unlike the governing board, primary attributes of these people may be only interest and motivation. They may provide technical skills in such fields as law, accounting, surveying, and public relations. They may provide social and organizational skills for special events, political liaison, or the creation of a docent program, if appropriate. They can be close to the land and provide credibility to the mission. Particular attention should be paid to bringing in younger, yet-to-be-discovered (or overloaded) community leaders into this group. This broad, diverse group of people can also provide a candidate pool for future board nominations. In using these and other volunteers effectively, it's important to limit what is expected of them, to make sure they know what is expected of them, and to offer great praise and acknowledgment when they come close to achieving what is expected of them.

Long-term continuity is best assured by the people involved and the leadership they provide. The membership of the board and an advisory group is the single most important decision to be made.

DEVELOPING an EFFECTIVE AGRICULTURAL LAND TRUST PROGRAM

Paul D. Maxwell

Protection of America's farm and ranchland from conversion to nonagricultural uses will become a very important issue in the 1980s. In the United States agricultural land is being taken out of production at the rate of 3 million acres per year. At the same time, domestic and export demand for agricultural products will require a steady increase in production over the next twenty years. In addition, the increased cost of producing food on the farm, along with increased land use competition for housing and nonagricultural goods and services, will place continued pressure on our agricultural resource base.

The local land trust can play an important role in the mitigation of agricultural land loss. Many of the methods used by land trusts for the protection of natural, scenic, and wildlife areas are also applicable to farmland. The critical ingredient, however, in a workable agricultural land protection program is the support of the farm community.

To gain support from the ranchers and farmers the land trust must make a sincere effort to understand the problems and complexities of the agricultural industry. Unless this is done, the trust will not be sensitive to the special needs of the farm/ranch operators and will find it difficult to seek creative ways to keep them on the land.

One of the best ways to gain support of local farm industry is to get them involved in the design of the program from the very beginning. The trust should encourage leaders of the farm community to develop the program themselves, using their knowledge of agriculture combined with the trust's experience in land conservation.

The trust should consider inviting an agricultural representative to sit on the trust's board of directors. In addition, formation of an agricultural advisory committee, to board and staff, would provide the trust with continued feedback on the evolution of the program.

At first, the land trust may be greeted with skepticism and looked upon as an outsider. It will take patience and a great deal of sales ability to present your ideas. After it has been established that the trust and the agricultural community do have common goals, the program can be started.

Once you have involved the key farm production people in support of the land trust concept, then you have to sell the idea to the supporting agribusiness organizations, lending institutions, and professionals. After they are behind you, it is time to go to the community at large and tell them the farmland preservation story.

The protection of agricultural land will mean dealing with property that must remain economically viable in the face of spiraling land and production costs. To accomplish this, it will be necessary to consider new tools for the land trust's bag of tricks. The use of limited development projects, transfer of development rights, partnerships between conservation buyers and farm/ranch operators, and other methods of creative financing may be the wave of the future in protecting agricultural land.

Eighty-eight percent of farms and ranches in the United States are owned by individuals or families. Ten percent are held by partnership or family corporations. Two percent of all farms are held by corporations that control 11.7 percent of the private land in farms. The most effective program at this time will be to deal directly with the individual or farm family and help keep them on their land.

If the trend of ag land loss continues, we not only reduce our base for food production, but weaken the fabric of the American family farm system that built this country. As the family farm is forced out of business, the land that does remain in production is more likely to be taken over by large corporate interests. This will reduce the diversity now provided under the family farm system and result in a monopoly of land control and food production.

In summary, the most critical issue is the fact that demand for food is increasing and our agricultural land decreasing. The National Agricultural Land Study estimates that 77–113 million *new acres* will be needed over the next twenty years if we are to meet the projected worldwide need for food.

Land trusts are in a position now to do something about the problem. Let us work together to meet the challenge.

SELLING YOURSELF as a LOCAL CONSERVATION ORGANIZATION

Mark C. Ackelson and Gerald F. Schnepf

Not only are our natural resources under increasing pressures, but the financial resources necessary to support the conservation of these natural resources is also under increasing pressure. Those of us concerned about the role of the "third sector," or private nonprofit conservation organizations, must assist by sharing philosophies and techniques that have proven successful.

The key to the successful initiation and development of new private nonprofit conservation organizations is in the handling of their early development programs. The founders of the Iowa Natural Heritage Foundation spent a great deal of time evaluating approaches prior to its incorporation. What we have found should be shared with others who are interested in establishing or (re)developing nonprofit, nonlobbying, local private conservation organizations.

Organizations and programs begin because of an unmet need. The seed of an idea germinates with one or more persons. These individuals must serve as a nucleus to provide some initial direction and program development. If this nucleus group does not include a widely recognized, respected, and effective leader, a part of your discussions may include gentle probing to identify such a person. A well-established and recognized leader is absolutely essential.

An approach or "idea" must be selected that has the highest probability of success based upon the opinion and judgment of this leadership. This idea or concept must be translated by the leadership into a program with a clear statement of objectives. The concept should be further reviewed with a peer group of additional community, government, and business leaders. "We have a concept in mind to respond to this particular need, and we would like to share it with you for your thoughts." Points to consider include:

Recognition of need(s) that precipitated the concept

Concept or approach to be taken in discussion of service area with clientele

Willingness to assist (no request for funds yet)

Suggestions of others to talk with

From these basic discussions, if the peer-group response reflected program support and has generated their interest, a refined game plan can be prepared and the organizational network established. Don't try to include too many people too soon. Concentrate on a limited number of effective leaders with a professional, geographic, and political balance. These founding sponsors should be prepared to lend at least modest financial support and time to the program. There must also be a balanced mixture of those who are "movers and shakers" and those whose name is critical for a stamp of approval (concept endorsement); some may have both attributes.

If the program is worthwhile, it deserves the best chance for success. The next key step then is establishing a somewhat broader base of supporters. This requires financial support and professional assistance. Financial support must be adequate to begin development, preparation, and distribution of informational materials, establishment of an office, and the initiation of project and fund-raising programs. The objective is to develop creditability.

Financial resources can be augmented by the efforts of dedicated professionals, retired persons, or volunteers. But professional staff expertise and a knowledge of the "turf" is necessary. Short-changing the effort at this point can be extremely detrimental to the short- and long-term success of the program.

Financial resources may be solicited from a selected group in the form of "seed money"—funds to develop informational materials, establish the program, and begin implementation of broader solicitations. Funds are needed for twelve–eighteen months of operations.

Your informational materials should be directed at several groups of constituents. This will require several different pieces of information. Don't forget that these materials are selling the organization and the program; poor-quality items suggest poor programs. Supporters are interested in successful programs, not losers. On the other hand, do not engage in mass distribution of high-cost materials as an attempt to cut corners in enlisting support. These materials should be long wearing and soft selling, with emotional appeal. They must clearly identify your program and financial goals, but you should be prepared to give to each contact a personal touch. The materials alone, in whatever form and regardless of quality, will not do the job for you.

With the "seed money," begin your program quickly and establish some early successes. Tell people about these successes. Switch the program from "what we intend to do" to "what we have done" as quickly as possible. Take your story to a variety of people and organizations and tell it with pride and enthusiasm. Again, remember, people like to be associated with success.

The organization should consider a series of informational dinners or meetings hosted by locally respected leaders. The program and successes can be reviewed with the attendees, and follow-up interviews made with selected attendees to gain feedback in the form of a feasibility study. The feasibility study should focus on the same points reviewed with the initial nucleus group. Keep accurate, thorough file notes as they will become increasingly valuable as you progress. Based on the follow-up interviews and subsequent fine tuning of materials and programs, a fund-raising goal and strategy can be refined or defined.

Having completed all of the above, our Foundation is now engaged in an endowment program, concentrating first on major contributors (trustees, individuals, corporations, and foundations), mostly developed from contacts made during the process of telling our story around the state. The long-term financial stability of the organization should be developed around a comprehensive planned giving program that can be used to build up a healthy endowment. The planned giving program success will require sustained effort over a considerable time and must have strong backing by the trustees. The organization must be prepared to invest the necessary time and effort in constituent education, prospect identification, and cultivation.

The Iowa Natural Heritage Foundation has established itself with a well-plotted course of action. Other organizations may benefit from the Foundation's approach. That approach is characterized by select leadership, professional staff, early success, and a concentrated development program. Each component is necessary for the overall success of the organization. The key is flexibility, development of an objective feedback system, and constant refinement of the programs.

FINANCING PRIVATE LAND CONSERVATION
H. William Sellers

In a changing economic climate and in the midst of major structural changes in our tax systems, it is difficult to address with any prescience this topic which has been so seemingly dependent on good times and high marginal tax rates.

Perhaps, if the land conservation movement adopts a strategy of financial planning for bad times, we will reexamine any fundamental problems in our philosophies and *modus operandi* that have cluttered our closets in the past.

This particular topic strikes to the heart of any organization because successful long-term financing of an organization is the result of other successes: (1) the formulation of and pursuit of clear and practical goals and objectives that will appeal to finance-oriented individuals; (2) development of a board whose members will provide funds or can assist in their acquisition; (3) recruitment of professional staff (or in the early years, skilled volunteers willing to work almost as much as staff) who have skills in land acquisition, management, and fund raising; and (4) development of a broad membership to substantiate the public nature of the organization and provide important contacts and spokesmen in the community. The first three are critical to getting started and remaining financially vital.

In a very real sense, a land conservation organization should consider everything it is and does from the point of view of how would a conservative banker view the organization and its track record. (In fact, establishing and building a relationship with a bank or banks should be one financing objective.) The important point, however, is that competition for private and public funds is going to be bitter in the years ahead, and the organizations that will succeed will be those who have done the most for themselves and have established a credit-worthy track record.

There are three major financing needs: (1) funds to acquire interests in land; (2) funds for staff and other operating costs of developing and implementing land conservation and acquisition programs; and (3) funds for staff and other costs of land management and public programs after and, possibly, before acquisition (as explained later).

The organization should always look at (1) above from the perspective of (2) and (3) and in doing so: Always view (1) as the last resort when donations or other methods of land conservation fail; and recognize that most acquisitions will require skills in and expenditures for (2) and (3) and that a realistic plan for securing or earning funds for such should be drawn up before negotiations begin.

The key to sound financing of land conservation programs is to reduce the extent to which the organization or donors of land interests are dependent on and/or expect purely charitable considerations. Recent tax law changes have certainly reduced the number of taxpayers who can make cheap donations of land interests or funds. This will put pressure on the operating budgets of organizations and may significantly reduce donation of land interests, absent a change in basic approaches. I believe that the solution to this problem is for the organization to define its mission as providing *expert* assistance to its community and to private landowners on land use and management issues, assistance that will be clearly compensated in cash, donated land interests, or both. In the past, many of us have assisted owners with gifts of land interests for conservation purposes. We have not concerned ourselves with how we can help a landowner with the disposition of land for development purposes or how we can assist him with present land management or land use questions. An owner should not be forced to choose between a pure conservation approach and a purely profitable approach.

Similarly, the organization must manage its land and public programs more productively and imaginatively in order to control costs, increase income, and cement its image in the community.

If we succeed in helping ourselves without crying "wolf" at every turn, foundations, private donors, and governments will know that when we ask for funds there truly is no alternative left to explore.

BUILDING an ORGANIZATIONAL BASE: Professional Staffing
Andrew Johnson

The need for professionally run organizations, active in the acquisition and management of open space areas, is finally being recognized as an alternative to government control. Progress made during the past ten years has been marred by the high price paid for land and the exploding cost of managing these lands.

The fundamental question is: What professions will emerge for the future and from what sector will they emerge? After Earth Day in 1970 people from many professions jumped on the bandwagon. Nonprofit organizations sprang up by the thousands, and most were "staffed" by volunteers.

To focus on those organizations set up primarily to "preserve" open space, we must analyze the work that is performed. In our work we run a mix of chores ranging from:

1. *Legal:* title search, quiet title actions, subdivision approvals, zoning changes, government regulations (i.e., flood plains and wetlands laws), mortgages, real estate tax exemptions, homeowners agreements, sales agreements, and so on

2. *Financial:* capital gains tax, mortgage rates, real estate market analysis, tax status, estate tax, government funding, and so on

3. *Management:* Wood-lot management, farm leases, endangered species management, trail construction, renovation of historical structures, posting, and so on

The organization dedicated to open space acquisition and management must have professional knowledge of all these areas if it is to successfully negotiate the purchase of land and then develop a strategy for its future management.

Often, nonprofit boards claim they cannot afford to pay professionals to manage their affairs, yet they proceed to purchase lands worth millions of dollars. Many organizations and foundations feel that it is somehow all right to spend millions on land and yet fail to retain professional level personnel to administer these purchases. Part of our work over the past few years has been helping nonprofits bail out of expensive purchases that they bought with little or no professional guidance and partial funding.

A major element of my past success in the last three organizations I have managed has been to attract professionals from commercial careers and retrain them in nonprofit work. One area I have yet to succeed in is to create the "profit motive" in the nonprofit arena. Somehow the word *profit* became an unacceptable motive for nonprofit work.

Provisions are in place within the IRS code to make money as a 501(c)3 without losing the nonprofit status (unrelated business form of the 990 called the 990T).

The business of buying and selling land is a very risky one and to properly decide what land should be purchased and for what price requires professional advice. To protect against losses, the nonprofit should structure each purchase in such a way as to make money (if all goes as planned).

In summary then, to build a firm organizational base, professional staffing is required. To attract professionals from the private sector with proven abilities in real estate matters is expensive; however, when compared to the potential losses that do occur when land is bought and sold, these personnel costs are minor. Volunteers have a role in the nonprofit, but their interest must be constantly stimulated and this requires professional leadership. Finally, long-term continuity can only come if there is money to provide such continuity. The sole reliance on contributions will not in itself ensure perpetuity of the organization.

DEVELOPMENT of a NONPROFIT ORGANIZATION
John R. Cook, Jr.

As an outsider who provides services to local land conservation organizations, I have several observations. I make these observations with a good general knowledge of the field, but not an insider's detailed understanding of the mechanics. While these observations are directed at land conservation organizations, they could very well be pointed at nonprofit organizations in general. This is also a difficult process because there is such a wide range of organizations in the field in terms of budget, staffing, level of organization, and size of operation.

MANAGEMENT

Local land conservation organizations have accomplished a great deal in their relatively short history. But to meet the challenges of the 1980s they must learn to do more with less resources. Much can be gained from an application of modern business practices to the local land conservation field. This includes such techniques as marketing plans, business strategies, financial planning, money management, telecommunications, budgeting, and accounting. Although it is dependent on the level of the organization, these practices can be applied to individual organizations in varying degrees. For example, in establishing a marketing plan, it is possible to produce a very sophisticated one in its development, application, and evaluation or one that is simple and direct in its approach. All of these business practices can be applied in varying degrees. This would accommodate the wide variety of organizations in the local land conservation field.

COMMUNICATION

There is a tremendous amount of activity occurring in the local land conservation field across the country. Unfortunately, this is being done on an individual and localized basis. This results in inefficiency and ineffectiveness due to duplication of action. With greater communication among these organizations, several goals would be accomplished. First, the transfer and exchange of techniques, experiences, problems, and even staff would greatly increase the effectiveness of each organization. This would significantly reduce the current practice of "reinventing the wheel" with each local organization. Second, the communication network would reinforce staff and other participants by providing morale and institutional support for its activities. Primarily, it is a self-awareness problem of realizing the breadth and size of action and activity of the collective field. Finally, communication would give organizations collective representation on deliberation of issues on the state and national levels. Laws, practices, and programs are being established on the state and federal levels on an annual basis that significantly affect the operation of local land conservation organizations. Currently, there is little or no representation of local land conservation organizations in the development of this new "action." The net result is that these organizations must deal with the results of this process rather than participate in its development. This can best be exemplified by the changes in the tax laws last year that changed the operation of these organizations. This happened with limited representation from local land conservation organizations.

PURPOSE

I believe that every nonprofit organization should periodically analyze its purposes and goals to determine if the reasons for the organization are still valid. With the fast-paced changes of our community today, the reason for setting up an organization can be solved or changed in the space of three to five years. It is important for the direction and morale of an organization to reassess itself to determine if its purposes and goals are still viable. This process, although a difficult and frustrating one, is extremely valuable for the well-being of an organization. It is through this kind of discussion that the staff and other participants have a clear understanding of their role and how they interact with the public.

I believe that there is an evolution to every organization. The first stage is what I would call the crisis stage. During this stage, the people involved in the development of the organization are operating in a constant state of crisis to keep it going financially and functionally. The next stage comes with the realization, on the part of the staff, that the organization is viable, stable, and will be around for some time. At this point, the emotion, zeal, and drive that established and operated the organization through its crisis period wanes, and complacency sets in. An organization is not operating on current goals and purposes but often just for the sake of operating.

With a scheduled periodic review of its operation, this complacency can be eliminated and avoided. Such issues as the need for the organization, its goals and purposes, public interest, financial viability, and many others can be analyzed, explored, and determined. In some cases, it may be determined that there is no longer a need for an organization. A big party can then be held and the organization seeks "early retirement."

BROAD BASE

It is important for local land conservation organizations and other nonprofits to seek a broader base in the community. This is true for political, financial, and public interest reasons. At the moment, there is no major motivation to do so unless this is part of the original purposes of the organization. The primary reason for this is that the financial sources and organizational origins are not directed in this manner. Yet if nonprofit organizations are to survive in the 1980s, I believe that it is important to have a broader base than currently exists. Further, there is much to be gained from interaction exchange in terms of techniques, experiences, and problems in other parts of the community.

To conclude, I am amazed at the quantity and quality of effort and results of the local land conservation organizations. In many ways, it is a true example of American entrepreneurship at its finest. Namely, they are creating markets and providing products and services in uncharted areas. To sustain this quality, each organization and each individual must look inward and outward to determine how they can do their job better and, indeed, meet the challenges and opportunities of the 1980s.

A CAREER IN LAND CONSERVATION?
Russell Cohen

I would like to discuss in this paper the economic and practical advantages and disadvantages of choosing a career in land conservation. As I have yet to officially enter the land conservation community as a full-time employee, I approach this topic with a bit of uncertainty. Nevertheless, I shall comment upon several issues that I myself have confronted in the course of choosing to specialize in land conservation and selecting what particular role to play within the movement.

ECONOMIC REALITIES OF A CAREER IN LAND CONSERVATION

As I am in my final year of schooling before embarking upon an expected career in land conservation, I have naturally developed an increasing interest in what positions are available and the degrees of remuneration they provide. I have noticed several trends in the current employment picture in addition to the long-prevailing characteristics. These latter items I shall address first. Land conservation, in common with most other altruistic pursuits, tends to be rather financially unrewarding. This would partially serve to explain that a large majority of local land conservation organizations are staffed partially or entirely by volunteers who derive their incomes from other sources.

However, one cannot ignore the considerable contribution of the "psychic income" that comes from acting in the public interest. In addition, positions in land conservation are often a pleasant alternative to normal desk jobs since they usually entail a large degree of personal contact with landowners with attendant traveling to and field inspection of proposed acquisitions. There is also a degree of cooperation and rapport among persons working with different land conservation groups that isn't as common among competing businesses. I suppose that it is up to each individual to discover upon taking a land conservation position whether the potentially higher job satisfaction sufficiently compensates for the less than optimum emolument.

The current employment picture for job applicants seeking work in land conservation is being shaped by several major factors. First of all, funding cuts, hiring freezes, and James Watt's attempted sabotage have seriously limited federal job opportunities in land conservation as well as having struck fear in the hearts of those currently employed therein. Second, there has been a significant increase in the financial and membership support for many private non-profit conservation organizations, a part of which is due to the incidents occurring at the federal level. It is not certain that the growing support for the private conservation movement will in itself result in a significant expansion of the number of land conservation jobs. Third, there appears to be continued modest growth of environmental jobs at the local and state level, with the delegation to them of duties formerly undertaken by the federal government being cancelled out by local and state budget cutbacks. Lastly, the effect of the ecology movement of the late 1960s and early 1970s on young minds has currently resulted in a substantial crop of graduates seeking environmental jobs, including most aspects of land conservation. Unfortunately, the number of these applicants seems to surpass the number of available jobs.

Job security is also an issue because of the financial precariousness of many land conservation projects and organizations. In summary, then, even if one could obtain and hold a land conservation job, it may be necessary to supplement whatever salary is paid with income from another source. This could be done by working part-time in land conservation and part-time in a more lucrative occupation or by the receipt of investment or other unearned income.

PRACTICAL CONSIDERATIONS FOR A LAND CONSERVATION CAREER

Given the fact that a person feels philosophically justified in choosing land conservation as a career and is willing to try his or her luck in the job market, the next issue is to decide what type of position to apply for, whom to work for, and if no suitable potential employers appear on the horizon, how to perceive a need for your services within the land conservation community.

Both public and private land conservation groups function at national, regional, state, subregional (e.g., intrastate watershed), and local levels. Both public and the larger, private national-level organizations are prone to excess bureaucracy although they often offer more adequate compensation than the smaller-scale programs and organizations.

Most local land conservation groups operate on low budgets with funds supplied partially or entirely by donations and cannot afford to hire staff. This does not indicate, however, that these groups couldn't benefit from some staff support when needed for a particular situation. Even where a group such as a local land conservation trust has experienced and capable members supporting it, they are often too tied up with their primary occupations, their families, and obligations to other volunteer groups to devote much time to preserving land.

As a closing comment, then, I would like to say that a career in land conservation has an advantage that for me outweighs the disadvantages: It is the opportunity to protect undeveloped land and help others observe a land ethic, the tenets of which I hold a great amount of respect for.

BUILDING for the FUTURE:
A Service Bureau
Suzanne Wilkins

A coordinating body that provides technical assistance and improves communications is one successful mechanism for improving the operation of local land trusts. Such a "service bureau" will prove effective if there is a demonstrated need or perceived recipients for it and if it can serve a geographically manageable area.

This service bureau can provide information to existing trusts—both base data (via comprehensive written materials and conferences and workshops) and periodic updates (via newsletters).

In Connecticut, the Connecticut Land Trust Service Bureau is currently compiling a handbook that covers: how to form and operate a land trust, how to acquire and manage land, how to obtain and maintain tax-exempt status, and how to work with local officials. In addition, the Connecticut Service Bureau sponsors meetings to heighten trusts' awareness and improve their acquisition and management skills. Through newsletters, it informs the Connecticut trusts about pertinent legislation, tax forms, and the like.

A service bureau can also assist individual trusts experiencing operational or management difficulties, and it can work with those regions or communities interested in establishing a trust.

Funding a service bureau is a challenge, since it is often difficult to demonstrate the need for it and its resulting effectiveness. Even in areas such as New England, where numerous trusts exist, outside funding sources must be sought.

There is a divergence of opinion on when and to what extent the trusts themselves should support a bureau. If membership is a prerequisite for service, trusts in greatest need of help often suffer, since they can least afford to belong. This problem may be solved by instituting a sliding scale or encouraging the wealthier trusts to contribute to special projects (e.g., as cosponsors to a workshop). In Connecticut, the Service Bureau has been established as a 2½-year initial project; trusts have not been asked to contribute at this time. After it has demonstrated its value, it may solicit their support.

Nevertheless, if a service bureau is to be staffed, major funding must come from external sources. Since many private foundations are interested only in local needs, community foundations serving metropolitan areas are more likely supporters. National conservation organizations and corporations should also be approached for seed money.

The role that national conservation organizations play in the local land trust movement is the key to its future. They should be encouraged to support this effort as a method to supplement and enrich the entire land conservation movement. (In addition, local organizations often have greater flexibility in land acceptance and operational procedures and thus can work in situations that a national organization cannot consider.)

Both the Trust for Public Land (TPL) and The Nature Conservancy (TNC) have made commitments to the local land trust movement. TPL has established its Western Land Trust Program. TNC has sponsored a pilot project in Connecticut, the Land Trust Service Bureau, and has provided a low-cost insurance program, available to qualified conservation organizations nationwide.

A service bureau is a strong tool that can improve the operational capability of local land trusts and may function well in areas throughout the country.

NATIONAL/LOCAL CONSERVANCY RELATIONSHIPS
Douglas R. Horne

The American Farmland Trust is a relatively new farmland protection organization—one year old—yet it has initiated efforts in three major program areas: (1) policy development and reform; (2) information clearinghouse; and (3) conservancy. Each of these areas has been staffed, programs have been developed, and the outreach work has begun.

The AFT program is initiated by our headquarters in Washington, D.C., although implementation may occur in cooperation with local conservancies and other farm-related organizations. The delivery system for AFT services is being shaped now, as we respond to requests by local groups who seek assistance in developing their conservancy, public education, or land planning and policy efforts. The scope and substance of these requests indicate that, oftentimes, local capabilities need to be augmented, although it is equally clear that institutionalized, permanent affiliation is not always necessary or preferred by either AFT or the local group. Consistent with this view, AFT is proceeding currently with a delivery system that allows (1) institutionalized affiliation in which the local group is a formal arm of AFT and (2) project-by-project cooperation with local conservancies. The latter of these approaches will prevail in most instances; therefore, the comments that follow apply to the relationship of our national organization to existing, independent groups.

Not surprisingly, our experience has shown that the most valuable service that AFT can provide to local groups is "bridge" financing for land acquisitions. Similarly, AFT is called upon to help identify charitable investors for conservation purchases. Through a revolving line of credit with a New York bank, we are able to help save parcels that would otherwise be lost due to the inability of local conservancies to arrange financing quickly. This fast-strike capability is probably the paramount feature of a national group like AFT and is directly dependent on the ability of the national group to secure large-amount grants and contributions for acquisition. A related service is the review of legal instruments pertaining to conservancy transactions that AFT staff and legal consultants can provide. This extra layer of legal scrutiny has been solicited by local groups, particularly in instances where there is a question of an IRS ruling on a contribution of interest in farmland. Thus far, bridge financing has been made available to conservancies, on a selective basis, at prime plus a small service fee. In the future, AFT hopes to make available bridge funds to additional groups through a revolving fund that is being established now through a special fund-raising effort. Future AFT acquisitions will be tied to states or regions in which farmland protection policy initiatives are taking place, and the purpose of the acquisition would be to demonstrate the fit between public and private preservation programs.

Other cooperative ventures have been requested of AFT. These projects include planning for limited development, staff training on technical conservancy and public policy matters, conference planning support, preservation information and research, and assistance with public education programs. For each, AFT can provide direct technical support and can help develop proposals or fund-raising efforts that augment local staff capabilities. Throughout, AFT is called upon, by virtue of its national perspective, to help assemble coalitions among conservancies that share similar interests and that can answer questions of mutual concern.

In summary, we believe that the best conservancy solutions to farmland conservation problems are local solutions. Yet local actions frequently require the financial, legal, and technical assistance that a national organization can muster. In certain instances, the very participation of a national group in a conservancy transaction is necessary to assure the landowner of the long-term security of his or her action—a reverter clause is frequently demanded by the donor. The national group also can be very effective in shaping a favorable statewide policy context for local conservancy activities. Beyond that, through a presence in Washington, D.C., the national group can represent conservancy interests in helping to shape federal policy and legislation. Through its national overview, the national group can collect and disseminate information of interest to all, including staff training materials. Last, but certainly not least, the national is often better positioned to successfully conduct major fund-raising efforts that can channel funds, in a coordinated manner, to local programs.

FEDERAL GOVERNMENT'S ROLE in PRIVATE LOCAL LAND CONSERVATION

Glenn F. Tiedt

The primary role of the federal government in private local land conservation is to provide a suitable institutional environment for citizen action. The principal way to do this is through the charitable contribution deduction in the Internal Revenue Code. This deduction allows taxpayers to donate land, interests in land, cash, and other resources to local land conservation organizations and subtract the amount of their gifts from their taxable incomes. The tax benefit to the donors has helped generate the financial support necessary to create a sound land conservation community. The public benefit to the community has helped improve the quality of life across the nation. The benefits to the public have far outweighed the costs to the Treasury.

Ideally, the statutory authority for charitable contribution deductions should be broad enough to permit local land conservation organizations to experiment with a broad range of techniques and activities. This ideal has been eroded by recent amendments to the Internal Revenue Code, and more erosion is possible through Treasury regulation. Both the federal government and local land conservation organizations should guard against too many federal limitations on public-spirited citizen activities.

A secondary role of the federal government in private local land conservation is to provide technical assistance in land protection activities and techniques. The Bureau of Outdoor Recreation initiated such a program in the mid-1970s, and its successor, the Heritage Conservation and Recreation Service, continued the effort until that agency was abolished and the statutory authorities were transferred to the National Park Service.

The technical assistance provided by the federal government for land conservation has spanned the entire range of activities from organizing for citizen action to negotiating for specific projects using highly sophisticated land protection techniques. It has included institution building through training of both staff and membership of qualified nonprofit organizations in the latest tax laws and legal tools, and it has helped many local organizations accomplish specific projects. Similar assistance has been provided in some cases by national conservation organizations to local groups, but the national organizations' own fund-raising needs limit their ability to engage in activities that do not have an immediate and direct bearing on their own programs. Only the government has seemed to have the breadth of responsibility and flexibility of action to assist everyone engaged in land protection activities.

Although the role of the federal government in private local land conservation is very limited, the opportunities for federal agencies to work with local land organizations to accomplish mutual objectives is virtually unlimited. Many of our national parks, for example, now face threats from outside their boundaries that are far greater than the threats from within. The National Park Service has no jurisdiction over the external threats, but local land conservation organizations working with local landowners and citizens could reduce or remove the threats using easements and other land protection tools. Some writers have described the parks as ecological artifacts rather than environmental systems. Local land conservation organizations could develop programs to protect systems using the national parks as the focal points for their efforts. National wildlife refuges, wilderness areas, and other natural resource lands face threats from outside their boundaries that can be addressed best by local efforts rather than expanded federal acquisition.

SHARE-ING INNOVATION:
National Park Service Provides Technical Assistance to Land Trusts
Michael S. Batcher

PARK AND RECREATION TECHNICAL SERVICES

The National Park Service, through the Park and Recreational Technical Services (PARTS) program, is engaged in a venture to provide high-quality information and technical services in land saving strategies to state and local public and private organizations including land trusts. This information takes the form of technical publications in the use of both real estate transactions (donations of land, bargain sales, conservation easements, etc.) and regulatory techniques (zoning, subdivision controls, performance standards, etc.) that can be used at the state, regional, and local levels to preserve open space, protect critical ecological areas, and conserve natural resources. This information is then presented through direct consultations and through educational workshops. By providing information and technical follow-up, the National Park Service is able to foster state and local efforts in conserving land without creating a rigid and hierarchical system. This avoids the traditional federal role of overseeing grants and controlling the allocation of financial resources.

With the cuts in federal and state expenditures new types of organizational relationships must be developed. The current environment is ripe for land trusts to fill the vacuum while holding onto their local roots and constituencies. Yet how will local organizations develop the knowledge and skills to fill this void? Many local land trusts possess vast resources and experience in the use of land-saving strategies and have pioneered the use of donations and conservation easements. Many others (and probably the majority) are small groups of concerned citizens that have organized as a 501(c)(3) organization and have acquired some land. Still others are organizations of citizens that have the potential to become a land trust as an expression of their concern for the land. Can innovative approaches be dispersed to this audience? Besides creating technical materials and providing consultation services and workshop sessions, NPS has designed the SHARE system.

SHARE

SHARE is a computer storage and retrieval system for the storage of brief descriptions ranging from 200 to 300 words on innovative projects in the provision of park and recreation services. Case studies are placed into a format (an abstract) for storage. Through the use of key words, the SHARE system can be used as a library for use in researching subjects in topical areas. Once a given case description is retrieved, the user may follow up by contacting the person or agency whose activity is described in the case study for more specific information or materials. At present the SHARE system is in a start-up phase with approximately 100 case studies in a variety of subject areas but with virtually unlimited storage capacity.

SHARE AND LAND CONSERVATION

The SHARE system has several applications to the land conservation effort. As a source for information storage, case studies could be collected in several topical areas:

Protection of specific resource areas such as coastal areas, forests, farmlands, wetlands

Use of specific techniques to preserve open space including direct acquisition, acquisition of easements, performance controls, agricultural zoning, transfer of development rights, land banking, and all of the techniques included in both real estate transaction and regulation

Management of each of these techniques and the positive and negative aspects of each technique in terms of effectiveness, organizational structure, and system design

Efforts of state, regional, and local governments to preserve land for purposes such as aesthetics, resource protection, and growth control

Efforts of state and particularly local organizations to preserve lands with which they are concerned, including local land trusts, conservation commissions, and watershed associations

These case studies would then be used by a variety of users including:

Park and recreation administrators, planners, and agencies

Local conservation groups, particularly land trusts, conservation commissions, and others in developing land-saving skills and a repertoire of land-saving strategies

Researchers who may require the analysis of case studies in order to evaluate or propose strategies for protecting specific resources

Large conservation organizations that may provide assistance to local groups in preserving land

State, regional, and local government agencies in their land use planning efforts

In order to upgrade this system, the National Park Service, along with the American Land Forum is currently investigating the possibility of collecting approximately 100–200 case studies of innovative projects in the use of land-saving strategies from around the country. Those projects would be described in the short abstracts for inclusion in the SHARE computer as well as printed in 4–5 page versions for distribution to groups and organizations on request. As a source of information, the SHARE system applied to land conservation would foster state and local control of land use issues related to the preservation of open space. As a "shared" system, it would foster a communication network that provides information and support without a rigid and politicized organizational base.

SUMMARY

The National Park Service, through its technical assistance program, is seeking to provide information and services to constituencies in land conservation. This effort is being done as a partnership with existing organizations that have the skills and ability with a goal of spreading and dispersing this critical information on the use of conservation techniques to a wide audience that needs to make use of innovative land-saving techniques. It is hoped that this model of information distribution can help build upon a pluralistic tradition of preserving land and resources.

BUILDING a TECHNICAL ASSISTANCE and COMMUNICATION NETWORK
Robert Augsburger

Since the local land conservation movement has its roots as a volunteer effort, the formation of a technical assistance and communication network should be similarly based. The ability to do so is enhanced by the wide diversity in the backgrounds of existing professionally staffed local organizations and the resources available to them.

This model envisions the formation of an association similar to those of trade or professional organizations. While a modest staff may be required to coordinate scheduling, production of output, and distribution of materials to members, the substantive work would be done by the members.

This model contemplates the formation of several standing working committees in a number of areas common to all members. For example:

Administration: Articles and by-laws, tax-exempt status, insurance, accounting, computers

Finance and tax: how to apply existing law, tax issues, creative transaction packaging, Treasury Department liaison, communication of tax benefits to landowners

Public policy: how to communicate the local land conservation movement, government liaison, non-tax legislative issues

Fund development: opportunities for foundation funding, successful special events and membership programs, fund-raising materials, deferred giving, training

257

Environmental management: Effective landowner programs, for example, registration, technical service, techniques for priority evaluation, easement monitoring, land management

When volunteer talent is not available to address an important issue or to prepare technical materials, the committees should be in a position to retain professional assistance for the project.

The benefits of the above approach lie in strengthening the national movement through the development of mutual commitments and the close working relationship stemming from committee assignments. People with like backgrounds will stimulate each other's thinking with the potential for improved results. And the resulting product should be more effective, having been developed by practitioners. The major weakness lies in the inefficiency of a volunteer effort—the risk that some critical opportunity will be missed, that the output will not be timely, or that the work just won't get done at all.

To get such a model off the ground, initial funding should be derived from foundation grants of sufficient amount and duration to permit the acquisition of staff support, organization and development of committees, and preparation and publication of initial material. Subsequent funding on a continuing basis should come from membership dues. If the work of the national organization isn't beneficial enough to justify financial support from the local land organizations that it serves, it probably shouldn't continue to exist. Funding for special projects, for example, training programs and conferences, could probably be obtained from foundations or perhaps governmental grants or contracts.

NEXT STEPS
Allan D. Spader

At the Consultation in October, I was requested to assist the participants in considering how the energy and commitment of that meeting can be carried forward. This paper sets forth some thoughts on the organization of a mutual support network to serve the land trust community.

The problem of organizing a national land conservation network has been approached in four parts: first, it identifies the potential participants of the networking process; second, it examines the needs for such a network; third, it outlines a proposed program of activities; and, finally, some funding and organizational questions are raised.

THE PARTICIPANTS

The network will serve two groups. First, and most important, are the more than 450 local and regional land conservation groups themselves, including the thousands of volunteer and professional leaders who make them work. The second group consists of those individuals and organizations who contribute to the movement from outside its ranks.

Land conservation organizations (i.e., land trusts, conservancies, reliances, foundations, and councils) operate in three spheres:

1. Regional programs (approximately 18) that:

   a. Serve states or parts of states

   b. Have achieved (or are achieving) relatively firm organizations and fiscal bases

   c. Are generally self-sufficient regarding technical and professional resources, and, in some cases, are capable of providing services to their community/region

2. Established local programs (approximately 150) that:

   a. Serve smaller geographic areas, generally no larger than counties

   b. Have achieved a relatively stable organizational base, often financially able to employ a limited staff, but still heavily dependent on volunteer effort

3. Emerging local and regional programs (approximately 300) that:

   a. Depend totally on volunteer effort

   b. Are typically organized in response to a specific threat to a particular tract of land and thus have not achieved a sense of long-term commitment

   c. Have limited access to technical, organizational, or fiscal support

Beyond the local trust programs described above, the network would serve a number of organizations and individuals who contribute to the land conservation community. These include:

   4. Individuals, who provide various professional services to local trusts or who provide analysis of land conservation issues, for example, environmental specialists, tax lawyers, land planners, bankers, appraisers, and developers

   5. National and regional conservation organizations, who work directly with local land trusts, for example, The Nature Conservancy, the National Trust for Historic Preservation, the American Farmland Trust, the Trust for Public Land, state Audubon societies, and the Isaac Walton League

   6. Public agencies, whose activities directly affect local trust programs, for example, state and local conservation, recreation, wildlife and land planning agencies, the National Park Service, and the U.S. Forest Service

THE NEED

Private land-saving efforts are protecting substantial properties of special natural, aesthetic, cultural, economic, or social value. The local land trust draws its *strength* from:

A diversity that reflects and responds to a wide variety of local and regional land-saving needs

An innovative and self-reliant spirit that is less constrained by the bureaucracy and politics than related national public or private programs

A unique ability to inspire and draw upon (1) the commitment of individual volunteers, (2) the provision of private financial support, and (3) the confidence of property owners seeking to protect land resources

On the other hand, local land-saving programs remain, in many cases, quite fragile. To varying degrees, most local organizations share the following *weaknesses:*

Limited capacity to develop fiscal self-sufficiency, especially when the competition for private funding is intense

Limited funds and professional resources to execute increasingly complex land-saving techniques needed in the future and to expand the institutional capacity to undertake, for example, greater responsibility for land management

Vulnerability to public legislative and regulatory actions, particularly in the tax field

Limited ability to communicate benefits and accomplishments to the general public, to the business, corporate and financial communities, and to local, state and national leaders

Relative isolation that severely limits technical interchange, moral support, and co-operative actions

The network would be designed to enhance the strengths of this movement and over-come its potential weaknesses. The most immediate goal should be to overcome the relative isolation of the individual local trusts. Isolation is a fact of life not only for those programs that have emerged in scattered locations in the South, the Midwest, and the West, but also in the Northeast where local land conservation programs have existed in close proximity to each other for some time. Beyond providing access to technical, professional, and organizational support, perhaps the most important goal is to reinforce and encourage the commitment of individuals in local situations and help each local volunteer and staff member know he or she is part of a larger whole.

THE PROGRAM

The proposed network program will have two elements, an information clearinghouse and a series of working task groups. The heart of the program would be the exchange of information for those participating in land trust activities. The *information clearinghouse* is con-ceived in two parts:

1. A bimonthly *newsletter* to serve as the central communications link among all 450+ land trusts. It would provide a regular medium for exchanging experiences, technical information, and policy analysis among the trusts themselves as well as for those who work with them. This publication should be designed so that most of its content would be contributed by individuals who are directly involved in local land-saving situations. It would also include regular columns devoted to specialized subject areas of importance to land trusts, such as tax law, transactional techniques, and appraisal.

2. Development of a *data base* to provide ready access to (a) detailed information about individual local land trusts and related support organizations and individuals, (b) technical assistance resources, (c) bibliographic reference materials and (d) a case-study file of land preservation methods and tools. The foundation of this data base already exists in the microcomputer-based inventory of local land conservation organizations compiled in the *Directory*.

The second element of the proposed network involves the organization and support of a series of *working task groups* on both a national and a regional basis. These groups would bring together individuals from within the land trust community to (1) address policy issues facing the community as a whole, (2) study specific technical problems encountered by selected trusts, and (3) design projects to be undertaken on a cooperative basis by groups of land trusts.

The staff of the network would: (1) provide logistic support to each of these groups and their projects, (2) when necessary, provide travel funds to assure participation from organizations with limited budgets, and (3) mobilize academic and technical resources to accomplish task-group objectives.

Potential topics to be addressed by these task groups might include:

1. Evaluation of recent and impending changes in federal tax law and IRS regulations as they affect the donation of conservation easements. This evaluation would include analysis of the potential impacts of these changes and the formulation of alternative strategic responses by local organizations, both individually and collectively.

2. Exploration of the potential role of private local land trusts as participants in public/private efforts to secure lands for regional hiking trails. Similar consideration could be given to the role of land trusts in implementing the so-called green-line concept being discussed in some parts of the country.

3. Development of tools to communicate more effectively the concept of private land saving to potential land donors, funding sources, public agencies, various professional groups, and the public at large. Initial consideration might be given to the design and production of some type of audiovisual presentation of the land trust message.

4. Organization of regional (multistate and intrastate) mutual support systems among local land conservation organizations. These systems could address such needs as board-member development and undertake analyses of land-saving issues particular to a particular part of the country. Priority might be given to an assessment of technical assistance needs—particularly those of small and emerging programs—and the mobilization of technical assistance resources on a regional basis.

5. Investigation of the problems associated with the valuation of land subject to conservation easements both in terms of research into the long-term effects of easements on land value and in fostering improved understanding of this issue among professionals in the land appraisal field.

6. Evaluation of the need for greater self-regulation within the land trust community in defining and meeting standards of "public interest" in the application of various land protection devices. This issue involves both the selection of lands to be protected and the determination of the appropriate level of public access to such lands once they are secured. A related issue of concern here is the responsibility of the local trust for management of the lands under its protection.

FUNDING AND ORGANIZATIONAL CONSIDERATIONS

The discussions at the Cambridge meeting revealed considerable ambiguity among the participants about the creation of "another national organization" as a means of getting themselves together. As a practical matter, the creation of the network described above will require some organizational structure; however, it can be accomplished without creating a full-blown, autonomous, nonprofit organization—at least until the proposed concept can demonstrate its usefulness and feasibility. In this light, it is suggested that the proposed land trust network be organized as a subsidiary trust and attached to an existing certified nonprofit organization that would serve as the legal recipient designed so that it has sufficient administrative insulation to head off any concern about its potential domination by the host organization. Consideration might be given to asking a group of local land trusts (3 or 4) representing different regions of the country to serve in the host capacity.

The funding requirements of the proposed land trust network should reflect the need for a small staff to function and travel as well as phone, postage, and other costs that go with a program operating on a national scale. In addition to one person to manage and carry out the overall program, the information clearinghouse element as proposed would require one professional person on virtually a full-time basis as well as one person to provide secretarial support. In addition, the acquisition of a microcomputer/word processor would substantially expand the capacity of these three persons to carry out all parts of the proposed program. The minimum funding base should also be sufficient to provide limited travel subsidies to facilitate contacts and participation for those land trust staff and officers with limited travel budgets.

RESOURCES

NATIONAL ORGANIZATIONS:
A Resource for Local Conservation Organizations

Barbara Rusmore, Jon Roush, Vincent Marsh, Douglas Wheeler, and Jennie Gerard

This meeting was scheduled to enable conference participants to acquaint themselves with our national organizations and how they might assist the local land trusts. Representatives for these groups with us today are: Jon Roush of The Nature Conservancy; Vincent Marsh of the National Trust for Historic Preservation; Doug Wheeler of the American Farmland Trust; and Jennie Gerard of the Trust for Public Land.

Jon Roush

The Nature Conservancy has a very specialized purpose. We are interested in protecting genetic diversity of rare and endangered species through protection of habitat, a fairly limited slice of the preservation pie. Though we have a national office in Arlington, Virginia, we are a decentralized organization, and regional and state field offices have great authority. I want to encourage you to get in touch with the Conservancy and establish a good working relationship with your local representative. We support cooperation between organizations, and though we do not have a formal networking program, we do cooperate with local groups in several ways:

1. Referrals and deferrals; properties with conservation values that do not fit the Conservancy's narrow guidelines often get referred to other more appropriate groups, and at times the reverse situation is true.

2. Being designated in deeds as the beneficiary of a reverter clause; when a property donor wants the added security of a national organization backing up a local.

3. Cooperating on joint fund-raising or legislative lobbying through the local office.

4. Utilizing our project revolving fund to help a local group acquire properties that fit the Conservancy's guidelines. This pool of money was established to buy properties and must be paid back (at expensive interest rates), generally with fund-raising monies recruited for that piece of property.

263

We are very interested in cooperating for appropriate conservation objectives and enjoy adding our capabilities to the conservation network.

Vincent Marsh

The National Trust for Historic Preservation is a private, nonprofit membership organization that was chartered by Congress in 1949 to hold historically significant property and to help Americans preserve buildings, sites, and objects important in history and culture.

Our headquarters is located in Washington, D.C., and during the 1970s six regional offices were created to serve a growing national preservation constituency. The Western Regional Office was established in San Francisco in 1971 to make its technical assistance programs more accessible to the western states. Subsequently, five additional regional offices—in Boston; Oklahoma City; Charleston, South Carolina; Chicago; and Washington, D.C.—were developed to assist in preservation efforts in all fifty states, Puerto Rico, and the U.S. Territories.

The National Trust is governed by an elected board of trustees and supported by more than 150,000 members, plus 2,400 member organizations.

Through timely information, technical assistance advice, and, when the need is critical, grants and loans, the National Trust serves private preservation organizations, individuals, and government units at all levels. It collects information on successful preservation projects, helps solve specific problems, provides guidance to those initiating preservation programs and groups, and initiates special projects that not only result in the preservation of target areas but also yield techniques that can be used elsewhere.

In addition, the National Trust owns and operates a number of properties, some of which are open to the public as museums. The Trust also holds easements on other properties to protect them from development or alteration.

The primary way in which the National Trust can assist you is through our Rural Conservation Project. This special project was established in 1979 to provide technical assistance and advice to rural communities on integrating the protection of rural historic resources with the protection of natural, agricultural, scenic, and other community resources. The Rural Project's work to date has been centered within two Northeastern rural towns but within the next two years the staff of the Rural Project who are based within our Mid-Atlantic Regional Office in Washington, D.C., will be working within other regions of the country. To date, the Rural Project has published a series of three National Trust information sheets, which address rural conservation issues. These three information sheets, namely, "Rural Conservation," "Establishing an Easement Program to Protect Historic Scenic and Natural Resources," and "The Development of Rural Conservation Programs: A Case Study for Loudon County, Virginia," are available free from all of the Trust's regional offices. Currently the Rural Project is writing a book on rural conservation techniques to assist private organizations and local governments and anticipates publication in 1984.

Staff of the Rural Project with assistance from the regional offices of the Trust can provide technical assistance to local communities and regional or statewide agricultural, environmental, or land trust organizations on a variety of rural conservation techniques. A Rural Project fact sheet details additional information on this program and is available through the regional office network or directly through the Rural Project office.

Douglas Wheeler

The American Farmland Trust was organized in 1979 in anticipation of the release of the National Agricultural Land Study (NALS). NALS is a federal assessment of the extent and causes of farmland loss in the United States. It makes two recommendations:

1.   That public policy be developed which will be more sympathetic to preservation of farmland; and

2.   That private sector initiatives or techniques be devised to achieve farmland preservation.

Following these recommendations, it is our goal to support the local and statewide organizations that will carry out farmland preservation activities.

We actively solicit support from individuals and organizations; we publish a bimonthly newsletter and at present are headquartered in Washington, D.C., with hopes of establishing a network of state organizations in the future.

Our objectives are as follows:

1.   We pursue public policy work recommended by NALS, as a national focus for local groups.

2.   We attempt to employ the middle-ground conservancy activity techniques utilized so successfully by The Nature Conservancy and the Trust for Public Land and apply these techniques to farmland preservation.

3.   We serve as a national clearinghouse on information regarding farmland preservation and farmland preservation techniques.

Jennie Gerard

The Trust for Public Land is a national organization headquartered in San Francisco that undertakes several different land preservation activities, primarily through land transactions. We have a land trust program specifically to provide assistance to local groups. We can provide training and technical assistance to local land trusts in three ways:

1.   Providing initial presentations on what a land trust is and an evaluation of the potential feasibility of a trust in an area

2.   Providing training on the role of a land trust, its board and members, and the rudiments of land transactions

3.   Actually demonstrating a land transaction, especially for agricultural land retention or major recreational land resources

We also sponsor regional workshops for land trusts and publish technical bulletins. These bulletins respond to specific questions and are published in order to share the information gained.

We are interested in being able to provide training and technical assistance throughout the United States, though our program is currently strongest in the West; and are happy to work cooperatively with existing organizations.

These national organizations provide a wealth of useful and diverse resources for local groups. This conference has also clearly pointed out what a strong resource the local organizations can provide for each other. By working cooperatively for common goals, we have the capability to accomplish much more than any of us can do alone.

RESOURCES for LOCAL ACTION
Barbara Rusmore

Much of this book is a dialogue between people actively involved in private land conservation. While there is a great deal of information about techniques and organizational strategies, there is not much about getting started. What if you would like to know more about this topic? Perhaps you are interested in setting up your own organization or protecting your property. Keep in mind that the work described here has all been done by people like yourself, often people with little or no previous experience in land preservation. All they had to go on was their desire and determination. Their successes are proof of the saying that "if you want something bad enough, you can do it."

Where to start? First find out if there is someone in your area already. The easiest way to begin is to contact the Land Trust Exchange. The Land Trust Exchange provides a referral service for local groups across the country, and it is their business to help people get in touch with each other. They can also provide beginning organizations with assistance in getting established. If you are interested in setting up an organization or contacting an existing one, they are the place to start. Their address is: Land Trust Exchange, 3 Joy Street, Boston, MA 02108; telephone number—(617)227-5039. The National Wildlife Federation publishes a directory annually (see bibliography) listing organizations by state. By using the Land Trust Exchange, the National Wildlife Federation directory, and your native curiosity, you can find out what organizations exist locally and approach them.

It is also worthwhile to contact the larger national groups working in land conservation that may have a branch office in your area, such as The Nature Conservancy, Audubon Society, Trout Unlimited, American Farmland Trust, and National Trust for Historic Preservation. These groups are all involved in land conservation activities, and one of them may be able to assist you. Your particular interest may fit perfectly with already existing programs.

The San Francisco office of the Trust for Public Land runs a land trust program in the western part of the country with a focus on agricultural issues. If your interests and location fall within that sphere, contact the Trust for Public Land. They also have programs in New York and other more urbanized areas of the country and have a commitment to working with local organizations.

When you talk with organizations, you will want to find out what their interests in land conservation are. Do they match yours? What level of organization have they developed? You may find that a group has been formed in your area, but it is working on getting established and has not yet completed a land transaction, not an unusual situation because it can take several years to transact the first land protection. Or perhaps a group has been there for fifty years, but it works with such a low profile that you had not heard about it. As you find out more about the various groups in your area, you will begin to see how you can fit your concerns with those of others.

Perhaps there is no organization that matches your interests, or perhaps there is no organization at all in your state. Particularly if you are in the Intermountain West, Midwest, or the South, there may not be a group for you to work with. You may have to start your own. Again, the best place to begin is with the Land Trust Exchange. They can give you information on the process that other organizations have gone through in getting set up and can put you in touch with others that can give advice and, possibly, other kinds of help.

Establishing an organization is a major undertaking involving complex legal, financial, and administrative issues. Some of the questions that must be answered are: What are the goals? What are you trying to accomplish both over the long term and immediately? Will the organization be run with volunteer or paid staff? How much money can you realistically expect to raise? It is very worthwhile to have experienced advice. The Land Trust Exchange may not be able to give you all the information you need to start, but they will point you in the right direction. From there, you can begin to discover interested people within your area who can also provide you with the kinds of expertise and assistance that you need. Just keep in mind that all local organizations have had to go through the process of getting set up. Though getting established can seem tortuous, frustrating, and very slow-going at times, perseverance furthers. If you keep at it, eventually you will have a local organization that will be able to protect land through a variety of private market techniques.

NATIONAL ORGANIZATIONS CONCERNED with LAND PRESERVATION

This is a preliminary compilation of resources for the land conservation community to be further developed as a service of the Land Trust Exchange; please tell the Land Trust Exchange of other groups or individuals who should be listed. University geography, planning, and environmental studies departments can also help. For additional sources, please see *Building an Ark*, by Phillip Hoose, and the National Wildlife Federation's *Conservation Directory*.

American Farmland Trust
1717 Massachusetts Ave., NW
Washington, DC 20036
(202) 332-0769
Publication: *Farmland*

American Land Forum
5410 Grosvenor Ln.
Bethesda, MD 20814
(301) 493-9140
Publication: *American Land*

Center for Environmental Interns Programs
637 Statler Office Bldg.
Boston, MA 02116
(617) 797-4375

The Conservation Foundation
1717 Massachusetts Ave., NW
Washington, DC 20036
(202) 797-4300
Publication: *Conservation Foundation Letter*

The Foundation Center
888 Seventh Ave.
New York, NY 10019

Friends of the Earth
124 Spear St.
San Francisco, CA 94105
(415) 495-4770
Publication: *Not Man Apart*

The Grantsmanship Center
11031 S. Grand Ave.
Los Angeles, CA 90015
Publication: *The Grantsmanship News*

Institute for Community Economics
151 Montague City Rd.
Greenfield, MA 01301
(413) 774-5933

Izaak Walton League of America, Inc.
1800 N. Kent St., Suite 806
Arlington, VA 22209
(703) 528-1818
Publication: *Outdoor America*

National Association of Conservation
Districts
1025 Vermont Ave., NW
Washington, DC 20005
(202) 347-5995
Publication: *The Tuesday Letter*

National Audubon Society
950 Third Ave.
New York, NY 10022
(212) 832-3200
Publication: *Audubon*

National Recreation and Park Association
1601 B, Kent St.
Arlington, VA 22209
(703) 525-0606
Publication: *National Parks and Conservation Magazine*

National Society of Fund Raising Executives
Investment Bldg., Suite 831
1511 K St., NW
Washington, DC 20005
(202) 638-1393

National Trust for Historic Preservation
(NTHP)
1785 Massachusetts Ave., NW
Washington, DC 20036
(202) 673-4000
Publications: *Preservation News, Historic Preservation*

(NTHP)
Rural Project
1600 H St., NW
Washington, DC 20006
(202) 673-4204

(NTHP)
Mid-Atlantic Regional Office
1600 H St., NW
Washington, DC 20006
(202) 673-2403

(NTHP)
Midwest Regional Office
407 S. Dearborn St., Suite 710
Chicago, IL 60605
(312) 353-3424

(NTHP)
Northeast Regional Office
Old City Hall
45 School St.
Boston, MA 02110
(617) 223-7754

(NTHP)
Southern Regional Office
456 King St.
Charleston, SC 29403
(803) 724-4711

(NTHP)
Southwest/Plains Regional Office
210 Colcord Bldg.
Oklahoma City, OK 73102
(405) 231-5126

(NTHP)
Western Regional Office
681 Market St., Suite 859
San Francisco, CA 94105
(415) 974-8420

Natural Resources Defense Council
122 E. 42d St.
New York, NY 10017
(212) 949-0049
Publication: *Newsletter*

The Nature Conservancy (TNC)[1]
1800 N. Kent St.
Arlington, VA 22209
(703) 841-5300
Publication: *The Nature Conservancy News*

(TNC)
Eastern Regional Office
294 Washington St., Rm. 850
Boston, MA 02108
(617) 542-1908

(TNC)
Midwest Regional Office
328 E. Hennepin Ave.
Minneapolis, MN 55414
(612) 379-2134

(TNC)
Southeast Regional Office
1800 N. Kent St.
Arlington, VA 22209
(703) 841-5300

(TNC)
Western Regional Office
425 Bush St.
San Francisco, CA 94108
(415) 489-3056

(TNC)
Great Plains Field Office
328 E. Hennepin Ave.
Minneapolis, MN 55414

(TNC)
Long Island Chapter
P.O. Box 72
Cold Spring Harbor, NY 11724

(TNC)
Lower Hudson Chapter
R.F.D. #2
Chestnut Ridge Rd.
Mt. Kisco, NY 10549

(TNC)
Adirondack Conservancy
P.O. Box 188
Elizabethtown, NY 12932

(TNC)
Eastern New York Chapter
196 Morton Ave.
Albany, NY 12202

Rural America
1346 Connecticut Ave., NW
Washington, DC 20036
(202) 659-2800
Publication: *Rural America*

Sierra Club
530 Bush St.
San Francisco, CA 94108
(415) 981-8634
Publication: *Sierra*

Soil Conservation Society of America
7515 N.E. Ankeny Rd.
Ankeny, IA 50021
(515) 289-2331
Publication: *Journal of Soil and Water
Conservation*

The Trust for Public Land (TPL)
82 Second St.
San Francisco, CA 94105
(415) 495-4014

(TPL)
Northeast Regional Office
254 W. 31st St.
New York, NY 10001
(212) 563-5959

---

1. In addition to the regional offices listed below, The Nature Conservancy has field offices in AZ, CA, CO, CT, FL, HI, IA, IL, IN, MA, MD, MI, MN, MT, NM, NY, NC, ND, OH, OR, PA, SC, TN, TX, VT, VA, WA, WV, and WI.

(TPL)
Southeast Regional Office
219 E. Fifth Ave.
Tallahassee, FL 32303
(904) 222-9280

(TPL)
Ohio Field Office
The Old Arcade, Rm. 342
401 Euclid Ave.
Cleveland, OH 44114
(216) 241-7630

(TPL)
Northwest Field Office
Rt. 2, Box 37-A
Burton, WA 98013
(206) 463-3847

(TPL)
Oakland Field Office
5848 Foothill Blvd.
Oakland, CA 94605
(415) 568-8595

(TPL)
Southwest Field Office
106 S. Capital St., Suite 8
Sante Fe, NM 87501
(505) 988-5922

U.S. National Parks Service
Interior Bldg.
Washington, DC 20240

Urban Land Institute
1200 18th St., NW
Washington, DC 20006
(202) 331-8500
Publication: *Environmental Comment*

The Wilderness Society (WS)
1901 Pennsylvania Ave., NW
Washington, DC 20006
(202) 293-2732, (202) 828-6600
Publication: *Wilderness Report*

(WS)
Western Office
4260 E. Evans Ave.
Denver, CO 80222
(303) 758-2266

CONFERENCE PARTICIPANTS

Gordon Abbott, Jr.
The Trustees of Reservations
224 Adams St.
Milton, MA 02186
(617) 698-2066

Mark C. Ackelson
Iowa Natural Heritage Foundation
Insurance Exchange Bldg., Suite 830
Des Moines, IA 50309
(515) 288-1846

Herman C. Allmaras
Mesa County Land Conservancy
3544 E. One Half Rd.
Palisade, CO 81526
(303) 464-7686

Cecil Andrus
537 W. Bannock, Suite 101
Boise, ID 83702
(208) 343-7676

Bill Ashley
Kellam Real Estate
P.O. Box 3466
Jackson, WY 83001
(307) 733-3523

Robert Augsburger
Peninsula Open Space Trust
3000 Sand Hill Rd.
Menlo Park, CA 94025
(415) 854-7696

George Ballis
2348 N. Cornelia
Fresno, CA 93711
(209) 233-4727

Michael S. Batcher
National Park Service
600 Arch St., Rm. 9310
Philadelphia, PA 19106
(215) 597-1585

Alexander Bill
Sara Bill
San Juan Preservation Trust
Rt. 1, Box 1426
Lopez, WA 98261
(206) 468-2925

Darby Bradley
Vermont Natural Resources Council
7 Main St.
Montpelier, VT 05602
(802) 223-2328

Terry Bremer
Lincoln Institute of Land Policy
3 Joy St.
Boston, MA 02108
(617) 826-5050

Russell L. Brenneman
Murtha, Cullins, Richter & Pinney
P.O. Box 30197
Hartford, CT 06103
(203) 549-4500

Craig Britton
Midpeninsula Regional Open Space District
375 Distel Circle, Suite D-1
Los Altos, CA 94022
(415) 965-4717

John C. Brooks
Savannas Wilderness Trust
3050 Sunrise Blvd.
Ft. Pierce, FL 33450
(305) 287-0478

Joseph Brooks
Emergency Land Fund
564 Lee St., SW
Atlanta, GA 30310
(404) 758-5506

Carl Brown
Jayne Brown
Kellan Real Estate
P.O. Box 634
Lake Fork, ID 83635
(208) 634-5228

Kingsbury Browne, Jr.
Hill & Barlow
225 Franklin St.
Boston, MA 02110
(617) 423-6200

Paul Brunner
ECO Realty
325 E. Broadway
Missoula, MT 59801
(406) 728-4230

Peter Capen
San Juan Preservation Trust
P.O. Box 711
Friday Harbor, WA 98250
(206) 378-4761

Richard Carbin
Ottauquechee Regional Land Trust, Inc.
39 Central St.
Woodstock, VT 05091
(802) 457-2369

Joan Carter
Volusia Land Trust
122 W. Michigan Ave.
Deland, FL 32720
(904) 734-1300

Davis Cherington
Massachusetts Farm & Conservation Lands
    Trust
527 Essex St.
Beverly, MA 01915
(617) 927-4097

Marie Cirillo
Model Valley Land Trust
Clairfield, TN 37221

Story Clark
Jackson Hole Alliance for Responsible
    Planning
P.O. Box 2728
Jackson, WY 83001
(307) 733-9417

Russell Cohen
c/o 41 Field Pond Rd.
Weston, MA 02193
(617) 899-8048

Dave Conine
Utah Environment Center
State Planning Coordinators Office
124 State Capitol Bldg.
Salt Lake City, UT 84114
(801) 533-4974

James M. Connor
Connor AgriResearch, Inc.
24 W. 500 Maple Ave.
Naperville, IL 60540
(312) 369-0880

John (Jeff) R. Cook, Jr.
Center for Environmental Intern Programs
629 Statler Office Bldg.
Boston, MA 02116
(617) 426-4375

Lew Cook
Cook Ranches
635 W. Indian School Rd., #211
Phoenix, AZ 85013
(602) 248-0660

Robert Currie
The Ohio Conservation Foundation
307 The Arcade
Cleveland, OH 44114
(216) 771-4100

Robert T. Dennis
Piedmont Environmental Council
28-C Main St.
Warrenton, VA 22186
(703) 347-2334

William H. Dunham
Montana Land Reliance
P.O. Box 355
Helena, MT 59624
(406) 443-7027

Dave Ebenger
P.O. Box 217
Winthrop, WA 98862
(509) 996-2206

Benjamin R. Emory
Maine Coast Heritage Trust
P.O. Box 426
Northeast Harbor, ME 04662
(207) 276-5156

Betty Feazel
Upper San Juan Land Reliance
At Last Ranch
Star Rt. 2
Pagosa Springs, CO 81658

Mickey Fleishner
Humboldt North Coast Land Trust
P.O. Box 457
Trinidad, CA 95570
(707) 677-3131

June M. Foote
Napa County Land Trust
6110 Silverado Trail
Napa, CA 94558
(707) 944-2597

Bill Gay
Trust for Public Land
82 2d St.
San Francisco, CA 95570
(415) 495-4014

Jennie Gerard
Trust for Public Land
82 2d St.
San Francisco, CA 95570
(415) 495-4014

Phil Gerner
CorLands
53 W. Jackson, Rm. 850
Chicago, IL 60604
(312) 427-4255

Herbert Grench
Midpeninsula Regional Open Space District
375 Distel Circle, Suite D-1
Los Altos, CA 94022
(415) 965-4717

Ralph Grossi
Marin Agricultural Land Trust
4025 Novato Blvd.
Novato, CA 94947
(415) 663-1158

Linda Hewitt
Plymouth County Wildlands Trust
290 Elm St.
Pembroke, MA 02359
(617) 826-5050

Jean Hocker
Jackson Hole Land Trust
P.O. Box 2897
Jackson, WY 83001
(307) 733-4707

Douglas R. Horne
American Farmland Trust
1717 Massachusetts Ave.
Washington, DC 20036
(202) 332-0769

Maggy Hurchalla
Savannas Wilderness Trust
P.O. Box 130
Stuart, FL 33495
(305) 287-0478

William Hutton
28 25th Ave.
San Francisco, CA 94121
(415) 392-8308

Gordon Jacober
Upper San Juan Land Reliance
P.O. Box 96
Pagosa Springs, CO 81127

Andrew Johnson
Philadelphia Conservationists, Inc., and
    Natural Lands Trust
1339 Chestnut St.
Philadelphia, PA 19107
(215) 567-5590

Jane Karr
Cook Ranches
635 W. Indian School Rd., #211
Phoenix, AZ 85013
(602) 248-0660

David Katz
Center for Sustainable Agriculture
9585 Rio Vista
Forestville, CA 95436
(707) 887-7732

George Kelly
Carmel Realty
P.O. Drawer C
Carmel, CA 93921
(408) 624-6482

Vince Lee
Jackson Hole Land Trust
P.O. Box 107
Wilson, WY 83014
(307) 733-3600

Ann Leonard
Land Trust of Santa Cruz Co.
P.O. Box 1287
Santa Cruz, CA 95061
(408) 426-0922

Mary Lester
Trust for Public Land
82 2d St.
San Francisco, CA 95570
(415) 495-4014

Johnathan Libby
California Native Plant Society
312 Emeline St.
Santa Cruz, CA 95060
(408) 423-4748

William Long
Montana Land Reliance
P.O. Box 355
Helena, MT 59624
(406) 433-7027

Jan W. McClure
Society for the Protection of New
    Hampshire Forests
54 Portsmouth St.
Concord, NH 03301
(603) 224-9945

Vincent Marsh
National Trust for Historic Preservation
681 Market St., Suite 859
San Francisco, CA 94105
(415) 974-8420

Chuck Matthei
Institute for Community Economics
120 Boylston St.
Boston, MA 02116
(617) 542-1058

Paul Maxwell
Marin Agricultural Land Trust
P.O. Box 809
Point Reyes Station, CA 94947
(415) 663-1158, (415) 897-3320

Merle L. Meacham
Jefferson County Conservancy
Rt. 1, Box 672
Port Ludlow, CA 98365
(206) 732-4334

Wendy Mickle
San Juan Preservation Trust
Rt. 1, Box 1410
Lopez, WA 98261
(206) 468-2925

David P. Miller
Maryland Environment Trust
510 St. Paul Place, Suite 1401
Baltimore, MD 21202
(301) 659-6440

Lee Miller
Winthrop Realty
P.O. Box 323
Winthrop, WA 98862
(509) 996-2121

Thomas Mills
Urban Land Program Trust for Public Lands
82 2d St.
San Francisco, CA 95570
(415) 495-4014

Steve Moody
Vice President of Investments
United States Trust
40 Court St.
Boston, MA 02108
(617) 726-7250

David Moore
New Jersey Conservation Foundation
300 Mendham Rd.
Morristown, NJ 07960
(201) 539-7540

Samuel W. Morris
French & Pickering Creeks Conservation
    Trust
Box 360, RD 2
Pottstown, PA 19464
(215) 469-0150

Hans Neuhauser
Barrier Islands Coalition
4405 Paulsen St.
Savannah, GA 31405
(912) 355-4840

Pat Noonan
The Nature Conservancy
1800 N. Kent St.
Arlington, VA 22209
(707) 841-5300

Steve O'Brien
40 Mile Loop
2744 N.E. Bryce
Portland, OR 97212
(503) 285-2531

Douglas D. Peters
Yakima River Regional Greenway
    Foundation
P.O. Box 156
WA 98942
(509) 697-7201

Don Price
Eagle County Land Conservancy
P.O. Box 742
Vail, CO 81658

Alice H. Rand
Maine Audubon Society
1222 Shore Rd.
Cape Elizabeth, ME 04107
(207) 799-4292

Jon Roush
Drawer A
Florence, MT 59833
(406) 273-0484

Donald Rubenstein
California Coastal Conservancy
1212 Broadway, Rm. 541
Oakland, CA 94612
(415) 464-1015

Barbara Rusmore
Montana Land Reliance
P.O. Box 355
Helena, MT 59624
(406) 443-7027

Thomas Schmidt
Western Pennsylvania Conservancy
316 Fourth Ave.
Pittsburgh, PA 15222
(412) 288-2766

Gerald F. Schnepf
Iowa Natural Heritage Foundation
830 Insurance Exchange Bldg.
Des Moines, IA 50309
(515) 288-1846

H. William Sellers
Brandywine Conservancy, Inc.
P.O. Box 141
Chadds Ford, PA 19317
(215) 388-7601

Karen Smith
Bear Creek Greenway
Southern Oregon Land Conservancy
80 E. Stewart
Medford, OR 97501
(503) 776-7004

Allan D. Spader
Lincoln Institute of Land Policy
26 Trowbridge St.
Cambridge, MA 02138
(617) 661-3016

Brian Steen
Big Sur Land Trust
P.O. Box 1645
Carmel, CA 93921
(408) 625-5523

Peter R. Stein
Urban Land Program
Trust for Public Land
254 W. 31st St.
New York, NY 10001
(212) 563-5959

Irmine Steltzner
Sausalito Land Trust
110 Spencer Ave.
Sausalito, CA 94965

Julie Stewart
California Coastal Conservancy
1212 Broadway, Rm. 514
Oakland, CA 94612
(415) 464-1015

Judith M. Stockdale
CorLands
53 W. Jackson Blvd.
Chicago, IL 60604
(312) 427-4256

Michael Swack
15 Marie Ave.
Cambridge, MA 02139
(603) 485-8461, (617) 492-0442

Alexandra Swaney
Montana Land Reliance
P.O. Box 355
Helena, MT 59624
(406) 443-7027

Edward Thompson, Jr.
American Farmland Trust
1717 Massachusetts Ave., NW
Washington, DC 20036
(202) 332-0769

Glenn F. Tiedt
National Park Service
Box 25287
Federal Center
Denver, CO 80225
(303) 234-6457

Roger Tilkermeier
Eagle County Land Conservancy
P.O. Box 742
Vail, CO 81658

Joan Vilms
Sonoma Land Trust
1217 14th St.
Santa Rosa, CA 95404
(707) 545-7572

John Wade
Peninsula Open Space Trust
3000 Sand Hill Rd.
Menlo Park, CA 94025
(415) 854-7696

Don Walker
1877 Broadway, #406
Boulder, CO 80302
(303) 447-9080

A. Elizabeth Watson
Rural Project
National Trust for Historic Preservation
1600 H Street, NW
Washington, DC 20006
(202) 673-4204

Douglas Wheeler
American Farmland Trust
1717 Massachusetts Ave., NW
Washington, DC 20036
(202) 332-0769

Suzanne Wilkins
Connecticut Land Trust Service Bureau
Box MMM
Wesleyan Station
Middletown, CO 06457
(203) 344-0716

Leonard Wilson
Vermont Environmental Board
P.O. Box 224
Waitesfield, VT 05673
(802) 496-2230

Steele Wotkyns
315 E. 9th
Davis, CA 95616
(916) 756-8985

Jack Wright
Bruce Bugbee & Assoc.
111 N. Higgins, Suite 300
Missoula, MT 59802
(406) 928-4176

BIBLIOGRAPHY

Agricultural Preservation Task Force, with the Lancaster County Planning Commission Staff. *A Deed Restriction Program to Preserve Farmland in Lancaster County, Pennsylvania.* Lancaster, Pa.: Lancaster County Planning Commission, 1979. (50 N. Duke St., P.O. Box 3480, Lancaster, PA 17604)

Allen, Paul. *To Preserve a Heritage: Conservation Easements.* Rev. ed. Baltimore, Md.: The Maryland Environmental Trust, 1976. (501 St. Paul Pl., Suite 1401, Baltimore, MD 21202)

American Association of University Women. *AAUW Community Action Tool Catalog: Techniques and Strategies for Successful Action Programs.* Washington, D.C., 1981. (Sales Office, 2401 Virginia Ave., NW, Washington, D.C. 20037)

American Law Institute. *A Model Land Development Code.* Washington, D.C., 1976.

America the Beautiful. Pleasantville, N.Y.: Reader's Digest Press, 1970.

Andrews, Richard N. L. *Land in America: Commodity or Natural Resource?* Lexington, Ma.: Lexington Books, 1979. (125 Spring St., Lexington, MA 02173)

Arabe, Michael. *Foundations: A Handbook.* Heritage Recreation and Conservation Service, U.S. Department of the Interior, October 1979.

Ashcroft, Mary. "Designating Scenic Roads—A Vermont Field Guide." Montpelier, Vt.: State Planning Office (Prepared by the Vermont Scenery Preservation Council), 1979. (Vermont State Planning Office, Montpelier, VT 05602)

Baker, R. Lisle. *Taxing Speculative Land Gains: The Vermont Experience.* Cambridge, Ma.: Lincoln Institute of Land Policy, 1980. (26 Trowbridge St., Cambridge, MA 02138)

BIBLIOGRAPHY

Barns, John C. "An Alternative to Alternate Farm Valuation: The Conveyance of a Conservation Easement to an Agricultural Land Trust." *Agricultural Law Journal* 3, no. 3 (Summer 1981): 308–322.

"Barrier Islands." *Environmental Comment*, February 1981.

Barrows, R., et al. "Mapping to Preserve Agricultural Land—Alternatives for Local Officials and Citizens." Madison, Wis.: University of Wisconsin Extension, 1980. (Agricultural Bulletin Building, 1535 Observatory Dr., Madison, WI 53706)

Batie, Sandra S., and Robert G. Healy, eds. *The Future of American Agriculture as a Strategic Resource.* Washington, D.C.: The Conservation Foundation, 1980.

Beldon, Joe, et al., eds. *New Directions in Farms, Land and Food Policies: A Time for State and Local Action.* Washington, D.C., Agricultural Project, Conference on Alternative State and Local Policies, n.d. (2000 Florida Ave., NW, Washington, D.C., 20009)

Blackmore, John. "Community Trusts Offer a Hopeful Way Back to the Land." *Smithsonian*, June 1978, pp. 87–106.

Boyce, David E., Janey Kohlhase, and Thomas Plaut. *The Development of a Planning Oriented Method for Estimating the Value of Development Easements on Agricultural Land.* Philadelphia, Pa.: Regional Science Research Institute, 1978. (P.O. Box 8776, Philadelphia, PA 19101)

The Brandywine Conservancy. *Green Is as Good as Gold: Preserving Natural Areas.* Chadds Ford, Pa., forthcoming. (P.O. Box 141, Chadds Ford, PA 19317)

Brenneman, Russell L. *Private Approaches to the Preservation of Open Land.* New London, Conn.: The Conservation and Research Foundation, 1967. (Box 1445, Connecticut College, New London, CT 06320)

———. "Techniques for Controlling the Surroundings of Historic Sites." *Law and Contemporary Problems* 36, no. 3 (Summer 1971): 416–22.

———. "Should 'Easements' Be Used to Protect National Historic Landmarks?" A Study for the National Park Service, 1975. (Available at special libraries)

———. "Historic Preservation Restrictions: A Sampling of State Statutes." *Connecticut Law Review* 8, no. 2 (Winter 1975–76): 231–47.

Brink, Peter H. *Commercial Area Revolving Funds for Preservation.* Information Series, National Trust for Historic Preservation. Washington, D.C.: Preservation Press, 1976.

Browne, Kingsbury, Jr. *Federal Tax Incentives and Open Space Preservation.* Lexington, Mass.: Lexington Books, 1982. (125 Spring St., Lexington, MA 02173)

Browne, Kingsbury, Jr., ed. "Family Lands." *Trusts and Estates, The Journal of Estate Planning and Administration*, April 1976, pp. 238–40 *passim.* (Communications Channels, Inc., 461 Eighth Ave., New York, NY 10001)

———. *Case Studies in Land Conservation.* Boston: New England Natural Resources Center, 1977.

Browne, Kingsbury, Jr., and Walter G. Van Dorn. "Charitable Gifts of Partial Interests in Real Property for Conservation Purposes." *Tax Lawyer* 29, no. 1 (Fall 1975): 69–93.

Burchell, Robert W., and Listokin, David. *The Environmental Impact Handbook*. New Brunswick, N.J.: Center for Urban Policy Research, 1975. (Center for Urban Policy Research, Rutgers University, New Brunswick, NJ 08903)

Burchell, Robert, and Listokin, David, eds. *Future Land Use: Energy, Environmental and Legal Constraints*. New Brunswick, N.J.: Center for Urban Policy Research, 1975.

Carney, William. *A Citizens' Guide to Maintaining Neighborhood Places*. Heritage Conservation and Recreation Service, U.S. Department of the Interior, 1981.

Chamberlin, Constance K. *Waterford: The Challenge*. Waterford, Va.: Waterford Foundation, 1980. (Waterford Foundation, Inc., Waterford, VA 22190)

Changing Times. "Unrest in the West: Who Owns This Land?" 31 July 1981.

Citizens' Action Manual. *A Guide to Recycling Vacant Property in Your Neighborhood*. Heritage Conservation and Recreation Service, U.S. Department of the Interior, 1979.

Civic Action Institute. *Community Land Banks and Land Trusts, a Neighborhood Action Guide*. Washington, D.C., 1979. (1010 16th St., NW, Washington, DC 20036)

Clark, Charles E. *Real Covenants and Other Interests Which "Run with the Land."* 2d ed. Chicago: Callaghan and Co., 1947.

Coffey, J. Steven. *Revolving Funds for Neighborhood Preservation: Lafayette Square, St. Louis*. Information Series, National Trust for Historic Preservation. Washington, D.C.: Preservation Press, 1977.

Cohen, Russell. *Guide to and Directory of Massachusetts Land Conservation Trusts and Similar Organizations*. Lincoln, Mass.: Massachusetts Audubon Society, 1981.

———. "Progress and Problems in Preserving Ohio's Natural Heritage Through the Use of Conservation Easements." *Capital University Law Review* 10, no. 4 (Summer 1981): 731–58.

Commonwealth of Pennsylvania. *Exploring the Use of TDR in Pennsylvania: Conference Proceedings*. Harrisburg, Pa.: Bureau of Environmental Planning, 1978. (DER, Bureau of Environmental Planning, Division of Planning Assistance, P.O. Box 2357, Harrisburg, PA 17120)

Connor, Tom. "Preserving Open Spaces Through Land Trusts." *New York Times*, 3 June 1979, p. 1.

"Conservation Conference: Conference Papers and Statistics from Cooperating Organizations." (Conference held in Green Hills, Pa., 9 June 1979, sponsored by the Berks County Conservancy.)

Conservation Law Foundation. *Conservation Restrictions*. Boston, Mass.: n.d.

———. *Floodplain/Wetlands Protection—A Guide*. Boston, Mass.: n.d.

_____. Gifts of Land for Conservation. Boston, Mass.: n.d.

Correll, Mark R., Jane H. Lillydahl, and Larry D. Single. "The Effects of Greenbelts on Residential Property Values: Some Findings on the Political Economy of Open Space." *Land Economics*, 54, no. 2 (1978): 207–217.

Coughlin, Robert E., and John C. Keene. *The Protection of Farmland: A Reference Guidebook for State and Local Governments*. Washington, D.C.: National Agricultural Land Study, 1981.

Coughlin, Robert E., and Thomas Plaut. "Less-Than-Fee Acquisition for the Preservation of Open Space: Does It Work?" *Journal of the American Institute of Planners* (now *Journal of the American Planning Association*) 44, no. 4 (October 1978): 452–62.

Council for Agricultural Science and Technology. *Preserving Agricultural Land: Issues and Policy Alternatives*. Report No. 90. Ames, Iowa, 1981. (250 Memorial Union, Ames, IA 50011)

Council on Environmental Quality. *Environmental Quality*. Washington, D.C., annual.

Daugherty, Arthur B. *Open Space Preservation: Federal Tax Policies Encouraging Donation of Conservation Easements*. Washington, D.C.: U.S. Department of Agriculture; Economics, Statistics and Cooperatives Service; Natural Resources Economics Division, 1978. (National Technical Information Service, 5285 Port Royal Rd., Springfield, VA 22161)

Dunham, Allison. *Preservation of Open Space Areas: A Study of the Nongovernmental Role*. Chicago: Welfare Conference of Metropolitan Chicago, 1966.

"Edited Proceedings of the New Hampshire Bar Conservation and Preservation Restriction Seminar." *New Hampshire Bar Journal* 16 (1975): 304.

Eshman, Rob. "In Land We Trust." *New Roots*, July–August 1981, pp. 19–22.

Farley, Virginia. *A Survey of Vermont Land Protection Efforts Through the Private Sector*. Woodstock, Vt.: Ottauquechee Regional Land Trust, 1981.

Fenner, Randee Gorin. "Land Trusts: An Alternative Method of Preserving Open Space." *Vanderbilt Law Review* 33 (1980): 1039.

Fletcher, W. Wendell, and Charles E. Little. *The American Cropland Crisis*. Bethesda, Md.: American Land Forum, 1981.

Fox, Timothy. *Land Conservation and Preservation Techniques*. Washington, D.C.: U.S. Department of the Interior, Heritage Conservation and Recreation Service, 1979. (HCRS Information Exchange, U.S. Department of the Interior, Heritage Conservation and Recreation Service, Washington, D.C. 20243)

Fraser, Elisabeth A., and Morris, Anne F. *Getting It All Together: The Application of Environmental Information to Land Use Planning*. Mendham, N.J.: Association of New Jersey Environmental Commissions, 1980. (300 Mendham Rd., Rt. 24, Mendham, NJ 07915)

French & Pickering Creeks Conservation Trust, Inc. *Voluntary Preservation of Open Space.* Pottstown, Pa., 1974. (Box 360, RD 2, Pottstown, PA 19464)

_____. *Proceedings of the First and Second Conferences on Voluntary Preservation of Open Space.* Pottstown, Pa., 1974, 1979.

_____. *Pickering Creek Valley: A Preservation Opportunity.* Pottstown, Pa., 1976.

Goetsch, Charles C. "Conservation Restrictions: A Survey." Comment. *Connecticut Law Review* 8, no. 2 (Winter 1975–76): 383–411.

Gold, Seymour M. "Social and Economic Benefits of Trees in Cities." *Journal of Forestry* 84 (1977): 84–87.

Goodman, Collette C. *Legal Considerations in Establishing a Historic Preservation Organization.* Information Series, National Trust for Historic Preservation. Washington, D.C.: Preservation Press, 1977.

Gove, Greg J. *Bargain Sales of Land.* Leisure Technical Assistance Publication (Leisure TAP) no. 8. Harrisburg, Pa.: Pennsylvania Department of Community Affairs, 1977. (Bureau of Recreation and Conservation, 104 South Office Bldg., P.O. Box 155, Harrisburg, PA 17120)

_____. *Easements for Recreation and Conservation.* Leisure Technical Assistance Publication (Leisure TAP) no. 6. Harrisburg, Pa.: Pennsylvania Department of Community Affairs, 1977.

Guitar, Mary Anne. *Property Power: How to Keep the Bulldozer, the Power Line, and the Highway Men Away from Your Door.* New York: Doubleday, 1972.

Gunther, Jack. "Preserving Small Natural Areas." *The Maine Manual for Conservation Commissions.* Cooperative Extension Service Bulletin no. 589, 1977, pp. 90–94.

Guth, Chester K., and Stanley S. Shaw. *How to Put on Dynamic Meetings.* Reston, Va.: Reston, 1980.

Hammer, Thomas R., Robert E. Coughlin, and Edward T. Horn. "The Effect of a Large Urban Park on Real Estate Values." *Journal of the American Institute of Planning* 40 (1974): 274–7.

Healy, Robert G., and James L. Short. *The Market for Rural Land: Trends, Issues, Policies.* Washington, D.C.: The Conservation Foundation, 1981.

Hendler, Bruce. *Caring for the Land, Environmental Principles for Site Design and Review.* Chicago: American Society of Planning Officials, 1977.

Heritage Conservation and Recreation Service (HCRS), U.S. Department of the Interior, with Massachusetts Continuing Legal Education—New England Law Institute, Inc. (MCLE-NELI, Inc.). *Historic Preservation, Conservation and Recreation—Federal Income Tax Incentives.* Boston, Mass.: MCLE-NELI, 1979. (44 School St., Boston, MA 02110)

BIBLIOGRAPHY

Heritage Conservation and Recreation Service. *Land Conservation and Preservation Techniques.* Washington, D.C.: U.S. Department of the Interior, 1979.

Historic Annapolis, Inc. *Easements.* Annapolis, Md., 1976. (18 Pinkney St., Annapolis, MD 21401)

Hite, James C. *Room & Situation: The Political Economy of Land Use Policy.* Chicago: Nelson-Hall, 1979.

Hocker, Jean, and Story Clark. *Jackson Hole: Protecting Public Values on Private Lands.* Jackson, Wy.: Jackson Hole Project, Izaak Walton League of America, 1981. (P.O. Box 2443, Jackson, WY 83001)

Hoose, Philip. *Building an Ark: Tools for the Preservation of Natural Diversity Through Land Protection.* Covelo, Calif.: Island Press, 1980.

Howe, Robert. "Techniques of Open Space Preservation: A Survey from a Canadian Standpoint." *University of Toronto Faculty Law Review* 32 (1974): 123.

McHarg, Ian L. *Design with Nature.* Garden City, N.Y.: Doubleday, 1971.

Maryland Environmental Trust. *Conservation Easements.* Baltimore, 1974. (8 E. Mulberry St., Baltimore, MD 21202)

Maryland Historical Trust. *Preservation Easements.* Rev. ed. Annapolis, Md., 1977. (21 State Circle, Annapolis, MD 21401)

Miller, James Nathan. "The Happy Landgrabbers." *Readers's Digest*, June 1981, pp. 148–57.

Milne, Janet E. *The Landowner's Options: A Guide to the Voluntary Protection of Land in Maine.* Augusta, Maine: Maine Coast Heritage Trust, 1978.

Montana Land Reliance. "Conservation Law Seminar—Conservation Easements and Related Charitable Conveyances." Helena, Mont., 1981. (P.O. Box 355, Helena, MT 59601)

Morales, Dominic, Byrle N. Boyce, and Rudy J. Favsetti. "The Contribution of Trees to Residential Property Value: Manchester, Conn." *Valuation* 23, no. 2 (1976): 27–43.

Mundie, Roberta M. "Can We Have Housing and a Greenbelt Too?" *Urban Land* 40, no. 8 (September 1981): 3–4.

Murray, Linda. *Land Trusts.* New York: Open Space Action Institute, 1968.

Natural Lands Trust. *New Options for the Owner of Natural Lands.* Philadelphia, Pa., 1981. (711 Widener Bldg., 1339 Chestnut St., Philadelphia, PA 19107)

Natural Resources Defense Council, Inc. *Land Use Controls in the United States: A Handbook on the Legal Rights of Citizens.* New York: Dial, 1977.

National Rural Center. *A Directory of Rural Organizations.* Washington, D.C., 1977.

––––––. *Private Funding for Rural Programs.* Washington, D.C., 1978.

––––––. *Resource Guide for Rural Development.* Washington, D.C., 1978.

National Trust for Historic Preservation. *Basic Preservation Procedures*. Information Series. Washington, D.C.: Preservation Press, 1979.

National Wildlife Federation. *Conservation Directory*. Washington, D.C., annual. (1412 16th St., NW, Washington, DC 20036)

The Nature Conservancy (Jacqueline Lansing, Project Director). *Preserving Our Natural Heritage*. 3 vols. Washington, D.C.: U.S. Government Printing Office, 1977, 1981.

Netherton, Ross D. "Environmental Conservation and Historic Preservation through Recorded Land-Use Agreements." *Real Property, Probate and Trust Journal* 14, no. 3 (Fall 1979).

Neuhauser, H., and J. Clark, eds. *Proceedings of the Workshop on Cooperative Managements of Coastal Ecosystems*. Savannah, Ga.: The Georgia Conservancy, 1981. (4405 Paulsen St., Savannah, GA 31405)

Northeast Environmental Design. *The Vermont Backroad—A Guide for the Protection, Conservation, and Enhancement of Its Scenic Quality*. Woodstock, Vt., 1974. (Ottauquechee Regional Planning and Development Commission, 39 Central St., Woodstock, VT 05091)

Paxton, Lynn, Lisa Cashdan, and Mark Francis. *The Making of Neighborhood Open Spaces: Community Design Development and Management of Open Spaces*. New York: Center for Human Environments, City University of New York, April 1981.

Payne, Brian, and Steven Strom. "The Contribution of Trees to the Appraised Values of Unimproved Residential Lots." *Valuation* 22, no. 2 (1975): 36–45.

Pennabecker, James H. *Open Space Lands Preservation Techniques: A Literature Review of Innovative Methods, An Update*. Exchange Bibliography no. 1393. Monticello, Ill.: Council of Planning Librarians, 1977.

People for Open Space. *Endangered Harvest: The Future of Bay Area Farmland*. San Francisco, Calif.: The Report of the Farmlands Conservation Project, 1980. (46 Kearny St., San Francisco, CA 94108)

Peskin, Sarah. *Guiding Growth and Change*. Boston, Mass.: Massachusetts Audubon Society, 1976. (South Great Rd., Lincoln, MA 01773)

Platt, Rutherford H. *Open Land in Urban Illinois: Roles of the Citizen Advocate*. Dekalb, Ill.: Northern Illinois University Press, 1971.

Popper, Frank J. *The Politics of Land Use Reform*. Madison, Wis.: University of Wisconsin Press, 1981.

Proudman, Robert D., and Rajala, Reuben. *AMC Field Guide to Trail Building and Maintenance*. Boston: Appalachian Mountain Club, 1981. (5 Joy St., Boston, MA 02108)

Raymond, George M. "Structuring the Implementation of Transferable Development Rights." *Urban Land* 40, no. 7 (July–August 1981) 19-25.

Reilly, William K., ed. *The Use of Land: A Citizen's Policy Guide to Urban Growth*. New York: Crowell, 1973.

Reynolds, Judith, and Anthony Reynolds. *Factors Affecting Valuation of Historic Property.* Information Series, National Trust for Historic Preservation. Washington, D.C.: Preservation Press, 1976.

River Conservation Fund. *Flowing Free, A Citizen's Guide for Protecting Wild and Scenic Rivers.* Washington, D.C., 1977. (317 Pennsylvania Ave., SE, Washington, DC 20003)

Roe, Charles E., and Richard H. Sussman. *Forming a Conservation Foundation in North Carolina.* Heritage Conservation and Recreation Service, U.S. Department of the Interior, 1979.

Rubin, H. "Reserves, Preserves, and Land Trusts." *Sierra*, November 1979, p. 27.

Sampson, R. Neil. *Farmland or Wasteland: A Time to Choose.* Washington, D.C.: National Association of Conservation Districts, 1981.

Sargent, Frederick O. *Rural Environmental Planning.* South Burlington, Vt., 1976. (330 Spear St., South Burlington, VT 05401)

Shands, William E., and Robert G. Healy. *The Lands Nobody Wanted: Policy for National Forests in the Eastern United States.* Washington, D.C.: The Conservation Foundation, 1977.

Sheaff, Richard. *The Formation of Land Trusts and Watershed Associations.* 2d ed. Concord, N.H.: Society for the Protection of New Hampshire Forests, January 1973.

Sheail, John. *Nature in Trust: The History of Nature Conservation in Britain.* Glasgow: Blackie, 1976.

Shopsin, William C. *Saving Large Estates: Conservation, Historic Preservation, Adaptive Re-Use.* Setauket, N.Y.: Society for the Preservation of Long Island Antiquities and the New York State Council on the Arts, 1977. (93 N. Country Rd., Setauket, NY 11733)

Silverman, Jane. "Rural America: Love It or Lose It." *Historic Preservation*, 1981, pp. 22–31.

Sleeper, David. "Working for the Rural Public Interest." *Country Journal* 8, no. 12 (December 1981) pp. 60–67.

Small, Stephen J. "The Tax Benefits of Donating Easements in Scenic and Historic Property." *Real Estate Law Journal* 7 (Spring 1979): 304–319.

Solomon, Louis M. *Leasing Public Land: A City's Investment in the Future.* Cambridge, Mass.: Lincoln Institute of Land Policy, 1978. (26 Trowbridge St., Cambridge, MA 02138)

Steiner, Frederick. *Ecological Planning for Farmlands Preservation: A Sourcebook for Educators and Planners.* Pullman, Wash.: Washington State University Cooperative Extension Service, 1980.

Stipe, Robert E., ed. *New Directions in Rural Preservation.* Preservation Planning Series. Washington, D.C.: Heritage Conservation and Recreation Service, U.S. Department of the Interior, 1980.

Stocker, Frederick D. *Farm-Use Assessment Revisited*. Cambridge, Mass.: Lincoln Institute of Land Policy, 1979. (26 Trowbridge St., Cambridge, MA 02138)

Stokes, Samuel N., and Joe Getty. *Rural Conservation*. Information Series, National Trust for Historic Preservation. Washington, D.C.: Preservation Press, 1979.

Stone, Edward H. *Visual Resource Management*. Washington, D.C.: American Society of Landscape Architects, 1978. (1900 M Street, NW, Suite 750, Washington, DC 20036)

Stover, Emily Jane, ed. *Protecting Nature's Estate: Techniques for Saving Land*. Washington, D.C.: Bureau of Outdoor Recreation, U.S. Department of the Interior; The Nature Conservancy; and New York State Office of Parks and Recreation, 1975 (December). U.S. Government Printing Office Stock No. 024-016-00082-2.

Strong, Ann L. *Private Property and the Public Interest: The Brandywine Experience*. Baltimore, Md.: Johns Hopkins University Press, 1975.

_____. *Land Banking: European Reality, American Prospect*. Baltimore, Md.: Johns Hopkins University Press, 1979.

Sutte, Donald T., Jr., and Roger A. Cunningham. *Scenic Easements: Legal, Administrative and Valuation Problems and Procedures*. National Cooperative Highway Research Program Report 56. Washington, D.C.: Highway Research Board, 1968.

Swann, Robert. *The Community Land Trust: A Guide to a New Model for Land Tenure in America*. Ashby, Mass.: International Independence Institute, 1972.

Taylor, Susan Westwood. "Citizens Taking Action: A Collection of Case Studies." San Francisco, Calif.: The Trust for Public Land, 1980.

Thurow, Charles, et al. *Performance Controls for Sensitive Lands: A Practical Guide for Local Administrators*. Chicago: Planners Press, 1975. (American Planning Association, 1313 E. 60th St., Chicago, IL 60637)

Toner, William. *Saving Farms and Farmland: A Community Guide*. Chicago: American Society of Planning Officials, 1978. (American Planning Association, 1313 E. 60th St., Chicago, IL 60637)

Treusch, Paul E., and Norman A. Sugarman. *Tax Exempt Charitable Organizations*. Philadelphia: American Law Institute–American Bar Association, Committee on Continuing Professional Education, 1979.

The Trust for Public Land. *Annual Report 1981*. San Francisco, 1981. (82 Second St., San Francisco, CA 94105)

_____. *Negotiated Land Development Proceedings*. Cambridge, Mass.: Lincoln Institute of Land Policy, 1982. (26 Trowbridge St., Cambridge, MA 02138)

The Trustees of Reservations. *Conservation and Preservation Restrictions: A Summary of Opportunities for Property Owners*. Milton, Mass., n.d.

BIBLIOGRAPHY

U.S. Department of Agriculture, Soil Conservation Service, Committee on Land Use. *Land Use Notes*. Edited by Warren T. Zitzmann. Washington, D.C., n.d.

U.S. Department of Agriculture, Economic Research Service. *Rural Zoning in the United States: Analysis of Enabling Legislation*. Washington, D.C., 1972. (U.S. Government Printing Office, Washington, DC 20402. GPO Stock No. 0100-2519)

"Urban Forestry." *Environmental Comment*, November 1980.

Vineyard Open Land Foundation. *Looking at the Vineyard*. West Tisbury, Mass.: 1973.

Warren, Rebecca. *Case Studies, Local Land Conservation in Maine*. Northeast Harbor, Maine: Maine Coast Heritage Trust, 1979. (MCHT, P.O. Box 426, Northeast Harbor, ME 04662)

Watson, A. Elizabeth. "Establishing an Easement Program to Protect Historic, Scenic and Natural Resources." Information Sheet no. 25, National Trust for Historic Preservation. Washington, D.C.: Preservation Press, 1980.

_____. *The Development of Rural Conservation Programs: A Case Study of Loudoun County, VA*. Information Series, National Trust for Historic Preservation. Washington, D.C.: Preservation Press, 1981.

_____. "*The Use of the Conservation Easement: A Survey and Analysis of Selected Programs*." Master's thesis, Pennsylvania State University, 1981.

Whyte, William H. *Securing Open Space for Urban America: Conservation Easements*. Washington, D.C.: Urban Land Institute, 1959. (1200 18th Street, NW, Washington, DC 20036)

_____. *The Last Landscape*. Garden City, N.Y.: Doubleday, 1968.

Wilkins, Suzanne C., and Roger Koontz. *Land Trust Handbook*. Middletown, Conn.: Land Trust Service Bureau, 1981. (Box MMM, Wesleyan Station, Middletown, CT 06456)

Williams, Hugh. "The Case of Island X." *Down East*, June 1979.

Winthrop, Frederic, Jr. "Saving Farms, Massachusetts Style." *Country Journal* 8, no. 12 (December 1981): 86–93.

Wood, Peter. "Business-Suited Saviors of Nation's Vanishing Wilds." *Smithsonian*, December 1978.

Woodruff, Archibald M. *The Farm and the City, Rivals or Allies?* Englewood Cliffs, N.J.: Prentice-Hall, 1981.

Wrenn, Tony P. *Woodbury, Connecticut: A New England Townscape*. Washington, D.C.: Preservation Press, 1975.

Zube, Ervin H., Robert O. Brush, and Julius Gy Fabos, eds. *Landscape Assessment: Value, Perceptions and Resources*. Stroudsburg, Pa.: Dowden, Hutchison, Ross, 1975.

INDEX

Also available from Island Press,
Star Route 1, Box 38, Covelo, California 95428

Building an Ark: Tools for the Preservation of Natural Diversity Through Land Protection, by Philip M. Hoose. Illustrations. $12.00

The author is national protection planner for The Nature Conservancy, and this book presents a comprehensive plan that can be used to identify and protect what remains of each state's natural ecological diversity. Case studies augment this blueprint for conservation.

Tree Talk: The People and Politics of Timber, by Ray Raphael. Illustrations by Mark Livingston. $12.00

A probing analysis of modern forestry practices and philosophies. In a balanced and informed text, *Tree Talk* presents the views of loggers, environmentalists, timber industry executives, and forest farmers and goes beyond the politics of "production versus protection" to propose new ways to harvest trees and preserve forest habitats in a healthy economy and a thriving environment.

Pocket Flora of the Redwood Forest, by Dr. Rudolf W. Becking. Illustrations. $15.00

The most useful and comprehensive guidebook available for the plants of the world-famous redwood forest. Dr. Rudolf W. Becking, a noted botanist and Professor of Natural Resources, is also a gifted artist. The *Pocket Flora* includes detailed drawings, a complete key, and simple, accurate descriptions for 212 of the most common species of this unique plant community, as well as eight pages of color photographs. Plasticized cover for field use.

A Citizen's Guide to Timber Harvest Plans, by Marylee Bytheriver. Illustrations. $1.50

California state law permits any interested citizen to learn the details of proposed timber cutting on private or public lands. This report instructs citizens on their rights concerning timber harvesting, the procedures for influencing the details of proposed logging operations, and the specialized vocabulary surrounding the Timber Harvest Plan. A resource for action.

An Everyday History of Somewhere, by Ray Raphael. Illustrations by Mark Livingston. $8.00

This work of history and documentation embraces the life and work of ordinary people, from the Indians who inhabited the coastal forests of northern California to the loggers, tanbark strippers, and farmers who came after them. This loving look at history takes us in a full circle that leads to the everyday life of us all.

The Trail North, by Hawk Greenway. Illustrations. $7.50.

The summer adventure of a young man who traveled the spine of coastal mountains from California to Washington with only his horse for a companion. The book he has made from this journey reveals his coming of age as he studies, reflects, and greets the world that is awakening within and around him.

America Without Violence: Why Violence Persists and How You Can Stop It, by Michael N. Nagler. Foreword by Louis Jolyon West, M.D. $8.00

Challenging the widespread assumption that violence is an inevitable part of human existence, *America Without Violence* asserts that it *is* possible to live in a nonviolent society. The choice, Michael Nagler says, begins with each individual. In personal, practical language, *America Without Violence* explains how to make the changes in our private lives that can counteract the forces of violence throughout our society.

The Book of the Vision Quest: Personal Transformation in the Wilderness, by Steven Foster with Meredith E. Little. Photographs. $10.00

The inspiring record of modern people enacting an ancient, archetypal rite of passage. This book shares the wisdom and the seeking of many persons who have known the opportunity to face themselves, their fears, and their courage, and to live in harmony with nature through the experience of the traditional Vision Quest. Excerpts from participants' journals add an intimate dimension to this unique account of human challenge.

Wellspring: A Story from the Deep Country, by Barbara Dean. Illustrations. $6.00

The moving, first-person account of a contemporary woman's life at the edge of wilderness. Since 1971, Barbara Dean has lived in a handmade yurt on land she shares with fifteen friends. Their struggles, both hilarious and poignant, form the background for this inspiring story of personal growth and deep love for nature.

Headwaters: Tales of the Wilderness, by Ash, Russell, Doog, and Del Rio. Preface by Edward Abbey. Photographs and illustrations. $6.00

Four bridge-playing buddies tackle the wilderness—they go in separately, meet on top of a rock, and come out talking. These four are as different as the suits in their deck of cards, as ragged as a three-day beard, and as eager as sparks.

No Substitute for Madness: A Teacher, His Kids & The Lessons of Real Life, by Ron Jones. Illustrations. $8.00

Seven magnificent glimpses of life as it is. Ron Jones is a teacher with the gift of translating human beauty into words and knowing where to find it in the first place. This collection of true experiences includes "The Acorn People," the moving story of a summer camp for handicapped kids, and "The Third Wave," a harrowing experiment in Nazi training in a high school class—both of which were adapted for television movies.

Perfection Perception, with the Brothers O. and Joe de Vivre. $5.00

Notes from a metaphysical journey through the mountains of Patagonia. The authors share their experiences and discoveries in using their powers of perception to change the world. Their thoughts are mystical at times, but their basis is firmly experiental and parallels the most theoretically advanced works in modern physics.

The Search for Goodbye-to-Rains, by Paul McHugh. $7.50

Steve Getane takes to the road in an American odyssey that is part fantasy and part real—a haphazard pursuit that includes Faulkner's Mississippi, the rarefied New Mexico air, and a motorcycle named Frank. "A rich, resonant novel of the interior world. Overtones of Whitman, Kerouac."—Robert Anton Wilson

Please enclose $1.00 with each order for postage and handling.
California residents, add 6% sales tax.
A catalog of current and forthcoming titles is available free of charge.